JUST JESUS

JUST JESUS
A Glimpse of the Three Volumes:

Volume 1 (chapters 1–51): Jesus goes to the Jordan to listen to John the Baptist. There he meets Peter, John, and Andrew. The news of John's imprisonment kindles his desire to do something for his people. Thus the spark: He must take over, and with a group of friends, he must awaken the spirit of the poor, telling them that God is on their side, fighting shoulder to shoulder with them. He forms his group in Capernaum, and through words and signs presents God's plan for humankind. Jesus gradually finds himself at the helm of a people hungry and thirsty for justice, who in turn see in God a Father, a Liberator, and a Friend.

Volume 2 (chapters 52–99): Jesus' activities in Capernaum and in the towns of Galilee, including his journeys to Jerusalem in the company of his twelve friends, where people meet them and follow them, prove that Jesus is a true leader of the people, a great prophet. His word becomes more and more intense as he criticizes the ambition and egoism of the rulers, while proclaiming the liberation of the poor. It is a liberation that will find realization in a new society that is communitarian and fraternal, where everyone is equal, where no one has more and others less. The conflicts among the ruling class — the priests, landowners, and officials — become more accentuated day by day. Jesus and his friends are fully aware of the calumny, the threats, the persecution, and the clandestine activities against them.

Volume 3 (chapters 100–144): Jesus' last journey to Jerusalem culminates in his arrest and death. The Romans as well as the religious authorities of the capital join hands to silence the threatening voice of the prophet. Jesus became prisoner, was tortured, and in his death experienced the weakness and helplessness of those who have fought for justice against the seemingly powerful and invincible rulers of this world. The God of life who does not allow the unjust to have the last word resurrected Jesus from the dead: this is the experience that Jesus' friends transmit to us. The first Christian community is built on this faith.

JUST JESUS

Volume 1:
A People Starving for Love

José Ignacio López Vigil
and
María López Vigil

Translated by
Trinidad Ongtangco-Regala

A Crossroad Book
The Crossroad Publishing Company
New York

The Crossroad Publishing Company
370 Lexington Avenue, New York, NY 10017

Originally published in Spanish as *Un tal Jesús*. First translated into English as *A Certain Jesus* by Claretian Publications, a division of Claretian Communications, Inc., U.P. P.O. Box 4, Diliman, 1101 Quezon City, Philippines; this edition has been adapted from the new Claretian edition, with biblical and liturgical references for pastoral use, copyright © 1998 by Claretian Publications.

Printed in the United States of America

Library of Congress Cataloging-in-Publication Data
López Vigil, José Ignacio.
    [Tal Jesús. English]
    Just Jesus : the scandalous gospel of Jesus of Nazareth, vol. 1: a people starving for love / by José Ignacio and María López Vigil.
        p. cm.
    ISBN 0-8245-1836-5 (v. 1 : alk. paper)
    1. Jesus Christ – Fiction. I. López Vigil, María. II. Title.
PQ6662.O664 T313 2000
863'.64 – dc21   99-050688

1   2   3   4   5   6   7   8   9   10   06   05   04   03   02   01   00

Contents

Foreword

I

Dorothy Day was the cofounder of the Catholic Worker. This was a house of hospitality in the poor area of New York City which was a haven for the outcasts of society. On any given day, one could find alcoholics, drug addicts, prostitutes, and petty thieves gathered around the table to share a big pot of soup and day-old bread. Adding water to the soup when unexpected visitors arrived (nearly every day) was a common occurrence. Dorothy herself had been arrested more times than anyone could remember. She was already in her seventies when she refused to take shelter in a mock nuclear attack and walked around the virtually abandoned streets to make a statement with her life that nuclear safety was an illusion, and the production of nuclear war material, sheer madness. Once she was introduced on a Catholic campus where she was to give a talk as "a living saint," to which she retorted, "you don't get rid of me that easily." A point well taken. There's something about elevating a person or a message to the spiritual that removes its bite. Peter Maurin, cofounder with Dorothy of the Catholic Worker, used to say that the gospels were dynamite but the church kept the dynamite wet so that it would never explode.

Every Good Friday within recent memory, in the City of Manila, the urban poor have enacted their own version of the suffering and death of Jesus. Carrying a large cross, banners, and cardboard replicas of their shanties, they do their own stations of the cross in front of government, business, and even church offices with the message that Jesus continues being crucified today in the urban poor, whose shanties are brutally demolished, they themselves seriously injured and often left "without a place to lay their head." Often enough, they meet a procession emanating from the church replete with members of mandated organizations and regular churchgoers. Though externally not radically different in appearance, they represent quite different messages: one, transcendent (Christ died for our sins); the other emphasizing the immanent (Christ has made a preference for the poor and continues to suffer when they are oppressed, beaten down, despised).

On Good Friday of 1980, Alex Garsales and Herman Moleta, two active lay leaders in basic Christian communities, took the parts of Jesus and an apostle in the passion play of Kabankalan, Negros Occidental, in the Philippines. Very much aware of the part that Jesus was exercising in the life of the community, Alex stated that more than a historical event was being commemorated in that celebration. As if to underline the truth of that statement, their bullet-riddled bodies were found in the cogon grass on Easter Monday.

What other country in the world has the number of martyrs that the Philippines has offered in the past twenty-five years, proving that the gospel has lost nothing of its bite, which caused the death of God among us two thousand years ago? A few years ago, I decided to make a calendar and recorded on the calendar all the men and women of faith who died because of what they believed in, that God continues to act in this world among the poor to bring about a kingdom of justice for all (only those who died for justice, not persecuted); and there were more than enough names for every day of the year.

This book, then, is for those who believe that the gospel has lost nothing of its bite and that it continues to disrupt and disturb our comfortable, cushioned Christianity. The Jesus presented here enters our lives as the great disturber, confronting the afflicted and afflicting the comfortable. May he continue to do so.

EDWARD M. GERLOCK*

II

Just Jesus is a work of art, at the same time a theological undertaking and a pastoral effort. One must insist on its worth, without looking at it as if it were just another book. This text is of great literary and dramatic quality, a proof of the seriousness and capability of the authors.

The content proves to be even more interesting. The theological back-drop presents relevant questions to us. This is not a new children's story about Jesus; nor is it written for entertainment; rather, it is a profound theological exposition.

---

*Edward M. Gerlock is a free-lance theologian, sociologist, and photographer. He is currently a part-time editor for Claretian Publications. He also ministers to the elderly.

We are accustomed to see the figure of Jesus from this side of his resurrection and ascension to heaven; we are used to seeing him in liturgical rituals, mythicized by painters, musicians, and other artists. *Just Jesus* focuses on him from another angle, prior to the resurrection, showing him as the historical Jesus, a human figure as seen by his contemporaries, his friends, his adversaries, and (this may be judged as more debatable) just as he saw himself from his human conscience.

These two perspectives on Jesus, however complementary, are radically different. To project onto Jesus of Palestine all we believe him to be, all we have thought of him as the Risen Jesus, is an error in historical perspective, confusing levels and bringing false and tragic consequences in understanding the entire phenomenon which is Jesus. If we reduce the total Jesus to the Palestinian Jesus, we cut off a very important part of that totality. Likewise, if we reduce the total Jesus to the Risen Jesus we also amputate an important part of that same totality. The first amputation may discredit Jesus' divinity; the second, his humanity. Both are equally heretical and dangerous.

This book may seem to underemphasize the perspective of those who totally believe in the risen Christ. The good thing is that this book will force them to go to the Palestinian Jesus, the historical Jesus, which is the real form Jesus adopted to preach the Kingdom and to bring people to the Father. What might be disturbing to them is the tremendous demand of this earthly Jesus who emptied his divinity in a concrete and historical way. These believers hide themselves not so much in the Risen Jesus, but in the ritualized and mythicized Jesus.

This book gets us totally into the scandal of Jesus according to his enemies — that Jesus, being a man, claimed to be the Son of God, the Messiah, greater than Moses, and so on. The Risen Jesus turns out to be less scandalous and more fitting if the intrinsic unity between the living Risen Jesus and the Crucified One is broken. For these people, reading *Just Jesus* can be of much help if they try to better understand this scandal more than looking for reasons for their faith.

For those who do not quite know who this certain Jesus is, those who know him only through ideological manipulation passed down through the centuries, this book will also be very good. It will bring them back to a necessary initial experience, faithfully situating them side-by-side with the Palestinian Jesus in whom it was indeed difficult to see God in person. Will they remain there, focusing on the purely human aspect of the complex reality of Jesus? Is it not necessary to proclaim Jesus of Nazareth as the Risen One, as the God-chosen One? Does not the text underscore the difference between Jesus and his disciples?

This brings us back to what the gospels are meant to be. *Just Jesus* is written from the accounts of the gospels and, obviously, situated before the gospels. It is a fact that the gospels are not purely historical narratives; they are the expression of the memory and faith of the first communities, many of whom witnessed the experience of the Risen Christ more intensely than the memory of the Crucified One. The gospels are narratives in which the expression "Jesus is Lord" is very explicit, yet at the same time the concrete experience of what had been Jesus' historical life is not clearly stated.

Just Jesus is situated in the tangible experience of the historical life of Jesus. For this reason, an attempt must be made at a literary re-creation, just as the gospel stories strive at a theological re-creation. Both are based on historical data, used for example by Josephus (though he ignored many of the details transmitted more or less elaborately by the gospels). It is obvious that the theological re-creation proves to be more authoritative than the literary reconstruction this book presents. *Just Jesus* does not try to replace the gospels, but shows how these should be read, deepened, and lived.

An important point is the pastoral relevance of this book. It is, indeed, a pastoral work even if some theological problems may arise on account of the option taken by the authors in their approach to Jesus. It is certainly not a novelistic narrative of Jesus' life; it is a tool for evangelization — a proclamation of the good news not only for the poor but also for those who have heard it but need to be reimmersed in it. The book is certainly shocking, as it jolts the reader and recovers the vitality of the evangelical message, which has become somewhat mummified in translation. This might likewise be disconcerting to simple believers for whom the uncovering of faith and not necessarily faith itself has a very different character from that presented in *Just Jesus*.

For those very much steeped in traditional religiosity (with traditional and popular not being necessarily synonymous) the shock may be a bit violent. It could be a positive and necessary element to help place their faith on the level of Christian praxis. This should be done with care and vigor. For better assimilation the book may require a well-planned system of pedagogy and a sharing in community.

The style, the mood, and the contents of *Just Jesus* are derived and lived from the theology of liberation and from the preferential option for the poor. This is where some may stumble, not so much simple folks who may disagree with the form perhaps, but more so the educated and the Sadducees who question more its content. They tend to see in *Just Jesus* a politicization of the faith and a revolutionary radicalism, a form of class struggle, the same way some view the theology of liberation. They confuse "class struggle" with the prophetic struggle against sin. I am aware, though, that neither in the theology of liberation nor in this book is everything prophetic struggle, even though the consoling call is addressed mainly to the poor.

In conclusion, *Just Jesus* is a great challenge and can be of practical benefit to a great number of people. Sometimes a direct reading of the Bible in ecclesial communities is sufficient to recapture the living word of God and to stimulate people to action. However, this is not always possible. A greater catechesis is needed which can be done through a discussion in community of books like *Just Jesus*.

IGNACIO ELLACURÍA, SJ*
Extract from the preface to the Spanish edition

III

For a number of years I had been toying with the idea of writing a life of Christ.

About ten years ago, a Jesuit friend of mine who has been working as a missioner in the mountain villages of Honduras urged me to get my hands on a copy of a book entitled *Un tal Jesús*, a creative retelling of the gospel story developed for the people of Latin America. My friend's enthusiasm proved to be more than justified. *Un tal Jesús* blends together Christology, contemporary New Testament studies, and liberation theology in a way that highlights, skillfully yet simply, both the immensely attractive humanness of Jesus and the overarching divine commitment to liberating human beings from every form of oppression.

This was the book, I soon realized, which I had secretly been wanting to write all along. "That's the way it actually was!" I kept exclaiming to myself as I made my way, chapter by chapter, through this version of the gospel

---

*Ignacio Ellacuría, SJ, along with three other Jesuits, their housekeeper, and her daughter, were assassinated at their residence in El Salvador on November 16, 1989.

story. For reasons I cannot altogether account for, I had the queer yet firm recollection of having been "there" before, as if, after two thousand years of lapsed memory, I had somehow awakened to the startling realization that I had been present to these scenes and events centuries ago. The work so excited me that it was all I could think or talk about for several months afterward. The first time I devoted a seminar to *Un tal Jesús*, the students did not want to see the course come to an end.

The theology of *Un tal Jesús* arises out of the experience of men and women fighting to surmount enormous poverty, economic exploitation, and political violence. The story "works" by drawing a parallel between the situation of injustice in many parts of Central and South America today and the life and time of Jesus. Jesus becomes a campesino whose awareness of himself as a prophet grows and develops, whose basic message is about the Kingdom of God being a kingdom of justice, whose humanity is never eclipsed by divinity, and whose good news is as much the attractiveness of his own personality and humanity as it is the message about God's Kingdom. He tells jokes and stories. He sings and dances. His hands are callused from hard word, and, like so many in South America, he even has a nickname, "Moreno" [in the original Spanish], "the dark one," because of the color of his skin.

There were two things which my students enjoyed about the book. First, they fell in love with the figure of Jesus. From week to week, they would remark about how human Jesus appeared there, so unlike the portrait of him they had grown up with. His story assumed a kind of naturalness, indeed, a believability, which drew them into the gospel. They would never again be able to read or hear many gospel passages the same way as before. *Un tal Jesús* had made the gospel story come alive without reducing it to the genre of religious fantasy. Jesus had feelings and emotions, as did his companions and his mother. He lived and breathed in this world. However prophetically he would react to the things he witnessed, Jesus never came across as mysterious, otherworldly, or serenely ascetical. Even the Jesus who was raised from the dead still remained the companion and friend; he had not suddenly become a distant, elevated supernatural being. The book helped some of them to relate to Jesus, really and earnestly, for the first time. For the first time, they heard a Jesus who laughed.

The second thing the students liked about the book was the way it deployed the theme of justice and God's "preferential love for the poor" throughout Jesus' ministry. For, just as the figure of Jesus as they knew it had seemed remote and unreal, so too his mission and work seemed un-connected with the pressing concerns of ordinary men and women. The Jesus they had been raised with was completely divorced from history, more a citizen of heaven than of the earth. He was a model of moral be-havior, a teacher of high spiritual ideals and values, their point of contact with the unseen God, and the one who had rescued them in some inex-plicable fashion from their sins. In fact, their understanding of salvation and redemption was so focused on the remission of sin and eternal life that the good news about Jesus himself amounted to little more than a pious curiosity or a soothing tale for world-weary souls; it had as much relevance as a statue of the Infant of Prague.

To put the matter bluntly, *Un tal Jesús* had given the story of Jesus back its guts. There really was something worth proclaiming and worth laboring to help men and women understand. There really was a "divine cause" which Jesus had taken upon his shoulders after being baptized at the Jor-dan. The gospel, fully lived, could make a difference to history, not merely in the private space of the individual's own spiritual development but in the public space of communities, politics, society, and culture. The matter of human sinfulness, which ultimately came to account theologically for why Jesus was crucified, was absolutely inseparable from the concrete mis-ery, powerlessness, and injustice that had caused the prophetic voices of old to blaze out against the rich and powerful of the land; the same evils would have stirred the soul of Jesus.

Many people find it difficult to comprehend why the church, in talking about Jesus, makes so much of sin when forgiveness comes so easily. And the reason for their bewilderment is that the forgiveness of sins is not so much a matter of sacrament and ritual as it is a matter of doing justice and promoting reconciliation among men and women. The real work of redemption, in other words, involves throwing oneself, heart and soul, into confronting and transforming all the forces, structures, relationships, and institutions which rob human beings of their freedom and suck away their life. This task is something to which we can devote our lives, too, just as Jesus did. His story has compelling reason for being retold.

The reader comes away from *Un tal Jesús*, then, with two graces which have worked one over intellectually and morally. One discovers a new way of relating to "a certain person named Jesus," and one senses that the real purpose of Jesus' life was both more complex and more exciting than the claim that he came to take away the sins of the world generally sounds.

Furthermore, these graces suggest two focal points for talking about Jesus today. Jesus was fully and attractively human, more so, perhaps, than any of us might ever hope to be; and God had chosen the side of those who counted as nothing in the eyes of the world: those chronically hungry, those who thirst for righteousness and justice, those whose basic rights had been violated, those burdened by poverty, guilt, and sin. What is there left for us to do, except to want to be with Jesus and to continue doing what he has begun?

WILLIAM REISER, SJ*

---

*Father William Reiser is a member of the Society of Jesus. He teaches theology at the College of the Holy Cross in Worcester, Massachusetts. He has written a number of books, including *An Unlikely Catechism* (Paulist Press), *Into the Needle's Eye* (Ave Maria Press), and *Renewing the Baptismal Promises* (Pueblo Publishing Co.). This section is an excerpt from the introduction to the book *Talking about Jesus Today: An Introduction to the Story behind Our Faith* (Paulist Press).

It All Started in Galilee

I'd like to tell you of what I saw with my now-failing eyes, what I heard, what my callused fisherman's hands did along with that One who lived with us. . . . I am John, from Patmos, a little verdant island lost somewhere in the Greek Sea. I'm always reminded of the son of Mary, Jesus of Nazareth, a very close friend of mine. I spent the best years of my soon-to-be-ending life by his side. Today, I will relate to you the good news he brought us so that we will all be united in one single effort and be happy in one single hope. You know, everything started in Galilee. . . .

Galilee is the northern province of Palestine. Jews from the south despised us. They would say that we Galileans were a gossiping, dirty, and boisterous people. They could be right. But they would also say that out of envy, because our land was the most beautiful in the whole country. Galilee is a vast garden, especially during spring, when the flowers cover the valley of Esdraelon; when wheat and grapes grow and olive groves and date palms bloom; when the blue and round Sea of Galilee is teeming with fish. There are important cities in Galilee: Sepphoris, Capernaum, Magdala. . . . But everything began in one small village called "the Flower" — in our Aramaic language, Nazareth means "the flower."

Susanna: Mary, have you heard that Rachel's son already left?

Mary: Yes, Susanna, I heard.

Susanna: When a palm tree comes out crooked, not even God can straighten it. That boy had a bad start.

Mary: And he will end up worse, Susanna.

Susanna: I guess the mother is to blame. A child reared well lives well. But think about Rachel's bad example. . . .

Mary: No, not the bad example, Susanna. The thing is, young people today just don't know what they want. Look at my son: no permanent job, no future.

Susanna: Don't talk like that about Jesus. That bronze-skinned son of yours is one treasure of a young man.

Mary: What treasure? Look at him: thirty years old and nothing. All his friends are already married and they have kids.

Susanna: My dear Mary, the thing is, your son is not so easily swayed. For sure, he's looking for a girlfriend somewhere outside Nazareth. Well, tell me, what future does Jesus have in this little town?

Mary: Yes, that's true....

Susanna: Hey, little girl, it's now my turn with the water!

Girl: Then quit talking and hurry!

Susanna: Don't push me, girl! What a monster! Hey, Mary, before I forget, tell your son to pass by the house because the wall is breaking down again. Don't forget, Mary.

Mary: Yes, I'll tell him.

Nazareth was just like that: a small rural town lost in an obscure corner of Galilee. It could only boast of twenty houses and a small synagogue. No one from that small community ever became famous. "Nothing good comes out of Nazareth," people from Canaan would say. People in Nazareth were very poor. They walked barefoot, and nobody seemed to know how to read and write. They made their houses from the caves in the hillsides. In one of those houses lived a widowed, but still young, country woman: her name was Mary. She lived with her only son, a burly and ruggedly handsome man with bronze-colored face burnt by the sun and a black beard. His name was Jesus.

Mary: Jesus, lay that hammer down and come; the food is getting cold!

Jesus: Yes, Mother.

Mary: Didn't you hear me? Quit pounding; come and eat. Come on.

Jesus: All right. Oh no! Who ever made me think I could make these useless tools? I told that Roman I knew how to make tools. But now, this one is longer than the other.

Mary: Oh, Jesus, my son, you always poke your nose into everything. If there's a wheat harvest, you're there. If an animal is gonna be butchered, you're there too. Then, you're somewhere else, putting up tiles and hammering at doors. Now, you're even trying to make tools!

Jesus: Don't worry. We're gonna have lentils on the table because of those tools. The Roman paid me a denarius in advance.

Mary: Poor Roman. Poor horse, especially.

Jesus: Didn't you say the food was getting cold? Come on, let's eat! Ah this smells good.

Mary: Come now son, say grace. And make it short.

Jesus: Short?

Mary: Because it will also take a short while to finish the food. Bread and lentils, nothing more. Go on, say grace, I'm hungry.

Jesus: Well ... Bless, Oh Lord, this bread and these lentils. Amen. Now, Mom, please pour me some wine because my throat is as parched as the desert.

Mary: There's no more wine, son. Why can't you just be content with fresh water?

Jesus: I'll end up like a frog with a lot of fresh water.

Mary: You know, son, Naphtali's wife is sick. She has fever again. This afternoon I'm gonna make her some soup. Poor woman, and with so many kids. Don't you wanna eat, Jesus? Are you sick?

Jesus: Me, sick? Why do you say so?

Mary: You're not eating anything. You've been a little strange these past few days. Come now, tell me what's wrong.

Jesus: Nothing's wrong with me, honest.

Mary: You're holding something back.

Jesus: Well, I have those tools which are driving me crazy!

Mary: Don't lie. Look, I know something's wrong because that Benjamin went to the Jordan to see the prophet. And you're rarin' to go too. Am I right?

Jesus: You guessed right. I didn't wanna tell you — I didn't want you to get sad.

Mary: No, I won't be sad. I'm just worried. There's lot of bandits along the way.

Jesus: Well, there isn't much they can get out of me, if you're worried about that.

Mary: Look, Jesus, before I forget: Susanna wanted me to tell you to drop by her house because the wall in her house is falling apart.

Life in Nazareth was a routine: eat, work, and sleep. The women enjoyed chatting and gossiping among themselves as they fetched water from the well. The children were used to running away from the classes that the old and blind rabbi would organize for them, and they would go instead and steal fruit nearby. The men would rather be at the small square adjoining the synagogue, waiting, as usual, for stingy Ananias to hire them for a planting or harvesting job. When there was no work available, they preferred to pass the time playing dice and placing bets they didn't have money for. Or they would think of some way to earn a living, just like Jesus would do.

Jesus: Hey, Susanna, this wall is now stronger than the walls of Jerusalem.

Susanna: You're finished? Oh, you're wonderful. Come, bring this hen to your mother....

Jesus: Thanks, Susanna. Bye!

Susanna: Bye, Jesus. Say hello to Mary for me!

In the evening, everyone would retire into their respective homes, warm themselves by the stone furnaces, drink some soup, and lie down atop the straw mats that served as their beds.

Jesus: Susanna paid me with this hen. Now we've got something for tomorrow.

Mary: Tie it to this pole. Then, let's have dinner. It's getting late. Say grace, my son.

Jesus: But Mother, these are the same lentils left over from lunch!

Mary: And so?

Jesus: Well, they've already been blessed!

Mary: How long will you be away?

Jesus: I don't know.

Mary: But my son, why do you have to go to a place so far away? What good would you get over there?

Jesus: Nothing...But everybody wants to see and listen to John the prophet. I also wanna go. Besides, didn't you tell me that he was a close kin of yours?

Mary: Yes, Isabel was my aunt. But in Galilee, we're all related to each other.

Jesus: Well, I wanna meet that cousin! He's already a somebody, and I heard people travel all the way from Jerusalem just to be baptized by him. They also say that John talks, shouts, and spits fire from his mouth.

Mary: Careful or you'll get burned. That's dangerous.

Jesus: What's dangerous?

Mary: What John is doing, agitating the people. Let him keep on talking and he'll end up with his head chopped off like anyone claiming to be a prophet.

Jesus: I wish there were a thousand men like John, a thousand gutsy men who would tell people the truth.

Mary: Then there would be a thousand heads chopped off and a thousand mothers grieving for their sons. Remember the massacre in Sepphoris. We almost suffered something similar.

Jesus: Age seems to have made a chicken out of you.

Mary: First, I'm no chicken. And, second, neither am I that old. Come now, eat... Seriously, Jesus, why do you really want to go there?

Jesus: I'll be back soon, promise.

Mary: I don't think so. You get there, you start kiddin' around, you become a friend of all those crazy people you meet, and you don't want to leave them.

Jesus: Mother, I want to go. I don't know how to say it to you, but I just don't like the way things are going here. Fix a door today, install three bricks tomorrow, earn four denarii crushing grapes... Then afterwards, what?

Mary: I was heading in that direction. Then, what? That was what I wanted to say. What is it that you want, Jesus? A year passes by, another year ends, and you haven't yet decided what to do.

Jesus: I want to do something so things might change. Or don't you see it? The Romans are oppressing us; people are getting hungrier all the time; the taxes are higher each time. And to top it all, the priests in Jerusalem are condoning all these abuses. What's next? Shouldn't we young Israelites join hands?

Mary: Yes, my son, I understand it now. But what can we poor people do? Listen: forget those dreams and face reality. You're already thirty. Now is the time to put your feet on the ground. I'm already alone... How I wish your father were still around... Oh, my good Joseph, may he rest in peace. Jesus, my son, where would I end up if something happened to you?

Jesus: Just as I said: you've become a coward with the passing of time. Well, then, weren't you the one who always said: God will put down the proud and lift the humble ones; God will feed the hungry and leave the rich ones with empty hands?

Mary: Yes, Jesus, I know I said that, and I believe in that. Everyday I pray to the Lord to enable us poor people to get rid of this misery.

Jesus: Mother, praying isn't enough. One has to take risks. One has to do something like John is doing.

Mary: So you've really made up your mind. You want to go to the Jordan and join those revolutionary radicals. I won't be surprised if one day they tell me: Mary, your son has become a prophet. He's roaming around and preaching too.

Jesus: Me, a prophet? Don't worry about that. Words more useless than these tools would come out of me. No, I'm not cut out for that. Now, let's finish these lentils because tomorrow, we'll have chicken.

A few days later, Jesus rose early, folded his old tunic, grabbed a dry branch to serve as a cane, and went on his way to the Jordan River where John the prophet was.

•

Jesus' origins were as humble, poor, and rustic as Nazareth was then. Nazareth was an unknown speck in the land of Israel, a land mentioned not even once in the Old Testament. But "it" started there (Acts 10:37). From there came the one who announced that good news which was excitedly heard by the poor in Israel.

The narrative above begins with the same words with which John, Jesus' friend, begins his first letter to the Christian communities: he refers to what he saw with his own eyes. He was one of the apostles, one of the witnesses to the life and passion of Jesus who brought that story forth to our time through their writings and through the communities that created the good news. Two thousand years ago, it echoed all over Israel.

During Jesus' time, Nazareth — "flower" in Hebrew — was a small village in the interior of Galilee where some twenty families lived. It being a village founded on a hill, the people used the openings on the slopes to build their dwellings. There was extreme poverty. The "possessions" of those families were not more than a pair of straw mats and some clay containers in which they could store grain, oil, and food for some animals.

The Galileans (who lived up north) were considered by the Israelites of the south (Judea) as a quarrelsome people, with little respect for religious laws and traditions. The region was a lair of activist guerrillas who regularly organized revolts against the Romans. Nazareth did not boast of anything, and being a notorious village, it was an unlikely place for the Messiah to come from (John 1:46).

In modern times, owing to Christian history, Nazareth has become the capital of Galilee, where some thirty thousand people live, most of them Christian Arabs. The biggest building in modern Nazareth is the Basilica of the Annunciation, which Pope Paul VI inaugurated in 1964. What used to be the "walls" (rear part of the cave) of the house where the family of Mary, mother of Jesus, dwelled are preserved inside. An inscription dating to the beginning of the second century was discovered there. It reads: "Xe Maria" (God save you, Mary). It gives credence to the historical authenticity of the place. The well to which Mary and her neighbors would daily go to fetch water, and which has always supplied water to the village, has been preserved. The source is located inside a small Greek Christian Orthodox Church. Moreover, one can see the remains of what was once the cemetery in Nazareth during Jesus' time and where, no doubt, his ancestors were buried.

Mary was around forty-five years old when Jesus began to announce the good news. Like all rural women, she would have been, at that age, a woman spent by hard work, yet full of common wisdom regarding the usual sorrows and joys in life. Her hands would have been callused; she would have been modestly dressed; and like all women of her class in Israel, she would have been illiterate. She was a poor woman who, like the faithful people belonging to "Yahweh's poor," had placed all her faith in God. Like all mothers, she worried about her son running into danger, "entering politics."

Susanna, Mary's friend, is one person whose name is recorded by the gospel of Luke when it talks about the women who accompanied Jesus when he preached in the villages and towns of his country (Luke 8:3). Community relationships in a small town were marked by strong bonds, and everyone was practically a member of the family, or, at least, people knew everyone's life and problems quite well.

Jesus' profession, like Joseph's, has been limited traditionally to being a carpenter. However, the original word used by Mark means more like a "handy man" (Mark 6:3). Jesus would work on wood, making tools and fixing doors. He would also plant and harvest as a daily wage-earner. For our culture, his social condition would be more like that of the underemployed.

In the Spanish original of these volumes "Moreno" (brown-skinned) is the fond nickname given to Jesus. Jesus' Semitic origins suggest a dark brown complexion and some features which, like those of Arab extraction, would have little to do with the images that make him appear as a fair-complexioned, blond-haired, and blue-eyed person.

Mary is a widow at this point in Jesus' life. There are no data to prove this, but Christian tradition has assumed her widowhood. Her being a widow makes her more cautious, more "cowardly." Likewise, she would be closer to her son.

Jesus went hungry and sweated while working. He had friends; he cried, laughed, and got tired like all of us. And like us, he sought his place in the sun and entertained doubts regarding his own destiny, surrounded as he then was by weakness (Heb. 5:3). John's prophetic preaching was a calling for him, a decisive moment during his search for a place in the sun. He slowly discovered his vocation, the same way as it happens to many individuals who, in their giving up everything to God and to their brothers and sisters, deepen their commitment and become what God wants them to be.

2

On the Way to Jordan

At that time, many went to the Jordan to see John the Baptist. The prophet's powerful voice drew a lot of people to fill the dry and dusty roads of Judea. The same happened on the roads of Galilee, though to a lesser degree. In springtime, these roads were filled with flowers, with new blossoms and very tall green grass that was at times waist-high.

Philip: I'm dying to see that prophet! Some people told me that he's the straightest guy who's walked on earth in a long time. Others say, though, that they couldn't hack his terrible temper.

Nathanael: Oh! Philip, I'm worn to the bones. What I want to do now is fall dead on the hay and snore the time away. . . . We got up so early today.

Philip: Don't you sleep, Nathanael, we've gotta reach Magdala before lunch. We barely have enough time. Jason, the tavern owner, offers the nicest fish in town during the first hour. If we get there late, he's gonna treat us with rotting fish. He always does that, and I'm pretty well used to that. I was there last week and I had to eat the leftovers of those who had come in early.

Philip and Nathanael were old friends. They knew each other from way back. They had played together and, at times, had also worked together. Years ago they had gone into separate trades. Philip hopped from town to town selling a little of everything: amulets, combs, scissors, fish hooks, pots and pans, . . . while Nathanael had a shop in Canaan, Galilee. There he worked with wool and, from time to time, fashioned things of leather.

Nathanael: Well then, cheer up, man!

Philip: I'm cheerful, Nathanael, I really am. That's what I'm saying: if John the Baptist is, as they say, a prophet, the time of hope for us empty-bellied folks has come. I've already taken note of that. I've never sold so many things before. You hit the road; you meet people on the way to Jordan, and, without your noticing it, you sell them something for the

9

trip. See what I mean? That's why I say John is a prophet. He's brought me luck.

Nathanael: Quit fooling around, Philip. I still don't understand how so many stupid thoughts slip out of that big head of yours.... But do you seriously think he's a prophet?

Philip: It isn't a stupid idea, Nathanael. Don't you think the Messiah will start a world far better than this one? Will he not bring justice? Well, justice is my being able to drop coins into my bag.... I've suffered much hunger. God's time should also be my time. Look, Nathanael, I brought these to see if I can sell them. I'm grabbing opportunities opening up during the trip, don't you see?

Nathanael: Well, what do you have there? Necklaces?

Philip: What do you think? Aren't they beautiful? Look at this one.

Nathanael: Philip, who are you going to sell these necklaces to?

Philip: Oh, they say Jordan is full of women — you know the kind I mean... The very stupid ones are easy to fool. I'm gonna be doing them a real favor by offering them this beautiful stuff. I'm gonna help them improve their business....

Nathanael: Do many prostitutes come to see the prophet?

Philip: A lot! That's according to those who have been there....

Nathanael: Blessed be the Most High! What ever made me come with you? I already told you that that prophet is....

Philip: What? What about that prophet? He's a prophet of the poor. He announces great changes for the earth, Nathanael. We've gotta listen to him. We should always listen to the voice of God.

Philip and Nathanael arrived at Magdala by noon. Magdala was a city whose air was thick with the smell of wine, women, and fish. It lay on the banks of the great Sea of Galilee. From the hills up north, many traveling caravans and camels entered the city. They stopped at Magdala and continued their trip into Galilean territory.

Jason: Hello, Philip!... It's been a long time since we bumped into each other in this tavern, you shameless fellow! What? What are you going to sell us today? I tell you, when the full moon begins, and it started yesterday, it is a bad time to do business!

Philip: I didn't come to sell, Jason. My friend and I, we're just passing through.

Jason: And who is your friend? I've never seen him here before.

Philip: Well, he seldom comes this way. He's busy with his wife, his children, his mother-in-law, and his shop. He's from Canaan, and he hardly goes out from there. You know, he has lots of work....

Jason: What brings you to Magdala, friend? Are you fed up with your wife? Here in this city, you know, there are women who can heal all sorrows.... Hey, you seem to be a serious man. What's your name?

Nathanael: Nathanael.

Jason: Nathanael. Very well. And what do Philip and Nathanael want? Are they going to spend the night here? I can find two nice beds for both of you....

Philip: We won't be spending the night, Jason. We gotta get going.

Nathanael: I'm so sleepy, but, well, we'll just sleep for a while under some tree.

Jason: And where are these friends heading to that they are in such a hurry?

Philip: We're going to Jordan to see the prophet.

Jason: By Moses' beard! Two more guests who've also been fooled! Even you, Philip? Oh, the prophet!... Now come, did you lose something at the bottom of the river that you are now going to put your head into that murky water? Well, surely, this little bald guy with a little-boy face has really put the craziness in you! Hike more than a hundred miles just to see that long-haired man!

Philip: Look, Jason, let's quit arguing. We're hungry.

Jason: You'll get more hungry when you get to where the prophet is! They say John is flesh and bones, that he only eats locusts, and he makes people fast and do penance. I'll whip you up something that will load your stomachs for a week!

Philip: Hey, Jason, make it fresh fish, will you?

People began to fill Jason's tavern. The smell of fish and grape wine was getting stronger. People were eating on the floor, some on top of rocks. The first ones to arrive grabbed the few available wooden stools. Philip and Nathanael went into a corner with their freshly broiled fish, olives, and hot sauce. After a while, when only fish bones remained on the plate, they saw someone enter. It was someone they knew.

Philip: Guess who's here!

Nathanael: Who's that?

Philip: Jesus of Nazareth, the son of Mary! What could he be doing here? Hey, Jesus! Jesus! Come over here!

Jumping over plates and taking care not to topple a wine jar, Jesus approached the corner where Philip and Nathanael were.

Jesus: What's up, Philip? How are you, Nathanael? I didn't expect I would meet somebody I knew here.

Philip: And so? Do you have work here in Magdala?

Jesus: No, I'm going to Jordan.

Philip: You're going to Jordan? You too?

Jesus: Aren't you two going to see John the prophet?

Philip: That idea entered his head, and it took hold of me also...

Jesus: What have you done, Nathanael? Have you closed your shop?

Nathanael: No, but I have little work these days. I left my wife to take care of it in case something crops up. I think it won't be long till we get to the Jordan....

Philip: Hey, Jason, bring over another serving of fish and a glass of wine! Now, it's gonna be the three of us who will go and see the prophet!

Nathanael: Don't yell, Philip! Must everybody know where we're going? They'll be laughing at us.

Philip: Let them laugh. Probably some of them are also going to the Jordan. Hey, my friends, is there anyone among you who's going to the Jordan?

Nathanael: Shut up, Philip, please! What a jerk you are!

Philip: This prophet has shaken the entire nation of Israel. I've seen it because I travel north and south. To be able to move so many people is a sign that one comes from God. Don't you think so, Jesus?

Jesus: I think so. That's why I'm going there.

Jason: Oh boy! So you're also going to the river? Where are you from?

Jesus: Nazareth.

Jason: Nazareth? I don't think many from that God-forsaken place have gone to the Jordan There are more rats than people in that village!

Jesus: A few days ago, Benjamin, the son of Rachel, left for the Jordan. He's a friend of mine.

Jason: And where are you going now? What kind of people are these? Just like sheep, all go where one goes! What crazy people! One can dream of prophets and divine signs while staying here and having a great time! You, Nazarene, don't you like that? I have very good wine and a few women.... There's nothing like that in your town. Why don't you hang around a few days and leave these two south-bound nuts?

Jesus: Look, I want to meet the prophet. I'll be hanging around Magdala some other time, promise.

Jason: What thick illusion-filled skulls! Hey, Nazarene, munch those fish bones and chat with me later! Let's see if you don't change your mind. I gotta go now because I got a lot of things to do.

Philip: The fish is very good, Jesus; they are the best in the lake.

Jesus: I can see that, Philip; you're swallowing them head, tail, and bones!

Philip: Jason's wife is a whiz when it comes to cooking.

Nathanael: But Jason is a rascal. He makes fun of prophets. That's very bad; it's the worst thing to do in the world.

Philip: Hey, Jesus, you believe that John will be the savior of Israel? Many people say so, and there are those who disagree.

Jesus: I don't know, Philip. One has to see him and hear what he says first.

Nathanael: Israel's savior should clean this nation of all stupidity. They say John immerses people's heads in the river and you become a new person when he pulls you out.

Philip: Hey, I like that! It's been seven months since I had my last bath!

Jesus: I'm sure that John is a prophet. It's been a long time since a man who said so many truths appeared in this country.

Nathanael: I'm not sure of anything. I've never seen a prophet. Prophets belonged in another time when God remembered his people and ruled them....

Jesus: Well, Nathanael, I think God has remembered us again and has sent us John.

Philip: It's all the same to me whether it be God or the devil! What I want to see is that baptizer shouting the word....

Nathanael: What word, Philip?

Philip: That which is needed here, my goodness! That we the downtrodden poor need someone to come and tell us: "Wake up, slumbering people, the time has come!"

Nathanael: Shut up, Philip!

Philip: Girdle your loins. This time it's for real!

Nathanael: Philip, by God!

Philip: Everyone united march onward as one!

Nathanael: Hush, Philip! Instead of going to Jordan, we might end up in jail! Hey, Jesus, finish those bones and let's get going!

Jesus: Yes, Philip, let's get going! Leave those speeches for another time. We still have two more days of travel before getting to see John the Baptist!

John was baptizing people in Bethabara, in Perea, south of the old city of Jericho, near the Dead Sea. Many people then came to listen to his words, seeking to find Israel's savior in his person.

•

John the Baptist's preaching of justice aroused the nation of Israel's hopes in the coming of the Messiah. It launched a true people's movement. People from all of Judea and also from the neighboring province of Galilee in the north traveled to the Jordan to hear John and prepare themselves for baptism in the river and to receive the hoped-for redeemer.

"Messiah" is an Aramaic word which means "anointed." The Greek word is equivalent to "Christ." In Israel, kings, when they ascended to the throne, were anointed with oil as a sign of sanctification and blessing from God (1 Sam. 10:1). Throughout its history — a history filled with failures, defeats, and slavery — Israel hoped for a redeemer from God who would bring lasting peace. Some hundred years before Christ's birth, this hoped-for savior began to be called "Messiah," in the belief that he would be a powerful king who would make Israel a great nation and drive away foreign masters from its land and give justice to the poor. When the first Christian communities recognized the Messiah in Jesus, they also began to call him "Christ," meaning God's anointed, his envoy, his blessed one. Among the four gospels, Matthew's is the one that marks Jesus' messianic character the strongest because it was especially written for Jewish readers. The coming of the Messiah, what this person would do, how to recognize him, where he would come from — some thought he would be an angel, while others thought he would be a great priest — were topics of conversation among the people during Jesus' time.

For the people of Israel, prophets were people of God who spoke in his name. They interpreted events, denounced injustice, and announced God's plans. They were feared by kings and rulers. After years of not having a prophet in the country, the people saw in John a prophet. Some even came to the point of seeing the hoped-for Messiah in him. This explains the mobilization of the masses who were aroused by the words of the Baptist.

In this episode, we see two of Jesus' disciples: Philip and Nathanael. Little is known about Philip: he was from Bethsaida, and he is mentioned only five times in the gospel texts. Much less is known about Nathanael: John only mentions him twice. In the lists of the twelve apostles, Nathanael has always been identified with Bartholomew. Philip, the itinerant vendor, happy, ingenious, and always preoccupied with his retail business, and Nathanael, the tanner, the older one, disillusioned and indecisive, were poor men who lived the insecurity that marked their social class. John the Baptist's message of salvation caught the imagination of the lower class.

Magdala was a city located on the banks of the Sea of Galilee, along the caravan route which entered Galilee from the mountains of Syria. Because it was a trade route, taverns and brothels sprang up there, as they still often do in similar places. There are few archeological remains dating back to the Magdala of gospel times.

(Matt. 3:5–6; Mark 1:5; Luke 3:7)

3

A Voice in the Desert

In the fifteenth year of Emperor Tiberius's reign (while Pontius Pilate was the governor of Judea; Herod, the viceroy of Galilee; his brother Philip, the viceroy of Ituraea and Trachonitis; Lysanias, the viceroy of Abilene; and under the administration of the high priests, Annas and Caiaphas), God spoke to John, the son of Zechariah, in the desert. John had spent many years in the monastery of the Dead Sea. When he felt that he was called by God, he left the monastery to preach along the banks of the river Jordan, proclaiming a baptism of conversion.

Baptist: The prophet Isaiah said it and I am repeating it! Make way for the Lord! . . . The Liberator of Israel is coming soon! . . . Don't you hear his footsteps? Prepare the way; make his paths straight that he may come to us!

John's voice echoed throughout Bethabara and the neighboring city of Jericho, extending to Jerusalem and spreading like wildfire in the whole country of Israel. We were anxious to hear that voice proclaiming justice and freedom from the Roman yoke. All of us came from the north and south to see the prophet from the desert. . . .

My brother James and I traveled from Capernaum. We came with our constant companions, brothers Peter and Andrew, who were also fishermen from the Sea of Galilee. Like us, they supported the zealot movement.

James: He's the man we need, Peter! Hell, this prophet minces no words and speaks out the truth as brutally as he can!
Peter: Then what are we waiting for, James? Call your brother and let's go approach him. Come on, Andrew, let's go, and I don't care if we have to elbow our way through, in order to get near him.

Long live the movement!
For seventy years, our country had been a colony of the Roman Empire. Consequently, the people became desperate because there was hunger everywhere, and they were made to pay taxes. That is why many of us sympathized with

the zealot movement, as it aimed to overthrow the Romans. Besides, there were guerrillas scattered all over the country.

Peter: Long live the movement!
All: Long live the movement!
James: Death to the Romans!
All: Death to the Romans!

The zealots were well organized, especially in Galilee, our province. Peter, Andrew, my brother James, and I formed a small support group in Capernaum. We talked to the people about the movement, and, yes, we joined in every protest and rally in the place.

Well, some of the protests we initiated. . . . I remember it was because of this that we decided to see the prophet John. Then, having heard him speak, we realized that we were of the same cause.

Baptist: Those who are in power shout: "Peace, peace, let there be peace!" Tell me, how can there be peace without justice? Can peace exist between the lion and the lamb, between the rich and the poor? On the other hand, the people below shout: "Violence, violence!" But they say it out of ambition, because they also desire to go up and commit abuses against those who are left behind. They are lions too, hiding under the skin of a lamb. . . . Thus, the Lord says: "All must change their ways! Everyone must be converted!"

The heat was exhausting. The mosquitoes were hovering like a cloud above our heads. People came from all walks of life peasants — artisans from the towns, wool traders, tax collectors, beggars, the sick people, prostitutes, and soldiers. Vendors were also present, pushing their carts through the people, selling their wares of little cakes and dried fruits.

Baptist: Repent, before it is too late! Those who want to be free from the wrath of God, be baptized in this river as it cleanses the body and purifies the soul! Do it now or the fire will convert you into ashes!

Piles of sandals and sheets were seen on the gray sand along the riverbank. John, whose back was supported by a rock, the water reaching up to his waist, baptized the people, holding them by the head. He immersed them into the water until they almost drowned, then pulled them out toward the shore. There were hundreds of us who received this baptism of purification.

Peter: Andrew, did you notice how his eyes glow, like two burning coals?

Andrew: This prophet is the same Elijah who came down from heaven in his chariot of fire. He is Elijah in person!

Peter: This is the end of the world!

James: Out of my way, you dupes! Let me see the prophet!

The prophet was a big man, whose skin was burned by the desert sun. He was clothed in camel's hair and wore a black belt around his waist. He had never had his hair cut, and it reached down to his waist. When the wind blew, his mane seemed that of a wild beast. It was the prophet Elijah talking through his mouth. Well, actually, John was not talking: he was bellowing, and his words bounced like stones hurled at our heads.

Baptist: Make way, make his paths straight, so that the Liberator will not delay! Fill up the holes that he may not stumble! Level the mountains if necessary, that he may not have to turn around and be delayed! ... No, he will not delay, for he is coming! ... Don't you hear his footsteps? Don't you feel his scent in the air? The Messiah is coming, the Liberator of Israel!

Peter: Pff! ... All I can smell here is the stink of urine. I'm going to faint.

Andrew: You're a pig, Peter. Shut up and listen to the prophet.

Peter: But it is true, Andrew. I don't understand why I'm here. People get immersed in the river and they do whatever underneath. They become even dirtier when they come out of it. And the prophet claims that the water cleanses and purifies! Pff!

James: You're right, Peter. The water seems like soup to me already, and the people's heads are like chick peas.

Peter: Let's go to the other side. I can't stand all this filth.

Andrew: Now look who's talking.... Peter, you are the one who stinks!

Peter: Go to hell, Andrew! Better take back your words!

John: Come on, that's enough, Peter. Let's get away from here, the heat is sickening.

We stayed away a little to be able to breathe some air. Peter was mad at Andrew, who was mad at me. James was angry at everyone. The four of us were good friends, in spite of the fact that we were always quarreling.

James: So, what do you think? On whose side is the prophet? You heard him say that all — those who are up and those who are down — must be converted.

John: That's nothing but sweet talk, James. He should tell exactly who he is. Is he supporting the zealots or not? That is what he should tell us.

Peter: Very well said, John. Long live the movement!

Andrew: Shut up, Peter. You're like a parrot!

Peter: The baptizer seemed to have dumbfounded you, Andrew.

Andrew: I'm for the prophet. Whatever you say, whoever you support, I'm for him.

John: But is he supporting the movement or not? That's what I want to know, Andrew.

Andrew: Why don't you ask him, John? Go immerse yourself in the water and ask him whose side he's on. You're his namesake — perhaps he'll answer you.

John: Well, yes. I'm not afraid of this prophet, nor of anyone. If he sides with the zealots, well and good, but if he's for the Romans, may he drown himself in this stinking river!

Andrew: Not so loud, John. It's not that easy.

James: Oh, yeah, it's easy, Andrew. You just have to kick all the Romans in the ass. That's all.

Peter: Anyone who hears you speak, James, will think that you're one of the seven leaders. Tell me, redhead, what have you done for the movement? Surely, you made noise in some four towns?

James: Likewise, what have you done, Peter? Hurl stones from the rooftop? Don't you flaunt again how you spat at the Roman captain, because here, even the children can spit on the soldiers!

Peter: You're a braggart. I better shut you up....

John: Stop the argument, damn it!...Now let's see who among us will dare ask John whose side he's on....

Peter: Why don't we all go a little farther away from here? I can smell the stench from here and it makes me dizzy. Come on, let's go....

The four of us left, and we ate some olives. We got a big surprise along the way.

Peter: Isn't that big head coming over here that of our friend Philip, the vendor? Philip!...Blazes! Now we're headed for trouble!

Philip: Peter, Peter, the stone thrower!...How's life treating you? Hey, James, the big mouth! And here is John, the troublemaker!...What are you up to this time, sons of Zebedee?...And look who's here too, the skinny Andrew....I swear, I'm so delighted to see you!

John: And so are we, Philip, the greatest chatterbox in all of Galilee!

James: Hey, Philip, don't be rude.... Why don't you introduce your pals?

Philip: Yeah, that's right. Nat and Jesus, I want you to meet these four rascals. They're fishermen from Capernaum, while these two scoundrels are even worse than you! Nathanael is a true-blooded Israelite who lives in Cana. He's a wool maker and is more cunning than a fox. He's got a wife who is unbelievably unbearable. The other fellow, this nice hick from Nazareth, is called Jesus. He can repair doors, just as he can make horseshoes. He's a jack-of-all-trades. Ah, and when he lends you money, he never charges interest! ... The problem is he's always penniless, and you end up lending him some money instead!

Peter: Well, it seems like we have known each other for a long time. But now, let's fill our stomach, as it's getting late!

All seven of us ate and had a chat amid the huge crowd. When night fell, we dispersed and headed for the riverbank. Every one gathered some dried twigs and started to build a bonfire. Some cut down palm leaves to make into tents so they would not sleep in the open air. The river Jordan was teeming with people who came in search of the prophet John, who, in turn, continued to look for the Messiah, the Liberator whom he was proclaiming.

•

The gospel of Mark, as well as John's, starts with accounts of Jesus' life, as preached by John the Baptist, along the banks of the river Jordan. This is one way of highlighting the link between the prophet's message of justice and the good news of Jesus.

On the one hand, the Baptist's preachings contained in the gospel accounts are searing indictments of injustice and the corrupt situation in the country, starting with Herod himself, the king of Galilee, who was publicly criticized by John. On the other hand, John considered his mission as preparatory for the coming of the Messiah, who was to found a new world based on the equality of all people and the sovereignty of God.

In order to prepare this new world, notwithstanding his preachings and proclamations, John employed a ritual which became very popular: baptism. People came to listen to him and confess their sins. Afterward, John submerged them into the waters of the river Jordan. It was a symbol of purgation. Water cleanses the unclean. It was likewise a symbol of rebirth, of starting all over again, leaving behind the ancient world of fatalism and injustice: from the water springs life, which begins in the water. Baptism by John was not a magic ritual. It was nothing without a real transformation in the attitude of those who were baptized. It was a mass baptism. The masses — particularly the poor Israelites — took to heart John's message and got into the water in preparation for the coming of the Messiah.

John preached and baptized in the desert, along the banks of the river Jordan, at a place commonly called Bethabara. The Jordan ("that which descends") is practically the only river that waters the land of Israel. It comes from the north, near Mount Hermon, and flows into the saline waters of the Dead Sea, the lowest place in the planet, about four hundred meters below sea level.

John the Baptist's simplicity, as reflected in his food and clothing, made him popular among the people. When they looked at this sun-burned and uncouth man, they saw the prophet Elijah coming back to defend his people. John's long and disheveled hair was typical of those who committed themselves to a total service to God: the vow of the Nazirites (Judg. 13:5; 1 Sam. 1:11).

For about seventy years, Palestine was a Roman colony. Rome was then the most powerful empire on earth, as the United States is today. Many nations during that period were under the Roman Empire. For the occupied provinces, this meant occupation by foreign armies and exploitation of the people, on whom heavy taxes were imposed and who were denied participation in decision making. Rome, the empire's capital, was destroyed about five hundred years after the birth of Jesus. There was great discontent with the Roman domination in Galilee, as well as in Judea. The zealots were known to be one of the oppositionist groups. They were engaged in clandestine activities; some were into the guerrilla movement, especially in the northern region of Galilee, where the movement was strongest. The zealots were nationalists, preaching about God as the only king. Furthermore, they were opposed to any foreign power, which was why they refused to pay taxes and to submit themselves to a census ordered by the empire. Weighed down by the burden of paying taxes, the peasants and the other poor people of Israel sympathized with the movement and protected its members. Similarly, the zealots had their own agrarian reform program: they declared that property should be distributed equitably, as the social gap was extremely wide. Debts must be written off, in accordance with Mosaic law on the Year of Grace. The zealots movement was said to have been founded by a certain Jude of Galilee, shortly after the birth of Jesus, when the people began to refuse to pay their taxes. The people's rebellion was suppressed by the Romans at the cost of blood and fire. The word "zealot" comes from "zeal." They were zealous of God's honor, passionate, and fanatic. The "sicarios" were an active group within the zealot movement. These were terrorists who always carried daggers (*sicas*) under their robes, which they used to murder the Romans.

It is probable that among Jesus' disciples many belonged to the zealot movement. The gospel very clearly expresses this when referring to "Simon, the zealot" (Luke 6:15). Judas's nickname ("Sicaria") implies his affiliation. Further, the moniker given by Jesus to the brothers James and John, "Boanerges" (sons of thunder), and that of Simon Peter, "Barjona," are attributed by some as referring to the zealots. The words may also refer to the theme of the zealots and the struggle engaged in by the disciples.

(Matt. 3:16; Mark 1:1–8; Luke 3:1–6)

4

God's Justice

People from the land of Judea and the city of Jerusalem, even those from faraway Galilee, came to listen to John the Baptist. When they repented and confessed their sins, the prophet baptized them in the waters of the river Jordan. My brother James and I, Peter and his brother Andrew, Philip, Jesus and Nathanael were also there.

Baptist: It is the Lord who said to me: "Raise your voice like a trumpet and denounce the sins and rebelliousness of my people. Shout out the injustices committed against the poor throughout the countryside and the cities!" ... Go back to the Lord! Be sorry from the bottom of your hearts, and the gift of life shall be given back to you!

Philip: This prophet keeps on saying the same thing. I wonder if he doesn't tire of himself. We have been here for two hours, and he sings nothing but the same song. . . .

Nathanael: Shsss! Quiet, Philip; I'm listening.

Philip: But Nathan, don't you see I'm bored?

James: Don't be silly, Philip. You've got to shout out these things to the people so they get it into their heads.

Philip: Be converted, be converted. . . . Blah-blah-blah . . . But what the hell does it mean to be converted? I don't understand it.

John: It means "to change." And to change means to topple the Romans and kick them out of our land.

Andrew: Come on, Philip, ask the prophet what should be done in order to be converted. He'll tell you. John wants people to ask him questions.

Philip: You think so, Andrew?

Andrew: Why, of course, man. Come on, ask him anything.

Philip: Eh, prophet of God! Prophet John!

Nathanael: Hey, Philip, for your mom's sake in Bethsaida, shut up! Don't make trouble. . . .

Philip: But I gotta ask the prophet. . . . Hey, prophet John!

23

Nathanael: You'll make a mistake, as always.

Baptist: Who called my name?

Peter: This big head over here wants to ask you something! . . . Here!

Baptist: What do you want to know, brother?

Philip: John, you keep on talking of conversion, of changing one's ways, of preparing the way, for the one who is to come. . . . Tell me, how should I prepare myself? We who are hungry, how can we do this? What are we gonna do?

Baptist: First of all, there must be justice. You hear me? There must be justice!

Philip: Better explain that further, prophet. You see I'm a stupid man and . . .

Baptist: How many blankets have you got?

Philip: Well, I feel embarrassed to say this, but . . . I only got one at home, plus this other one on me. . . .

Baptist: So you have two. You have an extra blanket. Give it to the one who has none. In Israel, there are a number of naked people with not even a rag to cover themselves! . . . You want me to be more specific? . . . You, the one on the side, . . . yes, do not hide yourself — How many pairs of sandals do you have? . . . Two? Three? What you are not wearing are the extra pairs. In Israel, so many walk barefooted, with not even a pair of sandals to wear. Share what you have with them. Have you got two pieces of bread? Share it with the hungry. Let no one have anything in excess so that no one will be in need. This is what the Lord wants. This is the meaning of conversion: sharing. Justice, brothers and sisters, justice! I am preparing the way for the Lord, and the Lord speaks through my lips: that everyone may eat, that everyone be clothed, that everyone may live. . . . Oh, he who turns his back on another, turns his back on the Lord! . . . Woe to him who closes his door to the traveler, who turns out to be the Messiah, who comes knocking at your door!

James: Very well said! This is exactly what we zealots are asking for. Justice!

Philip: Well, Peter, you may now hand me that blanket you have on. . . . The prophet tells us to share what one has. I say you must begin with your friends. Charity begins at home, don't you think so, Andrew?

Andrew: This man is indeed a prophet. All prophets before spoke of justice. The message of the prophets is always the same.

Nathanael: Well, speaking of giving half of what you have . . . For example, I have a shop, with four tools, but . . . this does not mean I am rich. I simply have enough to . . .

James: Don't worry, Nathanael. The rich are something else. Look at those people coming. . . . They are traitors!

Amid the crowd, two men with silken turbans passed and headed for the shore. The tall one had pockmarks on his face. We knew little about this man and more about the other. His name was Matthew, and he collected taxes in our city, in Capernaum. He was slightly limping and had a short gray beard full of bare patches. As always, he must have been drinking. . . . We all hated Matthew because he was helping the Romans.

James: Traitor to the country! Get outta here! Out!

All: Out! Down with the traitors! Outta this place. Leeches!

Jesus: This man looks drunk.

John: Of course, otherwise he wouldn't have dared come here. We know him very well, Jesus. Believe me, in this country you won't find a man more cowardly than Matthew.

Philip: Hey, James, my ears are already buzzing. For heaven's sake, quit yelling! As far as I know, this is a place for sinners, right? Matthew must be the greatest bandit of them all, but he too has the right to see the prophet.

James: The only right he has is to be hanged!

Matthew and his companion were able to reach the shore. At that time, John was baptizing a few heavily made-up prostitutes. Matthew waited a while for them to get out of the water. . . .

Matthew: Prophet of the most high, we have heard that Galilean ask you what he had to do.

All: Stay away from here! You traitor to the country. Traitors!

Baptist: Quiet! I want to hear what this man has to say. God wants to listen to him too. Speak up!

Matthew: Prophet of the most high, What must we do? We are Jews, but . . . we collect taxes for the Romans. What must we do?

Baptist: Let not your hands be stained by collecting more than what is prescribed by law. The Romans have laid a heavy burden on our people. Do not compound this burden by robbing the people of the little that they have. The Romans have trampled on our lands. Don't make the yoke heavier, nor the hand of the foreigner more oppressive.

Matthew: Will there be salvation for us?

Baptist: Salvation is for the one who seeks it. The one who will come after me will separate the grain from the chaff. He will keep the grain in his barn while he will burn the chaff with unquenchable fire. But there is still time to repent. Get converted and be cleansed with purifying water!

The two tax collectors went near the water. Matthew was staggering due to fear and, perhaps, for being drunk. Then John the prophet held them by the hair and submerged them in the warm and dirty water of the Jordan, where the sins of the prostitutes, the poor, and the usurers were floating in disarray: big sins and small sins, all the faults of our people....

One Soldier: Master! John! Speak to us!

Baptist: What do you want?

Soldier: You have spoken before the Romans. We are Roman soldiers. We have come to see you because your word has also reached us. We wear the uniform of those who have made themselves masters of this land, but we wish to be baptized too. What must we do in order to save ourselves from evil?

Baptist: The only owner of this land and of all the countries of the world is God! You may be the strong ones now and you punish the weak. Tomorrow, the stronger ones will come and they will beat you. Today, the kings and the rulers of this earth are like a herb which is green, but it will dry up tomorrow and get burned. God is the only king! The only law is that of the Lord! And God's law is justice!

Peter: Beware, prophet! If you keep on talking like that, you'll soon be brought to Pilate!

Baptist: God is the master of all lives. It is not Pilate, nor Herod, nor the Roman army. Soldiers, you must not threaten the people, nor accuse anyone of things they haven't done. Don't tell lies in court or abuse your power. Be content with your wages and don't rob the poor of their shelter or their food. All these, you must observe, you, Roman soldiers...!

Philip: I'm beginning to like this prophet. He yells at me, and also at the Romans. This John is one helluva brave man....

Philip: Come on, let's go.... Today we've had enough of the yellings of this John, the baptizer.

Jesus: Just a moment, Peter.... I would like to ask the prophet something.

Peter: Did you say you're going to ask him something?... But you know what his reply will be: "Justice, justice, and justice..." I'm leaving now.

Jesus: Just a minute, Peter.... John! I want to ask you something!

Baptist: Speak up, Galilean. I'm listening to you.

Jesus: Prophet John, ... I ... I do not know if I am meddling in some-thing I am not aware of, but ...

Philip: Speak louder, or he won't hear you!

Jesus: I was saying that ... Oh well, you were saying: Feed the hungry. You also say: Don't cheat in your taxes. Likewise: Do not use violence. All this is good, but ... these are only the branches.... What about the trunk?

Baptist: What do you mean?

Jesus: I believe that if the branches yielding bad fruit are pruned every time, they will continuously bear bad fruit, because the trunk is bad, and the roots are rotten.... Prophet John, what must we do in order to pull out these roots so that no one will ever starve, no soldier will ever use force, no ruler will ever collect taxes?

Baptist: Who are you?

Jesus: My name is Jesus. I came yesterday, with my two friends from the north. I have heard you speak; that is why I'm asking you.

Baptist: I cannot answer what you are asking me. Somebody else will. I baptize with water, but after me will come someone who will baptize with fire and the Holy Spirit. I only trim the branches. He uproots the tree, burns the bad roots, and rids the garden of all weeds.

Jesus: And who is this One that is to come? Who are you talking about?

But John did not reply anymore. The wind began to blow along the river Jordan. The bamboo trees swayed, and the waters formed into small and giant whirlpools. John stayed on top of a rock, looking afar. His eyes were burning on account of the sun and blazing with hope as they gazed through the horizon, in anticipation of the One who was to come.

•

Justice is an essential topic in all Scripture. That God is just, as the prophets have said again and again, means that he is a liberator who takes up the cause of the poor and demands that the rights of the oppressed be respected. He is upright and does not allow himself to be corrupted by any deceitful word or any meaningless cult. The Kingdom of God that is to come and is announced to the people is a kingdom of justice. A kingdom where there is equality, where the hopes of the people will be realized. Knowing God, which in biblical language is the same as loving him, is doing what is just (Jer. 22:13-16). True religion consists of recognizing the rights of the poor and maintaining just relations among people (Isa. 1:10-18; Jer. 7:1-11).

In proclaiming justice, John the Baptist demanded "conversion" from the people who were listening to him. The biblical meaning of this word is not "to confess, to repent, to have remorse of conscience." Rather, it refers to a change of ways, a return to the Lord who is just and, like him, doing what is just. There is no conversion before God without conversion before others, and especially before the poor. Conversion means sharing. He who does not share is not within the justice of God.

With regard to the Roman soldiers, John concretizes conversion in terms of nonabuse of power. The soldiers, foreigners as they were, were recruited from the masses. As servants of imperialism, afflicted with the system's corruption and emboldened by the arms provided them, they continued to oppress the people. The tax collectors like Matthew, who were officials of the empire or local officials, because of their position, extorted money from the poor. John denounces cheating in the collection of funds. Conversion has to pass through one's pockets. It always involves rejection of power. Good intentions are not enough.

The question that Jesus asks John concerns the matter of structural sin and personal offense. One can trim the old branches of a tree, but when the roots are rotten...Sin and injustice are not only individual transgressions which can be amended by way of individual conversion. There are also situations of sin: for example, an economic regime that is profit-oriented, benefiting only a few, a system in which, in the process of competition, the poor become poorer and the rich become richer. This is the structure of sin. A political regime that allows no participation of the people on the matter of decision making, utilizing torture, crime, fraud, and corruption for its survival, is likewise an institutional sin. An integral liberation, more than individual change, is needed in order to defeat sin. The gospel is a transformation of society.

(Luke 3:7-18)

5

The Broken Bamboo

The voice of the prophet shook the desert of Judah and echoed in the hearts of the crowd that gathered to listen to him along the banks of the river Jordan. John was announcing a new world that we were all dreaming of. . . .

Baptist: The fire of the Lord shall wash away all crime and abuses that afflict this earth like leprosy! And God will then do marvelous things that are unheard-of. He will create new heavens and a new earth, where justice will finally reign. There shall be no more tears nor moanings. . . .

While John was speaking, Jesus moved away from us and started to walk. He was going far from the crowded river Jordan, heading toward a place where there were less people. Andrew and I glanced at each other and started to follow him. I remember it was four o'clock in the afternoon. . . .

John: Where do you think he's going, Andrew?
Andrew: What do I know? Perhaps he wants to take a breather. One can hardly breathe down there, John. . . . Hey, what did Philip say his job was?
John: Bah, he said he could "fix anything." Just imagine, he wouldn't have to work hard in the neighborhood of Nazareth . . . because there, even rats die of hunger. . . . Ah . . . ah . . . achoo!

After I sneezed, Jesus looked behind and saw Andrew and me following him. . . .

Jesus: Oh, I didn't notice you. . . .
John: Achoo! . . . Damn it! I got this cold when I had myself baptized in the river. . . . Ah . . . Ah . . . When I got out, there was this cold draft that . . . Achoo! . . . Damn!
Jesus: Where are you going, by the way?
Andrew: Where are you going?

Jesus: Nowhere. It's too warm over there, and the mosquitoes are all around. I decided I should take a walk.

Andrew: Well, same here.

John: Andrew is right.... The stench from the river is nauseating. At least here, one can still breathe.

Andrew: That's right. The truth is, it's getting warm.

John: I would say it's like a furnace in Babylon.

Andrew: Let's say it's a kind of heat that ... ehrrmm ...

Jesus: Say, why don't we all sit down for a while, under those palm trees?

John: That's a good idea, Jesus, because ... oh, well, let's go ... this heat is ...

The two of us wanted to have a chat with Jesus, but certainly not about the weather. I don't know, but this tanned man from Nazareth had caught our fancy, ever since we saw him with Nathanael and Philip. We wished to know more about him....

John: Philip claims that you're a "jack of all trades." Are you a mason or something?

Jesus: No, ... well, yes, and an iron smith, and a carpenter. I also patch holes; well, I do anything. In Nazareth, it's difficult to have a fixed job.... Have you been there? It's a small town. You must always be ready to do anything that comes up.

Andrew: Who do you live with? Are you married?

Jesus: No, I live with my mother.

Andrew: And your father?

Jesus: He passed away when I was about eighteen years old.

John: So, don't you plan to get married?

Jesus: You see, I met a girl before.... How shall I put it ... ? I wasn't sure.

John: I can just imagine. In Nazareth, with four ugly ladies in your midst, it must be difficult to find someone deserving. You should go to Capernaum where jobs are good and life is more interesting.

Jesus: You're all fishermen, aren't you?

Andrew: We do business with Zebedee, the father of this guy, who has a very bad temper. He's doomed, you know!

John: Hey, you, skeleton! Why don't you leave my father alone?

Andrew: Okay, okay. So, you work as a blacksmith, is that all you do, Jesus, nothing more?

Jesus: Hey, do you know what it means to go out everyday in search of a job?...It's never easy.

Andrew: Certainly not. I don't mean that.... Well, about the move-ment...is it functioning in Nazareth?

Jesus: Are you zealots?

John: No, we're not.... Well, yes...I mean...The movement is our only hope to get rid of these damned Romans! Don't you think so, Jesus?

Jesus: I really don't know.... Honestly.

John: How come you don't? You should know!

Jesus: That's true, John, but...

John: There's no excuse. You should know.

Jesus: Okay. But you must also know which animal has its legs on your head, and yet, you don't know.

John: How's that?

Jesus: I'm asking you which animal has its legs on your head.

John: I don't know. Which is it?

Jesus: The louse!

John: What! Oh, yeah, its legs are on my head. Now, that's a good one, eh?

Jesus: Tell me, Andrew, in what way is a louse similar to a Roman?

John: A louse being likened to a Roman?

Jesus: Why not? Even the Romans have their feet on our heads!

John: Right! And they are considered animals too. That's really a good one! Give us another, Jesus....

I remember that day like it was today. As I close my eyes, I still imagine Jesus smiling, with many friends around him. He told us four jokes, a few stories, and with much ease shared his worries with us. We seemed to have known each other all along. Funny, but this tan-skinned man was one of those you come across and never forget all your life.

John: Wait till I share these jokes with Peter...!

Andrew: Where do you get all your stories, Jesus?

Jesus: Since the nights are very long in Nazareth, my friends and I often get together. One cooks up a story, another a legend...our way of killing time, you see.

Andrew: What do you intend to do now? Are you going back to Nazareth just to kill time?

Jesus: Well, that's what I don't know. On one hand, I like it there; besides I must look after my mother, who is alone....But sometimes, I don't understand why I feel the urge to run away...to escape....

Andrew: To escape from whom?

Jesus: Not really to escape...I don't know, maybe to travel, go to Jerusalem, see the world. Get what I mean?

John: Why don't you do what Philip has done? Buy yourself a cart and a horn and start selling amulets and other knickknacks around the whole city.

Jesus: It's not for me. I'd like to do something else....Whenever I hear the prophet John I tell myself: This is something worth doing. This man is helping the people....But I...what do I do for others?

John: And what do I do?...And this skinny man?...We're all hopeless cases here. But listen, since you have a gift of words, you can buy yourself a camel skin and you can also begin baptizing on the other side of the river....That's it. Be a prophet!

Jesus: Stop that foolishness, John. Can you imagine me as a prophet, ...a peasant like me, who has never studied the Scriptures and whose knees tremble every time he's asked to read in the synagogue?

John: Bah, that's only true at the start. One gets used to everything. Before, I was scared of the sea. And now, for thirteen years, I've been casting nets into the sea.

Andrew: How would you like to be a fisherman like us, Jesus?

Jesus: Sure, but I can't swim. I'd drown!

John: Come to Capernaum. There, only the cats are scared of the water.

Jesus: Well, if you only knew...that last night, I dreamed of the sea....

Andrew: Really? Come on, tell us about your dream, Jesus.

Jesus: It was a strange dream, and it worries me. Look, I was facing the sea, just like now. Then from the water I saw the prophet John. He looked at me and pointed out some bamboo to me along the bank of the river and then headed for the desert. After that, I saw him no more.

Andrew: What happened afterwards?

Jesus: Then a strong wind came, jostling the bamboo along the shore and knocking it down....Then a whirlwind came and I felt that the wind was grabbing me by the hair, just like when John holds those who are going to be baptized, lifting me and taking me to the site of the broken bamboo....

John: So what did you do?

Jesus: I leaned over to straighten them up.... There were a number of them.... I raised them one by one. It was a difficult thing to do, but I enjoyed doing it and I was happy. Then I woke up.

John: There, there, but why does it bother you, man? It's just a dream, and a lousy one, at that.... Your jokes are a lot better....

Jesus: But I was happy fixing the broken bamboo. I have never felt that way before....

John: Well, of course, each one of us finds enjoyment in whatever way he can....

Jesus: No, it's just that when the prophet John was talking a while ago, about the new heaven and earth, I felt the same joy.... That's why I remembered the dream....

John: I guess after listening to John the Baptist about the Messiah and liberation, we all dream of the same thing. And with his long hair, this liberator will certainly be a character! Surely it's that type that will create a new earth.... Do you know how I envision the new world of the Messiah? Without the Romans. No more taxes and abuses. Out with Herod and his cohorts.... They're all rotten leeches! They have to be crushed! Out with the treacherous publicans too...!

Jesus: Say, in the new world, there'll have to be room for many, but you keep throwing out so many people....

John: That was what the prophet said: that the Messiah would burn all trash and uproot the old branches....

Jesus: What about the bent bamboo, the almost-broken bamboo?

John: Of what use is broken bamboo? I don't think the Messiah will straighten them up, like you did in your dream....

Andrew: Say, Jesus, how do you imagine yourself to be in this new world?

Peter: Where are they? Where could they have gone?

Andrew: It's my brother Peter. I can hear his voice from here....

Peter: Hey, where are the Capernaum people?

John: Over here, Peter!

Peter: But where have you been all this time?

Andrew: Talking to Jesus...

John: Look, big nose, this tan-skinned man called Jesus knows some jokes...!

Peter: What the heck! Jokes! Time is never wasted here. We went down to the river and discovered a site full of crabs. Nathanael made soup that tasted...mmmm. Don't you feel hungry? Come on, let's go.

Jesus: Hey, Peter, you're called Peter, aren't you? I was thinking about it yesterday. I had never heard of that name....

John: But his name is Simon!

Jesus: Then why do they call you Peter?

Peter: Ah, that's another story to tell....Have you told Jesus about the movement?

John: This guy Peter gets himself into all sorts of trouble. All he does is yell and throw stones....That's why we gave him the name of Peter: *petros* means "rock."

Jesus: So your name is Simon, but they call you Peter....

Peter: Oh well, why don't you just stop talking about me and join the others so we can eat the crab soup?...I can smell its delicious aroma from here!

Night fell on Bethabara. The riverbank was glowing with bonfires, and the whole countryside smelled of recently cooked food. The truth was that Andrew and I could not fully comprehend then the impact of Jesus' dream. Now that I am old, I recall that day when Jesus became my friend. After I'd met him, when I found myself far from that place where I met the tan-skinned man, everything just became clear to me.

The ancient writings of Isaiah announced it: he straightened the broken bamboo and extinguished not a single wick emitting a spark of light.

•

Jesus, like all of us, was a searcher. He searched for an answer to questions about life and reality. He looked for basic answers, such as relating one's service to God and people in circumstances of conflict experienced by others. Jesus realized this quest through reflection and prayer and, at the same time, sharing his preoccupations and questions with his friends. To pursue one's own vocation is an individual process. Our brothers and sisters and the community help in our discernment, and their solidarity is the source of our strength that helps us undertake decisions that God expects of us by being part of this reality. Jesus' manner of expressing himself, as the gospel has shown us, gives us a picture of a man who was amiable and witty, a man never wanting in anecdotes and stories to tell, jokes and other puns to share.

People of ancient times (as well as today) gave a lot of importance to dreams. They believed that dreams enabled people to get in touch with God, and by way of dreams one could look into the future. In Israel, certain dreams were given special meanings. Some of these dreams even figure in the Old and the New Testaments as revealers of the future or God's plans for his people (Gen. 27:5-10; Dan. 7:1-28; Matt. 1:18-25). Short of superstition, these beliefs lead us to a profound truth: God is near us in our wakeful moments or in our dreams, by way of our psychological make-up and the complexities of our mind. A believer ought to discover God by way of any of these experiences.

Jesus' dream, as told to John and Andrew, captures one of the most beautiful messianic prophecies of Isaiah (42:1-4), where the prophet describes the Messiah as a harbinger of the infinite patience and mercy of God, a just but not intolerant man, a fighter but not a subduer.

(John 1:35-39)

6

An Ax Is Laid to the Roots

At that time, Joseph Caiaphas was the high priest in Israel, the religious head of the country. Caiaphas lived in a sumptuous palace in Jerusalem. Everybody hated him because we were aware of his dirty dealings, and we knew that he was a pawn of the Romans who were then occupying our land. . . .

A Priest: We are here to consult you about a matter of importance.

Caiaphas: Yes, I know. It's about the new taxes. That's all right. I'm giving my approval. After all, I'm not the one who has to pay. On my behalf, please tell Governor Pilate to do everything he can to maintain peace and order in our country. Ah, and tell him, too, that I haven't forgotten his invitation: I'll be at the Antonia Tower to savor that famous wine he ordered from Rome.

Another Priest: We will tell him, Your Excellency, but we came here for another purpose. . . .

Caiaphas: Listen carefully. If you were sent by my father-in-law to collect payment for the lambs on the feast of the Passover, tell him I can't pay him even a single denarius. I incurred a lot of expenses in constructing my palace in the countryside. Besides, I see no reason why he's in such a hurry. . . .

Priest: We did not come to collect anything, Your Excellency. It's about John, the son of Zechariah. . . .

Caiaphas: So, it was about something else. . . .

Priest: By this time you must have heard about the disturbance caused by this fool along the river Jordan. . . .

Caiaphas: Unfortunately, I'm well-informed about it. . . .

Priest: People go in droves to listen to his ravings. They say he is a prophet of God. Others claim he is no other than the Messiah, the Liberator that our people have been waiting for. . . .

Caiaphas: What? This shaggy man is the Messiah . . . ! or the Prophet! . . . A filthy, stinking man — that's what he is, just like any gang of galley slaves.

Priest: You ought to do something, Your Honor. It might spread like wildfire. . . .

Caiaphas: Well then, go see for yourselves. That's right, you go to the Jordan and find out what's behind all this. Ask this guy the reason for all the uproar and all these baptisms, and by what authority is he agitating the people. And tell him to be very careful with his actions. This is my warning to him. . . .

The eyes of Caiaphas, big and watchful as those of an owl, remained fixed on the wooden door of his palace as he watched the two priests leave. Then, slowly he sat down on the silk-covered armchair. In a few days, he would be receiving news about this prophet, a troublemaker and a rebel, giving him, the high priest of Jerusalem, a lot of problems. . . .

Everyday, more and more people headed for the river Jordan to listen to John and be baptized. That morning, before the priests sent by Caiaphas from Jerusalem arrived at the Jordan, four Pharisees came to Bethabara. These Pharisees thought of themselves as pure and holy, because they prayed three times a day in the temple and fasted in accordance with Moses' law. They despised us, but we simply laughed at them. . . .

Pharisee: Deliver me, Lord, from evil men, keep me from infidels, whose tongues are deceitful and whose hearts are sinful. Do not corrupt me like them, oh Lord of Israel, nor stain my cloak with the impurities of these lawless men, who know not your commandments nor respect the sanctity of your temple. Deliver me, oh Lord . . .

Four Pharisees, all wrapped in their black and white striped cloaks, made their way among the people. With their heads bowed, they were praying ceaselessly. They did not want to stain their reputation by mingling with us. . . .

James: And why are the Pharisees here? These wicked men can all go to hell!

Philip: Leave them alone, James, and let us see what they want. . . . Here, everyone is free. . . .

James: They're here to spy on the prophet John. . . . What a disgusting sight! They think they're saints! . . .

One Pharisee: John, son of Zechariah, we came all the way from Bethel in order to know you and to receive the baptism of purification....

Another Pharisee: We are followers of the Law, prophet John. We observe the Sabbath. We give alms in the temple, pray daily, and fast.

Pharisee: We are obedient to God. What more do you ask of us?

Baptist: Nothing. It is the Lord who asks for justice.

Pharisee: Prophet John, you must know that we have always been just. Our hands are clean.

Pharisee: We, too, want to prepare the way for the Messiah.

Baptist: Nobody ever prepares the way for the Liberator of Israel by proclaiming that he is clean. Your hands shall always remain clean due to constant washing, but not your hearts! For they are proud and pretentious! Hypocrites! You are no better than the peasants gathered here or the prostitutes weeping for their sins and asking forgiveness from the Lord!

Pharisee: With whom are you trying to liken us? We are Abraham's sons!

Baptist: No! You are all sons of a viper. You are like serpents: hiding your venom in your belly!... Stop claiming that you are Abraham's sons.... The sons of Abraham are just and do not dominate others. You blind Pharisees: cleanse your hearts not your hands! Be upright with your work and don't recite so many prayers! Heed me well, or else you'll not escape the fire that is soon to come....

James: Very good, John! Be hard on them.... *This man calls them like he sees them!* Damn these Pharisees! Why do they have to poke their noses into everything?

Philip: Listen, guys, I know of a Pharisee, the youngest of them, who's a very good man. He helps me and...

James: Come on, Philip, you don't have to defend them now before these people.

Philip: But all I wanted to say was that the Jacobite...

James: Don't push, you creep. There's room for everyone here!

A Priest: Give way, Galilean!

James: Hey, what brings you here, anyway?

Another Priest: Clear the way, for we have to go back to Jerusalem!

While John was denouncing the hypocrisy of the Pharisees, the priests sent by Caiaphas arrived from Jerusalem. They were wearing yellow robes, and they smelled like incense or sandalwood.

Baptist: God says he will catch all of you like fish in the river and no one will escape the day of cholera!

Priest: John, son of Zechariah! . . . Who gave you the authority to speak those things?

Priest: Who do you think you are?

Baptist: And who are you?

Priest: We were sent by Caiaphas, the high priest from Jerusalem and keeper of God's laws, to ask you this question: By what authority do you speak in this manner? Who do you think you are? Why don't you speak up? Eh? . . . You have caused a stir among these people with your cries, and now you are speechless.

Priest: What do you think of yourself? . . . Do you think you're the Liberator of Israel, the Messiah?

Baptist: I am not the Liberator of Israel.

Priest: Then who gave you permission to be talking to these people about the fire of God that will come down to purify *them?* Do you think you are the prophet Elijah who seared the earth with his burning words?

Baptist: I am not Elijah! He was the greatest of the prophets! I am not he! I only announce and make way for the one who is to come.

Priest: And how do you make way for him? By baptizing these wretched ones and feeding them with stories? . . . And who are you to baptize them? We are already purified as it is written in the Law, whose custodian is the high priest. Who are you to introduce a new way of life? Are you like Moses who can introduce new laws to these people?

Baptist: I am not Moses!

Priest: What are we to tell Caiaphas, the high priest? In whose name, shall we tell him, are you doing this?

Baptist: Tell this to Caiaphas: "In whose name are you doing what you are doing? In the name of God you stain your hands in the dirty business of your father-in-law, Annas! And in God's name, you sit at the same table with the oppressive Romans!"

Priest: Shut up! You are offending the high priest! You are insulting God!

Baptist: No, it is the high priest who has offended the Lord with his crimes and other acts of injustice. I am not going to shut up. I cannot be silenced! I am the voice that cries in the desert: Make the path straight for the Lord! Go tell Caiaphas that his throne is wobbling. A Galilean who was with you yesterday already said it: It is not the branch that is rotten, but the trunk, and therefore, the entire tree. And when the tree is rotten, you have to uproot it.... Look at what I have in my hand....

Philip: It's a cane. I see it from here!

Baptist: You may be seeing a cane, but look at it very well.... It's the ax of the Messiah! Look very well and tell Caiaphas what you have seen. The Lord laid an ax in my hands, and I must put it in the hands of the one who is to come after me. I only lay the ax to the root of the tree, so that he who is to come after me shall finish the job. When he comes, he will raise the ax and with only one thrust, cut the rotten tree. The day of the Lord's fury has come! The ax is ready and sharpened! It is just awaiting the one who is to come. He will not delay, for he is already in our midst.... Where are you, Messiah? Where do you hide, oh Liberator of Israel? My hand gets weary holding the ax. Let me know if you are not coming, so that I can give the first blow. Come, Liberator, and make haste! Let the earth be opened and spring forth the Liberator! Let the heavens break loose, and may we be showered with the salvation of the Lord!

A few days later, the priests returned to Jerusalem....

A Priest: Your Reverend Highness, dear Caiaphas,... that man is a crazy fool!

Caiaphas: If he is a furious madman, then he is not dangerous. His madness will pass.

Another Priest: He goes down to the river surrounded by all this crowd, shouting and screaming. In his hand is a cane which he claims to be the ax of the Messiah, for cutting the rotten roots of the tree....

Caiaphas: I'd rather cut his long hair with that!

Priest: And not only that; he is also an agitator. He has spoken very harshly against Your Excellency.

Caiaphas: Really? What did he say about me?

Priest: That the throne of Your Excellency is about to fall, for the day of the Lord's fury is near. He says he is the voice that cries in the wilderness.

Caiaphas: Let him scream as much as he wants. Agitators don't last in this country.... Leave him alone in his preaching. John has very little time left....

John wasted no time baptizing the people who went to the river Jordan. More than anyone, he knew fully well that his days were numbered. He was in great haste, but feared no one. He had the inner strength of the prophets, from Elijah, the greatest of all, to Zechariah, who was killed before the altar, inside the temple.

•

John the Baptist's activity bothered the political as well as religious author-ities, who were all fearful of any popular movement. That is why the central authority, represented by the high priest Caiaphas, sent an investigating commission to Jordan.

The high priest was the greatest religious authority of Israel. From the temple of Jerusalem, he controlled the whole theocratic system through which religious and political matters passed. On him depended the temple personnel, composed primarily of priests and Levites.

Annas had been the high priest earlier and maintained a powerful po-sition even after formally out of office, functioning as a kind of high priest emeritus. He was from the powerful priestly family of Bete (Beto) and was very influential, politically and economically. He was succeeded in his post as high priest by his five sons and, finally, by his son-in-law, Joseph Caia-phas, who sentenced Jesus to death. If at one time the high priests had represented the religious sentiments of the people, in the years narrated to us by the gospel, this institution was totally corrupt. The high priest was no less than a collaborator with Roman imperialism, the major symbol of a religious system that was oppressive to the people through the laws and through a policy of fear. The high priest likewise enjoyed great economic benefits from this post. John the Baptist, possessing an authentic, coura-geous, and truly religious character, made everyone tremble within the whole system.

To any institution, be it religious, political, or cultural, the voice of the prophet is always a threat. A prophet is born outside the institution and situates himself or herself along its borderline. The institution represents the law, the norm, security, and power. The prophet personifies risk, audacity, freedom, and imagination. The conflict between the institution and the prophet has always existed, even in the church.

A group of Pharisees also approached John. In the gospel narrations, they are always presented as the most determined enemies of Jesus. The word *pharisee* means "separated." The Pharisees were not priests. They constituted a lay movement led by the learned and the scribes. Their reli-gious practice centered on the strict observance of the law, and, therefore, they despised the people and "isolated" themselves from those who did not share or observe the same scruples.

This mentality of the Pharisees still persists in people who think of God as a "banker" who takes into account our good and bad deeds, whom we can "buy" through meritorious works (sacrifices, promises, vows...). It is present especially among individuals who consider themselves the best and look down on others. One of the most revolutionary elements of the message of Jesus is his proclamation that the self-righteous shall be the last and that the last, the "sinners" (prostitutes, drunkards, cheaters), shall be the first before God.

John explains to the investigating commission the coming of the day of the Lord. God's fury, his wrath, is a biblical issue taken up by the majority of the prophets. It is not the sort of anger which is capricious or arbitrary. Neither is it a form of God's passionate revenge against those who have offended him "personally." The fury that the prophets speak of refers particularly to the day when God exhausts his patience before the oppressors and intervenes, with all his power, in favor of the oppressed. One must not think, however, that the God of the Old Testament was a vindictive God, surpassed by the God of Jesus, all-loving and merciful. The texts of the New Testament, as found in the gospels as well as in other books, have adopted the theme of wrath (Rom. 2:5–8; Rev. 6:12–17), just as the ancient prophets likewise spoke of the endless mercy of God (Exod. 34:6–7; Isa. 49:13–16).

(Matt. 3:7–12; Luke 3:7–20; John 1:19–28)

7

Baptism in River Jordan

It was dawn that morning in Bethabara, where John was baptizing. The sky was clear, with no trace of clouds, and the desert wind was blowing intensely above our heads, agitating the waters in the river Jordan. Although there was no sign of it, that morning proved to be very significant. We would recall this a few years later. . . .

Baptist: I am just one voice, a voice that cries in the wilderness! Make way, clear the road, for the Lord is coming soon! He is coming! He will not delay! Be converted! Cleanse yourselves, change your hearts of stone to hearts of flesh, new hearts prepared to accept the Messiah of Israel!

On that day, Philip, Nathanael, and Jesus decided, finally, to get baptized. The three fell in line, jammed among the crowd of pilgrims, and waded through the muddy waters of the river.

Baptist: Come on, you better decide now. Do you want to be baptized or not?
Philip: Well, I . . .
Baptist: Do you want to promote the Kingdom of God, so that justice will prevail on earth?
Philip: Of course, but the trouble is . . .
Baptist: What is the matter with you, Galilean?
Philip: Nothing. It's just that I'm not very fond of the water, you know. . . . It's been months since . . . wait . . . wa . . . !
Baptist: May the God of Israel remove the filth from your body and soul, that you may see with your own eyes the great day of the Lord! And now, let me see . . . Who are you? What is your name?
Nathanael: My name is Nathanael, from Cana of Galilee.
Baptist: Do you want to be baptized? Do you want to be clean for the coming of the Messiah?

Nathanael: Yes, John, I want to.... I also want to prepare the way for him and ... assist the Liberator of Israel....

Baptist: Well, you said yes. This word will hang over your head. When the Messiah comes, follow him. Don't betray him, or God will betray you for the words that you have just uttered. Are you decided now?

Nathanael: Yes, prophet, I ... I am....

Baptist: Come closer, and be sorry for your sins.... Even if your sins are as red as blood, they will be as white as snow; even if they are as dark as charcoal, they will remain as clear as rain water....

The prophet submerged the hairless head of Nathanael in the river, just as he did to our friend Philip and the others. Jesus' turn came....

Baptist: You, where are you from?

Jesus: I am a Galilean, like the other two. I live in Nazareth.

Baptist: In Nazareth? In the neighborhood between Nain and Cana?

Jesus: Exactly. Do you know the place?

Baptist: I have some relatives there.... What did you say your name was?

Jesus: Jesus.

Baptist: You're not the son of Joseph and Mary, are you?

Jesus: Exactly. My mother said we were distant cousins.

Baptist: That's it. It's indeed a small world! Will you stay here at the Jordan for some time?

Jesus: Yes, a couple of days....

Baptist: Will you be baptized?

Jesus: Yes, John. That's why I came. You are preaching justice. I also wish to comply with God's justice.

Baptist: Have you repented of your sins? Truly and with all your heart?

Jesus: Yes, John. I am sorry for everything, ... especially for this fear....

Baptist: What fear? Do you fear anyone?

Jesus: I'm afraid of God, because he is exacting. At times he wants to harvest where nothing has been sown. He scares me every time he demands what I am not capable of giving him.

Baptist: If you get baptized, will you promise to prepare the way for the Messiah? Think about it first.... God accepts no excuses. If you say yes, then that's it. If you say no, so be it. Make up your mind.... Do you want to be baptized?

Jesus: Yes, John, I want you to baptize me.

Baptist: Very well. You will be one of those who will assist the Liberator of Israel.

Jesus: You always talk of this Liberator, John. But where is he? Who is he? You told the emissaries from Jerusalem that you are not the Messiah that we are waiting for.

Baptist: Of course I am not the Messiah. He comes after me, a lot stronger than I. He comes after me, but he is before me. This I assure you, Jesus: if he appeared before me, I would not dare untie his sandals.

Jesus: But who is he, John? When is he coming?

Baptist: He has come. My heart tells me that he is already in our midst, the Redeemer of Israel, although I have not seen him yet.

Jesus: How do we recognize him when he comes?

Baptist: The Holy Spirit will rest upon him, like a dove, quietly. The Spirit of God never makes noise. . . . The Messiah will come like a light breeze. He will not cut the almost broken bamboo, nor will he extinguish the flickering wick. . . . Have you not read what the prophet Isaiah says: "This is my beloved Son, with whom I am pleased"? This is the Messiah, the chosen son of God. . . . What is wrong with you, Jesus? . . . You are trembling.

Jesus: Nothing . . . I'm okay.

Baptist: You tremble like the boats in the river when the desert wind blows over them.

Jesus: I'm just feeling cold. That's all.

Baptist: But it is not cold. . . . And how is that possible when you look flushed?

Jesus: I'm nervous, John . . . , so please baptize me now, while fear has not taken me over, or I might change my mind. Please do baptize me now. . . .

The prophet John, that sun-burned giant, vigorously raised his arm, held Jesus by the hair, and submerged him in the rushing waters of the river Jordan. . . .

Baptist: Lord, give us our freedom; send us the Liberator. Blessed is he who comes in the name of the Lord!

Shortly afterwards, Jesus was taken out of the water. . . .

Jesus: Thank you, John. I feel more relaxed now. I feel . . . happy. I don't know why, but I'm happy! . . . Hey, John, what's the matter with you? You're trembling. . . . John, do you hear me? . . .

But the prophet was not listening. His eyes were fixed on the sky, as if he were looking for something, scrutinizing the clouds, examining the flight of birds....

Baptist: I hear the voice of the Lord above the waters! The God of glory is coming like thunder!...His forceful voice is calling....

Jesus: What are you saying, John?

Baptist: Nothing, nothing...For a moment, I thought I heard...The birds in the desert speak a mysterious language, and they are like a mirage on the horizon....It's nothing, don't worry....

A Man: Hey, let's get this over with! Why all this big talk just to soak one's head?

A Woman: Shut up, you dope! You should be ashamed of yourself to be talking that way....

Another Man: Hey, stop pushing, woman, it's my turn now!

Jesus: John, I would like to talk to you when there is less confusion here. I need to talk to you.

Baptist: It is I who need to talk to you, Jesus. Now, go back to the shore. The people are getting impatient with this heat....

In a short while, Jesus returned to the shore....

Peter: What happened, Jesus? What took you so long?

Jesus: I took the opportunity to ask him some questions....

Philip: I thought you drowned in the river, ha, ha, ha! Look at my hair. It's still dripping. What the heck, this prophet has arms like a pair of pliers; he gets hold of you, submerges you in the water, and presto! You're baptized.

Peter: What did you ask him, Jesus?

Jesus: How's that again, Peter?

Peter: I said, what did you ask the prophet?

Jesus: What everyone wants to know, like, who the Messiah is, and when the Liberator of Israel is coming.

James: And what did he tell you? Did he say something new?

Jesus: No, James, his answer was the same....

Nathanael: There is a certain glow in your eyes....

Peter: Come on, Jesus, tell us. What did the prophet tell you...? You were chatting with him for a long time....

Jesus: He said nothing to me, Peter. Well, he said that the Holy Spirit comes quietly, like a soft breeze; you will feel it in your face, without knowing where it comes from and where it is going.

James: And where does that lead to? Isn't it John who was talking about the fire, the ax, and the fury of God...? The Messiah cannot be a soft breeze! He will be a hurricane, and will come as flashes of lightning!

Jesus: I'm not sure about that, James. Look at the bamboo. A hurricane would destroy the broken bamboo and extinguish the flickering wicks.... All of us here are not like that.... What would become of us if God came like a hurricane? Who among us would survive before him?

Nathanael: Hey, what's the matter with you, Jesus? You're talking strange.... What else did the prophet tell you?

Jesus: That the Liberator has already come. That he is in our midst.

Peter: Then let him come out in the open! Did he tell you where he's hiding? Let's look for him, and carry him on our shoulders.

James: Friends, the only thing that's clear to me is that in this stinking river, the Messiah won't find anything. Look at those people by the riverbank.... What has the Messiah got to do with them? To form an army of scalawags and prostitutes?

Philip: Now look who's talking. The son of Zebedee, who's got more lice than hair in his beard!

James: Go ahead and laugh, Philip. When the Messiah comes and finds you with your mouth wide open, he will shut it with a big punch! Look at the group we have here — people who stink, prostitutes, and foolish men. A very good group to welcome the Messiah!

Jesus: They are like broken bamboo, James. The Messiah is coming to straighten them, not to give them punches.

James: Look, Nazarene, that sounds pretty good, but what is needed here is...

Philip: Enough of these bickerings! I've just been baptized and won't allow my lips to be tarnished by cursing.... Damn, it's already getting late, and somehow we have to feed our stomachs.

Peter: Yeah, that's better. First, let's have lunch, and continue with the discussion later. Hey, Andrew, John, Nathanael! Come on, guys. Are you coming too, Jesus?

Jesus: Of course, Peter. Let's go.

The sun was at its peak, enveloping the parched land with its scorching heat. That morning the river, the wind, and the desert birds became witnesses to how

God made his presence felt in the river Jordan. The Lord sought Jesus, who in
turn listened to his voice. Something marvelous happened to us, but at that time,
we were not aware of it.

•

The baptismal rite made popular by John signified a public acknowledg-
ment that marked the beginning of a way to justice while awaiting the
coming of the Messiah. Jesus, who was one of the many, joined the
people's movement by adhering to John's message. His baptism would
be the starting point of his life of service to the people.

After that, Jesus, as a true human, began to understand what God expected of him, by way of his contact with his people and his various
experiences. He grew in age, according to the biological process that we
all undergo. He grew in wisdom: by opening up to the Lord and to others,
he came to realize his mission. He grew in grace: remaining faithful to God
strengthened his commitment to service, to the point of giving up his own
life. This whole process is, in a way, highlighted in the gospel narration of
Jesus' baptism — at that point he, having been aware of the character and
message of John, underwent a decisive inner experience of faith.

Sometimes, during intense moments of our lives, we ask ourselves, in a
very special way, what we ought to do, what our vocation and responsibility are. These are moments when we are touched by the pain and injustice
around us; and with our strength, we share something in the hope that
things may change. This is the time when we certainly experience the guid-
ing hand of God leading this world toward a future full of hope, making
us realize that all men and women in our midst are brothers and sisters.
This is the moment when reality "speaks" to us, and we become so en-
lightened as to understand its meaning. It is not easy to explain or translate
these experiences into words. And this was how Jesus felt when he was
baptized in the river Jordan.

In order to describe this inner experience and appreciate the significance of this moment in Jesus' life, the writers of the gospels had to
resort to external symbolism. The heavens open: this means that God is
near Jesus.

A dove descends: something new is going to happen, and like the Spirit
hovering over the waters on the first day of creation, now it is flapping its
wings over Jesus, the new human. Then God's voice is heard, choosing
Jesus as his beloved Son.... All this notwithstanding, we are not to forget

that Jesus' commitment, all through his life, was marked by simplicity and humility, without grandeur. It is through humility that the Lord wished to reveal himself.

Baptism among Christians is not intended for salvation; it is rather an initiation similar to what Jesus underwent. Christian baptism is a rite, witnessed by the community, in which one breaks away from sin (rejecting Satan and his works), and it adheres to the good news of Jesus by means of the baptized person's commitment to put into life the new values taught in the gospel.

The early Christians who lived in Israel were baptized by being submerged in the waters of the river Jordan. In other places, the people would take a bath in a river or in a pond. Through the centuries, this custom has vanished among most Christian groups, and nowadays in those groups only a small amount of water is poured on the head of the new Christian. The Orthodox Christians and other groups, however, still practice baptism by immersion.

(Matt. 3:13–17; Mark 1:9–11; Luke 3:21–22; John 1:29–34)

8

The Last Night in Bethabara

Andrew, Peter, James, Philip, Nathanael, Jesus, and I were baptized by the prophet John. We felt we were ready for the coming of the Liberator of Israel. We had to return to our province. I remember that night, the last that we spent along the bend of Bethabara, when we were all gathered in a tent to say our farewell. . . .

Peter: This jug is for Philip, who hasn't had a bath for three years!

Philip: And mine goes for Nata, who, after that plunge into the water, is now beginning to grow hair! See for yourselves, folks, how this is happening to a bald man, thanks to the waters of the river Jordan.

Nathanael: Leave me in peace, Philip. Don't be such a bore. . . .

James: Seriously now, fellows, didn't you notice how the prophet John was behaving? . . . He was restless, going to and fro like a bloodhound smelling his prey, but knew not where to catch him. . . .

John: That's right. The prophet was behaving strangely since yesterday. His eyes are fixed on something that is to come that we are not yet aware of. . . .

James: Not something but somebody. They heard him say that the Messiah is closely following us. . . .

Nathanael: He's always said that, and yet, not even a shadow appears.

Philip: Couldn't he be the Messiah himself? Come on, tell me, who in this country possesses more guts than the Baptizer, to reveal what is true? I think John is the man!

Peter: I don't think so. He must be somebody stronger than John. He hasn't spoken yet, but when he does, even the gods will tremble!

John: The only quiet person here is the Nazarene. Hey, Jesus, what's the matter with you? Move closer, man. . . .

Jesus: I've gotta do an errand for a town-mate who's right now waiting for me. . . . I'll be back soon. . . .

Philip: Don't be long. Skinny Andrew has just left to get some wine. . . .

50

The town-mate Jesus wanted to see that night was the prophet John. Jesus knew where he was sleeping: inside a hollow rock whose tip touched the river. He went to talk to him. . . .

Baptist: That's how it is, Jesus. We are distant cousins. My mother always remembered your mother with great affection and the time she spent with her in Ain Karem, before I was born. Boy, how time flies! Later, I left home to enter the monastery and heard nothing about them. While in the monastery, I was informed of the death of my father, Zechariah. He was never in favor of my entering the monastery. Of course, he was a priest, and you know, the priests of the temple of Jerusalem were arch-enemies of the Essenes in the desert.

Jesus: How is your mother, Elizabeth?

Baptist: She died the following year. Uncle Joseph and Aunt Mary were there for the funeral. You must have been a little boy then.

Jesus: Oh yeah. I remember I was left alone in our house in Nazareth. Upon their return, there was trouble in Sepphoris. The city got burned, and so many were crucified. . . . It was terrible.

Baptist: That was the time your father, Uncle Joseph, died, wasn't it?

Jesus: No, that was a few years later. In Sepphoris there was always trouble, and since we lived very near, they punished him for having helped those who had escaped. They beat him up so that, . . . well, he didn't last long. Such a crime.

Baptist: Yes, these Romans are ruthless. . . . They are to be feared. . . .

Jesus: But you are not afraid of them. You can shout at their face anytime.

Baptist: Should I fear them? What can they get from me? Nothing. I have nothing to lose. I have neither money, nor a home, nor a family. I left nothing behind. Look, the only thing that they can take away from me is my voice. But I've already said what I wanted to say. . . . Now, we better talk about yourself. Tell me about your life. What do you do? Rather, what do you want to do?

Jesus: That's why I wanted to talk to you, John. I need your help. I'm confused.

Baptist: So you don't know what to do. You have this feeling that God is hovering above your head like a mosquito but doesn't tell you what to do. Is that it?

Jesus: Yes, sort of. I've been restless for several months now. As I see you now, I say to myself: hell, this John's really hitting the nail on the head. He opens the eyes of the people; he helps them. . . . He really does something. . . . On the other hand, what am I doing?

Baptist: Very well. You want to work? Stay with me. You can assist me when I baptize people. As you've seen, there's work for two, even for three hundred. Every day more and more caravans come, and I end up losing my voice because I talk and shout a lot. I tell you, I'm tired. Stay with me, Jesus. I think you've got what it takes to be a preacher.

Jesus: I, become a preacher? No way. I'm just going to stay in Nazareth with my tools and my bricks. I'm not good at talking to people.

Baptist: Moses stammered; and Jeremiah was a little boy when God called him. They said exactly the same thing as you did. I also trembled when I opened my mouth for the first time. . . . Now, it doesn't really matter whether I face a thousand or ten thousand people. Come on, man, make up your mind. Stay with me; the two of us will manage.

Jesus: But . . . I have a lot work in Nazareth . . . and I . . .

Baptist: That's all right. You don't want to be a preacher because you're scared of the people. Then go to the monastery. I spent more than ten years there. Do you see those rocks over there . . . and those mountains? . . . Behind them is the Dead Sea. The fishes that are carried away by the current from the Jordan die as they reach the salty waters. It's a place where there are no animals, no trees. . . . There you will find the monastery, away from the world but closer to God.

Jesus: And who said that in order to be close to God one should stay away from the world?

Baptist: That's what the monks of the desert have been saying. That's why they've hidden themselves in the monastery.

Jesus: That's why you left; you wanted to be with the people.

Baptist: Yes, you're right. God and the people are right here inside me. I don't have to get rid of one to accommodate the other.

Jesus: So don't talk to me about monks and solitude. I don't want to stay away from the people. I love to have friends, I like parties, and I love life. Isn't God in all of these, in joy and happiness?

Baptist: I believe so, Jesus.

Jesus: So?

Baptist: And so, what else are you looking for? Get married, raise a family of ten children, and, who knows, one of them might be the Messiah. Then, you may live the rest of your life in peace.

Jesus: Right, that's what my mother always tells me. I don't know, I'm really confused.

Baptist: You don't want to join the monks in the desert. Neither do you want to live a normal life like the majority of the people, nor wish to stay with me, as there is much work to do.... What is it that you want?... To fight? Then join the guerrilla movement of the zealots. These groups are well organized in Galilee.

Jesus: I...don't know. With the way things are, and knowing how powerful the Romans are, don't you think it's crazy to fight them? Is it really worth the bloodshed? Tell me.

Baptist: I see your point. I also ask myself the same questions....

Jesus: So?

Baptist: So you're not joining the zealots either.

Jesus: Help me, John, I'm confused. I don't want to be stingy with God. But he shouldn't be stingy with me either. What does he want from me?

Baptist: If you're so confused, then do what those who have searched for the Lord have done: go to the desert; go to the sandy mountain alone and there, between heaven and earth, shout to the Lord. He'll respond to you.

Jesus: You can also hear other voices in the desert, not only God's, but the voice of temptation.

Baptist: Yes, but the Spirit, who is more powerful, will be upon you. And,...Jesus, who are you?

Jesus: What is it, John?

Baptist: Nothing, excuse me. For a moment, I thought...Are you really the Nazarene whom I baptized this morning?

Jesus: Why, of course.... What's the matter with you, John?

Baptist: Nothing, forget it.... At times, I spend the whole night imagining how the Messiah will look.... Will he be blond? Will he have black hair? Will he have a thick or thin beard? I've been waiting for him for a long time. At times, I feel he's not coming anymore, that I'm going to die without seeing him.

Jesus: Don't say that, John. You're tired, that's all. Well, I'm going back to my companions in the tent. I'll heed your advice. Tomorrow I'm going to go to the desert.... Will I see you again, someday?

Baptist: I hope so. Say "hello" to your mom. Good luck, Jesus.... Have courage.

Jesus: Thank you, John. Goodbye!

Jesus got back to our tent a little late. We were all gathered laughing, playing dice, and most of all, we were pouring wine into our mouths....

John: At last you're back!...Come on, Jesus, tell us some good jokes.

Philip: We were celebrating the coming of the Messiah....Hik! And here you come at the right moment....Hik!...You must be our Messiah! ... Hik!

Jesus: How many liters of wine are needed to get such a big head drunk, Philip?

Peter: Well, if I were the Messiah, I'd squeeze all the Romans into a net, including their capes and shields, tie them up, and throw them in the middle of the lake for the fishes to feast on....

James: You're too good for nothing to become the Messiah, Peter. But if I were to become the Messiah, I'd transfer the capital to our province, and with the help of five hundred elephants, I'd pull the temple out of Jerusalem and drag it there....

Peter: Hey, Jesus, what would you do if you were the Messiah?...Do you hear me? What would you do if you were the Messiah?...

Jesus: Knock it off, Peter. Stop kidding....

Peter: But I'm serious, Jesus....Each one of us can be the Messiah. And why not? John says he is among us. He may be the bald one, or that skinny man, or...it could be you, Jesus. This is the Lord's thing. If he points to somebody, then that person is the Messiah. If he points to someone else, then that person is it. Anyone can be the Messiah. You might even be the Liberator of Israel, Jesus!...

John: Hurray! Tomorrow I can go back to Galilee and dance with the plainest looking dame....Tra, la, la, la...

Nathanael: Let's have a toast, for tomorrow I'm going to go back to my shop....Jesus, my dear brother, I'm so happy....

James: Hey, Jesus, we've decided to go back to Galilee tomorrow.

Jesus: That's wonderful. I'm going back a little later.

John: You're not coming with us tomorrow?

Jesus: No, first I've got to go to Jericho....

Peter: In that case, I'm going with you to Jericho, and we'll join these scoundrels on the road....

Jesus: No, Peter,...I mean...I'm not really going to Jericho, but to the desert.

Peter: To the desert? What for? Do you intend to go there alone?

Jesus: Yes.

Peter: Are you out of your mind?

Jesus: Well, yes, a little.

Philip: I drink to this hick who's a little crazy, and for all the silly men gathered here!

To tell you the truth, since we had too much wine in our heads, I can hardly remember what else transpired that night, our last in Bethabara.

•

John the Baptist's character had a great impact on those who listened to him and even among those who knew him through the news about him reaching all the nooks and crannies of the country. He ought to have had a great influence on Jesus, who, later on, would say that John was the greatest among those ever born of a woman (Matt. 11:11). At the height of the movement spurred by the Baptist, Jesus discovered his calling, and upon John's death, he would succeed him as the prophet. The relationship between John and Jesus, specifically referred to in the gospel of Luke, must be understood basically as a way to show the intimate link between the message of the previous prophet and that of Jesus.

It is very possible that John the Baptist lived for some time in a monastery of ascetics along the banks of the Dead Sea, near the place where he later baptized the people. The Essenes belonged to a religious congregation formed about one hundred thirty years before the birth of Christ. They lived in community and most practiced celibacy—although some of them belonged to married groups. They uttered special prayers, but did not offer animals as sacrifice. They also had a vow of poverty and shared common property. One of their concerns was to copy the Holy Scriptures. Some of these copies have reached us following the discovery in Qumran in 1947. They are the oldest manuscripts of some books of the Bible. The most important is the scroll of the prophet Isaiah. At present, one can still see the ruins of this monastery. Parts have been preserved, like its walls, stairs, the purification pools, and so on. Many objects found in these ruins are preserved in the Book Museum in Jerusalem, such as pots, sandals, coins, tables, and so on. The ascetics isolated themselves from the world in order to avoid sin and considered themselves perfect and favored by God. This made them proud and even intolerant. Possibly John left this group because of their elitist tendencies.

John the Baptist showed Jesus various ways to carry out his desire to serve: through a monastic life, through family life, and by joining an armed movement. Jesus, however, saw some obstacles in each. Not seeing himself in any of them, he did not become a monk or anything of the sort. Instead, he mingled with his own people and participated in all their concerns, their problems, their joys. Nor did he get married. Nor did he compromise himself with the zealots or any other political groups of his time. He did not end up as a priest or Levite. He was a layman and never was part of any religious structure of his era. He was not even a part of the secular movement of the Pharisees. Living independently up to the end of his life, he did not isolate himself from the social class into which he was born.

In this episode are recorded some details about the death of Joseph, Mary's spouse. There is no historical reference about the time or manner of Joseph's death. What is historically known is the siege and destruction of the city of Sepphoris during the youth of Jesus. Sepphoris was located near Nazareth and was then the capital of Galilee. The Romans burned the city as retaliation for the rebellion waged by the zealots.

9

Beneath the Desert Sun

Early the next morning, I saw Jesus coming out of the tent where we, the Galileans, spent the night. He took his walking stick and began to walk alone, away from the river toward the desert of Judah. Then, he suddenly disappeared. . . .

Jesus: Lord, what do you want from me? What do you expect of me? Speak to me, that I may overcome this fear and respond to you! . . . Speak to me, Lord! . . .

But he heard other voices inside him. . . .

Mary's Voice: What is it that you want, Jesus? One year has passed, and another year, yet you haven't decided on anything. Listen to me, son. Forget about your dreams and be realistic. You are thirty, and it is high time you put your feet on the ground. . . .

Innkeeper's Voice: Ah, some crazy men! They dream of prophets and signs from God when they could stay and enjoy the good life! Cheer up, Nazarene! I have very good wine for you, and some women . . . ! There's none of this stuff in your town.

Peter's Voice: I'm serious, Jesus. Anyone can be the Messiah. Why not? John says he is in our midst. It could be this bald man, or that skinny one, or . . . or, you, Jesus. You can be the Liberator of Israel! . . .

Jesus continued walking through the desert. He climbed the hills, descended through them, and passed along the mountainside. When evening came he lay flat on the sand, his face looking up to the sky, as if waiting for an answer. . . .

Jesus: Lord, what do you want from me? . . . What can I do for my people? John is a prophet, and he can speak, . . . but I . . . I . . .

How many days passed? . . . How long could someone, stricken by hunger and thirst, survive? Nothing. Not even a sign of life, nor a drop of water could be seen anywhere....Jesus, his lips parched and bluish, sat on a rock. He felt the blazing sun above his head, and became dizzy. Then he remembered nothing. He rolled over on the sand and was lost in deep sleep....

Devil: Tsssk...tsssk...Poor guy! Why did you come here without any food at all? You don't even have a camel! Do you know that only beetles and lizards inhabit this desert?

Jesus: Who are you?

Devil: It doesn't really matter. Let us say that I'm a dream....

Jesus: Bah, then I don't see any need of you....

Devil: Don't say that....Sometimes dreams can be realer than reality itself....You poor guy! You fainted because of hunger and exhaustion. I'll help you. But first, you've got to tell me clearly,...Why did you come here?

Jesus: I'm looking for God. I need him to speak to me and show me the road I ought to follow....

Devil: There are no roads in the desert. Not even in life. One makes a road with a bit of luck and a little ambition. I can be of help to you, Jesus of Nazareth.

Jesus: How did you know my name?

Devil: Only a few come here, so it's easy to know who's who.

Jesus: And what's your name?

Devil: Don't worry about that....Listen to me....I can give you good advice. Listen: Do you know that cats have seven lives, while crocodiles have four? How many lives have you got, poor man?

Jesus: Only one..., of course.

Devil: Then, enjoy it, my friend!...Why go look for a road? The way of pleasure is what most men and women take, and they like it.

Jesus: What must I do in order to enjoy life?

Devil: First, you must not think a lot. Thinking makes you sad.

Jesus: That's easier said than done....What about our country? There's so much injustice to correct. How can I stop thinking of these things?

Devil: It's nothing but the idealism of youth. With or without you, life will go on. Two thousand years will pass and the poor will continue to be poor, and the rich will become richer. The same abuses of the past will be committed again tomorrow.

Jesus: Perhaps you are right, but...

Devil: Listen to me, Jesus of Nazareth. Look at this rock....Imagine this rock to be a piece of bread, a recently baked piece of bread.... Oh, my good friend: to eat it is the first rule to enjoy life....

Jesus: Man does not live by bread alone....

Devil: Of course not! You need good food for the stomach, good wine to drink, and nice women to go to bed with!

Jesus: What about the word of God? People live by the word of the Lord too.

Devil: Uff, forget about God. God has his own problems in heaven, while you have yours on earth. Do you know what you really need? Money!...Money, my friend, is the key to happiness. You can buy everything with money. Listen to me: if you have a lot of money, then you'll enjoy a comfortable life and be happy.

Jesus: But where am I going to get such an abundance of money? It's not easy to be rich.

Devil: For you it is. You have a knack for business. I'm sure that if you transfer to Jerusalem and start business there, like putting up a small lending shop, or textile trading,...you'll progress, young man. You can convert stones into bread, and bread into money, and money can give you anything! Enjoy life and don't think of...So, you decide.... What else are you waiting for?

Jesus: I don't know, but...I'm looking for...If I have money, life's luxury and security,...then what?

Devil: Now, I realize, young man, that you're not like the rest who simply want to make money and be happy. You want something more than this. You want to dominate the world, be at the helm of the ship!...Am I right?

Jesus: I don't understand you.

Devil: Give me your hand and come with me....

Jesus: Where will you take me?

Devil: Look, I want you to observe from this mountain. From here, you can choose well. Take a look at all the kingdoms and governments in this world: Jerusalem, Egypt, Babylon, Athens, Rome...Which do you like most?

Jesus: What are you talking about?

Devil: You can be the lord of any of these empires, if you wish.... Or, if you are more ambitious, like Alexander the Great, you can rule the entire world.

Jesus: That's impossible. I'm only a peasant who wears a pair of broken sandals. . . . I don't even own a piece of land, and here you are talking about my being the lord or master of . . .

Devil: Everything is a matter of wanting it. Little by little you'll be scaling the ladder of power. Think about it, young man: politics is the art of stepping on the head of someone at the lower rung of the ladder.

Jesus: That's exactly where I am: at the lowest rung of the ladder. Whose head am I going to step on? What must I do to go up?

Devil: I'll help you. Trust me.

Jesus: Tell me, please. Who are you?

Devil: I'm the lust for power that's hiding in your soul, Jesus. You don't just aspire to money and other luxuries, because you want to rule and have power over others. That's natural. Look! . . . A person wages war against a neighbor, and will win, for sure, because of ambition. A person already has hundreds of thousands of people in subservience and still wants more who will obey and serve.

Jesus: I don't know, but . . . I prefer to serve than be served.

Devil: You're a dreamer, Jesus. Tell me, who do you want to serve?

Jesus: The Lord . . . and my country, Israel. . . .

Devil: Oh, I understand. I should have known that before. You're even prouder than I thought. Now, let's be clear on this, Jesus of Nazareth: you want to be the Messiah that all Jews have been waiting for, for many centuries. . . . Hey, don't put on that face. . . . You know damn well what I'm talking about. Money is easy. Power is likewise boring, I know, and you aspire to something special, like being the Messiah of Israel, the savior of the world. You want to be remembered through the centuries, have entire libraries of books written about you, and you wish to have several followers, with a very powerful organization of course. . . .

Jesus: How can you talk that way to me? I've never thought anything of that sort. . . .

Devil: Come on. You'll need a good starter for your career. Do you understand? . . . Let's go to Jerusalem, to the temple, to the pinnacle of the walls. . . .

Jesus: Leave me alone. I don't want to go with you. Let go! . . .

Devil: Look — four hundred cubits high! . . . Look down, . . . and look at those people. . . . Everyone has come to see the miracle.

Jesus: What miracle?

Devil: Yours! Close your eyes, and jump from here.

Jesus: Are you crazy? I'd kill myself!

Devil: Of course not! I'll go down and see to it that you don't strike a single stone. Trust in me.

Jesus: What good will that do for me?

Devil: That would be the first miracle. Then people will come, and they will applaud you. And you will ask: Who are you looking for? Are you looking for the Messiah? For the Liberator? I am he! And everyone will kneel before you, and you will be great. You will be known all over the world!

Jesus: But...

Devil: No more buts. Don't think anymore. Don't you hear the people calling for you? Come on, jump! I'll take care of the rest!

Jesus: Wait a minute.... This is tempting God. You are not to tempt the Lord.

Devil: God! God! Will you let God out of this, you idiot!

Jesus: You leave me alone! Go away! Go away!

Devil: I'm sorry for you, Jesus of Nazareth! You're taking the wrong road, fellow. All right, you hardheaded one. You will regret having ignored me. Anyway, we shall meet again. So long!

Jesus: Tell me who you are.... Who are you? What is your name?

Cameleer: My name is Nasim, and I am a Samaritan. I'm taking this road to get me to Jericho....

An old cameleer was passing through the place, and when he saw Jesus lying down on the sand, he approached him and helped him.

Cameleer: Who are you?... Did you lose your camel? Were you held up by bandits?... You know, brother, this place is treacherous. Even the devil trembles when he crosses through. You were shouting and I came near to see what was happening.... Come.... Uff! That's all right now.... You're almost dead, brother.... Here, drink this goat's milk, and let's go, for it's still a long way from here to Jericho.... Hoaa,... camel,... let's go...!

For how many days did Jesus stay on that gray and barren mountain? I would not know. In the desert, God put his people to test for forty years. Even Elijah crossed the desert, and for forty days and forty nights he waited to see the face of God. John the Baptist learned how to shout in that desolate place, proclaiming the coming of the Liberator of Israel.

•

Galilee, the northern region of Israel, is always verdant and has fertile soil. In contrast, Judea, Israel's southern part, has a dry area and scarce vegetation. Some parts are even desert lands, which are uninhabited. In these lands where Jesus roamed, thorns and thistles hardly grow. Rain is very scarce, and only caravans of camels are seen crossing the landscape. At present one can see in the desert of Judea, near the city of Jericho, the so-called Mount of Temptation, which Christian tradition has claimed for centuries as the place where Jesus was tempted. Alongside this mountain there live some Orthodox monks in an old monastery. The Israelites thought that the land was cursed by God, infertile, and that only wild animals and demons lived there. All these contributed to the belief that the place was extremely risky, where people were put to a test, but were able to resist temptation. The desert was thus considered not simply a terrible place. The long pilgrimage of the Israelites through the desert, through a span of forty years until they reached the promised land, converted the place into a special venue to see God and to know better the people's plans during solitude and in times of trouble. It is between these two meanings, the confrontation with evil and God's revelation, that the text on the temptations of Jesus is centered, as expressed in the accounts of the evangelists.

The gospel accounts of the temptations of Jesus must be read not as historical narrations, but as theological summaries of the challenges that Jesus, as a servant of Yahweh, had to overcome throughout his life in order to be faithful to the end: the temptation of security in a life without risk, of seeking one's advantage; the temptation of money-power with which to dominate others; the temptation of a Messiah who seeks to be served rather than serve. Jesus, like every human who takes commitment to heart, has to experience weakness and choose the path of generosity. Unceasingly, he renewed his own vocation, and in so doing he overcame temptations told to us in the gospels.

The key to understanding the accounts of the temptations is in the three phrases through which Jesus answered the devil. These three phrases appear in the narration of the pilgrimage of the Hebrews through the desert (Deut. 8:3, 16; and 6:13). What God asked his people in that march through the desert in order to test their faithfulness is renewed in Jesus. Jesus experienced the same temptations suffered by the people centuries earlier. But Israel failed God and succumbed to a temptation of distrust, accumulation, and power-hunger. Jesus, however, remained faithful. In this personal account, he redeems himself and his people, reaching the plenitude of collective history. The culture and literary style during the period of Jesus necessitated the use in these accounts of the figure of a tempter who was alien to the person being tempted. Thus, the figure of the demon appeared as the interlocutor of Jesus. The Bible often mentions the devil under different names: The adversary, Lucifer, Satan, Beelzebub, and so on. One must carefully discern in every occasion the narrator's intention in resorting to this character.

(Matt. 4:1–11; Mark 1:12–13; Luke 4:1–13)

10

In the Prison Cell in Machaerus

The voice of the prophet John, clamoring for justice and proclaiming the coming of the Liberator of Israel, was becoming more intense and pressing each day. Those who came to listen to him felt he was in a great hurry, as if he knew that his days were numbered....

Baptist: Open your eyes wide! Be ready, so that when he comes (he-who-is-to-come is already here), all of you will know him and will meet him!...No one is to say: "I have been baptized. I have been purified in the river; it is enough." Being baptized is not the end of the road, but the beginning! When the Messiah comes, he shall commence the liberation of Israel. All of us must follow him and be collaborators of the Messiah. That is, if he comes...

A Woman: I hear the trumpets of the Messiah! Don't you hear that noise, my countrymen?

A Man: Lady, will you stop that silly talk and listen to what the prophet is saying.

A Woman: You listen! I'm not deaf; I can hear. I'm telling you that the Messiah's caravan is coming here!

A Boy: Look there! The Messiah is coming!

All: The Messiah! Prophet John, the Messiah is coming!

On the road descending from Jericho, a long caravan of extravagantly decorated camels was seen coming, preceded by a group of slaves clothed in silk and blowing their trumpets. But no, it was not the Messiah who was coming, but King Herod and his court. They were to move to the palace in Machaerus on the other side of the Jordan, beside the Dead Sea. They had to pass through Bethabara in order to get there.

A Man: Lady, if this is the Liberator that we've been waiting for, then we can now die....But no, it's Herod and his men!

A Woman: Look how the carriage wobbles! How fat he is!

A Man: He's about to burst!

Herod Antipas was the governor of Galilee, the last of the sons of Herod the Great. We loathed his father for having imposed heavy taxes on us. A chip off the old block, the son was likewise an unscrupulous and unjust man, corrupted by vice, with utter disregard for the Lord and the sufferings of his people.

A Man: Hey, prophet John, King Herod is heading toward us!
A Woman: The nerve of this man! What does he want from us?
A Man: Let him be, lady. If he wants to be baptized, then we'll see how his weight will pull him down and drown him in the waters.
A Woman: That's right. Let us all drown him!

The prophet remained strangely quiet as he watched the approaching caravan. The carriage in which Herod was riding did not go near, for he was an extremely superstitious man. He was afraid of the prophet with long hair, and with a tongue like a sword, about whom he had heard many things. The caravan followed the road leading to the palace in Machaerus. While it was still a little way off, John broke his silence, and with the force of lightning, he faced the people who were milling around the riverbank.

Baptist: See how this man stinks! He smells rotten!...A decaying fish begins to reek a foul odor through the head. The acts of injustice committed in this country are so prevalent that the stench is unbearable. Who else but the leaders of this country are the rotten ones? Herod, as well as his administration, is corrupt. He lives by the blood of the innocent and the sweat of the poor....But his reign is not forever. The worms are eating him up. As I break this old walking stick, so will the Lord destroy his throne. Herod will fall, and he will be toppled amid joyful shouts, with the coming of the Liberator of Israel!...You are to witness this with your own eyes and there will be great rejoicing!

John exposed before the people all the crimes and abuses committed by the unjust king. Among those gathered, however, were followers of Herod who were spying on the people. And what was expected did happen.

Herod: So, he said all those things about me? Too bad, I would have wanted to hear it....Be that as it may, it is good that they talk about me.
Servant: He also said that...sss... sss...
Herod: Really? What an insolent man!
Servant: That you can not live with...sss...sss...

Herod: How dare this hairy man say that of me!...And in front of the people, at that!

Servant: That the queen is living in sin...

Herod: This man is conspiring against my government. He is dangerous....

Servant: They say he is a great prophet, the one sent by God, the Most High!

Herod: Silly! The time of the prophets ended long ago....If not, then, I'll finish him off now!...I want this John immediately, this son of Zechariah.

Servant: What if the people resist?

Herod: The people! They only bark; they don't bite! Tell the men to be armed, in case....

Servant: When must they leave, King?

Herod: Right away. The sooner, the better. I'm anxious to see the face of this famous prophet of the desert.

And so it was. John was ordered arrested by Herod, was bound and brought to the prison cell of his palace in Machaerus. More and more people gathered along the riverbank, as they saw him being dragged off by Herod's men. They wanted to prevent the soldiers, but were helpless. The women wept aloud and grieved: "Once again, the masters of power and might silenced the voice of the prophets."

In a few days, the riverbanks of the Jordan were abandoned and as silent as before John came with his powerful voice and filled them with hope and life.

John was shut up in the basement of the palace in Machaerus, in a dark and narrow cell where other prisoners perished while serving their sentence....

Herod: I have long wanted to see you, John, son of Zechariah.

Baptist: And I have waited a long time to see you, Herod Antipas, son of the wicked Herod the Great.

Herod: See how ironic life can be....Until yesterday, you were the "prophet," but now, you're no more than a mouse in my trap. What things have you been spreading about me? Come on...speak up!

Baptist: I only said what everybody already knew. That you are an unjust king, and that God will topple down your throne. The last thing I said was that you were living with your sister-in-law, your brother Philip's wife.

Herod: Herodias is my wife!

John: Herodias, who is as brazen as you, is Philip's wife. You stole her away from him. You must give her back to him.

Herod: How dare you speak to me like that!

Baptist: And how dare you fiddle with God's laws!

King Herod started to bite his nails. He was too afraid. The blazing eyes of the prophet terrified him. . . .

Herod: John, . . . prophet John, . . . Who are you? Who taught you to speak to the people the way you do? . . . Are you the Messiah? . . . Speak up!

John: I am not the Messiah. I proclaim the coming of the Liberator of Israel. He is already coming, and he will strip you of your crown, leaving you naked before the people. He will also tell you to your face the acts of injustice you have committed, as well as your vices!

Herod: And where is this Messiah that you're talking about? Who is this Liberator of Israel? . . . I want to meet him.

Baptist: You will not see him. You are too sinful to see him.

Herod: I'll see to it that they cut off your tongue to be thrown to the dogs!

Baptist: You are scared, Herod. You are carrying on your shoulders the burden of your abuses against the people. You are afraid because you know that God takes into account your sins.

Herod: I'm not afraid! I'm not afraid! I'm not scared of anyone! Neither am I terrified of you, you liar!

Baptist: You're afraid of the truth!

Herod: No, my soldiers are here to defend me. I have the armies, I have palaces, and I have the power. And now, I also have you, the prophet. Ha-ha-ha . . . ! Now, what have you got to say?

Baptist: I have already told you everything. First, you must return your brother's wife. Then, we'll talk.

Herod: But Herodias is my wife. I love her. She's mine.

Baptist: She isn't yours. You have no right to live with your brother's wife.

Herod: Neither do you have the right to raise your voice to me. What makes you think you have such a right? I am the king of Galilee and you ought to respect me!

Baptist: Respect you? Now you're making me laugh. How do you expect me to respect a man who's full of vice, who earned his throne through intrigue and all sorts of treachery and bribery, a man whose government wallows in blood?

Herod: I am the authority and you have to obey me!

Baptist: My authority comes from heaven. You were born of a woman, like everyone else, and you were born naked, like everyone else. The worms will eat you up like everybody else.

Herod: Shut up! You shut up!

Baptist: The only king I have is the one from above; him I obey!

Herod: John, wouldn't you like to leave this place ... and talk to the people again ... ? We can talk this over. Wouldn't you like to go back to the Jordan and be a prophet again? Do you know that your fate is in my hands, and if I will it, I can give you your freedom?

Baptist: No, Herod. You are mistaken. My fate is not in your hands, but in God's. Yours are empty ... and tarnished. Soon, they will be tied, and your power will be put to an end with the coming of the Liberator of Israel.

Herod: Give me a cup of wine, Herodias.

Herodias: You have drunk a lot today, ... Herod. Is anything the matter?

Herod: No, nothing. Nothing is wrong with me.

Herodias: I know you too well.... You cannot deceive me.... This "prophet" is worrying you, this John you have imprisoned in the dungeon.

Herod: Stop talking about prophets.... You know nothing about them. The prophets are sacred people.

Herodias: Sacred people! Ha! You know what should be done to them? Have their throats cut to silence them. Say, Herod, why don't you have John's head cut off?

Herod: Shut up!

Herodias: If you really love me, you'll do it for me. Do you love me?

Herod: You know I love you so much, Herodias, ... so much ...

Herodias: Are you afraid of him? Do not fear him. The moment you have him beheaded, you'll be the same powerful man as before....

King Herod wanted to kill John, to get rid of that voice that bothered him unceasingly. But he was afraid of the people in Israel who knew that John was a prophet who spoke on behalf of God.

•

The gospels speak of two Herods. Herod the Great, in alliance with the Romans, governed the country tyrannically from 37 BCE to 4 CE. He was known to be responsible for the killing of innocent people. When he died, four years before the birth of Christ, the country was divided among his three sons. Herod Antipas, the youngest, was the contemporary of John the Baptist and Jesus. He ruled Israel, Galilee, as well as the zone of Perea, along the eastern side of the Jordan. He was given the title "tetrarch," but the people called him "King Herod." Though married to a Moorish princess, Herod Antipas became the lover of Herodias, the wife of his brother Philip. This situation resulted in a war in which many innocent people were killed. The king was an ambitious man and without scruples. Historical accounts describe him as a squanderer, a tyrant ruthless to anyone opposing him (and there were many), and a very superstitious man. He also collaborated with the Romans, the lords and masters of the country, who had totally supported him in exchange for large monetary rewards: on behalf of the Romans, Herod Antipas collected taxes from the people in Galilee and Perea.

One of the many accusations hurled by John the Baptist against the corrupt system of his time was directed against Herod Antipas, whom he publicly charged with living adulterously with his sister-in-law. John's accusation was not a mere question of "morality." The king's adultery was like the last fruit on a tree that was completely rotten. Herod's reign was corrupt because of acts of injustice, squandering, theft, crimes.... There was not even a minimum of political or social morality. This was what John vehemently condemned.

Herod, in compliance with the Jewish religious norms, would go to his palaces in Machaerus and Jerusalem, to attend festivals and to go to the temple to pray. On one of these occasions, he ordered the imprisonment of John. Herod feared the people's movement instigated by the prophet, and he wanted to retaliate against John for making accusations against him in public.

Machaerus was a fortress built along the eastern shore of the Dead Sea in Perea. Herod the Great fortified it and built a magnificent palace about twenty years before the birth of Christ. Herod Antipas celebrated the great feasts in the palace. It was here that John the Baptist was imprisoned and ordered beheaded by the king. In the year 70, the fortress was destroyed by the Roman armies. To this day only its ruins are preserved.

Herod feared John, even when he was imprisoned, because the prophet, sensing great freedom within him, and fearless even before death, confronted the king and told of the king's acts of injustice to his face.

(Matthew 14; Mark 6:14–20; Luke 9:7–9)

11

Toward the Galilee of the Gentiles

When Jesus left the desert, his feet were swollen, his eyes dilated, and his hair and beard full of sand. He was happy, in spite of exhaustion and hunger. But he was in a hurry. He bade goodbye to the old Samaritan who had given him a ride on his camel and went back to the Jordan.

Jesus: I must see John.... I have to talk to him.... I will say: "John, I have finally decided to serve my people." How do I begin? What must I do? Do you want me to stay with you and baptize people too?... I'm ready for everything.... I'm not afraid anymore.... Well, I'm still afraid,... but I'm willing to do anything. God gave me the courage while I was in the desert.

When Jesus got to Bethabara, at the bend of the Jordan where John had been baptizing, he saw no one on the riverbank. The place was deserted. There was no baptism, nor were there caravans of pilgrims. John was not around either. From afar, Jesus saw two women, and he rushed toward them.

Jesus: Hey, wait, the two of you! Don't go away. I mean no harm.... Wait!
Magdalene: You look like a crazy man or a leper. Who are you?
Jesus: I just came back from the desert — that's why I'm so dirty. Please, don't be afraid. Wait for me.
Old Woman: What do you want? Are you also wanted by Herod's men?
Jesus: No, I came to look for the prophet, John, and... but what has happened here?
Old Woman: Now there are two of you asking the same question. She came when everything was over. Well, that's life.
Jesus: Tell me, what has happened here? Where is John? Where are the people?
Magdalene: The prophet was taken away by Herod's men. That's why the Jordan is deserted.

70

Jesus: Was John arrested by Herod?

Old Woman: Don't you know? The news spread like wildfire all over the land. What a great misfortune, oh Lord!

Jesus: But why? What right did he have?

Magdalene: By force. He sent his soldiers, with whips and swords. The prophet was tied to a horse and they took him away.

Jesus: Where did they take him?

Old Woman: To the worst of all prison cells, to Machaerus, beyond the mountains of Moab.

Magdalene: May the worms consume Herod like his wicked father!

Jesus: And the people did nothing to defend the prophet?

Old Woman: What could we do? We all fled, running; that was what we did. Who would dare lift a finger against Herod? Who is brave enough to open his mouth in this country?

Magdalene: The only man who could do that was John. He feared no one, not even Herod, nor the devil put before him!

Old Woman: They shut him up in prison, and one of these days, they will kill him. What a misfortune, oh my God! Well, what can we do? The prophet's life is over.

Magdalene: And that puts an end to your business of selling little cakes, old Ruth, which hurts even more than the shackles of the baptizer.

Old Woman: Look who's talking. Listen to this, young man. I'm a poor widow who earned a living by selling little cakes to penitents who wanted to be baptized.

Magdalene: And they got out of the water feeling more starved than contrite.

Old Woman: Fine, but if I could sell my wares, thanks to the people who came to listen to John, then what's wrong with that?

Jesus: You're right, old woman. The prophet helped some people by his preachings, and he has helped you by improving your trade.

Magdalene: He was not able to help me. I wasted this trip.

Jesus: Did you come to be baptized by John?

Magdalene: Well, yes, ... yes, ... that is ...

Old Woman: She's laughing because she, ... well, you can see from the make-up she has on her cheeks ... The men from Capernaum rushed here to see the prophet, while this woman ran after them, ha-ha. ...

Magdalene: And what else did you expect? I have to make a living.

Old Woman: She must have frightened away the clients. This place is deserted. Such bad luck for you, Mary!

Jesus: Your name is Mary?

Magdalene: Yes, and yours?

Jesus: Jesus, and behind this dirty face of mine, I'm a good man, I assure you.

Old Woman: You speak like the Galileans. Are you from there like this woman?

Jesus: Yes, I am from Nazareth, a small village inland.

Magdalene: I come from Magdala, by the lakeside.

Old Woman: There is no need to say so. All Magdalenes are known for their perfume.

Jesus: Didn't you say you were from Capernaum?

Magdalene: Well, I was born in Magdala, but when my mother died, I was left alone. Now I live in Capernaum. I do anything for a living.

Old Woman: She works as a whore for all those filthy fishermen on the wharf!

Jesus: What a coincidence! I recently met a group of friends from your place. Maybe you know them.

Magdalene: I guess so. I know all the men from Capernaum. . . . Tell me their names.

Jesus: They are Peter, James, John, and Andrew.

Magdalene: Hell! I know them. Andrew is a little serious, but the two brothers, James and John, well, I'd rather avoid them than see them. And I'd rather not talk about Peter.

Jesus: I thought they were fine.

Magdalene: Well, they turned me off. They were always pestering me. To hell with all of them. And I told them to their face: "You go your own way. I want to have nothing to do with you. And once and for all, be sure you wash your mouths before talking to me!"

Old Woman: You talk like you were a decent woman!

Magdalene: No, I'm not. But this fellow is. Look, just between the two of us: avoid their kind. If you only knew what I know!

Old Woman: Alas, the only decent person I knew was the prophet, John. Oh, the way he looked, and spoke! He was God sent. But now this country is doomed. Israel has become an orphan. There is no prophet to lend her a hand, to guide her, to lead the way. Now we are lost.

Jesus: Don't talk that way. John paved the way for us, and we must continue what he started.

Old Woman: No, young man. It's all over. John was the voice of the poor, of all of us. You never heard him speak? He was shouting. And do you know why? Because he had in his throat a thousand voices: he was speaking for the thousands of poor, downtrodden people who never enjoyed the right to speak. Tell me, who is now going to fight for justice for us?

Jesus: We must do it ourselves. Yes, why not? We ought to have our own voices heard, and we must do it. God will be on our side to fight for us.

Old Woman: John always spoke to us of a great and powerful Liberator who was to come after him. Now, he's locked up in prison, but the Liberator hasn't come.

Jesus: He'll come. The Messiah and the Kingdom of God will come. Let us not lose hope.

Old Woman: No, young man. What we need is someone who will take up the prophet's staff and talk to the people, like John did.

Magdalene: But who is brave enough to do this? Damn this country — it has no more men like John.

Jesus: On the contrary. I believe there are many who would be willing to die for justice. They're just waiting for a signal to start. They're waiting for someone to tell them: "Now is the time, brothers and sisters. The Kingdom of God is near, and so is our liberation!" John is imprisoned, but the Messiah is not. He is coming. Don't you feel it in your hearts? Rejoice, Grandma, and you too, Mary, for soon we shall be free!

Magdalene: What are you talking about? I'm afraid the heat of the desert sun has got into your head.

Old Woman: Come here, young man. You must be very tired. My hut is not far from here. Mary and I will make you something to eat. Let's go.

Jesus: Thanks for everything. No, I must go. They're waiting for me in Galilee.

Old Woman: Did you like my little cakes?

Jesus: They're really very good.

Old Woman: Then take some with you. Take them to your mother. Tell her they come from an old woman who lives by the Jordan and who is very fond of her.

Jesus: But you haven't met my mother.

Old Woman: It doesn't matter. I've met you and I'm very fond of you, young man. Your mother must be like you.

Magdalene: Goodbye, Jesus. I'll be in Galilee next week. If you happen to pass by Capernaum, . . . well, come and visit me, if you don't mind going to my house.

Jesus: Of course, I'll see you, Mary. Goodbye, Grandma! When the Messiah comes, offer some of your honeyed cakes. He'll be as delighted as I've been. . . .

Old Woman: Goodbye, young man, goodbye. Enjoy your journey!

Jesus undertook the long journey back home toward the north, toward the Galilee of the Gentiles. He was exhausted, his sandals worn out, and his tunic half-torn. Notwithstanding, he continued his journey and walked faster than ever.

Jesus: Somebody must take the place of John. Someone must give hope to the people. Lord, send us our Liberator now! Where is he, Lord? We can't do anything while we wait for him. The fruit is already ripe and we must harvest. I'm getting impatient. I ought to do something now. I must follow the example of John.

Jesus walked for several hours through the river valley. On the second day, he reached the heights of Gadara before dusk. From there he could see the Sea of Galilee. He was on Galilean land! Suddenly, it began to rain. The waters from the sky gave back to the earth its freshness and fertility. Jesus felt an immense joy in his heart, as if he were seeing his beloved homeland in the north for the first time. In his mind, Galilee, drenched by the rain, was secretly giving him a welcome that night.

Jesus: Galilee, here I am, back to you, my land!

Land of Zabulun, Land of Naphtali! On the way to the sea, by the other side of the Jordan, Galilee of the Gentiles! The people who walked in the dark saw a light; on those who lived in the shadow of death, a great light shone. You made great joy, and they delight in seeing you, like those who sing on the day of the harvest. Because you have broken the yoke that bound them and destroyed the tyrant's rod; and to the fire shall be cast the boots he wears with pride and his blood-stained cloak.

For a Liberator is born, and endless is the peace he'll bring to us!

•

Mary Magdalene, as mentioned several times in the gospels, was a prostitute. The name "Mary" was very common in Jesus' time. "Magdalene" refers to her probable birthplace, Magdala. The town, as mentioned earlier, was noted for the abundance of prostitutes and taverns. Prostitution there was more a reflection of an economic problem than a moral concern, just as it is in many places today.

In a male chauvinist society, a single woman who is jobless is constrained to sell herself in order to survive. Mary of Magdala was undoubtedly one of these women. She was probably very young then, since prostitution was rampant among girls thirteen or fourteen years of age. The stereotyped picture of a woman of the upper social class, well-attired, smelling of perfume, and with some sentimental indiscretion, has no relation whatsoever with the vulgarity of a low-class prostitute like Mary Magdalene.

When he learned about the imprisonment of John the Baptist, Jesus was given a new dimension to the realization of his own vocation. Israel was left orphaned without the prophet announcing its liberation by God. Jesus felt it was his obligation to take over where John had left off. He would take his message of justice and bring it to his land, to Galilee. He would not baptize like John did nor expect people to seek him; rather, he would mingle with the people and be one with them. From the streets, the poor neighborhoods, and the plazas, he would announce to the people the liberation that God had promised them. From the banks of the Jordan, Jesus started his journey to the north. It was a long stretch by foot, consisting of about three or four stops, passing through the river valley by way of Perea and Decapolis or by taking the mountain route through the region of Samaria.

"The Galilee of the Gentiles" is an epithet given by the prophet Isaiah about seven hundred years before Christ describing the lands in the north. He indicated that the region, the home area of Jesus which originally belonged to the sons of the old patriarch Jacob, appeared to have been forsaken by God and left to the "Gentiles" (pagans, foreigners). These were the times when the Galileans were made prisoners and were deported. In the midst of suffering, there seemed no future for them. The prophet told them of a light shining amid darkness. When Jesus began to preach the Kingdom of God in Galilean lands after his baptism in the Jordan, Matthew remembered this prophecy of Isaiah and included it in his gospel.

(Matt. 4:12–17)

12

Today Is a Joyful Day

Mary: Don't think I know everything. That's not true, dear neighbor. Jesus was a bit bothered when he left; he was teeming with strange ideas. But don't you ever think it was a matter of the heart. How I would have wanted it! Ay, this son of mine. I'm afraid you're wrong, my dear neighbor. I guess these are bad times. Please don't get up. Lie down. That's it. This hot soup will do you good. Take it while it's hot. My mother used to prepare this concoction. It's very good.

Ever since Jesus left Nazareth to look for the prophet John by the river Jordan, the days seemed very long for Mary. She spent her afternoons in the company of her neighbor, the wife of Naphtali, who was then a bit indisposed....

Mary: You know, I feel like I've aged seven years these days. Imagine, I eat all by myself. At night, there is silence all over this hut. Jesus snores a lot, all right, but it's at least a noise that keeps me company and lulls me to sleep. Now, I wake up at night and get startled in the dark. The other night, I heard a noise and I asked: "Who's there? Who's there?" I even lit a lamp to see who was there. Oh, my dear neighbor, when our children are away, half of our life seems to have been taken away too. Wait till I pour these mint leaves in the soup. This will cure you as if you were cured by the heavens above. What if Jesus stays in the Jordan and leaves me here? That idea has been here in my heart, pricking me like a needle. Well, God knows each one of us, and has a purpose for everyone. He knows what road he wants Jesus to take. All I pray is for God to protect him from all dangers, for my son is so stubborn. He took after his father, don't you think so, my friend? Oh, there you are, you have fallen asleep. I shall leave you now. Sleep well.

Mary left Naphtali's wife and walked to her house. Inside, she ate a few bites of black bread. She didn't much feel like eating. Then she lay down on a mat. She was so exhausted that day, and soon she fell asleep....

The sun was beginning to peep through the horizon, stripping the sky of the last of the stars that shone. The cool morning breeze greeted the plants on the farm and caused them to sway and dance. It was dawn in Nazareth. Jesus, though exhausted, was elated with what he had seen and heard in the Jordan and in the solitude of the desert. He was now on his way back home.

Jesus: Hey, what are you doing here so early in the morning, Tonin, my boy?

Tonin: I'm gathering some shells. It rained yesterday, and so many of them came out. Look....

Jesus: You would like the lizards I saw in the desert! They were this big....

Tonin: You've been in the desert?

Jesus: That's right. I came from there.

Tonin: Why did you go there?

Jesus: I just searched for something.

Tonin: Did you look for these lizards?

Jesus: Lizards, no, but something else.

Tonin: Did you find what you wanted?

Jesus: Of course. Goodbye, Tonin. Show me those shells later.

Tonin: See you around, Jesus!

Mary, as always, was already up very early in the morning. She was boiling water on the stove for the lentils. She sat on the floor to grind wheat to be made into bread flour.

Jesus: Madame, could you spare some milk for a poor traveler...?

Mary: Why, yes, but...Who are you?...Oh, Jesus, my son! It's you! You're back!

Jesus: Yes, I'm back, Mother!

Mary: Oh, thank you, Lord, thank you! I've been praying everyday for your well-being. Praise the Lord! I was so worried about you, Jesus. Why, it took you so long and...how is John? I heard he was taken prisoner. Were you there when that happened?

Jesus: No, I had already gone....Yes, they grabbed him. They finally silenced the prophet.

Mary: Just like I told you, Jesus. Do you think they will kill him?

Jesus: I don't think so. Herod won't dare. He'll eventually set him free.

In the meantime, someone will have to take his place. John has kindled the fire and we must keep it burning.

Mary: It's now up to God to bring us another prophet. You must be hungry and thirsty. What do you want to eat?

Jesus: Whatever you have.

Mary: Look, son. When you left, I went to Cana and bought some good wine. I told myself we would have a drink when you got back. Here you are! Here, take it ... and some dates to go with it.

Jesus: Ah, it smells very good. Drink with me, Mother. Today is a joyful day.

Mary: I see you are very happy. You have lost weight, but you look good.

Jesus: You're right again. There is nothing I can hide from you! Yes, I won't deny it, I'm happy, but I'm worried about John. He's great, this cousin of ours. . . . Mother, the truth is, God's hand was behind this whole trip.

Mary: You were so nervous. I was thinking about what you said, that you were confused, that you didn't know what to do. All this, I kept in my heart. Now what, have you found what you wanted?

Jesus: John helped me see things clearly. Do you know something, Mother? I was baptized in the Jordan. It was ... It was something great. I have lots of stories to tell you. I also stayed in the desert.

Mary: You were in the desert? But, what did you do there? Oh, my dear son, that explains why you lost weight. They say that only beetles can stand the heat of the desert sun.

Jesus: Bah, that's not true. I found a place where I meditated a lot. Mother, can you imagine how it would be to tell the poor that God is offering us his Kingdom, to proclaim to the unfortunate ones who weep in our land that they shall all be comforted soon? Can you imagine what it would be to fight for justice, knowing that God is our leader and is side by side with us?

Mary: That would be great, Jesus, very great! There wouldn't be enough wine in Cana with which to celebrate that day. Your joy is contagious. But, look, son, you must put your two feet on the ground. That day will come, but not for us to see. It will take a long, long time.

Jesus: John says the Liberator of Israel is coming soon.

Mary: Yes, and the zealots say so, too, and he will cut the necks of all the Romans. Watch your tongue, son. There are more soldiers now in

Galilee than you can imagine. With the prophet's imprisonment, they're afraid that people may retaliate, so everyone is being watched.

Jesus: Look who's coming, . . . your close friend, Susanna.

Susanna: Where is that brown one who just got back from the Jordan? Hey, young man, I missed you! Your mother and I were scared to death when we learned about John. They say they dragged him out from the river like a wild beast. Now what's to become of our country?

Jesus: Take it easy, Susanna. You don't have to be that scared. No one, not even Herod, can silence the prophets. We must continue shouting, with the voice of John.

Susanna: See what I told you, Mary. See what has become of him . . . a revolutionary. He even challenges King Herod!

Jesus: Easy, Susanna, easy. Why don't you try this wine a little, and see how it will make you happy.

Susanna: Tell us, Jesus, what happened in the Jordan? Tell us what you saw there.

Jesus: Great things. It's been a long time since the truth has been spoken in Israel, a long, long time during which Israel has not looked up to heaven with much hope.

Susanna: And what must come from heaven to make us look up to it? Young man, we must look on earth, for it is this land that Herod and Pilate are lording over. They are going to kill John, the prophet, and if you get involved with these troublemakers, they will kill you too.

Mary: Well, let's forget about it now, Susanna. Today is a joyful day. Let's rejoice now and don't dampen this party with . . .

Susanna: Now, now, Mary, don't get me wrong. Remember how you ate your heart out when you learned about John. Not for anything, young man. Why shouldn't we worry? We remembered your father, Joseph, and how he was beaten, all because he defended those who'd escaped and gone into hiding.

Jesus: My father was a just man who did not run away when the time came. I am proud of him, and so is the Lord. You know what it would mean, Susanna, to be announcing to the four corners of Galilee that he and all those who died for the sake of justice are the very ones paving the way for the Kingdom of God?

Susanna: Oh, my son, he who shouts gets killed! Don't scream too much. Don't poke your nose into other people's lives. Get to work and be calm. This is what God wants — peace and tranquillity.

Jesus: Or better, this is what some people want, that we continue in our slumber, like Noah inside his tent, leaving us stark naked.

Susanna: Don't talk that way, Jesus. Mary, you better advise this young man. He might give you trouble someday, what with having so much politics on his mind. Listen to me, Jesus, get rid of those strange ideas and concentrate peacefully on your hammer and nails. Learn from the example of your father, Joseph.

Jesus: You don't seem to know my father. Do you remember when Boliche and he went to Nain to protest the price of flour? Who rose to his feet in the synagogue when that skunk, Ananias, wanted to claim all the lands of Balthazar?

Susanna: But that happened a long, long time ago.

Jesus: That's right, but people have not forgotten.

Susanna: I didn't say that people have forgotten.

Mary: Well, well, enough of these discussions. You're like cats and dogs. Hey, where is the jug?

Jesus: Come on, Susanna, take some more wine and all your fears will be gone.

Susanna: Say, Mary, is this the wine you bought in Cana?

Mary: Exactly. They sell it very cheap there, and it's very good.

Jesus: If you wish, I can bring you some more liters of wine when I pass by the place.

Mary: Will you journey to Cana, Jesus?

Jesus: Yes. In a few days, I'd like to go to Capernaum. I will pass by Cana.

Mary: But there's work waiting for you here. I have three pending errands for you. Do you know that the Roman soldier came back and ordered more horseshoes?

Jesus: You mean they liked my work? Well, that means we'll have more dinars to buy lentils and oil.

Mary: You must do them soon.

Jesus: Sure, I will. Say, I met some friends from Capernaum near the Jordan. These are fishermen from the lake and we got along very well. I'd like to see them again.

Susanna: Could Simon be one of them, the one they call Peter?

Jesus: Yes, he's one of them. Do you know him, Susanna?

Susanna: Why, of course! He's the son of the old Jonas. I'm even a distant relative of his mother, may she rest in peace. As a little boy, he was already quarrelsome!

Jesus: This Peter is okay, just like his brother.

Susanna: They call him the skinny Andrew.

Jesus: That's right.

Mary: Were there many people by the Jordan, Jesus? Tell us more about it.

Jesus: The place was like an anthill. It was swarming with people. The river was filled with people, men and women who were full of hope, wishing for change in our land. I, too, believe that there can be change in this country, but we should make it happen!

Mary: I'm happy to see you so contented, Jesus. Don't you think he looks good, Susanna?

Susanna: I would say that the steam has got into his head, and...

Jesus: Come on, Susanna, let's not talk about it. Sit down here, for I have so many stories to tell about my trip.

Susanna: Wait, Jesus, I'll go run and tell Simeon and old Sarah,... Naphtali too, and the children.

Jesus: Yes, tell everyone to come.

The whole neighborhood gathered in Mary's house to hear the news about the prophet John. Jesus had lived in Nazareth for about thirty years in the company of his townspeople, doing some carpentry, iron work, tilling the land... For him, the time had come to clear the furrows for the Kingdom of God in Capernaum, along the Sea of Galilee. That spring morning, everything seemed new. The grain promised to yield bread, and the trees, fruit. A great hope was awaiting Israel.

•

One day, Jesus left Nazareth, his hometown, and lived in Capernaum, a city by the lake. During that time, it was a big and significant city. Although Capernaum was not too distant from Nazareth (about forty-five kilometers), the decision entailed a gesture of farewell to his mother and his townspeople. That moment, which was Jesus' initiation to "public life," is traditionally a topic of reflection for all Christians. Everyone making a decision must say goodbye and give up something. A vocation of service always signifies some form of sacrifice. It is the price of the Kingdom of God.

Jesus shared with his mother his experiences in the Jordan when he listened to the Baptizer and was alone in the desert. Mary, like Jesus, was growing in her faith, her understanding of Jesus' vocation, and her acceptance of the mission that God destined for her son. For her, this process meant uncertainties, sufferings, fears, anxieties, and insecurities, just as it has for many mothers who share their sons' commitment to fight for justice at the risk of their own lives.

The gospel hardly mentions Joseph as a "just man" (Matt. 1:19). On the basis of this very simple yet profound phrase, it is good to reconstruct Joseph's image so that it can serve as a model for Christians not only of honesty but also of commitment, courage, and dissent — in a word, everything that would mean being a just man. This exemplary life was the best legacy of Joseph to Jesus. He witnessed how his father sided with the needy and participated when necessary. There is no historical or theological basis for an image of Mary's spouse as an old, passive man who was resigned and totally lacking in dynamism.

13

The Fishermen's Village

The great Sea of Galilee was bordered by hills and plains rich with fruit trees and wheat, vineyards and orchards. Along its banks were crammed several fishing villages: Tiberias, the cursed city, where King Herod had his palace; Magdala, known for its women; Bethsaida, which means "the house of fishes," where we were all born; and Capernaum, the noisiest city, which means "the city of consolation," where we were all residing and working now, upon orders of my father, Zebedee.

Zebedee: Blazes! Everything has gone well today. James, tell your mom to separate the big salmon for our soup. It's been a long time since we've had such a good catch. This calls for a celebration!

James: Are you gonna let me try your soup, Dad?

Zebedee: Why not? Invite your wife. Tell that rascal Peter to come too. What we catch, we all eat.

My father, old Zebedee, learned to row even before he could walk. He had spent all his life fishing in the Sea of Galilee. He knew the depth of the water better than the palm of his hand. Sometimes, I would think that my old man had scales on his skin and fishbones instead of a backbone. He had formed some kind of a cooperative, together with Jonas, the father of Andrew and Peter, and two other fishermen. Zebedee was their head. We shared the boats and the nets. Everyone worked together, and at the end of each day we would divide what we had earned, which was not much.

Zebedee: The time will come and my eyes will witness this, when there will be enough fish soup for everyone, enough work for everyone, and true justice for the poor! Come on, let's go home, John. I'm already hungry!

When the sun hid itself behind Mount Carmel, the sea remained still. The seagulls returned to their nests after fluttering over the waters during the day. The ferryboats, with their folded sails, squeezed by each other in the quay of

Capernaum, anticipating another day of work the following morning. The stoves begin to burn in all of the fishermen's houses, which were jammed along the riverbank.

Zebedee: How is the soup, lady?

Salome: It will soon be done, old man. Relax!

Zebedee: [with sarcasm] Don't forget to put in some spices for flavoring!

Salome: Will you stop pestering me and leave me alone with my cooking.

My mother, Salome, was a short, thin woman. Yet she was strong, like the roots of a tree, and her skin was sun-burned. She was advanced in age, but there wasn't a single white hair on her head, and that was her reason for vanity. She enjoyed her household chores, as well as having a long chat with her neighbors. She did all these with such great speed so as not to miss anything. I am always reminded of those flying fishes leaping about the lake swift as lightning and clever. We never caught them.

Zebedee: Hey, Andrew, aren't you coming over? Where's your brother, Peter?

Andrew: He'll come later. He wouldn't miss Salome's cooking for anything. He's staying with the children, as the wife had to look for herbs for her sick mother. He's coming though.

While my mother was cooking, the smell of the fish permeated the house. Andrew, James, and I played dice.

James: There goes number five! It's your turn, Andrew.

Andrew: Four and two!

James: Your turn, John.

John: I win again! Hey, James, you owe me two turns. And so do you, Andrew.

Andrew: What bad luck! I'm left with nothing, not even a single cent.

John: James, I think you cheat.

James: Who, me? You gotta be kidding. I play clean!

John: You, redhead. You're a cheat.

Andrew: Don't mind him, John. He always does it.

James: Hey, what are you babbling about, Toothpick? I'm honest, do you hear?

Zebedee: Hey guys, don't waste your energy fighting among yourselves. Reserve it for the Romans.... By the way, it's been some time since we've heard anything from the movement. It's strange, very quiet.

John: The people are scared ever since they got John the Baptist.

Andrew: The zealots are waiting to see what they're gonna do to him.

James: What they're gonna do to him, what they're gonna do to him ...Why don't we see what we can do? Let's do something without being told. We can't just be looking at the clouds all the time.

Zebedee: What can you do, young men?

John: Nothing, because the Romans are everywhere. The whole of Galilee is being surrounded.

James: So much the better. The more birds on the loose, the more they're gonna fall into the trap. Why don't we act now and surprise them?

Andrew: Peter was thinking about it the other day, but...

James: Hey, you, Toothpick, will you stop worrying?

Andrew: Don't forget that this is the best time for fishing in the lake. If we make trouble now, then we'll have to go into hiding afterward. Have you forgotten what happened during the feast of the Passover? What about our job?

John: Toothpick is right. We who are starving to death must always think of our stomachs first before anything else.

It was already night when Jesus arrived in Capernaum. He passed through the neighborhood of the artisans and walked toward the quay. The smell of cooked food came from each house and fused with the smell of rotten fish in the streets. It was the noisiest and liveliest time of day in Capernaum. After asking where our house was, he finally reached our place.

Jesus: May I come in?

Zebedee: Certainly, my friend. Who are you?

John: Jesus! What are you doing here?

Jesus: As you can see, I came to visit you.

James: Oh, the brown one from Nazareth!

Jesus: I'm happy to see you again, James. Hello, Andrew.

Zebedee: I see you know each other very well.

John: Hey, we didn't know what happened to you after you went to the desert. We thought you'd been devoured by the scorpions!

James: When did you find out about John? We have to do something, Jesus.

Andrew: We were just talking about it and...

Zebedee: Dammit! But who is this man? He comes sneaking into my house, and here I am like a fool....

James: Don't act like that, old man. He's a friend we met at the Jordan.

Andrew: He's from Nazareth and his name is Jesus.

Zebedee: From Nazareth? Bah, a good-for-nothing man of that town, a farmer who wants to conquer the sea?

Jesus: Your sons invited me to come. They say I can find a job here in Capernaum. In Nazareth, things aren't so easy.

John: Jesus, this is Zebedee, our father. Every hair in his beard stands for an ordeal he's been through. Here he is: an old, experienced revolutionary.

Salome: I am the mother of these two rascals!

James: This is our mom, Salome.

Salome: Welcome, young man. You're just in time to try our special fish soup. You must be tired. Come, have a seat.

Peter arrived shortly, rowdier than the rest of the group. He was elated to see Jesus again. He was with his wife, Rufina, and little Simon, one of his four sons. They wanted to greet the man from Nazareth. My mother had to add more water to the soup for everyone to have enough.

John: Do you remember that afternoon when Toothpick and I were having a chat with you? Come on, Jesus, tell them the joke about the flea. That's a good one!

James: This is no time for jokes, John. You look silly. Weren't we talking about doing something? Why don't we discuss it with Jesus?

Peter: I was just thinking the same thing. Long live the movement!

Rufina: For heaven's sake, Peter. Don't get yourself into trouble. My mother is dying. Don't give me another problem. You're crazy! Holy God!

Peter: But Rufi...

James: How is Nazareth, Jesus? Judas Iscariot was there recently, and he told us that...

Little Simon: Say, you know that I'm gonna have a baby sister?

James: It seems that everyone in the whole valley is being watched.

Jesus: That's right. And that's because of John. In Cana, I saw a lot of soldiers too.

Little Simon: Say, you know that I'm gonna have a baby sister?

James: Now shut up, you little brat. Don't you see we're discussing something?

Rufina: Little Simon, come over here. Don't be nasty.

Little Simon: But I'm gonna to have a baby sister!

Jesus: Oh really? And how do you know it's gonna be a baby sister? How'd you guess that?

Little Simon: Because I know everything!

Rufina: Shut up, young man, and come over here.

Jesus: So you can guess everything. Now tell me this: What's the only fish that wears a necklace?

Little Simon: The only fish . . .

John: That's it, a joke!

Zebedee: Quiet, John. What was it you said? Have you ever seen a fish wearing a necklace?

Jesus: Yes, sir, there's one, and it even uses a scarf . . . and . . .

Peter: It must be a strange fish. What is it? Tell us.

Jesus: It's the neck. . . . [1] What about this other one: Everybody buys it because they need it for eating, but nobody eats it.

Andrew: They need it for eating, but nobody eats it.

Jesus: The plate!

All: That's right.

John: This is getting to be exciting!

Zebedee: Quiet and listen. Come on, tell us some more.

Jesus: Listen to this: There's a married couple; the wife leaves and the husband stays.

Salome: That must be you and I, Zebedee!

Zebedee: Shut your big mouth, idiot, and let me think. . . . How is that again? A married couple . . . The wife goes away and the husband stays behind. . . . I give up. What is it?

Jesus: The key and the padlock![2]

All: One more, one more!

Little Simon: Hey, how do you know so many riddles?

John: This brown one makes up one story after another. Why don't you tell them a long story, about the camels, remember? Pssst . . . Silence now, everybody and listen. . . .

---

1. An untranslatable pun. The Spanish has *pez-cuezo* (*pes-cuezo*). *Pez* means "fish" in Spanish.
2. In Spanish, "key" (*la llave*) is feminine; "padlock" (*el candado*) is masculine.

Jesus: A man had three camels. One of them went to a well to drink. When he reached the well...

Jesus began to tell us stories, one after the other. We had finished our soup and everyone felt sleepy, but we continued listening to him. What a gift he had for telling stories! Everyone understood him, even grandmother Rufa and the brat, Little Simon, also called Mingo. Then when he started to talk about the Kingdom of God, he did so by way of stories and parables. They all listened to him in Capernaum and in Jerusalem. His stories spread fast, and we proclaimed his words in the streets and in the markets, confident that what he started in a village of fishermen was good news for everyone in every nook and corner of the earth.

•

The Sea of Galilee (actually a lake) is called a "sea" because of its great expanse. The gospel likewise refers to it as the Sea of Tiberias or the Sea of Gennesaret, referring to the two cities found along its shores. In the Old Testament it is called the Sea or Lake of Kinneret (from *kinnor,* which in Hebrew means "harp"). Legend has it that the lake has a harplike shape and that the gentle sound of its waves are like the sound of a harp. From north to south, the lake measures up to 21 kilometers. Its greatest width is 13 kilometers. Like the Dead Sea, it is situated below sea level (212 meters), with a depth of 48 meters. Its waters taste sweet. All kinds of fish abound in it — about twenty-four different species are known. In Jesus' time and even at present, fishing is the principal activity in the cities along the banks.

Several cities have been established along the lake. During Jesus' time, one of the most important cities was Capernaum ("city of consolation" or "city of Nahum"), which was never mentioned in the Old Testament. The city had a customs house because it was a frontier town between Galilee, which was governed by Herod, and Ituraea and Trachonitis, which belonged to Philip. Likewise, it was located beside the great Roman highway that joined Galilee and Syria (the so-called Via Maris). Because of its strategic importance, it also had a Roman garrison, under the command of a centurion. In Capernaum, many stories of the preachings of Jesus in Galilee were developed. It was here that he lived after he left Nazareth. Matthew referred to this as the "city of Jesus" (Matt. 9:1).

During the gospel era, Capernaum covered a few square kilometers and had a few thousand inhabitants. Aside from fishing, the town was also engaged in the development of agricultural crops like olives, wheat, and other grains. The houses were made of black basalt stone with roofs of straw and clay that shielded the residents from the heat, especially during summer. About four centuries after Christ, Capernaum was destroyed, and its ruins were not found until the end of the nineteenth century. These ruins — consisting of a few house foundations and the lay-out of the town and streets of the old city — were one of the greatest archaeological treasures discovered from the gospel era. Present-day Capernaum still preserves a great synagogue built over the old one as well as objects that existed during the period (oil lamps, stone mills, and so on). Undoubtedly, the most important of all these is the foundation of Peter's house. The inscriptions found show that since the first century, the early Christians would gather there to celebrate the Eucharist. The house was beside the quay and together with other small houses formed a kind of common patio (or yard) for the neighborhood. The plan of these small houses clearly indicates the extreme poverty in which Jesus' friends lived. It is probable that Peter's family, Andrew's family, and Zebedee's family — including his wife, Salome, and his two sons, James and John — lived together in one of these groupings of houses of fishermen in Capernaum.

Oral tradition was common in all peasant culture, such as the gathering of neighbors to listen to one of their townspeople tell a story that had been repeated a thousand times; this was the way to transfer knowledge from one generation to another — through stories told by a father to his children. The grandparents were the expert narrators. Jesus, a peasant, was heir to this type of culture. Further, the Middle East has always been a cradle of stories with moral themes: fables, parables, and so on. Into all of these, Jesus would incorporate his personal mastery as conversationalist and narrator — the gospels are proof of this. Practically all his parables sprang from his family and peasant environment. He expressed himself a lot better with imagery than with abstract ideas. It is wrong to believe that in order to do this he had to "adapt himself" to his less intelligent listeners, so that he would be better understood. In his language, Jesus did not have to lower himself, because he was from the same class as his listeners, and he spoke like them.

The good news of Jesus began to bloom in the fishermen's district of Capernaum, a poor area whose people were hard-working. It is necessary

to preserve these origins of the gospel because, more often than not,
Jesus has tended to be identified as an urban rather than a rural dweller
with good manners — a condescending person who was patient toward
the rude and hardened people. No. Jesus belonged to the lower class of
that small land. He mingled with the filthy children of the place, as well
as with women with callused hands and townspeople who laughed and
cursed while enjoying a pitcher of wine.

(Matt. 4:13)

14

The First Five

All of us fishermen from Capernaum were already up even before the roosters could crow in the morning. One by one, we would leave the house still half-asleep. With our nets we would all gather on the small wharf where our fishing boats were moored and where the old men would divide the tasks among us every day.

Zebedee: What early birds, young men! Brrr . . . It's damn cold! Come on, shake a leg, the mountain breeze will be good for fishing. Jonas, my friend, join your own men. Twins, you and I will go down that bend, and you, young men, to the fishing boats! Cheer up, everyone, for this is gonna be a lucky day!

The rowmen thrust the boats through the calm waters of the lake until the north wind began to blow and the sails were unfurled. And there in the deep was cast a big net that would catch the best fish. Another group with their baskets and ropes remained on the shore in order to trap the small ones, the goldfish and the needlefish.

Jonas: Stretch out the net, you beast! Farther. Hold it, Peter! Over there! Over there! We have a school of fish on the left! Come on, young men!

Jesus was with us for one week in Capernaum. He looked for a job during the day; at night he went to the house to have a drink and to tell us stories. Jesus was a good friend. Soon he became close to the family and considered himself one of us. That morning, when he woke up, we were already battling with the wavy waters of the lake. Jesus crossed the fishing village, passing through the palm trees that surrounded the wharf and walked toward the shore.

Jonas: Andrew, lend Peter a hand! You too, frog face! Come on, boys, all together now! One, two, three! Yaaa!
Men: Yaaa!

Jonas: One more time!

Men: Yaaa!

Jonas: Hurray for the fishermen!

Men: Yaaa!

Jonas: Cheers to the brave men of Tiberias!

Men: Yaaa!

Jonas: Cheers to the strong men of Bethsaida!

Men: Yaaa!

Jonas: Hurray to the real men of Capernaum!

Men: Yaaa!

Jonas: Ya, ya, ya, ya!

Men: Ya, ya, ya, ya!

Peter: Damn this net! Its knots are all rotten! Uff!

Andrew: Hey, Peter, isn't that Jesus? Look...

Peter: Ah, yes, he's the one... Finally, the brown one of Nazareth has shown up! Obviously these peasants from inland aren't early birds. Hey, you, guy from Nazareth! Just wait for us there; we're coming ashore!

Jonas: Where are you going, Peter? Andrew, you dope, don't release the rope!

Andrew: The net is empty, there's nothing in it, not even little fish or slimy shells!

Peter: We have a visitor. Come, let's welcome him!

Jonas: To hell with all of you and the visitor! Ever since this fellow came, you do nothing but spend the time chatting! You charlatans!

Jesus: Well, yes, I slept like a log. Right now, I'm going to see Rufina's friend, whose house is about to fall down. If I put up the wall and nail the roof in place, I can earn a few dinars.

Peter: That can wait. There's always time for work. Let's go look for Zebedee's sons down the bend; then we can roast some fresh fish.

Jesus: But you have to work, Peter, and...

Peter: Don't worry about that, Jesus. I'm sick and tired of casting nets.

Andrew: This is Jonas, our father. He's the most stubborn man in town.

Peter: One can always catch a school of fish here, but then, he gets tired of casting the net, and so ends up catching nothing at all.

Jesus: That must be a difficult job. I've been watching all of you do it.

Andrew: Not really. It's a matter of getting used to it and knowing how to work with the group. As one pulls up the buoy, another tucks in the knots, while another attends to the baskets. Like this...

Peter: Toothpick, first we gotta teach him how to swim. Peasants can't even swim, you know!

Jesus: You're right, Peter. Let's put it this way: I'm never at home in the water.

Andrew: Well, do you plan to stay in Capernaum for some more days?

Jesus: I'm not sure. It depends.

Peter: What do you mean?

Jesus: It all depends on you.

Peter: That's no problem with us, right Andrew? You can stay with the Zebedees or with us, for as long as you want. You're welcome any time.

Andrew: And, as you've seen, there's always work for you here.

Jesus: No, it's not because of that. That's not what I'm thinking of right now.

Peter: Then what is it?

Jesus: Nothing, it's just that . . . You see, when I was in the desert, after we parted ways at the Jordan, remember? I had a chance to reflect. . . .

Peter: So?

Jesus: Listen, Peter. The prophet John is still in prison, and no one is demanding justice. What have we been doing? We talk a lot, that's right, and that's all.

Peter: That was precisely what I was saying yesterday: we talk about a lot of things: many stories, baptism, it's all words. But when the moment of truth comes, we leave the prophet in solitude. Tell me, what is the movement planning to do? Aren't the zealots going to save him?

Andrew: Machaerus is very much isolated by mountains. It would be very difficult to storm it.

Peter: Difficult or not . . . We can't allow the voice of John to be carried away by the wind. We must act now, and do something. Good Lord!

Andrew: What's your plan, Jesus?

Jesus: Nothing special, Andrew, but . . . I don't know. As I see you cast your nets, it just occurred to me that . . . Hey, why don't we do exactly what you're doing when fishing? I mean, you cast your nets and, together, you pull it. Why don't we do something together?

Peter: Exactly. Less talk but more work. We need stones, not words, to smash the heads of the Romans. That's a good idea, Jesus. We do something on our own. Let's not wait for orders from the movement. Let's take the law into our own hands!

Jesus: Forget about the stone throwing and the law, Peter. What's important is that we be united, as a group.

Peter: That's a good idea. I like it. One for all, all for one. Together we face all perils, and together we celebrate our victory. Well, then, we form a group, and we attack by surprise.

Andrew: Hold it, Peter. This isn't clear yet. Why are we forming a group, Jesus?

Jesus: Well, to continue the work started by the prophet John, to talk to the people and tell them: "The time of the Lord has come. He will cast his nets by the sea, and all of you should be alert. God is not pleased with the state of things. The time has come when the big fish will no longer devour the small fish."

Peter: Very well said. When do we start?

Andrew: Take it easy, Peter. What Jesus has said is fine, but, . . . but we must be very careful. It reeks of conspiracy around here. If we organize something, we've got to take some precautions.

Jesus: Are you afraid, Andrew?

Andrew: I'm not scared, Jesus. But neither do I want to be hunted like a criminal.

Jesus: And you, Peter, are you scared?

Peter: Who, me? Of course not. You don't know me yet, Jesus!

Jesus: Well, I'm scared. While in the desert, I discovered that I was scared, . . . scared to risk my life, you know what I mean? But God will give us the strength to move on, don't you think?

Peter: Why, of course! There's no place for cowards in this world. Come, let's talk to James and John. Let's see what those bandits have to say!

Peter, Andrew, and Jesus headed for the shore until they reached the bend, where Zebedee's boats were waiting. My brother and I were with our father, mending some old nets.

Peter: There they are. The one who's half-naked is James.

Jesus: Hey, James, yes, you, come over here, and hurry, redhead. We want to talk to you.

Peter: And there's that restless fellow John.

Jesus: Come over here, John! Leave your nets and come here.

John: We'll be right there!

Zebedee: Hold it, young men, you're not leaving! It's not mealtime yet!

Damn these young people! I swear they'll go to bed with an empty stomach, this pair of bums!

James: Fellows, today would be the right time to show our friend around. Since he came, all he's done is nail and lay bricks. Today, we'll have a little fun. Look, Jesus, Capernaum is known for being a happy city, and that is true. Here, there is always dancing and drinking. Plenty of women, also. In this village, a certain Mary of Magdala has got us all hooked up! Ayyaya! . . .

Andrew: Hey, redhead, forget about that for now; we've got something more serious to talk about. Jesus has a plan. We were planning to organize a group independent of the movement.

The five of us walked toward the wharf as we discussed the group and the plan of action we would take. At the wharf, we gathered wood, built a fire, and cooked some fresh fish.

James: I guess we need some weapons.

Jesus: What are the weapons for, James?

James: To kill the Romans with. You always say that the big fish devour the small fish, and this must be stopped. Then let's get rid of them!

Jesus: Hold it, James. You yourselves have said that a good fisherman does not make a lot of noise, so as not to shoo away the fish. What has to be done at this moment is to begin gathering the small fish, to make them strong, so they won't be devoured by the big fish. What do you think? God also began that way, when he told Moses to organize the dispersed Jews, so that together, they could defy the Pharaoh and flee from his anger.

Peter: Well said, Jesus. I believe many will unite if we know how to cast our nets well.

Andrew: We can inform Philip, the vendor.

John: And Nathanael, too, from Cana.

Jesus: So, what now? Have we decided to do something? What do you think, James?

James: Well, I'm joining the group. We will see where we should begin. Let's work hand in hand.

Jesus: Do you agree, John, the troublemaker?

John: Sure, you can count on me.

Jesus: What do you say, Andrew, you Toothpick?

Andrew: As I've said before, . . . yes, . . . but with open eyes. We must all work together with this.

Jesus: What does Peter, the stone-thrower, say?

Peter: Are you asking me, Jesus? Three times will I say yes, yes, and yes! Give me that hand! And now, your turn, brown one. What do you say? Are you joining the group?

Jesus: Yes, I also put my hand on this ground, and there is no turning back for me. This is the time for us to work as one.

And so it was that by the wharf of Capernaum, with everyone squatting by the bonfire waiting for the fish to cook, we formed our group. We were only five.

•

Fishing was the main livelihood in all the cities and small villages surrounding the Sea of Galilee. During those times, fishermen belonged to the lower social class. The upper classes viewed them as being without a culture, as lax in their religious duties, and as uneducated. Together with the peasants and other poor, they formed part of the so-called *amhaares* (primitively known as "people of the land," "countrymen"; later known as "sinners," "lawbreakers"). The fishermen by the lakeside either worked for a patron who got the lion's share of the earnings or constituted an independent group which, with the help of family members, formed small cooperatives that would help ease their enormous financial difficulties.

Parts of the small wharves of Jesus' time are still preserved at various points on the Sea of Galilee. Tabgha, for example, is about thirty kilometers from Capernaum, and its steps are about two thousand years old. The wharf at Capernaum is located in the reconstructed portion.

Jesus recruited his first disciples from among the fishermen who were his friends. With them he formed a group, a community, and gradually discovered his vocation, his mission to proclaim the Kingdom of God in a world where many changes were needed. The first five disciples and later on his twelve staunch followers became, in effect, the first ecclesial community.

At the start of any human endeavor, there is much groping, much immaturity as one continues with the search. Plans are never defined to perfection; neither are the objectives or the consequences clearly seen. Thus the risk and trust are placed in the Lord for the success of the undertaking. The same was true of Jesus and his group. The leadership of Jesus within the group was not imposed or established right at the beginning. Rather, it was something that would gradually develop and be nurtured.

Slowly, the first fishermen of Capernaum saw in Jesus a great companion, a great friend, a natural leader with a generous character and strong will, and finally a shepherd who would tend his flock and lead them as the Liberator they were waiting for.

The task that Jesus and his friends are to face, which is to catch people, is communal and demanding. The Kingdom of God requires collective endeavor. Like fishing, it takes much of one's time and patience, a keen sense of observation, strategy, and astuteness. Jesus likewise tells his friends that God, who is a fisher of people, will cast the nets in order to catch human beings. This is a scene that is found in the parable of the fishing net (Matt. 13:47–50), which refers to God's judgment of the world. The good fish will be separated from the worthless ones (which at that time were understood to be the "bad fish" because they lacked scales and fins, as in the case of conger eels, and therefore were not fit for human consumption). Jesus tells his first disciples that the time for God's judgment has come. The symbol of the big and the small fish is substituted for that of the good and the bad fish.

(Matt. 4:18–22; Mark 1:16–20; Luke 5:1–11)

15

The Junk Dealer

On the third day of the week, Capernaum Square was very colorful and raucous. It was market day. People from the neighboring towns came to trade their wares, like fruit, textiles, and honey-flavored cakes.

Philip: Combs, rings, chokers for sale here! Necklaces and lozenges! Wedding rings, earrings for married women, bracelets for widows! Amulets! Shoes, slippers, slippers, shoes! Buy now, 'cuz I'll be gone in a minute!

Our friend Philip would always go to the market of Capernaum with his wares. He wore an old and worn-out yellow striped turban on his head and could be seen pushing a dilapidated cart full of utensils. With the shrill sound of his horn, Philip was the noisiest man in the square. The women of Capernaum were his good clients. Although he always cheated them on prices, he managed to sell them new pieces of junk every week. He was always surrounded by women, haggling and rummaging through his wares.

Philip: Here, take a look at this mirror, Mam! You look a lot prettier here! No more than five cents! Small mirrors, big mirrors! I'm willing to trade in one new mirror for two old ones! Mary, Mary, I brought you some rouge. Here, young lady, take it! Okay, you can pay me next week. Hey, hey, give that back to me. Don't touch it, it's delicate! Herbs, I also have good herbs — a hot concoction of these herbs straight from the Orient!
Salome: Hey, Philip!
Philip: Yes, Mam Salome! What's up? Do you want a comb or some perfume? Come, take a sniff of this; it was brought from Arabia.
Salome: Spare me, please. I'm too old for that. Look, you can come to the house if you care to have some hot soup.
Philip: You never disappoint me, Mam! As a matter of fact, I am hungry!
Salome: Of course, you devil! After all this shouting and screaming, who wouldn't be famished?

Salome and Philip, pushing his cart, walked to the house, where Salome had been cooking.

Philip: Take these needles, in exchange for this soup!

Salome: Young man, I'm doing this because I love to. You don't have to give me anything in return. I'll tell you when I need something from you. . . . So, this Mary Magdalene bought some rouge from you. What a girl!

Philip: Mam, I treat my customers equally. I must be of service to everyone.

Salome: Her presence in the village has caused quite a stir among the men. What with those swaggering hips . . . and . . . what a scent! May a strong wind snatch her away from here!

Philip: The soup is very good, Mam! Say, where are John and James?

Salome: Where do you think? Sweating it out to earn a living. . . . There's no market day for fishermen like them. Each day is just like any other for them: to be with their boats, sails, and nets, day in and day out.

Philip: So there's nothing new around here, Mam Salome?

Salome: Well, yes, there is something new. Somebody from Nazareth is in town. My children met him at the Jordan. Weren't you there, too, to see the prophet, John? Probably you know him.

Philip: From Nazareth? That must be Jesus, the storyteller.

Salome: Exactly. He can tell very funny stories. For many nights, he has fascinated everyone with his stories. He seems like a nice man. He's staying with us here.

Philip: Where's he now?

Salome: Right now, he must be repairing the roof of the house of Rufina's neighbor.

Philip: Good heavens! I'd like to greet him. I'm going there now!

Salome: Finish your soup first. Here, take some olives and a piece of bread.

Philip: You're right, Mam Salome. I should fill up my stomach first. My friends can wait. Besides, I'm sure you'll like these necklaces that I'll show you. They're made of red stones. I'm giving them at a cheaper price!

Philip left Salome and went in search of Jesus, who was at work at the house of Rufina's neighbor.

Philip: Hey, Jesus! Jesus!

Jesus: Oh, it's you, Philip!

Philip: Jesus, brown one, how happy I am to see you!

Jesus: I've long wanted to see you, big head. I was told you were coming to Capernaum today.

Philip: Today is market day, and I came to sell my wares, as always.

Jesus: Where did you leave your cart?

Philip: Back at Salome's house. She told me you were here. I haven't seen Zebedee's sons yet; neither have I seen Andrew and Peter. . . . Well, what are you doing here?

Jesus: As you can see, I'm doing some house repairs, so I earn a few dinars. Look how rotten these pieces of wood have become. They could fall off anytime.

Philip: Salome said you were going to stay. Why? Are you bored in Nazareth? No, don't say it. I understand. Life is so quiet there. I'll never go there to sell my wares. No one would ever buy them.

Jesus: There's little money there.

Philip: So you've come to join us here. Welcome to Capernaum, Jesus! How happy I am. That means we'll be seeing each other more often. I come here every week.

Jesus: The truth is, I didn't come here because I was bored in Nazareth. I like it there, really. I like it here too, but I came because . . .

Philip: Because you fell in love with a girl from Capernaum! That's okay, I understand. You know, time is passing, and as one gets old, one thinks of having one's own home, a wife and children. . . . Man, I'm so happy! Really, I am!

Jesus: No, Philip, it is not because of that. Now, you listen to what I'm going to tell you.

Philip: Well, tell me. What is it?

Jesus: Yesterday, I had a good discussion with the sons of Zebedee, together with Andrew and Peter. You see, we'd like to do something. They have silenced John, the prophet, but we still have our tongues. We can continue talking to the people, like he used to do, proclaiming the Kingdom of God. To do this, we must all be united.

Philip: Hey, what are you talking about? John was capable of doing it, what with his long hair and thunderous voice, . . . but we, we can't do it. I think you've all gone crazy!

Jesus: No, Philip. We're not crazy, and we must do something. We can't wait for other people to do it. In a short time, there will be many of us. God is on our side.

Philip: Well, I'm happy about that. If you've come to introduce some changes, then I'm happy to hear that, and I wish you good luck.

Jesus: The thing is, we're all counting on you.

Philip: What? You're counting on me? Me?

Jesus: That's right. What's so strange about that?

Philip: But I'm no good at this, Jesus. The only thing I know is my trade. Of course I'd like this country to have justice. . . . But if I myself can't move forward, how can I make others do the same?

Jesus: We can do something, Philip, you'll see.

Philip: I'm a stupid man, Jesus. I don't know anything. John the Baptist had studied the Holy Scriptures, and he knew what he was saying. But how can we do the same? Well, I leave it to the rest. I don't interfere in whatever they say. You see, I don't read or write. I used to listen to the Scriptures in the synagogue when I was a little boy, but I was so bored that I didn't learn anything. I'm a good-for-nothing in this regard. Just leave me alone with the horn and my cart.

Jesus: But we're all the same bunch of ignorant men, Philip. Who is Peter, anyway, and James? And who am I? I remember a psalm that says: "God makes great things with the most humble and with the little children."

Philip: Then you're better than I am, because you remember something of the Scriptures. . . . Tell me, what do those words mean?

Jesus: That in the eyes of God, the people who are most worthy are the insignificant ones, like us, like you. We need you in our group, Philip.

Philip: Well, that's so nice to hear, but, please, leave me alone with my trade. I don't want any hassles. I tell you, I'm a good-for-nothing.

Jesus: What about Moses? Didn't he form our land with a bunch of filthy slaves who didn't even have a piece of land they could call their own?

Philip: Well, yes, that's true. But even if they had, I would say that . . .

Jesus: They were hopeful and they wanted to fight. That's all, Philip, and that's what we have now: hope and the will to fight.

Philip: You're right there, but you haven't convinced me yet. I have such a big stubborn head!

Jesus: Who was King David, Philip? A shepherd, a poor guy. And who was Jeremiah the prophet? A boy who could not even speak. What about the prophet Amos? A peasant tilling his land when he was called by God. . . . God chooses the weak, the poor, so the wise will not become proud. Listen, you stubborn one, we want you to be in our group. We're all shabby and ignorant men, that's true, but together, we can accomplish something!

Philip: But if I get involved in this, then what'll happen to my business? How can I go to the Jordan and baptize people in the river? What about my cart?

Jesus: We don't have to go that far. The people went to the Jordan to be baptized, in order to prepare the way for the Liberator of Israel. Now, we must do something else, I don't know what.

Philip: The only thing I can do is go from town to town advertising my merchandise. That's all.

Jesus: Then we can go from town to town proclaiming what the Lord has in store for us. Right, that's a very good idea of yours.

Philip: Man, in that case, then take me in the group. I might even be able to advertise my wares. As we proclaim God's plans to the people, . . . I might as well take advantage and sell some necklaces! Now you've convinced me, brown one!

Jesus: I'm gonna leave this work for a while so that we can look for our other companions.

Philip: Do you know where they are now?

Jesus: They must be by the wharf. Come on, Philip, follow me.

In a short while, on the wharf . . .

Peter: So you're in this, too, Philip?

Philip: Jesus has sweet talked me into it, and I've taken the bait.

John: He must've spoken a lot to fill up your enormous head with sweet words!

James: Listen well, Philip. This is a serious matter. We must do this on our own, and we can't count on the help of the zealots. Get me? We have to be brave. Do you hear me?

Philip: I'll do the best I can, James. Don't scare me now. I just told Jesus that I enjoy going from town to town, and with my horn and cart, I can take the opportunity to . . .

James: What has your horn got to do with our plans?

John: It's all right, James. Philip's a little stupid, you know.

Philip: Oh, yeah? So I'm stupid, huh? I dare you to say that again, come on . . .

Peter: That's enough, Philip. You wanna join us or not?

Philip: I've already committed myself, Peter, and I'm not leaving. If you kick me out, I'll give you each a nice punch.

Philip, who came from Bethsaida, of Galilee, joined our group. But then, we did not know where to begin, nor what to do. We were only six. We had only hope and the will to fight.

•

There is little information in the gospels about Philip, the apostle. He was from Bethsaida, a village situated along the northern part of the Sea of Galilee, by the eastern shore of the Jordan, which was not part, politically speaking, of Galilee. "Bethsaida" means "house of fish." The brothers Andrew and Peter were born there too. According to the story, Philip was a hawker, an ambulant vendor of junk. This was a common occupation during the period and was classified as "despicable," together with several other popular occupations, as they were degrading to those who engaged in them. One of the reasons that being a hawker was humiliating or degrading was the hawker's association with women, on account of the nature of his work. As such, he was always suspected of committing immoral acts. Those whose manner of earning a living was considered immoral were not given public positions.

The gospels show again and again that not even the laws of the land, its norms, its traditions, and the deeply-rooted customs of the people, could stop Jesus from including everyone, just as God does not look at appearances (1 Sam. 16:7). God reveals himself in Jesus as the God who chooses the humble in order to shame the arrogant and undermine the values of presumptuous people (1 Cor. 1:26–29). God's chosen one, his son, Jesus of Nazareth, is a poor and an uncultured peasant. Those whom Jesus has chosen are the poor, those of the lower social class, the *anawim* of Israel. The church of Jesus is called to be a community of the poor, a place for freedom and unity where people do not worship money or give importance to social titles or positions.

As Jesus reminded Philip, Israel was formed as a people out of a small group of starving slaves, beaten down by hard work, who entrusted their hope in God and in Moses. When the poor awaken and organize themselves, when they begin to act without being humbled by their limitations, when they draw support from God and are strengthened by their unity, God places himself in their midst. In the history of people's liberation, the Lord is an ally of the humble and stands up for them, because it is through the action, commitment, and hope of the people that the Lord transforms history.

(John 1:43–44)

16

Beneath the Fig Tree

*During those days we asked Philip, the junk dealer, to speak with Nathanael,
from Cana of Galilee, to persuade him to join our group. Without being told
twice, Philip headed for the road that passed through the valley of Esdraelon.*

*He arrived in Cana of Galilee about noon. The town smelled of wine and
quince jelly. He pushed his cart of utensils toward the small weaving and tanning
shop where Nathanael worked, ... but it was empty. There, in the yard, under
the shade of a fig tree, he found Nathanael sleeping. He tiptoed toward his friend.*

Philip: Nathanael ... Nat ... Psst ... Wake up, Nat. ... Nathanael!

Nathanael: What's the matter? Who are you? Hell, it's you, Philip!
What are you doing here? How'd you get in?

Philip: How else would I get in? Through the door. I wanted to surprise
you, but I found you snoring like a pig.

Nathanael: What a fool you are, Philip! You just ruined everything, at
the worst time.

Philip: But ... I ...

Nathanael: I can never forgive you for this, do you hear me? Never.
Now beat it, and don't you come back here, ever!

Philip: What's wrong with you? Is business that bad? Has a relative
died? My condolences then. Were you beaten by your wife? Then beat her
with a club, so she'll learn to respect you. Blazes, you shouldn't allow her
to ...

Nathanael: Shut up, will you, Philip! Uff, you're a bore, really, you are!
No one could be worse.

Philip: Were you dreaming, Nat? When you were sleeping beneath the
fig tree, I saw you smiling like an angel; like you'd been given the white
horse of Solomon.

Nathanael: It was better than that, Philip. It was something more.

Philip: Come on, Nathanael, go on! Tell me about this dream. I'm your
friend?

Nathanael: I dreamed I was playing dice and won a fortune. Can you imagine that, Philip?

Philip: Oh, that's fine. You deserve it, my friend. After all, you never cheat. You lose every time.

Nathanael: In my dream I had plenty of money, a sack full of silver. Then I went to my wife and told her: "Old lady, we're moving to Jerusalem. We're rich, do you hear? We're rich! From now on, we won't be walking barefoot, nor will we be eating any more onions!" So we went to Jerusalem, where I put up a big shop. My business prospered. I had mountains and mountains of wool, all kinds of leather, weeding hoes, weaving instruments, shuttles, a dozen looms, several kinds of textiles, multicolored tapestries. . . . I had everything, Philip! I owned everything! Business kept on booming. Money flowed like honey. Every Saturday, my wife and I would walk slowly, hand in hand, to the temple. Imagine that! I was wearing a white, linen tunic, while she had several necklaces on, and a pair of gold bracelets. Everyone was green with envy and said: "There goes that very wealthy Nathanael!" And then . . . then . . .

Philip: Then what?

Nathanael: Then you came, you idiot. And everything was gone.

Philip: But that was marvelous. Your story just gave me goose pimples. I congratulate you, my friend. Good fortune has just come into your house.

Nathanael: No, that was only a dream. As you can see, poor people like us can only dream.

Philip: On the contrary. It is for this reason that I came. To bring you good news.

Nathanael: Come on, tell me soon, and let's see if it can make up for the damage you've done.

Philip: He has come.

Nathanael: Who?

Philip: Shsss! Don't shout, Nat, we've found the man!

Nathanael: Hey, what are you talking about?

Philip: We found the man who'll make your dream a reality. You'll have not only a shop of wool, but a marble palace, bigger than that of Caiaphas! You'll be the wealthiest businessman in the city! And I'll be rich too, Nat. Do you see this cart of combs and amulets? Ha-ha! Soon it's going to be full of pearls, do you hear? A lot more than the pearl necklaces that the Queen of Sheba wore! I'm going to be selling the finest pearls, as big as my fist!

Nathanael: Are you crazy, Philip?

Philip: No, I'm not, but with this man I'm telling you about, things are going to change. He's a smart guy, the type we've been waiting for all along.

Nathanael: We're waiting for the Messiah, Philip. You're not talking of the Messiah, are you?

Philip: Well, I don't know if he's the Messiah, or another baptizer like John, or whatever. I don't care who he is, but he has good ideas. He knows the Scriptures to the letter; the psalms, like the palm of his hand. He speaks like Moses and the other prophets. I tell you, with him around, we're going to move!

Nathanael: Once and for all, Philip, tell me, who are you talking about?

Philip: I'm not going to tell you. Find out for yourself.

Nathanael: Are you making a fool of me?

Philip: I'm serious, Nat. Come on, guess who this guy is.

Nathanael: Okay, at least you should tell me where he comes from. From Jerusalem, maybe?

Philip: You're wrong. He's not from Jerusalem.

Nathanael: He must be from . . . I don't know . . . from Caesarea?

Philip: Far from it. You've gone very far. Go up north.

Nathanael: Is he from here, from Galilee?

Philip: Yes, sir, he's from Galilee, but which part of Galilee? A comb for you, for the right answer.

Nathanael: What do I need a comb for, Philip?

Philip: Come on, guess. Where is he from?

Nathanael: From Tiberias.

Philip: No.

Nathanael: From Sepphoris.

Philip: No.

Nathanael: From Bethsaida.

Philip: I can't believe this, Nathanael. He's almost a neighbor of yours, and yet you can't guess. He is a Nazarene!

Nathanael: From Nazareth?

Philip: Exactly.

Nathanael: Come on, Philip. Go kid somebody else, will you? You're saying he comes from Nazareth! When has any noteworthy person ever come from Nazareth? Only charlatans and bandits come from that good-for-nothing little town.

Philip: I tell you, this is the man we need.

Nathanael: But who is he?

Philip: Jesus! Remember? He's Jesus, the brown one, the son of Joseph. He was with us at the Jordan, the one who told us a lot of jokes.

Nathanael: Now, this is the height of your foolishness. Are you saying that he's to be our Liberator? Only your big empty head could conceive of such a thing.

Philip: That's all right. Say whatever you want, but tomorrow you'll come with me.

Nathanael: Go with you? Where to?

Philip: To Capernaum. He's there. We're forming a group, Nat, and you've got to join us.

Nathanael: No, no, I'm not joining. Leave me alone, will you? I developed a lot of corns on my feet after that trip to the Jordan, and I'm not moving from here.

Philip: You'll come with me to see Jesus.

Nathanael: I tell you to leave me alone with my wife. Besides, I've got a lot of work to do.

Philip, as always, ended up winning and convincing Nathanael. Very early the next day, the two headed for the road to Capernaum. Nathanael helped Philip push the dilapidated cart full of kitchenware.

Philip: Uff...! Well, here we are.... We can now see the palm trees of Capernaum. When we pass by Matthew's table, don't forget to spit on that filthy tax collector.

Nathanael: Damn, how did I get into this mess? Philip, you, always get me into trouble.

Philip: Oh, come on. Let's go to Zebedee's house. I'm sure we'll find the Nazarene there.

They reached the house of Zebedee and saw Jesus when they entered.

Jesus: Hey, Nathanael! It's been a long time since we journeyed to the Jordan!

Nathanael: I'm happy to see you again, Jesus. How was everything with you after our last night in Bethabara?

Jesus: Okay. And how was it with you? How's your shop?

Nathanael: So-so. One has to work hard in order to live.

Philip: I'm glad you came. We need you here, Nathanael.

Nathanael: How's that?

Jesus: We need you.

Nathanael: You need me?

Jesus: Yes. Didn't Philip tell you?

Nathanael: Well, I, . . . I don't get this.

Jesus: We're forming a group, and we're counting on you. We need people like you who don't care about money or comfort, who are willing to forgo everything for the cause.

Nathanael: Cause? What cause?

Jesus: For the cause of justice that John the prophet was talking about.

Nathanael: Er, . . . I . . . But who ever told you I was any good for this?

Jesus: I can see it in your eyes, Nathanael. You're a good Israelite, and I bet if you won a fortune by playing dice, you'd share it with those who are more in need than you. If you owned a big wool store in Jerusalem, you'd help everyone, so that no one would walk naked in Israel. Am I right, Nathanael? You wouldn't allow your wife to go around wearing gold bracelets while there was great misery in the country.

Nathanael: Yes, yes, of course . . . Well, I don't know . . .

Jesus: Don't you ever dream of becoming rich, Nathanael?

Philip: Come on, Nat, don't deny it. Remember when you were under the fig tree?

Nathanael: Shut up, Philip. You have no right to meddle in this.

Philip: Okay, okay, but . . .

Jesus: I'm sure you want to be rich, so that you can share your wealth with the less fortunate ones. For how can one be happy when others are hungry and suffering?

Philip: Exactly. This can't go on. God has to correct this situation.

Jesus: Everyone must get involved in this, Philip. We're God's hands. I mean, God is counting on us, don't you think, Nathanael?

Nathanael: What for?

Jesus: So that things will change. So that you and I, the poor of this world, can take a breather, so that everyone will have enough, and no one will ever be wanting. There will be equality in the Kingdom of God.

Philip: I told you, Nat. Those who are on top will go down, and those who are down will go up. That's how we'll progress.

Jesus: So, will you join our group now, Nathanael?

Nathanael: Let me think about it some more. The truth is, I really can't do much, but . . .

Jesus: We'll witness great things, Nathanael. I'm sure the Lord will not fail us.

Philip: Hey, Nat, cheer up. Didn't you say you wanted to win the lottery? Well, bet on a number! Didn't you hear what he said? That God never fails!

Jesus: Yes, we'll see God's promise being fulfilled on this earth, and the dream of the poor will become a reality.

With Nathanael, from Cana of Galilee, we became seven in the group.

•

Cana of Galilee was a small village, six kilometers from Nazareth. There was a certain rivalry between the two places. Cana, at present, is a small and completely Arab city. One church in the town reminds us of the first miracle done by Jesus, when he changed water into wine. Another small church nearby is dedicated to the memory of the apostle Nathanael, who was born in Cana and who was referred to in other traditions as Bartholomew.

Accounts tell us of Nathanael as a tanner of leather and a weaver. According to the government lists, these occupations were despicable, a social stigma, as calculated by those who considered themselves "pure" and involved in superior work. The job of a tanner was highly contemptible because of the stench originating from the leather being cured. It was so repugnant that wives were given the right to divorce their husbands if they were tanners. The job of a weaver (in Galilee one worked more with linen or flax; in Judea, it was wool) was also despicable because it was considered an exclusively woman's occupation. In Jerusalem, for example, the weavers' district was completely marginal, being situated alongside the public garbage dump. Like many poor workers, Nathanael was smitten with ambition to make much money and attain social prestige. At first, he understood that the Kingdom Jesus was telling him about was this, a form of personal uplifting, an individual liberation from his misery. Jesus disconcerted him: liberation was for the whole community. It was to be shared. The good news that the poor would cease being poor demanded a concerted effort toward a group struggle.

Jesus' disciples underwent a process of growth, daily, in their understanding of the meaning of the Kingdom of God. This was realized in their contact with their countrymen, their practice of sharing money, their plans and risks, and through the inspiring words of Jesus. No Christian community is mature in its beginnings and has members free from ambition, egoism, and failure. The heedful contact with reality, the reflection of the group on decisions, the specific work for each day, and the search for enlightenment in the evangelical word contribute to the growth of the Christian community.

The account of Nathanael's vocation in the gospel of John is replete with theological symbols: the dream (with reference to the dream about Jacob's ladder, Gen. 28:10–17), being under the fig tree (in relation to the prophecy of Hosea where the people's fidelity is symbolized, Hos. 9:10), and Jesus' prophetic look at Nathanael (a picture of God, choosing the remaining faithful of Israel for the messianic community, Zeph. 3:12–13). Having in mind such symbolism, the evangelical episode should not be taken as a proof of the prophetic power of Jesus over the hidden thoughts of people. It is enough that we see in him an intuitive man who perceives what is in the hearts of his friends and who is capable of inspiring them with an ideal, which are the typical qualities of a popular leader.

(John 1:45–51)

17

The Bride and Groom of Cana

Three days later, there was a wedding at Cana of Galilee, the hometown of Nathanael. His neighbor, Sirim the woodcutter, was getting married to Lydia, a poor woman from a nearby village. Mary, Jesus' mother, was invited to the feast. We were also all invited.

Philip: Here comes the bride!
All: Here comes the bride! Here she comes!

The most significant moment of the celebration was the arrival of the bride. Her face was covered with a blue veil, and on her head was a crown of orange blossoms. The groom went to welcome her, and everyone proceeded to the garden of the house lighted by several crackling oil lamps.

Jesus: Mother, I didn't expect so many people would come to the party.
Mary: You're right. Sirim's parents have always been very poor, but generous. If they have two pieces of bread, they'd give you the other piece. See, we don't know them that much, and yet they've invited us.

In Cana of Galilee, we met Mary, Jesus' mother. She was a peasant, short, with burned skin, and black hair. She was about forty-five years old. Her hands were big and callused, due to hard work. She wasn't a pretty woman, but cheerful and charming. She had a Galilean accent when she spoke, and when she smiled, she looked very much like Jesus.

Jesus: Well, mother, we're here to enjoy ourselves. That's what parties are for! So have fun!
Peter: The fried dishes are ready! Let's go!
John: Hold it, Peter. Wait until they serve you.
Peter: But I'm hungry, John.
John: Now you've got to really stuff yourself, because when dancing time comes . . .

Peter: It's been a long time since I attended a wedding. Oh, this is great! Dance, food, and wine! What more could you ask for?

For the wedding feast of Lydia and Sirim, his parents made great effort. They roasted some young goats and chickens and bought several types of fruit and olives. They also bought wine from Cana, which was famous in the whole of Galilee, because it went to one's head so quickly.

Jesus: A toast for the bride and groom!
Philip: May they live for many, many years!
Mary: For the bride!
A Woman: That she may give Sirim more sons than Leah gave Jacob!
Peter: For the groom!
John: That, from his family, the Messiah may be born, to crush the Romans!

After several toasts of wine that flowed throughout the feast, the dance followed in the small garden of the house. The men formed one circle, and the women, another. Everyone forgot all the cares besetting us. The wine helped uplift everyone's spirits, drinking and dancing all our woes away.

John: Come on, Philip, it's your turn!
Philip: To the newly weds of Cana! . . . I must tell you, this feast is a wonder. I don't want to leave you behind!
Peter: Your turn, Jesus!
Philip: To the center!
Jesus: How radiant is the bride, and the groom so dignified, how delicious is the wine, that's served to everyone!
All: Good! Very good!
A Woman: What a beautiful wedding, la, la, la. Long live the groom, la, la, la. Long live the bride, la, la, la. May they live happily, la, la, la. If all weddings lasted for a lifetime, la, la, la, I wouldn't get so weary of life, la, la, la!
Another Woman: Hey, Mary, we haven't danced like this for a long time, have we?
Mary: Uff! . . . I can't anymore! I've got to stop!

Mary stopped dancing and headed for the kitchen, where Sirim's mother was preparing the honey-flavored tarts.

Mary: How are the tarts coming, Joanna? We can smell the aroma from outside!

Joanna: Uff, I never thought marrying off a son would mean so much work. You'll see what I mean, when your turn comes.

Mary: Oh, that'll be the day! And when it comes, I'll be dancing with more gusto than you can imagine!

Joanna: Oh, nothing of the sort. You'll have to stay in the kitchen, like I'm doing now.

Mary: Say, can I give you a hand?

Joanna: Samuel has gone to get more wine. You can help him fill up the pitchers. The party is getting to be more and more enjoyable, isn't it, Mary?

Mary: Why, yes! There's so much excitement.

Joanna: We've done what we could to give them the best for their wedding. And little by little, we shall be able to pay our debts, don't you think so? Oh, here comes Samuel.

Samuel: The guests are drinking a lot, and we only have three-fourths of a barrel left. If it goes on like this, in no time we won't even have a drop left.

Joanna: Oh, this can't be. Have you looked into the other barrels?

Samuel: Of course I have. They're all drained.

Joanna: I'm sure you haven't looked well. There has to be more.

Samuel: What a distrustful woman! I told you we only have this much, and no more.

Joanna: What do we do now? Tell me, Mary, what can we do? Oh, God, what an embarrassment! How can I tell the guests that there's no more wine to toast, that they must all leave? Oh, my God, what can I do?

Samuel: I don't know. I can't buy more wine. We already owe for three barrels of wine. They're not going to lend us anymore.

Joanna: It's your fault for having invited the whole district! Poor people like us can't afford to hold parties, you know that, old man. See, now we've run out of wine!

Samuel: Hush, woman, they might hear you outside.

Mary: Hey, Jesus, will you come here for a minute? Jesus!

A Man: Jesus, your mother's calling you at the door.

Jesus: I'll be right back!

Mary: Listen, Jesus, something's happened.

Jesus: Are you feeling bad? Are you tired of dancing? What happened?

Mary: No, son, it's something else.

Jesus: You look so sad, Mother. This is a wedding party.

Mary: Jesus, there's no more wine for the guests.

Jesus: Oh, so...do you want me to buy more wine? The truth is, I haven't got a single cent.

Mary: No, son, it's not that.

Jesus: Then, why are you telling me?

Mary: Who should I tell? Can't you think of something?

Jesus: I don't know... Are you really sure there's no more wine?

Mary: Go and ask Sirim's mother, who's weeping like she was in mourning.... The party's over!

Jesus: What's happened, Samuel?

Samuel: Nothing, young man, except that there's no more wine to serve. What can we do? We just have to accept it, and this woman doesn't stop crying. Damn, you better shut up, you make me all the more nervous!

Mary: Don't shout at her, Samuel. She's as nervous as you are, poor creature.

Jesus: So there's no more wine. Are you sure of that?

Samuel: See for yourself, Jesus. There's only three-fourths of a barrel left. What am I to do? I can't make miracles. All the guests drank it, so they can't complain.

Joanna: The party was too beautiful to end this way!

Samuel: There you go again!

Jesus: Have you thought of something, Samuel?

Samuel: Yes, tell the people that this is all over, that they can leave. Now, if they don't want to, then they must make do with water. I have nothing else to offer. They can drink as much water as they like.

Jesus: I don't even have a cent to offer you, Samuel; I can't help you buy more wine.

Samuel: I know. All those who have come to my house are as poor as I am. There's no one to ask for help. If my guests want to continue dancing and having fun, then let them drink water with a little honey for sweetener, if they like. Tell me, Jesus, is there anything I can do?

Jesus: What you said exactly. Come, let's fetch water from the well and fill up some of the barrels. Or we can fill up the large earthen jars that are by the door. There are about five or six of them, if I'm not mistaken.

Joanna: What are you planning to do, old man? Have you two gone crazy, serving water to the guests? Oh, Mary, this is really embarrassing!

Samuel: What do you say, Mary?

Mary: Do as Jesus says. We have no other choice. Explain to the people what's happened.

Joanna: Oh, God, I can't stand this humiliation!

Jesus and Samuel, the groom's father, filled the earthen jars with water from the well. The dancing was beginning to stop. The smell of sweat and wine mixed with the women's perfume and the burned oil inside the lamps. Everyone expected to be served more and more wine.

Mary: Son, what will the people say when they find out about the water in the jugs?

Jesus: The party will go on, Mother. Don't worry.

So the party continued.

John: Blazes, this wine is better than the other stuff! Look how well they kept it! Let me have another glass!

Peter: This man, Samuel, is different. He does the opposite. He serves us the best wine when we're almost drunk!

Philip: Long live the newly weds! Long live Sirim and Lydia!

Samuel: Tell me, Jesus, where did you get all this wine? Where did you buy it?

Jesus: Forget it, Samuel. It doesn't really matter. Don't you see everyone is enjoying the party?

Samuel: Try this a little.

Joanna: Oh, how good it is! I knew you had something coming, old man! But why did you have to make me suffer so? You old man!

Mary: Jesus, what's all this about?

Jesus: The party goes on, Mother. God wants this party of the poor to last forever!

The joy in Sirim's house lasted for many nights. That wine delighted everyone; it flowed without end. Later we found out that the new wine had been water drawn from Sirim's well. It was Mary who told us. She also told us how she realized for the first time that day that there was something in Jesus, something that she couldn't easily figure out but that was as delightful as a wedding feast.

•

The wedding feasts in Israel lasted for seven days. Wine was an indispensable item, being the most popular drink, and a symbol of love. Red wine was commonly drunk. There was much eating, drinking, and dancing during these feasts. A lot of food and sufficient wine had to be prepared in order not to disappoint the guests who looked forward to this week-long celebration, considered the most awaited event of the year. Among the poor communities, wedding feasts entailed an enormous economic effort on the part of the grooms' families. Although these weddings in Cana are usually depicted as celebrations among the wealthy and the elegant, they had to have taken place in an environment of the poor, to which Jesus and his friends belonged. They were occasions for merrymaking, for excitement, typical of Oriental feasts, and were even a bigger hit among the lower class.

Only John gives us an account of the wedding at Cana. The very structure of his gospel, as well as his style, makes the account a theological synthesis of Jesus' message — every historical detail contains a symbolic meaning. Israel's tradition, its poetry, and the prophets' writings portrayed the Messiah's coming in the form of a wedding. In the messianic feast, wine flowed in abundance (Isa. 25:6). In Cana, Jesus changed the water into wine: the water represented purification as commanded by the Jewish laws, which dictated that religion, for many, should center on the fulfillment of external norms. All this ends with Jesus: the water is changed into wine, which is a symbol of feasting, of inner freedom, of the Eucharist, which is sharing. The sign of the coming of the Kingdom of God is not the oppressive law, but a communal life. We must read this account, therefore, not in the context of a miracle, but as an announcement of God's plan. The day of feasting for the poor has come, a celebration without end. There ought to be endless joy, for God will have more and more wine for toasts.

Jesus was a cheerful man with an open mind, one who sang and danced with his townspeople. He was not a mere spectator at their feasts who would simply bless the occasion with his presence. Rather, he was another participant in these happy gatherings. One does not have to go to the temple or to a quiet place in order to meet the Lord. God is in the midst of hustle and bustle, in a banquet or in a dance. He even organizes these feasts: Jesus once and again compared the heaven that God prepares for his children to a wedding feast.

Mary's intervention at this moment in Jesus' life has been used, at times, as an argument to boost the theological idea that we need Mary's intercession in obtaining God's favors: Mary would ask them from Jesus, and Jesus would ask them from God. Nevertheless, Christian tradition strongly insists that the only mediator between God and people is Jesus, the master of history, on account of his resurrection (letter to the Hebrews). On the one hand, Mary's presence at the wedding at Cana and her intercession before Jesus constitute a symbol: the faithful Israel (represented by the mother) acknowledges that "there is no more wine" in the stone containers (which represent the Mosaic law written on stone tablets). This means that the law has lost its value and is devoid of meaning.

On the other hand, the account in the gospel is a proof that Mary's life was like that of Jesus. She shared her daily chores with her neighbors, as well as the problems of her people and their joys. She did not stand out because of a miraculous sign.

Regarding what we call miracles, John, in his gospel always refers to them using the Greek word *semeion* (sign). This may serve as a clue for us not to reduce a miraculous act to a mere work of wonder that is more or less spectacular. A miracle is always a sign that God liberates or releases human beings: from sickness, from fear, and from the sadness of death.... In each of the accounts about the signs made by Jesus, it is necessary to determine what these signs indicate, what form of liberation they are referring to, and of what relevance they can be for us, rather than focusing on the significance of whether something extraordinary took place.

(John 2:1–11)

18

A Madman Wants to Enter

A month passed, and then another. Jesus stayed with us in Capernaum. Every night when work was over, we would gather in Peter's house to have a chat and make plans. Our friendship grew by the day, like the fruit in the fields of Galilee that ripened at the right time. One Saturday we went to the synagogue with Jesus. Bartholomew, the madman, was at the door.

Bartholomew: Pray to God! Pray to God! Look at theeeemm! Look at theeeem! Gori, gori, gori, uuuu! I want to go inside and pray to the Lord! I want to pray to the Lord! Gori, gori, gori, uuuu!

Bartholomew was always dirty and smelled like rancid wine. His eyes were yellowish and his voice like that of a squawking crow, as it crossed the sky. He clapped his hands and wept as he begged permission to enter the synagogue. Everybody in Capernaum made fun of him.

Bartholomew: Let me in! Gori, gori, gori, uuuu!
Peter: Here comes Bartholomew again, the one we saw at the market the other day.
Jesus: Oh, yes, I remember.
Peter: A truly cursed man, nobody can stand him when he comes bugging you.
Jesus: What if they let him in, in the synagogue? Would he be pacified?
James: How can you let that crazy man in there? He's dangerous, Jesus. Once, he stripped a lady naked right in the street.
Peter: On that same day, he wanted to drown himself in the lake.
James: I wonder why they saved him. They should have let him go right down to the bottom of the lake! Men like him are good for nothing!

After a little chat on the patio, we all went inside the synagogue, which was our temple. Every Saturday, we would gather in the temple to worship the Lord, singing psalms, asking the Lord of the heavens not to abandon his people. The women stayed on one side, behind the wooden grills, while the men stayed at the center. Everyone focused attention on the sacred Book of Law, which was located in a place looking toward Jerusalem, the holy city of God.

Rabbi: "Lord, who will enter your house? Who will reside in your sacred mountain? He who has no stain, he who is pure, he who has a clean heart, clean hands, he who does not taint his tongue with deceit..."

After the readings and the prayers, one of the men stood to explain the meaning of the Scripture we had just heard. That Saturday, it was Saul's turn, an old businessman from the village of artisans who never failed to go to the synagogue.

Saul: Brethren, we have heard, very clearly, the message in the psalm that in order to enter the house of the Lord, one must be pure and clean. Therefore, we must not forget that in the Lord's house, no slaves or orphans can enter. Neither are the lepers nor the lame allowed to enter. Not the prostitutes or the adulteresses, not the women in their period. Only the clean and the pure. The bastard children can't enter the house of God, not even the abandoned ones, nor the shepherds with their reputation as thieves. Neither can the castrated enter the house of God, nor madmen, nor those possessed by an evil spirit. The psalm says it very clearly: "He who has no stain, only he shall be able to enter the house of the Lord...."

Saul's homily was quite long and boring. When I looked on my side, I saw that James was already half-asleep, while Peter was snoring. So were the others. Outside, Bartholomew, the madman, continued to scream. At one time, his yelling drowned the nasal voice of Saul, and we could hardly understand what the preacher was saying.

A Woman: What an impertinent fellow. Will someone please shut him up!

A Man: Jair, will you tell him to keep quiet? We can't hear a word here.

Saul: As we were saying, the Lord's house is only for the clean and pure, in body and in spirit, and...

Peter: Let that man in, so he won't make noise!

James: Keep your mouth shut, Peter!

Rabbi: This man who is screaming outside is impure! In no way can he be allowed inside. It's the devil who has sent him to keep us from worshiping God. But the evil spirit will not leave him!

A Woman: Well, with all this yelling, how can we go on praising the Lord, rabbi?

Peter: If we allow him inside, I think he will be calm!

Jesus: I think so, too. So why don't we let him in?

Rabbi: That's enough. That man is not clean. He's crazy! Why, he can't even distinguish his right from his left hand. How can he know God so he can praise him?

Jesus: But God surely knows him!

Rabbi: The Lord only wants the pure in his midst!

A Man: The rabbi is right.

Jesus: Well, I believe the Lord wants everyone in his presence. He will take care of cleansing them. He loves all of us.

Peter: Very well said, Jesus! So, let Bartholomew in!

James: You're just wasting your time, Jesus. This crazy man is not worth your effort. And you, Peter, stay out of this!

Peter: Shut up, James, will you? Jesus is right....

While we were arguing whether or not to allow Bartholomew inside the synagogue, the door suddenly flew open, as if a hurricane had blown through. Rolling like a ball of yarn, Bartholomew, bathed in sweat and laughing boisterously, gained entrance to the synagogue.

Bartholomew: Ha-ha-ha! I'm here! Gori! gori! gori! uuuu!

The women started to scream and there was pandemonium in the synagogue.

Bartholomew: I wanna pray! I wanna pray! Gori! gori! gori! uuuu!

His eyes were blazing like burning coals.

A Man: Get him outta here! Why is everybody not moving? Damn!

James: Get outta here! Get outta here!

Bartholomew: I wanna pray! I wanna...Gori! gori!

A Woman: This is too much! We need a rope to tie him up!

A Man: With or without a rope, we'll get him out of here! Gimme a hand, fat man. Let's kick this wretched man outta here!

Bartholomew: Gori! gori! gori! uuuu!

James: But he's stronger than Samson!

A Woman: Then cut off his hair!

A Man: Tie him up good! Damn!

James: All you women! Stay away from him! He's dangerous!

A Man: Give him a punch to silence him!
Another Man: Outta my way, you idiots, and leave him to me!

Julian, the blacksmith, whose brown arms were as hard as steel, grabbed Bartholomew by the nape and dragged him toward the door. The madman resisted, kicking with all his might, on all sides.

Another Man: Out you go, intruder! Devil!
Jesus: Hey, let go of that man! Leave him alone!

Jesus finally gained his way through the crowd.

Jesus: Can't you see he's a miserable man? Leave him alone . . . and give way, so he can get some air.

Little by little, the crowd began to disperse. Bartholomew was panting like a horse after a race, whimpering, with his face flat on the ground.

Rabbi: Don't touch him! The man is impure. Stay away from him! I told you, no one is to go near him!

Jesus ignored the rabbi's warning and stayed beside the madman.

Jesus: Why should I keep away from him, rabbi?
Rabbi: Because he's impure. Such impurity sticks like scabies.
Jesus: He's not impure. He's a poor creature, who's tired of people making fun of him and rejecting him. That's why he's acting this way. But God doesn't want him outside his house.

Jesus leaned toward him.

Jesus: Bartholomew, Bartholomew, do you hear me? What is wrong with you?

The madman opened his eyes and looked at Jesus defiantly.

Bartholomew: Leave me alone! Leave me alone!
Jesus: Hey, didn't you say you wanted to pray with us?
Bartholomew: I know you! You wanted to kill me! I know you!
Jesus: Will you shut up!
Bartholomew: I know you! Gori! gori! gori! uuuu! I know you! You're a friend of God! You're a friend of God!
Jesus: And so are you, Bartholomew!
Bartholomew: Uuuu! Uuuu!
Jesus: Come on, man, be calm now. . . .

Bartholomew was weeping, and his body was shaking. Jesus bent over to help him stand.

Jesus: Come on, stand up and come with me. Okay, that's it....

When he was on his feet, Bartholomew gave a loud cry and then fell unconscious.

A Man: Bartholomew's dead!
Peter: He isn't moving! Jesus, what's happened?
A Woman: Poor fellow.
Rabbi: God has punished him for wanting to enter his house! He was a sinner! Impure! All of you, stay away from him!

Bartholomew, the madman, lay on the ground, pale as a sheet. He was motionless.

Jesus: He's not dead, Peter. Why should he die?
Peter: Yes he is, Jesus. Look at his face. He's gone. When he gave out that loud cry, his soul left his body.
A Woman: Did you hear what the rabbi said? God killed him.
A Man: That's right. God punishes the insolent!
Jesus: God didn't punish him. He's not dead....

Jesus went near him and shook him.

Jesus: Come on, brother, get up! You've scared all of us out of our wits, and we have to continue with our praying. Come now, Bartholomew!

The madman got up. He wasn't pale anymore. He looked tired but was smiling, showing a couple of broken and dirty teeth.

Jesus: Come with us inside, Bartholomew. You can stay with us.

The madman took a seat between Peter and me, and prayed and sang with us. From that day on, he would go to the synagogue, to the market, and to the plaza. He was more relaxed. Eventually, we understood that that man whom we had ridiculed and ignored all along had a place among us too. That poor man, wretched and dirty as he was, was a brother of ours.

•

During Jesus' time, as in ancient times in general, the lack of scientific knowledge and ignorance about the human body led to the practice of attributing certain illnesses to evil spirits. This was particularly true of various psychological disturbances — mental diseases in which the form of behavior of the patient (screaming, uncontrollable movements, attacks, etc.) was more evident.

To use the word "crazy" was equivalent to saying "possessed by the evil spirit," and therefore, it was just like saying "impure" (which meant dominated or possessed by an "impure spirit," the devil). A majority of the ancient religions were of the belief that there are pure and impure persons, actions, and things. Such impurity had nothing to do with external filth. Neither did purity have anything to do with cleanliness. Nor had it anything to do with what is moral, "what is good" or "bad." What was "impure" was related to unknown and dangerous forces, and what was "pure" was full of positive powers. He who was impure could not go near God. The idea of purity-impurity was basically a "religious" concept. Since ancient times, the religion of Israel assimilated this way of magical thinking. In fact, many of the existing laws then dealt with purity, with specific reference to: (a) sex (menstruating and hemorrhaging were considered forms of impurity); (b) death (a corpse was impure); (c) certain diseases (leprosy and madness were likewise impurities); and (d) some food and animals (the vulture, the owl, and the pig were, among others, impure animals). Most of these laws are preserved in the book of Leviticus. As the people were evolving from a magical religion to one that emphasized personal responsibility, these ideas became obsolete. Nevertheless, some groups observed them to the letter — thus the practice of long cleansing or purification to make themselves acceptable to God. Jesus dismisses these magic practices, and through his words and actions removes the barrier between what is pure and impure in the old religion. The good news is that what is really pure is found only in people's hearts and in just treatment of brothers and sisters.

Jesus' sign took place inside the synagogue at Capernaum. About five hundred years before Christ, when the temple of Jerusalem was destroyed and the people of Israel were deported, the Jews started to build "synagogues," houses of prayer, where they all gathered to pray and read the Holy Scriptures. In Jesus' time, although a new temple was built in Jerusalem, a number of synagogues already existed all over the country. A small one was built in Capernaum, over which, four centuries later, a bigger one was constructed, and whose ruins, with all its great historical value, are preserved up to the present time. All the people gathered at the synagogue every Saturday, to pray and to listen to their rabbi or to a countryman who wished to give a commentary on the texts of the Scripture being read. These synagogues were not exactly the equivalent of temples today. They were more familiar places, more lay-oriented, wherein people could express themselves freely without being interrupted, and where there was really no need for a holy person or minister to be present. The rabbi was a teacher-catechist (not a priest).

Nowadays, many persons who are sick in mind are pushed to the margins of the community. The sane make fun of them; some families conceal them as a scandal without giving them a chance to be rehabilitated. They are, like Bartholomew, the new impure ones.

Jesus' sign in this episode is an indication that the house of God, the Christian community, is open to everyone, including the less fortunate. It is a sign of liberation: God appreciates them, and he has a place and a mission for them.

(Mark 1:21–28; Luke 4:31–37)

19

Peter's Mother-in-Law

When we left the synagogue, James, Jesus, and I went to Peter's house. Rufina, his wife, was preparing a good dish of lentils for us.

Peter: Come on in, fellows, and sit here in the shade. Food will be ready in a jiffy, and I swear everyone will have a good share. Come, Jesus, let's get some olives while Rufina's tending the fire.

Simon Peter was a special type. Peter, the stone-thrower, as we all called him, had a curly beard and a nose as big as a tomato. He was the best rower on the lake and the noisiest, too. He smelled of fish, but was always in good humor. With four sons to feed, and a wife, he had to work himself to death. Peter loved Rufina, his wife, very much, in spite of their constant bickerings.

Peter: Hey, lady, when will those lentils be ready? These fellows are hungry! For God's sake, hurry up!

Rufina: What do you think I'm doing? You should have given me the money earlier, you tightwad! These lentils don't come from heaven. One has to pay for them, big nose!

Peter: And that witch of a vendor simply couldn't trust you?

Rufina: That witch, as you call her, has been lending us food for three weeks already, and if you don't pay her before Saturday, that's the end of it!

Peter: And what did you tell her?

Rufina: That she was right.

Peter: Oh, really?

Rufina: Yeah, she's right!

Peter: Hey, don't raise your voice when you're talking to me!

Rufina: And don't you raise that voice of yours, either, scandalous man! Now I know why my mother is sick — it's because of your screaming!

Peter: What? It's your laziness that made her sick.

Rufina: Oh, Peter, Peter...

Peter: Now what is it?

125

Rufina: Don't accuse me of being lazy; it's not true.

Peter: And don't you call me tightwad, you know I hate it.

Rufina: Oh, Peter, what would I do without you?

Peter: Hmm...That's for me to say....What would I do without you, Rufi?

Peter and Rufina had four sons: Little Simon was the first son. Then came Alexander, who was five years old; Reuben, three; Ephraim, two; and...well, another one was coming, whom we all hoped would be a girl. Peter's brother, Andrew, the skinny one, still unmarried, lived with them, as well as their father, Jonas, a grumpy old man, and his mother-in-law, Rufa, who had been ill for two months.

James: Well, Peter, where are the lentils? Are they coming or not? Maybe a goat has eaten them before they could get to our table!

Peter: Don't be impatient, my friends. The food will be ready soon. You see, my mother-in-law has been ill, and things have been difficult since...

Little Simon: Jesus, our grandmother is sick.

Jesus: Oh yes? Where is she, Little Simon?

Little Simon: Over there, in the corner.

Peter: Old Rufa is my mother-in-law. It's really sad, you know; a case of a bad fever...Say, why don't you greet her and tell her one of your stories, while my wife is cooking up the lentils?...Come inside, Jesus, the old woman is there lying down....Just don't mind the mess around you. You know how it is to live in only one room, with so many people around.

Jesus: How are you, Grandma? How do you feel?

Rufa: I can't sit. I'm dying.

Jesus: But how do you feel?

Peter: She's a little hard of hearing, Jesus.

Rufa: Who are you?

Peter: He's a friend from Nazareth. Do you hear me? I said, from Nazareth. His name is Jesus, and he's going to spend a few days with us. He knows a lot of jokes. Ask him to tell you a funny story.

Rufa: Will that make me laugh? I'd rather cry!

Jesus: Come on, Grandma. Don't be such a killjoy. What's ailing you? Tell me, please.

Rufa: Oh, my son, what do I know? I'm not a doctor!

Peter: Okay, Jesus, I'll leave the two of you. I'll go ask Rufina to hurry up. I'll let you know when the food is ready.

Rufa: It's somewhat strange, son. Look, I feel I have fever inside my body. Do you hear?

Jesus: Yes, Grandma, I hear you very well.

Rufa: Outside, I feel terribly cold; even my skin cringes because of the cold.

Jesus: It's nothing serious, Grandma. It's just a simple fever.

Rufa: But my son, how can the heat and cold go together, and then you say it's nothing?

Jesus: There's nothing strange about it, Grandma. Even affection and hatred go together. Didn't you hear the bickerings between your daughter and your son-in-law a while ago?

Rufa: I'm deaf, you know. I hear some noise, but I know not where it comes from.

Jesus: Directly from the kitchen, where Peter and Rufina were quarreling.

Rufa: Ah, those two are like cats and dogs. I don't understand the young people of today. They swear their love for each other, and yet, they never cease quarreling.

Jesus: Well, it's like that. Haven't you had that experience yourself?

Rufa: That was long ago. Now, my teeth are almost gone. Look, ahhhh, I'm like an old fishing net that wears out easily. I'm not good for anything anymore.

Jesus: Don't say that, Grandma. I'm pretty sure, if you just get up from there and fix yourself a little, and take a walk through the village, someone will certainly notice and give you a compliment.

Rufa: What did you say?

Jesus: Compliments, Grandma, words of admiration.

Rufa: Good heavens, my son. That might have been true before, when I had all my teeth, and my hair was smooth and . . .

Jesus:. And they were saying beautiful things as you walked through the streets of Capernaum. Is that right, Grandma?

Rufa: The last compliment I received was when I was forty years old, can you imagine? I was still attractive then.

Jesus: Really? Tell me, Grandma, what did they tell you?

Rufa: Bah, I don't remember. It was such a long time ago.

Jesus: Now I'm curious to know the secret of your charm, Grandma. Come on, tell me.

Rufa: Oh, one of those foolish things of men. Imagine, I was on my way to the market, with a rose in my hair...Then I heard someone say: "Every time I see you, I tell my heart: what a beautiful sight, a sight so beautiful it makes me stumble." It was a fruit vendor who told me that.

Jesus: Say, Grandma, you've got very pretty hair.

Rufa: And soon, it will be falling off too. Everything in us old people falls off like dried fig leaves.

Jesus: Their leaves fall during winter, but they grow again in spring and begin to have flowers.

Rufa: There's no more spring for old people like us. Now you see me here; when you come back tomorrow, perhaps, I'm no longer here.

Jesus: Our body wears out, Grandma, but not the heart. The spirit never grows old. What matters is to keep the spirit young. Look at our Lord. Oh, the years that he's lived since the creation of the world! God is young, for he is young at heart, just like you, Grandma.

Rufa: God does not remember old people.

Jesus: Don't say that, Grandma. God cares about all of us: the big and the small ones, the young and the old. God never abandons us.

Rufa: Well, sometimes I feel abandoned, my son, like those old dried logs floating in the water, with nowhere to go.

Jesus: No, Grandma. You're still strong enough to go on. And when the Lord finally calls you, don't be afraid, because we're not to stay on this earth. We're going to join the Lord in his big house, where there is a place for each one of us.

Rufa: You speak very well, young man. God bless your tongue!

Jesus: And God bless those bones that you may become still stronger.

Rufa: Thank you, my child. But that's no longer necessary. Nobody needs me in this world.

Jesus: How can you say that, Grandma? Your grandchildren need you. Your son-in-law would be more at ease right now if you were to give your daughter a hand in the kitchen. She's having a hell of a time cooking the lentils right now, which are taking forever.

Rufa: Ah, my son. No one will ever beat me in the kitchen. Until two weeks ago, I was kneading bread, gathering firewood, and attending to the laundry. Sewing is not for me anymore; my eyes are tired. But the rest of the household chores I still carry out the way a newly wed does.

Jesus: And you were saying that you are good for nothing anymore.

Rufa: Yes, but now I am down with this illness. I don't even have the strength to sing a tune.

Jesus: You mean you can sing, too, Grandma?

Rufa: Why, yes, my son. I loved to...I was a happy person before.

Jesus: My grandfather Joachim used to sing to us on the farm. His favorites were the songs of yesteryears, those of your time.

Rufa: Are you fond of old songs?

Jesus: Very much, Grandma. Say, do you happen to know the song "The Lilies of King David"?

Rufa: Sure! A friend of mine taught it to me, during our trip to Jerusalem for the fair.

Jesus: Can you sing it, Grandma?

Rufa: I am sick, young man. How can I sing?

Jesus: Of course, you can, Grandma. Come on, sing it, please. Maybe you'll be more comfortable sitting down. Come, give me your hand. Cheer up.

Rufa: Just a minute, young man. I feel faint.

Jesus: You look good, Grandma. Now, try to stand. Yes...uupp! That's right, slowly now...

Rufa: Hold it, young man, my bones are...oh...

Jesus: You see, you can do it! Don't you feel a little better now?

Little Simon: Grandma, are you well now?

Peter: Mother, why are you on your feet? Go back and lie down immediately!

Jesus: Leave her alone, Peter; she'll sing "The Lilies of King David" for us, won't you, Grandma?

Peter: "The Lilies of..." Now, I don't know which of the two of you is sick with fever. Or have the two of you gone crazy? You better see this for yourself,...Rufina!

Rufa: Leave me in peace, Peter, will you? I feel a lot better now.

Children: Grandma is cured! Grandma is cured!

Rufina: But, Mother, why are you up now? Go back and lie down on the mat!

Rufa: Go, lie down yourself, if you want, and don't pester me. I feel all right, and right now I'm going to the kitchen to give you a hand. Then they'll see that old Rufa can still be useful at something, my goodness!

Jesus gave old Rufa a strong desire to live. Peter's mother-in-law got up that day and succeeding days. She helped in the kitchen, did the laundry, and served at the table while she sang the melodies of old, as taught to her by her grandparents, which she, in turn, taught to her grandchildren.

•

Peter had a mother-in-law, which, obviously, meant that he was married. This is one detail of the gospel. The composition of the family (his wife, Rufina, and his four sons) is an elaboration of the episode. Jesus' disciples were men of flesh and bones, each engaged in his own occupation, with a family, a house, and a psychological make-up different from the others. The gospel gives us more data about Simon, nicknamed Peter (also called "stone-thrower" in this account), which helps us reconstruct his way of being. A protagonist in several episodes in Jesus' life, Peter appears as a vigorous man, impulsive, affectionate, very generous, and close to Jesus on account of their profound friendship. Peter's house, where Jesus meets old Rufa, is one of the historically authentic places among the more tangible remembrances of the life of Jesus. The foundation and threshold (over which Jesus certainly passed a hundred times) of Peter's house have been preserved. The foundation reflects the extremely small space in which Peter and his family lived in poverty.

In Jesus' time, there were less old people than today. Life expectancy was shorter. Most men and women died young according to present-day perception. Old folks were very much loved, and their presence inspired respect in the family. They were likewise responsible for transmitting family history, cultural traditions, and so on. Jesus does everything for everyone. He approaches Rufa in a manner we should use to treat our old folks: making them feel their worth, giving them the strength to confront their afflictions with hope, and preparing them for the hour of death with serenity and trust in the Lord. This "miracle" of Jesus is a sign of God's love for the old, who, at times, are rejected and deemed useless by the society of today.

(Matt. 8:14–15; Mark 1:29–31; Luke 4:38–39)

20

A Leper in the Village

Peter: Hey, John, James! Leave the nets and come here. Hurry!

One morning, while we were cleaning the nets, Peter called us aloud from the house of Caleb, a fisherman from the village. When we got there, he seemed to be in mourning, the women were screaming, the people were shoving each other at the door, and the house smelled of eucalyptus leaves burned near the sick. Caleb's wife, who was dressed in black, was weeping nonstop as she pounded her head against the wall.

Anna: This is a curse of God! A curse of God!

Eleazar: It's leprosy! It's leprosy! We'll call for the rabbi right away to examine you!

Caleb: Don't touch me! You're lying; this isn't leprosy. Don't touch me!

Eleazar: You've been hiding it all this time, you wretch. Why don't you remove those bandages and show us your arms?

Caleb: They're only wounds...so...leave me alone. This isn't leprosy. It isn't.

John: Peter, is Caleb a leper?

Peter: That's what they say. Imagine the hassle caused by Eleazar's news. He says Caleb has some stains beneath those bandages and claims they're leprosy.

James: Caleb is a liar! He told us he was bitten by a spider; he told us that's why his arm is wrapped with bandages.

Peter: Eleazar has spread this thing all over the village, and he wants to bring this to the rabbi, to make sure what it really is.

James: Well said, dammit! Let the rabbi come, and if this fellow really has leprosy, then he should get out of here! And what does he want? For us to catch the disease?

Anna: This is God's curse.

All of us were scared of leprosy. It spread through the flesh, like vines extending through the walls, devouring the body until it was eaten away. Besides, since leprosy could be contagious, the law demanded that those afflicted be separated from family and community, and that they not go near anybody. Leprosy was the most dreaded of all diseases.

Eleazar: You see? You see? These wounds are leprosy. They have the color of sand.

Caleb: This isn't leprosy, Eleazar. I swear to God Almighty, it is not!

Eleazar: Don't swear, you liar! You should've told us about it. This thing is contagious, and you know it.

Anna: This is God's curse! This is God's curse!

A Woman: Poor wife, she does nothing but pound her head against the wall....

Salome: If Caleb has leprosy, then the wife may just as well be a widow,...what with the three sons she has!

Another Woman: He must have done something to be punished by God. I never really liked Caleb. He must have something impure inside him.

Caleb's house was full of people. The news that he had leprosy spread like wild fire through the village of fishermen. Old Eleazar, after having removed the bandages around Caleb's arm and examined his wounds, went to the synagogue to look for the rabbi. It was he who had the last say. Soon after, the rabbi arrived at Caleb's house.

Rabbi: Okay, out of here! Out, everybody!

Anna: Ay, rabbi, we are cursed by the Lord!

Rabbi: Be patient, woman, and stop talking about curses until we know what this really is.

Caleb: This is not leprosy, rabbi. Old Eleazar is lying.

Rabbi: I said everybody out! Now, let me see your arm.

Caleb: I don't want to leave my house! I tell you, it isn't leprosy! I'm clean!

Rabbi: Well then, what are these stains, Caleb?

Caleb: They're wounds, rabbi, wounds that can be cured.

Rabbi: Have you put something on to cure them?

Anna: Rabbi, I applied oil with sunflower seeds and the intestine of crushed red fish.

Rabbi: Hmm...Since when did you have these wounds?

Caleb: I don't remember. About four months ago ... I don't want to go away from here!

Rabbi: Well, you have to leave your house, Caleb. Your wounds are stuck to your skin, and your hair has turned white. It's leprosy all right.

Anna: This is a curse of the Lord!

Caleb: No, no, no, I'm not going to leave!

Eleazar and the rest of the men threw Caleb out of the city. For fear of touching him, they tied him with a rope and dragged him out of the house like an animal. Caleb resisted, hitting them and kicking them, as he wept desperately. His wife and children saw how he was dragged through the wide streets of Capernaum, to the hill caves, where the lepers lived and died in solitude.

Anna: Ay, Salome, what has my husband done to be punished by God this way?

Salome: Don't ask me, woman, I haven't slept for two nights since I learned about it. How would I know why the Lord has punished him this way?

Anna: Tell me, what am I going to do now?

Salome: Look, I already told my husband, Zebedee, to give you some money, so that you can mend nets. With this, you'll have something to keep you going. If you need something, just let me know, and I'll help you. If we eat, so do you.

Anna: What will my poor Caleb eat in the caves? He will live at the mercy of the almsgiver.

Salome: Woman, don't weep. Your sons need you.

Two weeks passed since Caleb was taken away from Capernaum. One evening, while we were playing dice at home, my mother, Salome, brought in a pot full of dried fish and some pieces of bread.

James: There goes number four! You win, Jesus.

Peter: Six and three! It's your turn, James.

Salome: Hey guys, take this food to poor Caleb. His wife is sick and can't go. I have to take care of the boys. I told his wife not to worry, that we'd attend to it.

James: I'm not going, woman. You wouldn't want me to be taken to the caves as a leper, would you? You know it's contagious, don't you?

Salome: I know, I know, but you don't have to go near. Shout so he hears you, and leave the food in the middle of the road.

Salome: And you, Peter?

Peter: Well, lepers make me sick to my stomach. Something happens to me that...I don't think I can go near them, even if they pay me one hundred dinars!

Salome: That's very brave of you, big nose!

Peter: Say whatever you want to say, but I don't think there's anyone here who would dare.

James: Are you scared of lepers, too, Jesus?

Jesus: It's not that, James, but...

Salome: Well, you better decide, between now and tomorrow. I spent a lot of time preparing this food, which isn't for you.

Finally, after long discussion, Jesus and I decided to take the food to the caves. The sun had hardly risen when we started for the caves. They were at the exit of Capernaum, on the left side of the road leading to Chorazin.

Jesus: Call him, John. When he hears you, he'll come out.

John: Hey, Caleb! Caleb! Where are you? This is John, the son of Zebedee! Caleb!

Soon, a man whose body was covered with rags, with disheveled hair, came out from one of the caves. It was Caleb, the fisherman from Capernaum.

John: Look there, Jesus. But I can't just throw him this food, as if he were a dog.

Jesus: So what do we do now?

John: Maybe we can go a little closer. He'll be happy to see us, but it might be risky, because the disease is contagious. I don't know...If you don't want...

Jesus: Okay, let's go.

Jesus and I moved closer until we reached the clearing where Caleb was waiting. When we were just a stone's throw away, we stopped. Caleb wept.

Caleb: John, how's my wife and the kids?

John: Don't worry about them, Caleb. Anna's mending nets on the wharf, and earning her dinars. The children have to eat, you know. They're all right.

Jesus: How are you, Caleb?

Caleb: And how do you think I am? Dying of disgust! What with all these rags... A number of lepers are already rotting. If it weren't for this damned disease, I'd go back to fish in the lake. I want to be with everybody!

Jesus: Do you still have those wounds on your arm?

Caleb: Yes, but it's not leprosy! If only God would cleanse me! But God never passes through these caves.

Jesus: Caleb, look, Salome prepared this fish and bread for you.

Jesus went closer, to give him the food.

John: Be careful, Jesus!

Jesus: Let me see those stains, Caleb.

Jesus helped him remove the dirty bandages around his arm.

Caleb: I want to go back to Capernaum.

Jesus: But let me see those stains first.

Caleb: Look at me. Look! Look! There's nothing! Where are my wounds? I'm clean! The stains are gone! I'm clean!

John: Jesus, what happened? What happened?

Caleb: I'm healed! I'm healed!

John: What have you done to him, Jesus?

Jesus: But, John, I...

Caleb: I'm clean, I'm healed! Help me remove all these rags! I'm healed!

Jesus: Caleb, don't shout so loud. The others might come out of the caves. Come, let's go to Capernaum. You must show yourself to the priest, to make sure that you're clean.

Caleb: I'm clean, I'm healed!

The following day, the rabbi purified Caleb with the blood of a bird offered as sacrifice. He washed him seven times and declared him clean, and released another bird as a sign of his healing.

Rabbi: Yes, it's true. His flesh is clean and there's no white spots on it. Your leprosy is gone. You may now go back to the village, Caleb. You're healed. You may go back to your family.

Caleb was free again to live with everyone. That evening, we had a party in the fishermen's district to celebrate. Weeping with joy, Caleb recounted what happened: he said it was Jesus of Nazareth who cured him. The news spread so fast that Jesus had to stay away for a time from Capernaum.

•

Leprosy, which in the Bible includes many skin diseases (like rashes, bumps, stains, pimples, etc.), was a dreaded disease. It was always considered as God's punishment, obliging the leper to separate from family and from the community. The leper was, aside from being repugnant, impure from the religious point of view, so it was the priest who determined the disease as well as its cure, if there ever was any. The law on this matter was extensive and presented in detail in the Old Testament. Because it was such a horrible disease, it was the popular belief that it would disappear with the coming of the Messiah.

Lepers were to live isolated in caves. They could not go to cities, and when they were on the road, had to shout their impurity, to warn people. Such isolation was not only on account of the contagious nature of the disease, but also because of its religious implication — that the afflicted was "cursed by God." When Jesus went near the leper and touched him, he showed compassion. His gesture was a voluntary violation of the religious law that made liable anyone who touched an impure person (Lev. 5:3). This is a sign that with Jesus, all limits between the pure and the impure are gone, and that the God that he reveals to us disregards whatever external distinctions exist. God does not punish nor curse anyone with disease. Neither leprosy nor any sickness, no matter how terrible, is God's punishment or revenge on people. Its explanation is found in natural causes, and it is the field of medicine which determines origin and cure.

The bacteria that causes leprosy was not discovered until 1868. Nowadays, it is no longer considered an incurable disease, although there are still a number of Hansenites all over the world. Poor hygienic practices and lack of preventive care at the onset of the disease explain why the disease still continues to be widespread. Present-day Hansenites still live in separate communities, although it is a fact that leprosy is no longer a contagious ailment when minimal precautionary steps are taken. The four evangelists attribute forty-one miracles to Jesus. Matthew cites the greatest number: twenty-four. John gives the least: nine. The stories about the miracles are strictly related to what the evangelists narrate about the activities and mission of Jesus. In this sense, we can say that they are essential to the gospel. Most of these acts or miracles are related to the healing of different diseases. Even the severest of critics acknowledge that Jesus became a man with certain powers to cure the sick, to alleviate suffering, and to strengthen faith which would be the source of healing. These are powers that are difficult to determine to this day, especially over a distance of two thousand years. From the theological point of view, the miraculous act in the gospel narration must always be seen not as a manifestation of something "extraordinary," but as a sign of liberation. God sends his son as the Liberator. Jesus proclaims the good news of this liberation, making signs, at the same time, to indicate that this liberation has already come.

(Matt. 8:1–4; Mark 1:40–45; Luke 5:12–16)

21

Jasmine Street

On the other side of the wharf at Capernaum was a road called Jasmine Street. It was named thus because the street passed through a corner of the village — a neighborhood of dirty houses with faded paint — where the prostitutes lived, and they used jasmine for perfume. Jesus had met one of them at the Jordan. Her name was Mary, who was born in Magdala. A couple of months before, she came to Capernaum to do business with the seamen of the village. One evening, Jesus left Peter and Andrew's house and, passing in front of the wharf, the synagogue, and the market, headed in the direction of Jasmine Street. He was alone.

A Woman: Hey, you, stranger, over here! Come, come. I may not be the youngest here, but I charge the least!

Jesus looked for a rundown little house of adobe and black stones where, he was told, Mary the Magdalene lived. He pushed the door open and found a narrow and damp porch, where several men were waiting, in a squatting position. All eyes were glued on the bamboo curtains, behind which the young whore was arguing with a bad client.

Magdalene: Get out of here, you devil, and don't you ever come back if you got no money. Rubbish! Go do your thing with some other whore!
A Man: May the fires of hell devour you, bitch!
Magdalene: You first, you filthy man! Puah! Who's next?

An old man with yellowish teeth stood up from the floor and went toward the prostitute. Mary had her dress unbuttoned, and her hair was disheveled. The lamp on the porch illumined her face, a youthful face that was fully made-up. The old man pushed her and entangled himself with her behind the bamboo curtains.

A Man: She's a wretched woman! One unguarded moment and she bites you!

138

Another Man: She's one hell of a whore. Not even the devil can produce a better one!

Man: Hey, stranger, what's your name?

Jesus: Jesus.

Man: Is it your first time here?

Jesus: Yes.

Man: Let me give you some advice, man: since you're new here, she's gonna charge you double. Pay only half. If she yells at you, take out your knife. These creatures take advantage of strangers. Always keep an eye open and don't leave your clothes near her reach.

One man after another came and left. Jesus was the last in line. At the end of an hour, he was the only one left on the porch.

Magdalene: Hey, you, what's the matter? Are you coming inside or not? Come on, let's get it over with for today. Damn these sailors!

Jesus: Mary!

Magdalene: Who are you?

Jesus: Mary, don't you remember me? We were together at the Jordan, in the old woman's house. She even gave me those honey-flavored cakes!

Magdalene: Jesus! Is that you, Jesus?

Jesus: Yes, it's me. Bring the lamp closer.

Magdalene: With so many men I know ... But ... why are you here?

Jesus: I'm staying in Capernaum for a couple of days. I came to visit my friends.

Magdalene: But of course. I heard there was a new face in the village, a peasant who was half-carpenter or a bricklayer, but I never imagined it was you. Come on in. Gosh, am I glad to see you again!

Jesus: And it's good to see you. Yesterday, I was told that you live here, so I came.

Magdalene: So, what do you do? Are you working on the wharf, in the market, or ... where else?

Jesus: I'm doing odd jobs here and there. Just let me know if your roof caves in, or if you have broken stairs, or you might need some door locks.

Magdalene: Where do you stay here?

Jesus: In the fishermen's village. I'm staying with my friends I met at the Jordan, remember?

Magdalene: With Peter, James, and their kind?

Jesus: Yes, we're good friends.

Magdalene: Oh, what friends you have! I told you to avoid them. They're a bunch of cheats. They talk a lot. I know them very well!

Jesus: Let's not talk about them. I came to greet you. They told me you were staying here.

Magdalene: I was so surprised to see you here that I forgot about my job. Please excuse me. You wait.... I'll just take off my clothes.

Jesus: No, Mary, I didn't come here for that.

Magdalene: That's all right. I've come to like you since I saw you at the river. This time, I won't charge you anything. But it's my job, so next time, I'm sorry, you've got to pay, so I'll have some oil for my lamp. Business is business, you know.

Jesus: But I told you, I'm here simply to greet you, to have a little chat with you. Don't you believe me?

Magdalene: No man has passed through this door "just to greet me." What do you want? Why have you come?

Jesus: Nothing. I just want to talk to you for a while.

Magdalene: Say, countryman, is there anything wrong, huh?

Jesus: Nothing. What's your problem, Mary? Here I am wanting to visit you, and you treat me worse than Herod's bodyguard.

Magdalene: Come on, out with it. What do you want from me?

Jesus: Well, if my presence is bothering you, then I'll go.

Magdalene: No, don't leave, but ... really, I don't know what to say.

Jesus: Now, will you button up and take a seat? Tell me, how has everything been with you since our meeting at the Jordan? Hey, Mary, what's the matter with you? Why don't you say something? Are you afraid of me? I'm not carrying a weapon with me, and I don't know where you hide your money.... Mary...

Magdalene: Huh, what?

Jesus: No. Nothing. Lara, lara, lari... Do you know that tune? This is what they sing in my town when harvesting wheat and... I see you aren't familiar with the song.... Ahem... Listen to this other one: Loro, la, lalaa, la ... This they sing when harvesting grapes, when they crush the grapes. You don't know that song either, do you? Tell me, you've been here for sometime ... Where can I find a good shoemaker who doesn't charge much? I need a new pair of sandals. The ones I'm using are worn-out, and so full of holes a camel could pass through them! That's why I'm asking if you know someone.... Ahem... You know something, Mary? My mother enjoyed the honeyed cakes given by that old lady friend of yours from

Beth-barah, remember? Yes, what was her name again? Remember? Wait, it's on the tip of my tongue. Simphoriana? No not that. Simphorosa?

Magdalene: What're you talking about? Her name's Ruth.

Jesus: Ruth, that's it, Ruth. I knew it started with an R.

Magdalene: Oh, the river Jordan! It was such a pity, wasn't it?

Jesus: What was a pity, Mary?

Magdalene: That everything ended as it did. Any word about the prophet?

Jesus: Nothing new. He's still in prison. Herod won't dare release him for fear of his wife, neither will he dare kill him for fear of the people.

Magdalene: How disgusting! The prophets are languishing in jail, while the swine are seated on the throne.

Jesus: This prophet John seems to be a good man, doesn't he?

Magdalene: A good man? Better, a good foolish man. "The Kingdom of God is near, the Messiah is coming!" And those who came were the soldiers who took him prisoner and silenced him.

Jesus: He sowed a seed. Someone after comes to water it. Then, another one will come and harvest it.

Magdalene: You must be a little fool yourself, like the prophet.

Jesus: What do you think, Mary? Will the day of justice come to this land?

Magdalene: How's that?

Jesus: Will there be justice like the prophet John was saying?

Magdalene: What do I know, and what do I care? Whichever way it is, we'll always be at the end of the line.

Jesus: What line?

Magdalene: The way to the Kingdom of God, like you were talking about. They say that God covers his nose when someone like me passes in front of the synagogue. Oh, wait a minute.... The light at the porch is about to go out. I need to add a little oil.

Jesus: Do you leave your light on all night?

Magdalene: Do I have a choice? If they see that the house is dark, then they don't come anymore. With the high cost of living nowadays, you can't afford to refuse a client who comes during the wee hours. So you see, I wait all night for some disgusting client who'll slobber over me. Why are you so quiet?

Jesus: I was just thinking...Perhaps you're better prepared than any-one else.

Magdalene: For what?

Jesus: Nothing. Just some stupid idea of mine. Listen, Mary, when I was a little boy in Nazareth, I was afraid of thieves. Now, I just laugh about my boyish fears. What would have they robbed us of, my parents and me, in that hut? Nothing, just a pair of old pots. But I was scared of them. At times, I would spend the night with one eye open, watching for the thief.

Magdalene: And what does that mean?

Jesus: One evening I thought: God must be like a thief, who comes when one least expects. What is important is that the house shouldn't be dark so he can find the door. Then I told my mother not to extinguish the light during the night, for the Lord might come.

Magdalene: And what has that got to do with me?

Jesus: Don't extinguish your light, Mary. Maybe when you least expect it, someone unexpected might come.

Magdalene: Well, look, I never thought you would come today.

Jesus: I'm leaving now. It's getting late.

Magdalene: Please don't go. It's still early.

Jesus: For you, it's always early. I've got to start the day early, to fix a plow.

Magdalene: Are you sure you just wanted to talk with me?

Jesus: Yes, what's wrong with that? Has my coming bothered you?

Magdalene: No, no. The truth is, ever since I came to this damned city, nobody...

Jesus: Nobody what?

Magdalene:. Nobody ever came to ... to ... talk to me, and to greet me.

Jesus: Probably because they don't know you yet.

Magdalene: Or they know me too well.

Jesus: Goodbye, Mary. Now you can rest a little.

Magdalene: Wait, Jesus ... Will you stay long in Capernaum?

Jesus: I don't know yet. Most likely, I will.

Magdalene: Will you come again?

Jesus: Sure, woman. And when I do, I hope you'll have your lamp lit. Goodbye, Mary, see you soon!

Mary saw Jesus off. He passed through a dark street, the street of jasmine flowers, as the people would say. Then she went back to her room, fixed her make-up, and lay down on the mat on the floor. That night she waited, but no

*one came anymore. The lamp remained lit until the cocks of Capernaum crowed
to announce another day.*

•

The prostitutes were marginalized women, despised by all, not only because of the "impurity" of their occupation, but also because of their condition, which was one of the lowliest in the social structure of that time. Yet Jesus spoke of them as models of being open to the message of liberation, and therefore, the first beneficiaries of the Kingdom of God (Matt. 21:34). This word of Jesus, as well as his warm attitude toward the prostitutes — Mary Magdalene was one of his followers — constituted a very grave scandal among the religious men of his time. One of the most original things in the gospel was the good news for the marginal, for those "without morals," to whom the laws of the period shut the door firmly to all possibilities of being close to God. The God that Jesus proclaims, and this is what constitutes the novel part of the message, shows his preference for these "sinners."

Jesus not only opens the door of the Kingdom to these women; he especially approaches one of them, so much so that the gospels would make of Mary of Magdala the first witness of his resurrection. Mary's condition and the relevance given her in the gospel have given rise to novels and films, even to a new interpretation of her relationship with Jesus from the point of view of a frustrated love affair. Without entering into this hypothesis (whose only basis is a literary one), what ought to be highlighted here is the enormous capacity of Jesus to befriend and rekindle hope in those who, having been despised by everyone, likewise scorned themselves. God's forgiveness, through Jesus, is not only in words from a distance; it is translated into action which, in this case, is the act of going to the house of a prostitute and talking to her on equal footing, notwithstanding the scandal it would have brought to "decent" people. In doing so, Jesus fulfills the prophet's promise: God will search for the lost (Ezek. 34:16).

In those times, houses were illuminated by oil lamps. The lamps were usually made of clay, with two openings, one for the wick and the other for the oil. At times, these lamps would be lit the whole night: which was a way of driving away evil spirits. That is why many lamps were found inside the sepulchers of the period.

One of the most common topics in Jesus' parables is that of vigilance. The Lord will come at anytime, and one must be ready to welcome him. God is an unexpected visitor who surprises people, who must always be on guard, who must always be watchful. The parables of the vigilant servant, the thief, and the lamp (Luke 21:35–40) are along this line. Jesus employs them to speak of the Kingdom of God. Mary Magdalene, who was used to staying awake on account of her "nocturnal occupation," understood, better than anyone, such an analogy.

22

The Good News

We arrived in Nazareth, where Jesus grew up. I traveled with him from Capernaum. It was Saturday, a rest day. At the first hour of the morning, the Nazarenes were all jammed into their small and dilapidated synagogue. The men were wrapped in sheets with black and white stripes. Some entered the synagogue chewing dates to stave off hunger, a practice that was prohibited. The women, as was customary, stayed in one corner behind the dividing screens. Among the rest of the village women was Mary, the mother of Jesus.

All: "Listen, Israel. The Lord is our God, only the Lord. Love the Lord your God with all your heart, with all your soul and with all your might. Remember these words as I command you today. . . ."

We started the ceremony by reciting aloud the morning prayer. Then followed the eighteen ritual prayers. When it was time for the reading, the old rabbi signaled to Jesus, who was by my side. Jesus made way through his townspeople and went toward the lectern where the sacred books were kept.

A young man opened the sandalwood box and took out the scrolls where God's law was written in black and red letters. For over a thousand years, the wise men of Israel had scrutinized the meaning behind every word and every syllable in such scrolls, searching for the will of the Lord. Jesus took the book of the prophet Isaiah. He unrolled the scroll, raised it with his two hands, and started to read haltingly, the way peasants did, for lack of schooling.

Jesus: "The spirit of the Lord is upon me. The spirit of the Lord has called me to bring good news to the poor: their liberation! The broken hearts shall be mended, the slaves shall be set free, the prisoners shall see the light of day. I come to proclaim the Year of Grace of the Lord, the Day of Justice of our God: to console the weeping, and put a crown of triumph on their humiliated heads; they shall be garbed in party dresses and not in mourning suits; they shall sing songs of triumph and not lamentation."

Jesus finished reading. He rolled up the scroll and returned it to the assistant of the synagogue, then sat down in silence. All our eyes were glued on him, awaiting a commentary on the text. Jesus, likewise, seemed to be waiting for something. His head was cupped between his hands, and he was noticeably nervous. After a while, he stood up and began to speak.

Jesus: Brethren, I . . . I . . . The truth is, I don't know how to speak before so many people. Pardon me for not speaking like the priests or the doctors of the law. Well, I'm just a peasant like you, and I don't talk much. Still, I thank our rabbi for having invited me to comment on the Scripture.

Rabbi: Don't be nervous, young man! Say anything, whatever occurs to you. Then tell us what happened in Capernaum, about the leper. People keep on saying many strange things.

Jesus: Well, brothers and sisters, I would like to say that, . . . that these words of the prophet Isaiah are . . . You see I heard the prophet John say the same words in the desert. He said: "This is going to change. The Kingdom of God is near." And I thought: yes, if God has something in his hands, but . . . but what? What is it that God has to change? Where will the Kingdom of God begin? I don't know, but now, after reading the words of the Scripture, I think I have understood what it means.

The smell of sweat of the Nazarenes mixed with the burned incense, and one could hardly breathe. Everybody felt the warm air that enveloped the whole synagogue. Jesus was perspiring tremendously.

Jesus: Brothers, sisters, listen to me. I . . . I'm bringing you great joy: our liberation. We, the poor, have spent our whole life bent like animals over our land. The powerful have placed a very heavy yoke on our shoulders. The rich have robbed us of the fruit of our toil. The foreigners have taken over our country and even the priests have joined them and threatened us with a religion based on laws and on fear. And so we are like our ancestors in Egypt during the time of the Pharaoh. We have partaken of bitter bread, and drunk lots of tears. They have given us so many beatings that we even thought that God had forgotten us. No, my brothers and sisters. The time has come and the Kingdom of God is near, very near.

Old Ananias, the owner of a press house and an oil mill, and all the lands bordering the hills of Nazareth, which extended up to Cana, raised his cane like a long accusing finger.

Ananias: Hey, you, young man, son of Mary, what stupid things are you talking about? Will you explain to me what it is that must change? Who are you alluding to?

Jesus: Everything has to change, Ananias. God is a parent who does not want to see his children treated like slaves nor dying of hunger. God's like a carpenter who uses a plane to level off a wall: everyone shall be equal, there'll be no rich nor poor; no pharaohs nor slaves; everyone's family to everyone. God'll come down from heaven to be with us, the most trampled upon on earth. Haven't we always heard that God ordered the Year of Grace? Haven't we just heard it? God wants a year of truce every fifty years. God wants to tear up all titles of property, all debt contracts, and all deeds of sale and purchase; he wants the land to be divided equally among all of us, because this land belongs to God, and everything in it. There are not to be any differences among us. That no one shall have more nor less. This was what the Lord commanded Moses a thousand years ago, and is still waiting, because no one's complied with it. Neither the rulers, the landowners, nor the usurers wanted to fulfill the Year of Grace. Now's the time for it to be fulfilled!

Everyone was silent. We were all amazed at how well Jesus, the son of the carpenter, Joseph, and the peasant woman, Mary, had expressed himself.

A Neighbor: Those words sound beautiful, Jesus, but they can't be eaten. "Liberation, liberation!" But when? Is it for the other life, after death?

Jesus: No Esau. That would be too late. The Year of Grace is for this life. The Kingdom begins on this earth.

Another Neighbor: So when? When the rich take pity and distribute their accumulated stuff among us?

Jesus: Stones don't melt from the inside, Simeon. You gotta have a hammer for this.

Susanna: So when do we see the fulfillment of the word you've just read?

Jesus: Right now, Susanna. Right now. We're going to start today. Of course, this isn't a one-day struggle. You don't crush a stone by one stroke of a hammer. Maybe it's going to take us another thousand years, like Moses. Or it could even take two more thousand years. But we'll also cross the Red Sea and be free. We've got to start today!

Jesus was no longer trembling. With his large, callused hands, he firmly supported himself on the edge of the lectern, breathing deeply, like someone who was to take a deep plunge. He was about to say something significant.

Jesus: I'd like to tell you this: I feel, cramming up in my throat, like arrows in the archer's hand, the voices of all the prophets who spoke before me, from Elijah, that valiant one from Carmel, to the last prophet we've seen in our midst: John, the son of Zechariah, who that skunk, Herod, holds as prisoner in Machaerus. Brothers and sisters, God's patience has come to an end! The Scripture I've just read isn't for tomorrow, but for today. Don't you see? It's being fulfilled right before your eyes.

The old rabbi scratched his head with uneasiness.

Rabbi: What do you mean by, "It's being fulfilled right before our eyes"? I have before me the sacred book of law, praise the Lord Almighty. And you're right beside this book, commenting on what you've read in it.

Jesus: I claim those words written in this book. Pardon me for the way I've spoken, brothers and sisters, but...

Jesus paused. He looked at us slowly, as if asking permission to say what he was about to say.

Jesus: When John, the prophet, baptized me in the Jordan, I felt God was calling me to proclaim the good news. That's why, now, I want to...

A Neighbor: Watch your words, Jesus. Who do you think you are? From the way you talk, you're putting yourself on a par with the prophet Elijah and John the Baptizer!

Jesus: I'm not comparing myself to anyone. I'm simply proclaiming liberation for us, the poor!

An old man with a hunched back like a camel burst with laughter:

Old Man: Hey, doctor, heal yourself first!

Jesus: What do you mean by that?

Old Man: Because we're all bad, but you're the worst! What misery will you liberate us from, when you're the most miserable in Nazareth? Look at your mother over there, behind the dividing screen. Hey, Mary, don't hide yourself, for everybody knows you here. Who is your father, Joseph? May he rest in peace, ... a wretched man, like us. And look at your cousins here. For the love of Abraham, how can you free us when you don't even have a copper in your pocket?

A Woman Neighbor: I think this brown one has become presumptuous!
Rabbi: Wait, my brothers, let him speak! Let him speak!
Neighbors: Enough of that silly talk! Make a miracle!
Neighbor: That's it, a miracle!
Neighbor: Tell us what happened in Capernaum! Did you learn some witchcraft to cleanse the lepers and cure the widows with bad fever?
Neighbor: Tell us, Mary, who taught these tricks to your son?
Rabbi: One moment, one moment! Jesus, do you hear what they say? They're right, son. Aren't you talking of liberation? Well, it must start here in your town; after all, charity begins at home.
Neighbor: You cured the lepers in Capernaum. Why don't you cure the ones who're here?
Lady Neighbor: Come on, what are you waiting for? Do you know that my legs are full of wounds?
Jesus: Neighbors, history repeats itself. During the time of the prophet Elijah, there were a number of needy widows, but he was instead sent to the city of Zarephath in a foreign land. During Elijah's time, there were lots of lepers in Israel, and the prophet cured Naaman, the Syrian, who was also a foreigner.
Neighbor: Hey, what do you mean by that?
Jesus: Nothing, but this is what usually happens. No prophet is welcome in his own land. Fine, I'm going back to Capernaum.

The Nazarenes started to kick and whistle at Jesus.

Neighbor: No, you're not going back to Capernaum: You go to hell! Have you ever seen a charlatan worse than him?
All: You're a fake! A liar! Take him away from here! Out! Out!

The men with fists in fighting position rushed toward the lectern where Jesus was, while the women were yelling behind the dividing screens. The fight had begun, and the old dilapidated synagogue shook with the uproar of the Nazarenes.

•

It was in Nazareth, where Jesus grew up, that he made the first public proclamation of God's good news for the poor. This text—about the basis of the promise made by the prophet Isaiah seven hundred years before—is a summary of what Jesus' life was to become and what, in essence, is the gospel: a liberation for the oppressed. This is a fundamental passage and vital to the understanding of the Christian faith.

In present-day Nazareth, there is a small synagogue built on the remains of the one that existed in Jesus' time. The former must have been a lot smaller than what we see at present, as there were very few residents in the village. Like all synagogues, it was built in such a way that when the people prayed, they tended to look to the direction of the temple of Jerusalem, the seat of religious worship in the country. In the synagogue the women never mingled with the men. There was a specific place for them, which was separated by dividing screens. The women could neither read the Scriptures in public nor give the commentaries.

When people gathered on Saturdays in the synagogue, they always started their prayer by reciting the Shema ("Listen, Israel...," Deut. 6:4–9), one of the prayers preferred by the Jewish faithful. It was then followed by eighteen ritual prayers in anticipation of the reading of the Scriptures. The most sacred place in the synagogue was a nook facing Jerusalem. Here were kept all the rolled scrolls of the Torah (law), in which were written all the books we still read today in the Old Testament of the Bible. The scrolls were kept inside artistically engraved wooden boxes.

Jesus, like all the Israelites of his time, spoke Aramaic, of the same linguistic family as Hebrew. Aramaic is still spoken in some towns of Syria. It was spoken in the whole country of Israel as a popular and domestic language about five centuries before the birth of Jesus. Hebrew was exclusively spoken by the learned men of the law. The Scriptures were written in Hebrew. The scroll from which Jesus read in the synagogue was written in Hebrew. This explains Jesus' stammer — he was not at home in an educated language, since he was a peasant, and therefore not well read.

It was the custom for any man present in the synagogue to read an excerpt from the Scripture and comment on the same before his countrymen, based on how it inspired him. This was a mission of the laymen, and not exclusive to the rabbis. The text read and commented on by Jesus is taken from Isa. 61:1–3. Jesus' decision to speak of the Kingdom of God, of liberation, bothers his countrymen, who neither accept nor believe that a poor, rugged man from their kind could come and liberate them from anything. We usually refuse to accept as "savior" somebody who is near us, who is like us, who is ordinary and simple, as we begin to look for great signs, for saviors coming from outside, who are extraordinary and superior, before whom we render our admiration. But God's plan is the contrary. God chooses to be revealed in the poorest, in the most humble of creatures.

The Year of Grace was an ancient legal institution dating back to the time of Moses. It was also referred to as the Year of Jubilee, which was announced by means of an instrument called *yobel* in Hebrew. This Year of Grace was to be fulfilled every fifty years, during which time all debts should be written off, all properties acquired returned to their former owners (in order to avoid excessive accumulation), and all slaves set free. This law was a way of proclaiming that the only master of the land is God. From the social point of view, this law helped maintain unity among families who deserved a dignified life. It was likewise a memorial of equality that originally existed among the children of Israel upon coming to the promised land when nothing belonged to anyone and everything belonged to everyone (Lev. 25:8–18). The Year of the Sabbath existed in the same light, and was celebrated every seven years. These legal institutions were considered as laws of liberation, as Jesus proclaimed. True to the tradition of his country, he referred to the Year of Grace as a starting point to initiate immediate reforms in the country, because of the big gap between the rich and the poor.

In Nazareth, in the synagogue, Jesus manifested maturity of conscience. When he applied the phrase of Isaiah "The Spirit is upon me" to himself, it was a way of considering himself a prophet in the tradition of all the prophets before him. After the resurrection, the primitive church accumulated various titles for Jesus, in order to describe his mission: Lord, Son of God, Christ. History, as gathered from the gospels, shows, however, that the title unanimously acclaimed by the people and his disciples was that of prophet. The prophet is defined in contrast to institutions. We must not consider Jesus as a theologian or professional teacher. Rather, we must understand that he lacked what the trained teachers of his time had — theological studies. The training of teachers was rigid, and lasted for many years, starting in infancy. When Jesus was addressed as "rabbi" (teacher, master), the title was used in a colloquial way, not as referring to a teacher in the theological sense. Jesus, thus, was accused of teaching without authority (Mark 6:2). When he spoke in the synagogue, he did not do so as a theologian nor as a teacher, but as a lay prophet.

(Matt. 13:53–58; Mark 6:1–6; Luke 4:16–28)

23

A Prophet in His Own Land

That morning, when Jesus read the words of the prophet Isaiah in the small synagogue of Nazareth, his neighbors got mad at him. Immediately, there were shouts of protests and malediction. The uproar grew so intense that when the rabbi tried to maintain order in that mess, it was already too late.

A Neighbor: You, a prophet? Ha-ha-ha! A prophet in tatters!
A Woman Neighbor: He says he's gonna liberate us. Who the hell does he think he is? Hey, son of Mary, beat it, and leave us in peace!
Old Man: Get this troublemaker outta here! Out with him! We don't lose anything by getting rid of him.

The Nazarenes rushed at Jesus with their fists high. He felt four strong arms over him that brought him down from the lectern. In-between shovings they took him out through a narrow door at one end of the synagogue. Everybody followed behind, screaming and whistling.

Neighbor: To the garbage dump! Throw him into the garbage pit!
Woman Neighbor: Right! To the garbage dump!

The neighbors pushed Jesus toward a low cliff where the women burned their garbage every Friday.

Ananias: It's only when I become old that I hear such stupidity!

Ananias, the wealthiest man in the neighborhood, raised his cane into the air and, with all his fury, charged at Jesus.

Ananias: This is what you get for poking your nose . . .

Everything went bad, and I tried to calm them down, but . . .

John: Hey folks, please, listen to me for a minute, don't be . . .

Before I could finish what I was going to say, a fat Nazarene took off one of his sandals and hurled it toward me with all his might.

Neighbor: Lick this, friend!

The sandal hit my face and my nose started to bleed. Jesus was also bleeding, and his tunic was torn into pieces.

Woman Neighbor: To the dump! To the garbage dump! The charlatans into the garbage!

I remember that scuffle very well. Now I can laugh at it, but at that moment, we all got the scare of our lives. Jesus' neighbors were really furious and didn't want to have anything to do with him. Well, that was already obvious. When Moses went to talk to his countrymen in Egypt, he was also branded as meddlesome and kicked out. The same thing happened to David, who was persecuted by his own compatriots. Joseph, likewise, was sold by his own brothers. Well, this always happens. No prophet is well received in his own land.

Neighbor: We don't need anyone to solve our problems for us! Much less do we need you, storyteller!
Neighbor: Hey, you creep, don't push!
Neighbor: Wha'd you say?
Neighbor: You heard it, . . . that you're a creep!
Neighbor: You say it again and I'm gonna punch you in the mouth!
Neighbor: You're a creep.

Nazareth was a notorious and violent neighborhood. The sun never set without a Nazarene spitting out curses and getting embroiled in fights for some simple misunderstanding. In a few seconds, they forgot about Jesus and his pronouncements in the synagogue. The fight became a free-for-all.

Neighbor: Imbecile! I'll make you swallow those words!
Neighbor: Pay what you owe me or I'll chop off your head!

The boys also got involved in the melee. Some picked up a few stones and gave them to the old men who couldn't use their fists. The women, on the other hand, pulled away each other's head scarf and bun, and scratched each other's face.

Susanna: I'm gonna crush you, you filthy devil!

Susanna was knocked over the floor, while fighting with the girlfriend of the butcher, Tryphon. I also saw Mary, Jesus' mother, whose eyes were red and her hair disheveled, trying to come near us. Then we heard that stentorian voice behind us.

Judas: Stop fighting! That's enough!

They were two men, one clambering over the other man's back, like a jockey on a horse. The man under was a burly, freckled, blond man, named Simon. The man on top was also young and strong. He had a yellow scarf tied around his neck and was brandishing a knife in his right hand. His name was Judas Iscariot. The two zealots went near the Nazarenes.

Judas: That's enough! What do you want? To kill and destroy one another?

The fight was all over now.

Neighbor: And who are you, if I may ask?
Judas: I'm someone like you, my friend, like him and like everybody else.
Neighbor: And who gave you the right to interfere?
Judas: Nobody. I'm meddling because it hurts to see that the mice are killing one another while the cat is smiling and licking its whiskers.
Neighbor: What's that supposed to mean?

Judas kept his knife under his sweat-drenched tunic and never got off Simon's back. The Nazarenes forgot about their bickerings and listened to the man who had just arrived.

Judas: Listen, my friends: once there was a hungry cat and there were three mice. One was white, the other was black, and the third was brown. The three were well hidden in their holes. So the cat began to think: "What must I do so I can eat them all? My legs are too big to fit in the holes. What am I gonna do?" Then the cat quietly went near the first hole where the white mouse was sleeping and whispered: "Little white mouse, the black mouse says that you're a rascal." Then he went to the black mouse's cave and said: "Little black mouse, the white mouse says that you're a coward." And finally, to the brown mouse, he said: "Little brown mouse, your other two companions say that you're the most stupid of all."
Neighbor: So what did they do?
Judas: Exactly what we did. They came out of their caves and began to fight among themselves. They ended up so tired, they didn't even have

the strength to run nor hide. Then the grinning cat came, held each one by the tail, and zas! swallowed all of them. This is what the Romans want: for us to fight each other so they can swallow us whole. Folks, they want to divide us. "Divide and rule," thus says the two-headed Roman eagle. Do you see this scarf around my neck? This was given to me by Ariel, the legitimate grandson of the Maccabees. They were good patriots, who didn't waste their strength fighting each other.

Woman Neighbor: What Judas Iscariot says is true! Our enemies are other people!

Judas: Exactly, woman. Reserve the knife for the throat of the foreigners, and the stones for the heads of Herod and his men. Save your strength to fight them when the time comes.

Then Judas took out his knife. With one hand he took a lock of hair and cut it with the other. Then he threw the hair into the air swearing.

Judas: We want to be as free as these strands of hair. May the Lord of the army cut my body into two if I don't fight for my people's freedom, for the freedom of the people of Israel!

The Nazarenes already had a lot to talk about and amuse themselves with that afternoon. Each one returned home, shaking the dust from their cloaks. The melee had enlivened them. Judas and Simon, the two zealots, came to us.

Judas: How is the reckless son of Zebedee?

Simon: We recognized you from afar through your beard, John!

John: And so did I! What a surprise to see you around, Judas! Blazes, Simon, I haven't seen you for a long time!

Simon: How're you doing, John? And the rest of the boys? Still casting nets for crabs?

John: Look, let me introduce my friend: this brown one was born here in Nazareth, but right now he's staying with us in Capernaum. His name is Jesus and he's got good ideas in his head. Look, Jesus, this freckled giant is Simon, the most fanatic zealot in the movement. He gave a punch to a Roman guard, and before he could turn the right cheek, he gave him another blow to the left. And this guy with the yellow scarf is Judas, a patriot like no one else. He was born far from here, in Iscariot, but he can already spit in-between his teeth like we Galileans do.

Jesus: I'm happy to meet you, Judas, and... and I also want to thank you.

Judas: For what?

Jesus: For saving our lives, my friend. Had you and your friend not come, they would've killed us.

Simon: But didn't John say that they were your neighbors?

Jesus: Exactly. Didn't you know that he who eats from your hand is the first one to bite you?

Simon: You're right. That is how it is. Well, Judas, it's getting late. Let's go.

John: Are you going to Cana?

Judas: No, to Sepphoris. There's been a squealer in the group over there and we want to find out who he is. We can't allow treachery among the zealots.

John: Very well said, Judas. Be hard on traitors.

Judas: Hey, Jesus, I'd like to have a longer chat with you. Maybe you can help in our struggle.

Jesus: Probably you and Simon can give us a hand too. We also have plans.

Judas: Of course, my friend. That's what we're here for, to help one another. Well, so long, John. See you in Capernaum, Jesus.

John: See you soon, Judas. May the scarf of the Maccabees bring you luck!

Simon: Goodbye, boys. See you!

Jesus: Goodbye, goodbye! Come, John, let's go see my mother at once. She must be more worried than the bricklayers of the Tower of Babel!

Jesus and I walked to the house of Mary. Meanwhile, in Nazareth, tongues kept on wagging.

Old Man: Can you imagine that, friend? And he claimed himself to be a prophet, this Jesus I've seen since birth and whose nose I've cleaned forty times!

Woman Neighbor: These false agitators make me furious. They talk of peace but they also bring in the sword! They talk of love and bring in stories, but look at the mess they get us into!

Neighbor: To hell with Mary's son! He's always been such a good fellow, so complacent.... And what has he got into?... Well, he had it coming, bad company, and the mother is too soft on him.

We reached Mary's house.

Mary: For God's sake, son! How embarrassing!

Susanna: Better: what audacity! I can't believe it, Jesus!

Jesus: Okay, Mother. I'm going back to Capernaum. Don't worry about me.

Susanna: I warned you Mary. Tell me who your friends are and I'm gonna tell you who you are. Have you seen this hairy man he came with?

John: Look, Mam, I don't...

Susanna: You are one of them, one of those agitators in Capernaum. There's Peter, the stone-thrower, Andrew, the skinny one, and James, the red-haired... Such friends you have, eh? And didn't you see those two who came, one of them clambering over the other like a horse? Oh, they're trouble.

Jesus: Come on, Susanna, please stop it. You're also troublesome at times. I saw you when you were holding Tryphon's girlfriend by her bun!

Mary: I beg of you, Jesus, for my sake, please don't get yourself into any more trouble.

Jesus: But, Mother, I did nothing but explain the Scripture, and they began to throw stones at me. Is it my fault? Tell God not to speak so clearly. It seems to me that it's the Lord who wants to get himself into trouble.

The next day, very early, Jesus and I started back to Capernaum. We returned with welts on our bodies. We were happy though. We had started using our voice to proclaim the good news of liberation of the poor.

•

The opposition of Jesus' countrymen, which started when they wouldn't accept "that one of them" would introduce himself as a prophet and speak about liberation, deteriorated into a brawl. This unleashing of violence, where quarrels and revenge surface, is typical of small towns. One must also take into consideration that in Middle Eastern countries this type of tumult, the result of aggressiveness, is common.

Jesus' words in the synagogue make him into a symbol of contradiction and scandal among his countrymen, especially the rich, as his words reclaim justice and equality. Initially, his words were a scandal for the majority of the poor too, because they refused to accept that a poor man like themselves could become a leader. Long periods of suffering sometimes breed skepticism among the poor. Since the price that one has to pay to attain freedom is the risk of starting without knowing how well things will turn out, one is met with all sorts of resistance. At this moment, the prophet's task becomes difficult because opposition comes from the oppressor and the oppressed at the same time, as the latter has not yet shed off an attitude of passivity (Exod. 5:22). Christian faith, as proclaimed and lived, is always a sign of contradiction. The gospel is not an effective balm in attaining universal unity through love. It unleashes conflicts. Jesus said he came to bring war, not peace. If the evangelical word is double-edged, it is because it divides, cuts, wounds, and exposes hypocrisy concealed by false religion, inequality among people, injustice maintaining such inequality, and the fear of freedom in the hearts of the oppressed.

Judas Iscariot is introduced in the episode. Some claim that this moniker made reference to his place of origin: "Iscariot," a small village in the region of Judah. However, experts on the zealots see in "Iscariot" a deformed version of *sicario*. The *sicarios* were a group of fanatic nationalists from the zealot party who used the *sica* (dagger) in committing acts of terrorism against the Romans. Judas was accompanied by Simon, the "zealot," one of the twelve apostles. All this indicates that in Jesus' group there were men of various political tendencies.

Even the extremists, who never appear in the gospel, invited Jesus as a "partisan" — to put it in modern terms — to be a leader of a popular movement unrecognized by official institutions.

The fact that Judas betrayed Jesus has put him in a very bad light in the course of history. He has become a good example of perversity, of evil incarnate. The historical figure of this man has been mythified to the maximum, and generations of Christians have used him as a form of catharsis for their feelings of guilt, thus converting Judas into a kind of a "scapegoat." There are some towns and villages where the effigy of Judas is beaten, burned, or hanged every year. It is imperative that we remove this barrier that impedes us from looking at him as one who was more than a friend of Jesus, certainly more politicized than the rest, and therefore more practical, perhaps, and more efficacious.

In our account, Judas narrates to the people of Nazareth a story with all the characteristics of a parable. Explaining an idea and teaching a lesson by the use of images as in a parable was a manner of speaking not exclusive to Jesus. It is a Middle Eastern mode of expression, and very common especially among the popular class.

To show his political affiliation, Judas appears with a yellow scarf belonging to a grandson of the Maccabees brothers, heroes of the Jewish resistance against Greek domination in the country about 160 years before the birth of Christ. The Maccabees were organizers of the guerrilla struggle in Israel which achieved important victories against the powerful Hellenistic empire. In the people's mind, they were a symbol of courage, patriotism, and freedom.

(Luke 4:28–30)

24

Like a Mustard Seed

In the early morning of the next day, after that scuffle in Nazareth, Jesus and I traveled north to Capernaum. Soon the heat of the sun began to pervade the Galilean plains, made golden by the ripe wheat grain, promising an abundant harvest. There was a cheerful air in the field. We, too, were happy, in spite of the blows we received the day before.

John: I can't help but laugh every time I remember. When that old man, Ananias, raised his cane, he was furious. He was red like, ... like ...

Jesus: Like your nose, John, which is as red as a tomato.

John: The truth is, and this isn't because they're neighbors or relatives of yours, Jesus, they're an impossible lot, and damn them! They're all also starving like us. You tell them about the Year of Grace and the liberation for all, and instead of being happy about it, they kick you in the ass. Not even the devil can understand them!

Jesus: The laws of Moses are antiquated, John, but since they were never complied with, they look new. New wine bursts the skins. And that is what happens. Of course, they will always tell us that some will have more and others less, because that is life, and that is how God wants it. We ought to have more patience. And then somebody suddenly shouts no, because if all the laws of God were complied with, and the things of the world were available for everyone, the same poor people would be shocked and couldn't stand it. Well, they also claim that our grandparents complained to Moses, dreaming of eating the garlic and onions of Egypt!

John: Hey, Jesus, don't talk to me about food at this moment, because my belly's rumbling. We better walk fast so we can get there in time for the soup!

Although we were tired and beaten, the road seemed short. We were dying to tell our companions everything that happened in Nazareth. After crossing

the valley for several hours it was already noontime, and the palm trees of
Capernaum were already within our sight.

Zebedee: Look who's coming, the rascals! Just in time!

John: We're back, old man!

Jesus: How's life around here, Zebedee?

Zebedee: Very well, a lot better than yours, I guess. Here, we were
already thinking the soldiers had got their hands on you!

John: Not the soldiers, but Jesus' neighbors, who're more hostile than
a bitch giving birth.

Zebedee: Salome, leave that stove and come over here fast; your son
and the Nazarene are back! And how're things in your town, Jesus?

Jesus: Oh, in Nazareth . . . Well, the same thing happened to us there
that happened to King Neco, who went for wool, but came out sheared
himself!

Salome: Oh, John, my son, and you too, Jesus . . . Tell me, what
happened to you? You seem to have come from battle.

John: 'Twas a mauling session, Mother. In Nazareth, they gave us a good
beating!

Salome: Really? And may I know why?

John: For no reason at all, Mother. The truth is, we . . .

Salome: It must be something serious, I must say.

Jesus: They invited us to speak, Mam, and we did.

Zebedee: And what the hell did you say?

Jesus: Nothing. That the reason why there are poor people is because
there are rich people, and that the poor'll only go up if the rich go down.

Salome: And you claim you said nothing. Have you ever seen a more
vicious tongue than yours, Nazarene?

Jesus: But that was what Isaiah, Jeremiah, Amos, Hosea, and the rest
of the prophets announced.

Salome: Like I told you, Zebedee: this guy is going to get himself killed.
And look at this son of yours. . . . Look what's happened to your nose, John.

John: Don't worry, Mother, it doesn't hurt anymore.

Jesus: They hurled a sandal at us, Mam Salome. I bent over just in
time, while this poor guy nearly swallowed it!

Salome: Praise be the Lord! Let me get a piece of raw meat, it'll help
reduce the swelling.

Zebedee: I hope it's not the slice that I'll have to eat later, woman!

Salome: Come on inside. Better wash your feet, so we can cure those welts.

Zebedee: Then you can tell us about the squabble in your village! Damn! Had I known it, I would've gone with you!

That night, we got together to talk about the usual thousand things. It was not only our group that was present. The news that Jesus had returned spread through the whole village, and some fishermen and other neighbors from the market slipped into the house.

James: So, what now, Jesus? Are you going to stay here for good?

Jesus: Well, if you don't kick me out, can I stay?

Zebedee: I think Jesus likes it here!

Jesus: It isn't that, Zebedee. In Nazareth there's less work and...

Rufa: Poor guys!

Salome: Don't feel bad for them, Rufa. After all, who told them to get themselves into trouble, huh? Serves 'em right!

Peter: But Salome, you heard your son. Jesus and he didn't do anything.

Salome: You too, shut up, Peter, for not one of you's an angel! Tell me, folks, who among you would speak before so many people in a synagogue saying that this world is topsy-turvy and must be set right?

Jesus: And how do you suppose you'd say it, Salome?

Salome: You don't have to say it. It can't be said, Jesus, because in this country, they put a muzzle on whoever talks a lot!

John: Oh yeah? In other words, we just let them do their thing, while we huddle in a corner?

Salome: And what do you want to do, John? For this world to exist, there must be the poor and the rich. Even the rabbi says that in the synagogue.

Peter: No, Mam, not necessarily so. That's the story they forced down our throats to silence us. And don't tell me you're shocked. Okay, what did the law of Moses say? For every fifty years, a year of truce. Tear up those property titles, write off those debts, set the slaves free. Let's begin anew, the way it was at the start. Everything belongs to everyone and to no one. That was the Year of Grace that Moses wanted, do you hear? The year of Grace!

Salome: Well, that's funny! Look, Peter, don't you believe it — ever since Eve ate that forbidden fruit, things have been that way and will continue to be so.

James: It's very convenient to say that. Of course, it's easier to complain about the darkness than light a candle. And that's what happens.

Salome: That's not so. The truth is, there's a certain restlessness in your being, which I can't figure out, and I'm not happy about it. This feverish feeling has grown ever since this Nazarene came around. Yes, yes, and don't put on that face, Jesus, for you know damn well it's true. Look, listen to me, forget about these crazy ideas for now. If this time they just punched your noses, next time around they're gonna break all your bones!

Jesus: As John was telling you before, the wine is new.

Salome: What wine are you talking about, you fool?

Jesus: The Kingdom of God, Salome. He's talking about the Kingdom of God that's come, and will burst the old wineskins!

The moon shone during the night, as the south wind began to blow. Eyes sparkled with curiosity as they were illuminated by the flickering light from the lamps hanging on the wall. Jesus was sitting on the floor, with crossed legs, in the middle of the group. He was perspiring, but smiling.

Jesus: Friends, in spite of the beatings we got, John and I were very happy when we left Nazareth. We have this great feeling inside and don't like to keep it to ourselves. It's the good news that the prophet Isaiah wrote about, many years ago, and which we spoke about in my village and is now being fulfilled. The Kingdom of God has come! Yes, my brothers and sisters, the time has come. When the time comes for the sheep to rear its young, then the lamb is born, and she can't wait, for it is time. This is the time of the Lord, who can't wait. Small group though we are, God will show us the way and we'll move on if we can push one another onward!

Peter: That's well said! You have my support, Jesus!

James: That's the way to talk, brown one!

Salome: Just a minute, just a minute, you crazy bunch! The flute sounds beautiful, all right. All that's fine. And I'll be the first to lend a hand, if need be, in a fight. I'm well trained for this, what with all the blows I've had to give my rogue husband!

Zebedee: Hey, hey, now what are you saying?

Salome: Nothing, old man, but one has to put feet on the ground. Who's gonna set this world aright? You? You, with a hole in each sandal and two patches on your trousers? Come on, don't aim so high, because you don't know the consequences!

Peter: Well, Mam, one has to start somewhere.

Salome: Sure, by staying put, for God's sake, without interfering in places you're not needed!

Zebedee: You're wrong, old woman. These young men are right. We spend the whole day and half of the night complaining that things are going from bad to worse, and we don't lift a finger to improve them. Now, what does that lead to?

Salome: But, God, you've got to open your eyes, for you could end up in the grave. Since when have you seen a dove challenging an eagle? Tell me. Put that in your head, young men!

Philip: Well, I've done that already.

Philip, the vendor, who had been quiet all along, scratched his huge head and looked at everyone, as if seeing a bad omen.

Philip: I don't intend to sink the boat, but in all sincerity, Mam Salome is right. What the devil can we do, being the last in line? I think the best thing that we can do is forget all about this, and go back home. So, if there's nothing else...

Jesus: Hold it, Philip, don't leave yet. Come here, big head.

Philip: What do you want now, Jesus?

Jesus: Tell me one small thing.

Philip: Enough of those stories of yours, Jesus, we already know each other.

Jesus: No, Philip, just name me one small thing.

Philip: Oh, well, let me see...a comb...

Jesus: No, something smaller.

Philip: Smaller than a comb? Well,...a ring.

Jesus: Smaller still.

Philip: Let me see,...a pin! That's the smallest I have in my cart.

Jesus: That's still very big, Philip. Think of something as big as the size of the pin's head. What's the smallest thing a peasant can hold in his hand?

Philip: The smallest...

Rufa: A mustard seed!

Jesus: That's it, exactly, Grandma Rufa. A mustard seed.

Rufa: That was very easy to guess, Jesus. The mustard seed is so small it can hardly be seen.

Jesus: However, when it falls to the ground and takes root, it grows into a big tree, as tall as the height of two men. It is such a big tree that the birds come looking for rest and food.

Salome: I see your point, Jesus. A small group and yet, it can accomplish great things . . .

Jesus: Yes, Salome. The Kingdom of God is like a mustard seed.

Peter: Very well said! And we are the sowers, ready for anything! The cowards, like Philip, should stay for awhile. Blazes, we're already a small group!

We continued talking and arguing up to the wee hours of the morning. Outside, the wind stirred the waters on the lake and shook the dried leaves of the mustard trees that grew along the shore.

•

After that failure in Nazareth, Jesus undertakes his activity in Capernaum, in the small house of the old man, Zebedee, in the company of the group of first disciples and the residents of the village. He tells them the parable of the mustard seed. It is a story typical of the beginnings of Jesus' activities in Galilee. It is a classic parable of contrast: the beginning is small, insignificant; in the end, a beautiful bush will be the marvelous result of what God has in his hands.

The mustard plant grows wild in Palestine. Along the lakeshore, it grows as high as three meters. The image of a tree that serves as a resting place for the birds and provides shade to whoever goes near is a symbol of God's kindness and generosity (Ezek. 17:22–24). In the old sayings of the Jewish rabbis, the mustard seed was considered the smallest of seeds. Although the mustard plant is no more than a bush, Jesus calls it a tree, an exaggeration, to emphasize how God's plans surpass ours, take us by surprise, much more than we can imagine. When we undertake a difficult and risky project, and for our part put in all we can, God enriches and makes what is great out of the smallest. The Kingdom of God is born from small things. Working among the poor and with them, God forms his community. This community is a call to lead in the truly important events of history.

The Kingdom of God is new wine. Jesus proposes this idea in the beginning of his activity as the fulfillment of the social laws during the time of Moses. Those laws — the Year of Grace being one of them — focused on equality, the overcoming of social divisions, and the avoidance of accumulation of wealth by a few at the expense of those who were starving to death. These were old laws that turned out to be new since they had never been complied with. In Jesus' time, differences among the Israelites were still being ignored.

The existence of social classes, the rich and the poor, for many, is "God's will," a "fate," a natural event that defies change, an irremediable reality that can never be altered. This manner of thinking, like Salome's, is common among the rich, for it suits them to believe so. It is the same among the poor because the rich and their adjuncts (the school, false religion) have taught them this attitude of resignation, have made them believe that God wants it that way and promises heaven in the other life if on earth they accept their misfortune. Nevertheless, "in the beginning this was not so; poverty and wealth came to people later," according to St. Gregory Nazianzen. The Kingdom of God begins here on earth precisely when there exist no more differences among people, when the earth's resources are distributed equally among us, when human beings are no longer considered rich or poor. Instead, they are living as brothers and sisters, children of the same Father, enjoying the same rights and the same opportunities.

(Matt. 13:31–32; Mark 4:30–32; Luke 13:18–19)

25

The Tax Collector

On the outskirts of Capernaum, on the street coming from Damascus, was the customs house where Matthew, the publican, son of Alphaeus, collected taxes. All merchandise brought in by the caravans of businessmen through this route into Galilee paid their contributions here.

Matthew: Hey, you, with the red turban! Yes, yes, don't pretend you don't see me. Pay seven dinars!

Trader: Seven dinars? Seven dinars for two boxes of pepper? That's too much!

Matthew: That's what you owe. Don't argue anymore, my friend, or I'll call one of the soldiers.

Trader: What a wretched man! Thief! The tax shouldn't be that high!

Matthew: Are you gonna pay or not? Many are waiting.

Trader: Here, take it. And go to hell!

Matthew: Next... Let me see, you... How many sacks of wool do you carry with you?

Another Trader: Ten sacks, sir.

Matthew: Ten sacks, really? You're a liar! What about those four you're hiding behind the camels?

Another Trader: But those are not from the...

Matthew: Shut up, you cheat. Now you'll have to pay me four more, so you'll know how to respect the law. You can't deceive me, my friend.

Trader: But I didn't want to...

Matthew: Ten and four is fourteen, plus four more is eighteen. Come on, let go of your eighteen dinars.

Matthew dipped his pen in the inkwell and scribbled some numbers. Leaning over his table, he was more jittery than he had been before. His beard and fingernails were stained with ink. There was always a jug of wine beside his bunch of papers. Every time he spotted a caravan coming from a distance, or some traders along the way, he would rub his hands, have a few shots of wine, and prepare to collect a good amount of money from them. In all of Capernaum, there was no other man more hated than he. We would spit every time we passed in front of his stall. The women cursed him, and we never saw a child approach him.

Another Trader: Please don't charge me too much, sir. With this oil, I practically don't earn anything for my children's food.

Matthew: What're you telling me? I don't give alms here.

Trader: Could you just gimme a little discount? I really need it.

Matthew: Weep somewhere else and try to get some money. I'm just following orders.

Trader: You're taking advantage of our being illiterate, you son of a bitch! You're cheating us!

Matthew: Hey, you, cross-eyed fellow, who told you to poke your nose into this? Come on, gimme twenty, and beat it!

Taxes were a nightmare for us poor people. Rome collected taxes in the whole of Judea. In our land of Galilee, we had to pay King Herod, who had sold himself to the Romans. His officials, the tax collectors, who we called publicans, were positioned at all the entrances of the cities in Galilee, collecting customs duties as ordered by the king. The publicans even increased these taxes so they could keep the difference, thus enriching themselves. Soon they, too, earned the hatred of everyone.

Matthew: Well, let's see. You're the last. What do you have to declare?

Another Trader: Two sacks of wheat and three barrels of olives.

Matthew: Open that sack, you might be concealing something.

At midmorning, Matthew had finished with the day's early caravans. It was the time for him to count his collection. He separated what was intended for Herod's soldiers and for himself. Then he sat at the table with his jug of wine and book of accounts. He wouldn't know how to exist without the two. Near the stall were the soldiers who guarded the customs house. They played dice while waiting for new traders to arrive. At this time Jesus passed in front of Matthew's stall.

Matthew: Hey, you, come over here.

Jesus: What's the matter?

Matthew: What do you have in that sack?

Jesus: Horseshoes.

Matthew: Really? And where are you going, may I ask?

Jesus: To Chorazin.

Matthew: What for?

Jesus: To shoe some mules. I've been making horseshoes, and I'm going there to sell them. That's my work.

Matthew: Pay three dinars and then you can go. Are you deaf? I said three dinars.

Jesus: Why do I have to pay three dinars? I'm not going out of Galilee. I'm going to Chorazin.

Matthew: And I don't believe you. I'm not stupid, you know. You're one of those involved in smuggling, with the Syrians.

Jesus: What smuggling are you talking about? I'm going to Chorazin to shoe some mules.

Matthew: And I'm saying you are going out of Galilee and you are involved in smuggling! You can get yourself into trouble, as much as you like, but you have to pay three dinars.

Jesus: But what three dinars are you talking about? I can't pay you. I haven't got a single cent.

Matthew: Then you've got to pay me with those horseshoes.

Jesus: How can I do that? If I have to leave them here, there'll be no work for me, so what will I go to Chorazin for?

Matthew: Ah, that's your problem. Either you give me three dinars or the sack of horseshoes.

Jesus: This is crazy.

Matthew: It's the law, my friend. The law grabs smugglers, like you, by the throat. That's how I caught you.

Jesus: I'm sorry, Matthew, but I'm not involved in any smuggling with the Syrians. Neither do I have three dinars. Nor can I give you the horseshoes. I have to work. Please let me go.

Matthew: Don't ask me for favors when I'm talking about the law. Besides, I don't want to waste my time with you. Puah! You're a smuggler. You can't deceive me. These horseshoes will not leave the customs house. Everything has been said now, so do whatever you please.

Jesus: Pff! What a guy! That means I've gotta wait until you cool off tomorrow and listen to reason. Can I sit here?

Matthew: Do whatever you wish, and don't bother me anymore. To hell with smugglers!

Jesus sat on the floor, leaned on one of the walls of Matthew's stall, and stared at the road that vanished afar. The heat of the sun became intense, and soon enough he dozed off. Meanwhile, Matthew continued counting his money, scribbling more and more numbers on the papers. When Jesus woke up, the jug of wine was empty and the tax collector's eyes were red and sparkling. Just like every other day, before noon Matthew was already drunk.

Jesus: Hmmm...I fell asleep. Well, Matthew, have you solved my case? What? Are you allowing me now to proceed to Chorazin with the horseshoes?

Matthew: You don't get outta here! That's what I say! And let me work in peace!

Jesus got up and stretched his arms while yawning. Then, leaning over the table, he followed closely the direction of Matthew's pen.

Jesus: That must be difficult, huh, Matthew?

Matthew: Hmmm.

Jesus: I mean, writing. I can write only a few letters. I'd like to learn more. Why, you do it very fast.

Matthew: I had a teacher for this. In this job, if you can't write, you're nothing.

Jesus: If I stay longer in Capernaum, will you teach me?

Matthew: Hmmm...I can write, but I can't teach. Blazes!

Jesus: Say, Matthew, how long have you been in this job?

Matthew: Bah, many years. I don't remember anymore. One, two, three, four...I don't remember.

Jesus: Do you like your job?

Matthew: Of course. Who doesn't like to have money so he can buy what he wishes? Of course I like my job. Damn, you're messing up my computations. Will you shut up and let me work in peace!

Jesus: But you paid a price for this, didn't you?

Matthew: What?

Jesus: In order to have everything you want, you had to lose friends.

Matthew: What do I need friends for? No one is a friend to anyone. If someone is at your back, beware, he wants to get something from you. I don't believe in what you're saying!

Jesus: Well, but...Don't tell me you're used to having people spit at you when they pass by.

Matthew: Oh, let them. They can even blow their noses if they like. They spit at me, I curse them. They can insult me, but that's all, that's all they can do. I can extract their money, and that's more important. I can hurt them even more! What? You think I'm wrong? I couldn't care less.

Matthew momentarily set aside his work and, with his eyes swollen from having drunk too much alcohol, turned to Jesus.

Matthew: Hey, who're you, and why do you ask so many questions? Do you think I don't know you? I know your group here in Capernaum. This skinny one and the red-haired one and...

Jesus: And John and Peter.

Matthew: Yes, a gang of bandits. Smugglers, that's what you are. You, being the stranger, must be their chief.

Jesus: Enough! We're a group of friends, Matthew. I met them at the Jordan, when we went to see the prophet John.

Matthew: Another agitator! I want to know what you're up to. Be sure, I'm gonna find out. I have a way of doing so.

Jesus: If you really want to know, then you should come with us one day.

Matthew: Yes, yes, because you're concealing something. I know your kind very well. You're like chameleons, you change colors fast, and how!

Jesus: I'm serious, Matthew. Why don't you come to Salome's house one day, so we can have a chat?

Matthew: Why don't you come to the house, eh? Why, you and your friends wouldn't dare set foot in my house, would you?

Jesus: I wouldn't mind. If you invited me, then I'd accept. I'll tell my friends right away.

Matthew: Would you eat at my house?

Jesus: Yes, Matthew, if you say so.

Matthew: I see you can pretend pretty well, stranger. But, ... you see, for a long time, I haven't invited anyone to my house....

Jesus: Then I'll be your first guest. When do you want us to come? This coming Saturday? Or tonight, if you want?

Matthew: Are you serious?

Jesus: Of course, Matthew. After having been detained in this boring place, I'm hungry, and I can't stand it any longer. Let me inform the rest. We shall go to your house tonight, okay?

Matthew: Sure. But we're gonna need some wine for everyone. I can't eat without wine!

Jesus: I can see that.

Matthew: So better come with me to buy some wine.

Jesus: It's a deal. Let's go!

Jesus left his horseshoes beside Matthew's working table and walked toward the tavern of Joachim, who was blind in one eye. The tavern was located at the exit of Capernaum. Matthew, who was wobbling, followed him.

•

According to data from the gospels, Matthew, one of the twelve apostles of Jesus, was the son of a certain Alphaeus who was a tax collector at the customs house of Capernaum — a gateway for caravans coming from Damascus. In the gospels of Luke and Mark, Matthew is also called Levi. Since the second century, he has been considered the author of one of the four gospels. In our story, Matthew appears as a man of weak character, a pessimist, a skeptic, who finds in his drinking some refuge from the society that considers his job disdainful.

Since the time of Persian domination, Israel knew what it was to pay taxes to a foreign power. It was only up to the time of the Roman Empire that collections were unsystematic. Each Roman province was obliged to pay taxes to the Roman treasury, although some cities and prime allies of the empire could collect them for their own benefit. Such was the case with the Galilean tetrarch Herod Antipas, who collected them from the different cities of Galilee, among which was Capernaum. Matthew, therefore, was an official of King Herod, a great collaborator of the Roman Empire. Taxes were a big burden for the people and an important weapon of the rulers for political control. To the computed sums were added certain amounts, in the form of gifts and bribery to be given to authorities and to administrative personnel. There was corruption from the lowest level to the highest.

The tax collectors (publicans) belonged to the most contemptible social category of the country, which included usurers, money-changers, gamblers, and shepherds. In this job, aside from the strict collection of taxes — which was reason enough to earn the hatred of the people — all kinds of cheating occurred. Due to the numerous frauds and the vast number of those victimized by them, the publicans were socially stigmatized, which caused them to lose their civic and political rights. In the language of the people, the tax collectors were associated with thieves, pagans, prostitutes, assassins, and adulterers. They were indeed that society's excrement. All this highlights the great scandal of Jesus inviting a publican to become part of his group and reiterating on several occasions that the good news he was bringing along was primarily intended for the "publicans and sinners."

In all probability, Matthew was a rich man because of the fraud committed in his occupation. But he would not have belonged to any of the prestigious families, since tax collectors were no more than sub-lessees of wealthy contractors, usually of the upper social class. Matthew's occupation has, at times, been interpreted as proof that Jesus got followers from various social classes and that the gospel's goal was social harmony. This is not correct. The gospel's message is obviously directed to everyone, but not in the same manner for everyone. The good news for the poor is this: that they will cease to be poor. The rich are asked to renounce their wealth if they want to enter the Kingdom of Heaven. The message clearly shows that God takes sides, that God is not neutral. That Jesus associates himself with Matthew and invites him into his group signifies that he is breaking all socioreligious barriers of "decent" people of his time by befriending the undesirables and the sinners.

During that time writing was usually done on papyrus. Papyrus is an aquatic shrub that grew in the marshland. It was harvested in the northern part of the Sea of Galilee. Its fibers were made into baskets, boats, and a kind of paper that could easily be rolled. The color of ink with which one wrote was black, basically made of very thick soot. Those who could write would sometimes carry their inkwells hanging at the waist. Naturally, a tax collector had to master the art of writing, and normally should have some knowledge of Greek, because of dealings with traders from other countries. In the light of these qualifications of Matthew, Jesus' level of culture was notably inferior, for he was "semi-illiterate." In such a society, as in any other society, those who knew how to write had an edge over uncultured neighbors who were dependent on them for knowledge and whom they could assist or deceive.

(Matt. 9:9; Mark 2:13–14; Luke 5:27–28)

26

In the Tax Collector's House

Jesus: Aren't you coming?

James: Over my dead body, Jesus! Have you gone crazy? How can we ever eat with that bastard?

James's screaming resounded through the wharf at Capernaum where Jesus had come to talk to us about Matthew and to ask us if we wanted to go with him to his house. But we had hated the tax collector for so long that nobody wanted to go along.

Mila: You mean he's coming over to eat here?

Matthew: Yes. He's from Nazareth. I think he's weird. I suspect something, but...

Mila: He must be dangerous. Otherwise, why would he come to this house?

Matthew: I told you he's weird. Actually, he doesn't look bad, but I guess he's...

Mila: It's been such a long time since anyone from town has come to have lunch with us,... except once, those Roman captains. I'm sick and tired of them!

Matthew: You can't complain, Mila. My job comes from them.

Matthew's wife was a poor woman. Her husband's job, one of the most despised in our country, had alienated her from everyone in Capernaum. She shut herself up in their house and rarely went out. Whenever she went to the market, the other women would whisper at her back and make fun of her. She didn't have any friends. Nor did she have children. That's why, that evening, in spite of her husband's suspicions, she was happy — finally someone was going to be their guest.

Neighbor: Hey, Salome, Salome!

Salome: What's the matter, Anne?

Neighbor: Is it true what they said about that stranger living in your house?

Salome: Tell me what they said.

Neighbor: Mila, the wife of that brazen Matthew — may the fires of hell consume him — dropped by and told Naomi that the Nazarene was gonna have dinner in their house.

Salome: What? No kidding? That's a big lie. Why would he do that?

Neighbor: You don't believe it? Ask the people in the marketplace. Everyone's talking about it. I was told that Jesus was a decent guy. Then how come he's gonna have dinner with a tax collector?

At dusk, when the first star appeared in the sky, Jesus headed for Matthew's house. He was alone. The tax collector lived at the end of the fruit vendors' district. There was no other house around his. Nobody wanted to live near him. That was how much we hated the tax collectors in Israel.

Matthew: Come in, stranger. That one peeping out is my wife, Mila.

Jesus: Good evening, Mila.

Mila: Welcome to our house, sir. I mean, ... well, my husband told me you'd be coming, so ... We also invited Captain Cornelius to join us. I hope you won't mind. He's a friend.

Matthew: Hey, stop the small talk, woman! Go finish preparing the eggplant in the kitchen!

Mila: Okay, okay, I'm going.

Matthew: So, you've come alone, huh? Your friends didn't want to soil their sandals by setting foot in my house.

Jesus: Yeah, that's true. They didn't want to come. I told them, but ... but ...

Matthew: That's okay. Worse for them. The less mouths there are, the more food for us. Come on in.

Meanwhile, we gathered in the house of old Zebedee. We were indignant. My mother, Salome, who was always in control, did not prepare soup for us that night.

Salome: Even the rabbi knows about it! What shame! Everyone is talking about us! Wait till I get hold of you, Jesus!

James: There was no way of keeping him from having dinner with that swine.

Peter: I don't quite get it. What would Jesus want from that stinking tax collector?

James: Rather, what would he want from Jesus? There's something fishy here.

Salome: That's right. Something stinks here like rotten cheese.

James: Aren't we gonna do something? Shall we just sit around and do nothing?

Peter: Why don't we just go there and tell him the truth when he leaves? He's gotta have this clear in his head. What do you think, huh? Shall we go near Matthew's place?

At Matthew and Mila's house, the tax collector and his wife had been eating, drinking, and socializing with Jesus and Cornelius.

Matthew: So, the woman is telling this guy: "Yes, I want to take you!" Ha-ha-ha . . . What do you think, huh? Ha-ha-ha . . .

Mila: For heaven's sake, Matthew, will you stop those silly stories.

Matthew: Oh, come on, serve Jesus more meat, and more eggplant too. Look, his plate is empty. You came here to stuff yourself, well, do you understand? No one starves in my house!

Jesus: Well, okay, but that'll be the last. I'm full. You cook very well, Mam Mila.

Matthew: Yes, sir, she's a great cook. That's what Cornelius always tells her, but she never believes it. Of course, for one who is used to being spat at in the street, how can she believe she could do anything good? This wife of mine hides herself in a shell. She fears people. I tell her to ignore them and not mind what they say. Is that right, my friend?! Every one for himself. But she is a very stubborn woman, you know, ha-ha-ha.

Mila: That isn't the point, Matthew. It's just that . . .

Matthew: Shut up! Look Jesus, in my kind of job, when an account I'm working on gets smudged with ink, nothing can remove the stain and it remains there. The same thing happens to us tax collectors. The moment you get into this job, then you're stained forever. But one must get accustomed to it so as not to suffer, like this woman! There is never a day that passes without her shedding tears. She's a cry baby, you know! But this ain't no time for weeping. Attend to Jesus, woman. Let me tell you one more joke. There was a very tall woman who fell in love with a dwarf . . .

Andrew, Peter, James, and I went near Matthew's house. We were seated on the street, and from there, could hear the laughter of the tax collector. We couldn't imagine Jesus behind those walls having dinner with one of Herod's bootlickers. After a while, Eliab, the rabbi, passed by and saw us.

Rabbi: Well, look who's here.

Peter: Hmm...

Rabbi: So, this good friend of yours is now in the company of the tax collector. How come? This morning he was seen drinking with this fellow in the tavern and now he has joined him for dinner at his house. Now, what do you say to this? Or are you also expecting to be invited inside?

That was just what we were waiting for. Peter stood up suddenly and grabbed some stones in the street, and started to hurl them at the windows of Matthew's house.

Peter: Damn this tax collector, as well as you, Jesus, and everyone else!

Mila: Oh my God! What's that noise? Matthew, run!

Matthew: What's happening here? Dammit!

Jesus: Wait here, Matthew, don't leave. Let's go, Cornelius.

Jesus went to the door. Behind him was Cornelius, the Roman captain. At that moment, a stone zoomed between the two.

Jesus: What're you all doing here?

Peter: You, what are you doing here? Dining with that traitor, that leech?

The rabbi, Eliab, wrapped in his black cloak, defiantly approached Jesus.

Rabbi: How dare you break bread with sinners? Everyone in Capernaum is talking about you.

Jesus: Oh yeah? Let them, if they want.

Rabbi: You can't sit at a table with an unclean man.

Jesus: And who's forbidding me to?

Rabbi: The holy law of Moses, and our sacred customs. Are you not aware that he who sits with an unclean man becomes unclean too?

Jesus: Hey, rabbi, are you clean?

Rabbi: What?

Jesus: I'm asking if you're clean. You've lifted a finger against Matthew. Take care that God won't lift his finger against you.

Rabbi: Watch your words, you filthy man! You call me a sinner when I'm a teacher of the law!

Jesus: No, you were the first to call Matthew a sinner and all of us here seated at his table. So, Matthew's a sinner. Fine. People who are well don't need a doctor. Sick people do. Matthew is sick and he knows it. We need to heal him.

Rabbi: You're talking nonsense, you stupid peasant! So you are the doctor? And you've come to cure this poor fellow, Matthew? You are as sick as he is. You listen to me: he who gets into a pigsty becomes like a pig. Now you're as dirty as that filthy tax collector. Aren't you aware of what the Scripture says about that? Don't enter the synagogue without first offering a sacrifice for the forgiveness of your sins.

Jesus: And aren't you aware of what the Scripture says somewhere: "What I want is love and not sacrifice"? The Lord prefers love over penance.

Rabbi: How insolent! Damn you! Someday you're gonna eat your words!

The rabbi spat on Jesus' face. He was so red with rage, the veins in his neck were about to burst. Furiously, he shook his sandals before him and left.

Peter: You've betrayed us, Jesus. We never thought you could do this to us.

James: Once and for all, tell us: Whose side are you on?

Peter: This is all talk: "Things are going to change, things are going to change." And here you are, dining with a traitor and a Roman soldier. Then what?

Jesus: This is what we've been saying all along: people must change. Matthew is the most detested man in Capernaum, and we can be of help to him.

James: You can go to hell, Jesus! All right, do whatever pleases you, but beware of that man. He can throw us all in jail.

Peter: Let's get outta here. Continue your dinner. And may you all choke, damn it!

Jesus and Captain Cornelius went inside Matthew's house again and continued dining with him. We returned to the village without saying a word. As far as I can remember, that was the first serious fight we had with Jesus. We could not comprehend why he had done that, for then, we did not understand that in the Kingdom of God there was a place for a man as despicable as Matthew, the tax collector.

•

The tax collector, aside from being hated by the people, was an outcast. His testimony did not have any juridical value; and in a sense he was like a slave, as he found himself inferior before his countrymen. As a "sinner," he was morally rejected, to the point that the money coming from the tax collector's coffers could not be accepted as alms for the poor, for it was dirty money. Such contempt of the people likewise extended to the tax collectors' families. That Jesus not only befriended one of these men but also dined with him was a grave scandal for the residents of Capernaum. Jesus' friends combined this moral scandal with something political, since Matthew was a collaborator of the Romans.

In order to understand what Jesus did when he dined with Matthew, one must be aware of the fact that among Middle Easterners, to entertain a person and eat with him at the same table is a sign of respect, peace, trust, fraternity, and forgiveness. Sharing food at a table is a sign of sharing one's life. That Jesus dined with Matthew — as he did with other publicans and sinners — was not only a social happening where he manifested his extraordinary humanity or sympathy for despised people. Such a gesture also carried with it a profound theological meaning, as it gave the most meaningful expression of God's love for lost souls. It was a gesture in antic- ipation of the final banquet in history where God will seat at the principal places of his table those whom "decent people" rejected as the last.

The rabbi, the city's guardian of morality, is one of those most seriously scandalized by Jesus' conduct. This is not surprising. A prophet who spoke of God the way Jesus did and also contradicted religious laws at the same time was intolerable. To avoid "sinners" was the greatest obligation of the pious who wanted to please God. The rabbi thought God rejected the sinner and would only take him if he repented and mended his ways. Then and only then would he become the object of God's love: when he reformed himself. Jesus revolutionizes this false religious idea. For God, it is not only the moral aspect that counts. It is more than that. The process is reversed, and it is God who approaches the immoral by showing that person special love and preference. That was then — as it is even today — a scandal, the disintegration of what is "moral." Up to the end of his life,

Jesus would be accused of immoral conduct by decent persons, because he drank and ate with the "publicans and sinners."

The message of the gospel is always an announcement of change. It requires a readjustment in relationships among people leading to genuine equality. Likewise, it requires each and every one to reform attitudes and a thorough change in values, options, and so on.

There should not be any opposition between structural and personal conversion, favoring one person over another. Both aspects of this change-conversion complement each other and are necessarily mutual. The ideal the gospel speaks of is a new man and woman, in a new society.

(Matt. 9:10–13; Mark 2:15–17; Luke 5:28–32)

27

The Lost Sheep

Peter: For God's sake, Jesus, open your eyes! Can't you see? Matthew has been sold to the Romans, a bootlicker of Herod!

Jesus: Matthew is a man, Peter, like you and me.

James: Damn that man and damn you, too! Matthew is a traitor. Tax collectors are traitors, and they gotta be crushed like serpents!

Peter, James, and I stayed with Jesus at the wharf's inn beside the lake. The night before, Jesus was in the house of Matthew, the tax collector of Capernaum, and had dinner with him.

John: Haven't you noticed that this guy, Matthew, is always alone, as if he were a leper? No one in the city wants to be with him or go near him.

Peter: And you know why? Because he stinks and you can smell him miles away.

John: Is he the kind you want in the group, Jesus? What do you really want?

James: I agree with Andrew. If this good-for-nothing creature joins the group, then I'm out. I don't want to be with traitors.

Peter: Neither do I. May the One in heaven cut off my balls if someday I betray my kind!

Jesus: I wouldn't say that you are a traitor, Peter. Who doesn't know that Matthew is a traitor to the country? But, probably, we together can reform Matthew.

John: "Probably...probably..." Or he might spill the beans and get us all killed on account of your imprudence! I'm sorry, Jesus, but you don't have a lick of political talent. You don't even have a sense of smell. No one ever puts a wolf in the midst of sheep.

Jesus: Who ever told you Matthew is a wolf? Wolves are different, John. Matthew used to be like us. I know he's a crook now. But still, he isn't a wolf.

Peter: Oh really? Who then is the wolf?

Jesus: I don't know, but when I saw Matthew seated at that stall, alone, ink-stained, half-drunk, I remembered an ancient story told to me by Joachim when I was a little boy in Nazareth. He told the story like this:

Joachim: There was once a shepherd with a hundred sheep. When the sun rose in the morning the shepherd would get up and lead his flock to the mountain where there was greener grass and cooler water. All his sheep were strong, healthy, clean, and well taken care of, except one who was sickly at birth and had one leg shorter than the others. This sheep was always left behind because she was limping. Ever since she was born she was despised and ignored by everyone. No one ever played or ate with her. Nobody even went near her. She was always alone. One day, as the shepherd and his flock were going to the mountain, it began to rain. The shepherd started to run and his sheep ran after him to return to the fold. The sick sheep tried to run too, imitating her companions, but she couldn't keep up. She would trip, then would rise again, and would fall again. The shepherd and his flock lost their way at the turn of the road. The lightning flashed and the fog blurred the way. The weak sheep got lost, and dragged her lame leg looking for her companions' tracks. But the water washed away the road and she didn't know where she was or which way to follow. She went to and fro and was getting drenched in the rain, and got farther and farther away from the rest. It was getting dark. Meanwhile, the shepherd, followed by his flock, reached the fold. He always made them pass through the hole so he could count them one by one.

Shepherd: ...95...96...97...98...99...What happened? I'm missing one sheep. This can't be. Maybe I counted wrong.

Joachim: And he counted again.

Shepherd: ...95...96...97...98...99...There are only 99 of them! I'm missing one sheep! Maybe it's the sick and limping one. Good Lord, where could that poor creature have strayed?

Joachim: The other shepherds told him, "Hey, don't worry about her. She's sick and can't walk. She's of no use to you. Let her sleep in the open air, or just leave her to the wolves." Evening came, and the lame sheep, alone and lost, continued to go around and around the mountain. She cried but no one responded. She cried louder and louder, but alone in the mountains all she could hear from afar was the howling of hungry wolves. The lost sheep got very scared. She ran without knowing where to go and fell into a ravine. She rolled over sharp rocks doing somersaults, sliding down below, where the earth was muddy. She was beginning to sink. The shepherd was lying on his straw mat and keeping warm. He tried to sleep, but in vain; he was thinking of his lost sheep.

Shepherd: "Mmm ... What a time to get lost on a bad night like this! Why does she always have to be the last? Uff, ... well, what can we do? She asked for it, let her come out of it. I'm going to sleep."

Joachim: The sheep with the broken leg still had a spark of life in her. As she exerted her last effort to get out of the ravine she sank even more. The mud was slowly swallowing her. In the warmth of his hut, the shepherd finally fell asleep. And while he was sleeping peacefully the lost sheep went down, down the dark ravine. The mud covered her mouth and her whole body. She could neither shout nor move. She was dead.

Peter: What happened afterward?

Jesus: Nothing. That's the end of the story.

John: What?

Jesus: Yes, the story's finished.

Peter: But why should it end that way, Jesus? What did the shepherd do? He let her die?

Jesus: Well, the shepherd did what he could.

Peter: What he could! Tell me why he didn't look for the sheep.

Jesus: That's easier said than done, Peter, to go out in the middle of the night during a storm ...

John: Hell, he should've covered himself with a cloak!

Jesus: What about the other sheep, huh? He had to watch over his flock.

Peter: The good-for-nothing was sleeping!

Jesus: He had to take care of the ninety-nine sheep.

John: Bah, they could've been left alone. Didn't you say they were healthy and strong? But the poor, helpless sheep.

Jesus: Well, John, neither was she worth much. After all, she was only one.

John: No, no, no, it's not fair that way, Jesus. That story of yours has left a lump in my throat. I hate the ending.

Peter: So do I.

Jesus: I don't understand you guys, because that's just how you wanted the story to end.

Peter: We? But you were the one who told us the story, dammit!

Jesus: No, you did. You, John, and you too, Peter. So did you, red hair! Fortunately, God has given it another ending. Yes, God tells us the story in a different way. Listen: Once, when the shepherd reached the fold, he began to count his sheep:

Shepherd:....95...96...97...98...99...Well, well, I'm missing one sheep. I gotta go and look for it right away!

Joachim: But his companions told him: "How can you go out in this kind of weather? There's a heavy downpour. It's already night. You won't be able to find her. Anyway, she's only one. Are you gonna leave the ninety-nine behind for this one?" But the shepherd ignored them, took his staff, put on his cloak, and hurriedly left in the midst of darkness to look for the sick and stray sheep.

Shepherd: Starlight! Starlight, where are you? Starlight!

Joachim: He called her by her name. He ran from one side to another, went up and down the mountain shouting at the top of his voice until he was hoarse. He didn't mind the rain, the cold of the night nor his weariness. He was only thinking of his sheep who was in danger. He had to find her before it was too late.

Shepherd: Starlight! Where are you? Starlight!

Joachim: After having looked everywhere there was hardly a tinge of hope left in him, when he heard a bleating from afar. Yes, he knew that voice. Of course, he knew it was her!

Shepherd: Starlight! Starlight!

Joachim: It was his sheep, and she was alive! The shepherd rushed down to the bottom of the ravine and took the sheep. She was out of danger! He then carried her on his shoulders, covered her with his cloak, and returned her to his fold. He bandaged her wounds and lay her beside her sisters on the warm straw mat. That night, the shepherd was so happy that he woke his neighbors up.

Shepherd: My friends, I have found my sheep! I have found my sheep! She was lost and almost dead. But I have found her! Rejoice

with me, my friends! Come, let's all drink to this. I want everybody
to be happy tonight!

John: Well, that's better, dammit. But tell me...

James: Tell me, Jesus, after all is said and done, what's the purpose of
your story, huh?

Jesus: I don't know, James. Sometimes, sometimes I think God will be
happier to see a lost soul like Matthew going back to him and changing
his ways than to see the ninety-nine whom we believe to be good and just.

*Six centuries earlier, the prophet Ezekiel wrote in his book: "Thus says the
Lord: my flock is astray and there is no one to take care of them. That's why I
am here. I myself will take care of my flock and watch over them. I shall take
them from places where they go astray on cloudy and foggy days. I shall look for
the lost sheep and bring back the stray ones, cure wounds, and heal the sick. I
shall lead everyone to the path of justice."*

•

Jesus' friendship with Matthew, the tax collector, creates the first serious
conflict in the apostolic group. The other disciples do not know how to
interpret such a gesture.

If the gospel calls for a radical equality among people, it will necessarily
provoke conflict in society and even within the Christian community. It
is difficult to eliminate such prejudices, to accept the other person as a
brother or sister, and to overcome all types of discrimination. This is a long
process and, sometimes, a painful one. Even if properly channeled, these
pressures may give way to a real crisis of growth and maturity within the
community.

The parable of the lost sheep is one in which Jesus wants to explain
what God is like.

At the outset it is surprising that Jesus compares God's feelings and attitudes with those of a shepherd. Together with the tax collectors and others
of despicable occupation (usurers, money-changers, etc.), the shepherds
were known as people of ill-repute during Jesus' time and were undoubtedly considered among the "sinners." They were suspected of pasturing
their flocks in other people's fields and were believed to be involved in
much cheating and stealing.

Up to the present, it is the custom in Palestine for the shepherd to
count the flock at dusk before putting them into the fold to ensure that no

animal has been lost. The shepherd in Jesus' story has a hundred sheep. At that time, that was an average-sized flock. Among the Bedouins the flocks would ordinarily number between twenty and two hundred animals, consisting of sheep or goats. A herd of a hundred sheep was tended by only one shepherd who, because of his economic situation, could not afford to hire anyone to help him.

On the whole, the data of the evangelical text and the particular detail of a shepherd carrying the sheep on his shoulders make one think that this sheep was an especially weak animal. This is basic in the narration in order to get a picture Jesus makes of God: it is not the worth of the animal which compels the shepherd to look for her. It is enough that the sheep is his own and he loves her for her being handicapped. He also knows her; he is aware that the sheep cannot find her way alone. The good shepherd — says Jesus on one occasion — knows each of his sheep and calls each one by its name (John 10:1–21). This parable deals essentially with God's feeling — the joy of recovering the lost one. Such a feeling of joy will be fully manifest at the end of the story when the day of reckoning comes. God will be happier to announce the salvation of "one lost soul" than that of the many just ones. It hurts to see these erring ones all alone by themselves and being despised all their lives, but Jesus will be immensely happy to have them beside him. Jesus speaks of a joy defining God: that of salvation and forgiveness. He acts in the same manner as God, who has a preference for the weak and the despised. We see God in Jesus' words and works. The whole of Christian theology is embodied in this.

Jesus compares God to a shepherd and says the same of himself. In the gospel of John, Jesus appears as the good shepherd. Such analogies have a lot of antecedents in the Old Testament. The text of the prophet Ezekiel (34:1–31) announcing the messianic times is the most direct source of Jesus' being inspired by this parable. The image of the shepherd carrying his lost sheep on his shoulders is strongly emphasized by Jesus to his apostles. This, together with the fish and the bread, is also the most frequently used symbol of the first Christians. We find this image of the good shepherd in sculptures and sepulchers and on altars and catacomb walls — the image appears wherever the persecuted Christians gathered to pray and celebrate their faith.

(Matt. 18:12–14; Luke 15:3–7)

28

God Is on Our Side

At dawn it rained in Galilee. Dark clouds from Lebanon cloaked the plain of Esdraelon. Lightning, like arrows of fire, flashed through the sky and struck the crown of palm trees. Those were summer storms. We were confined to our houses and patched the roof holes as we awaited the end of the interminable torrent.

It rained the whole morning. The drenched earth could no longer soak up anymore water. Unabated, the clouds let loose their fury.

A Man: I'll be damned! Hailstones! Hailstones!

It was noontime when it cleared up. The crows reappeared and fluttered about the ash-colored lake. All of us fishermen hastily went to shake the wet sails of our boats and stretch the dripping nets. As we left, we heard screams from the fields. The women were running like crazy, lamenting and pulling out their hair. The men followed behind with bowed heads.

A Man: What happened? Why are the women weeping? Who died?
A Woman: The wheat! The wheat is destroyed!

The farmers left their houses and rushed to the fields where the storm had destroyed the wheat due for harvest. The grain had been battered by the violent storm and was scattered on the ground.

A Woman: The wheat's destroyed! The wheat's destroyed!
Another Woman: There won't be any bread for the poor this year!

The whole of Capernaum lamented the crop's loss as though they were mourning a child's death. The artisans, traders, fishermen, and even prostitutes on Jasmine Street all sympathized with the farmers in the fields. If there was no harvest, then no one would have anything to eat.

A Man: Damn this rain! What will become of us now?

187

A Woman: We'll all starve again and be at the mercy of the usurers, or beg on the streets!

Another Woman: Perhaps even sell our souls to the devil!

Peter, James, Jesus, and I were getting drenched among the ruined crops in the midst of those screams. Gradually, we managed to move away from the city. The farmers climbed the hill of the seven fountains and from there gazed at the vast flooded field that could pass for the Sea of Galilee.

A Woman: Ay, what sin have we committed to deserve such misfortune?

Another Woman: It's gotta be the sins of many taken together, because if it's not the rain it's the drought; otherwise it's the increase in taxes or a child getting sick. We're always the losers!

A Man: Look at the result of my labor for these past few months. Everything's lost, all ravaged . . . Dammit, they can bury me on this land, land which is not even mine!

Old Woman: We die with the wheat crops. Oh God, help us!

Another Man: Why do you have to call on God for help? Leave him alone in heaven — he's too busy counting the stars. God doesn't care!

Woman: Let's just accept our fate, my friend. Nothing can be done about it.

Man: Yes, let's be resigned to our fate. But what if my children cry again for bread tomorrow? Shall I tell them to accept this as our fate?

Old Woman: This is life, my son; the life of the poor. We simply bow our heads to accept everything that comes our way.

Man: Well, I can't take this anymore. I've suffered all my life, do you hear? Year after year it's always like this. Until when will this last?

Jesus: Hey, look above you! Look up!

At that moment a rainbow appeared in the sky. Jesus was the first to see it.

Jesus: That is the Lord's arch! It is the sign of peace after the deluge!

Woman: Will you stop that silly talk, stranger? There might be peace in heaven but on earth, all is hunger! Where there is starvation, there are tears and damnation!

Jesus: No, woman. The rain has ceased and so have the tears. Nothing can be solved by weeping and pulling one's hair.

Old Woman: And what else can we do, huh? Before, we had very little; now, we've got nothing. Nothing's left for us to do but weep!

Jesus: No, grandmother, we've got eyes to see the Messiah!

Man: Who'd you say it was? The Messiah? Ha! And where has this young man been hiding, that he doesn't even show his face? Tell the Messiah to hurry up, because, with the way things have been going for us, we might all be dead when we're supposed to welcome him!

Jesus: But he's coming soon! Look at the rainbow, brothers and sisters, God is coming down through it! Our liberation is near!

The people were milling around us. Jesus was beside me. His naked feet were sunk deep in the mud, and his beard was dripping wet. Up above, the rainbow crossed the purified air, bridging heaven and earth.

Jesus: Listen to me, my sisters and brothers: it rained so hard the whole night and day that we thought it would never cease. This was what Noah thought after forty days of heavy rain. But it stopped, and he came out of the ark. Likewise, this was what our ancestors in Egypt thought after four hundred years of suffering and subjugation, but they crossed the Red Sea and were freed. We have also spent four hundred years under oppression. The pharaohs have always crushed us to death like these wheat grains. We were ground into small bits and the flour that came out of our own sweat was made into bread that they ate. All this is over. God will wait no longer, and neither shall we!

Man: Hey, what is this idiot saying? Look, you, are you crazy or what?

Jesus: Neighbors! We have reason to rejoice, in spite of everything!

Old Woman: Are you mad, young man? Why the hell should we rejoice when we've lost everything?

Jesus: We have the Lord, grandmother. We still have him. He's on your side! He's offered his Kingdom to us, understand? To us, who are starving, downtrodden, the losers — to all of us!

The people kept on shoving one another in order to hear what Jesus was saying. The women stopped weeping, squeezing their mud-stained and rain-drenched skirts to dry. The men shook their heads, cynical and sarcastic, but also drew closer to listen to Jesus.

Jesus: Yes, indeed, we have reason to rejoice! Happy are we, the poor, for ours is the Kingdom of God!

An old man wistfully supported his chin with his cane.

Old Man: I think you're playing a joke on us, young man. It's misfortune and not joy to be poor. No one ever goes to the wake to congratulate the dead.

Jesus: Please listen to me, old man. God doesn't commend you for being poor. He will commend you though, by ending your poverty. This includes you and everyone else. A new world is about to begin! The Kingdom of God has come! For us who lament to see our sick and undernourished children, for us who wet the earth with our tears. God's joy shall be for us! Now, we hunger; but on the day of liberation, no one will be wanting in bread or wine. We shall soon eat and drink in his Kingdom, and that will be very soon. We, the hungry, shall receive God's justice!

Woman: "Soon, soon." When will that be? In heaven perhaps? Yes, in the other life, because we will all have perished of starvation!

Jesus: No, we will have no need for food in the other life. This is for our time on earth. The Kingdom of God is coming to this world!

Jesus leaned over and picked up some wet mounds of earth. His eyes sparkled as if he were holding a treasure in his hand.

Jesus: This earth belongs to us. The land, the wheat, and the wine are God's legacy to us, the humble!

Old Woman: Say whatever you like, my son. I'm eighty years old now and have yet to see a hairy frog or a poor person defeating a rich one.

Jesus: That we shall see, old woman, with our own eyes! Have faith. Happy are those whose eyes are pure, for they shall see the coming of the Kingdom on earth!

Some of the men squatted to hear him better. The sun began peeping behind the clouds and was reflected in the pools of water. Despite the havoc done to the crops, it seemed to us that not everything was lost.

Jesus: The Messiah is coming to level the earth. No longer will there be hills or ravines. Nothing shall be high or low. All shall be equal and be brothers and sisters. No one shall have more than the other. Happy are those who share what they have: God will share his Kingdom with them!

Woman: That's what I have always been saying. Goodness! If we were only less selfish we would have lived in peace and without such anguish! But the rich believe the world is all their own and we are what we are now, fighting for a handful of wheat grains while their barns are filled to the brim. Do you think this is right, stranger? Tell me.

Jesus: That's why there can never be peace: because the wealthy's abundance is not shared with those who are always in need. Many talk of peace: their lips utter sweet and beautiful words, yet they steal and kill with their own hands. They talk of peace yet are children of war. God commends not them but the true artisans of peace: those who work for justice, the children of God!

All: Good! Good!

Jesus: The rich are blind. The blind can't see the rainbow's radiance, much less our sufferings, simply because they refuse to see. What ambitious people! They shall be ruined when the time comes. Soon we shall hear them scream just as we have wailed now. They may be laughing now, but soon they shall weep and grieve in excruciating pain when the Lord empties their chests; the Messiah strips them of their rings and robes, starves them and swipes their money the way they did to their workers. Yes, my companions, things will change: the last shall be first and the first shall be last.

All: Good, that's the way to talk!

John: Beware, Jesus. There are so many people here. There will always be a squealer around. We will be accused of troublemaking and...

Jesus: Let them do what they want, John. My friends, when the powerful hate us, when they persecute us in every town and drag us to courts, we must rejoice too! That is always the fate of those who seek justice. Elijah and all the prophets were persecuted and that is why John is still in prison. This doesn't matter though. God commends those who fearlessly speak and risk their lives to defend others. Yes, my friends, let us proclaim all this to the world, for the peasants of Chorazin to hear, for Bethsaida's artisans, for Tiberias's fishermen, and for the prostitutes of Magdala. Let the news spread throughout the valley for everyone to hear, from the fount of Dan to the arid lands of Beer-sheba. God is on our side! He is with us, the poor people; God is fighting on our side!

Jesus said this on the Mount of the Seven Fountains that faces the lakes near Capernaum.

•

The Beatitudes — one of the best-known parts of the gospels — best summarize the fundamental preachings and activities of Jesus: the proclamation of the good news to the poor. The Beatitudes are not a collection of conduct norms (such as "we must" be poor, "we must" be merciful). They are joyful news intended for the poor, the losers, and the oppressed. In order to highlight this aspect of the good news — which is very concrete — and not to reduce the Beatitudes into mere moralizing and abstraction, Jesus in this episode discourses on the Beatitudes in the concrete situation of hopelessness and pain — when the peasants of Capernaum lost all their harvest.

The so-called Mount of Beatitudes or the Mount of the Seven Fountains is situated about three kilometers from Capernaum. Although it is not high — about a hundred meters — one can see the whole Sea of Galilee from its peak in an exceptionally breathtaking view. The Church of the Beatitudes was constructed there in 1937. It has eight walls in memory of the eight Beatitudes as cited in the gospel of Matthew. On various occasions the Beatitudes were adopted as a formula for consolation. Those who weep and suffer from hunger should not despair. God will wipe their tears, feed them, and fill their hearts with joy, up to the world beyond. If everything has been bleak for them on earth, then their fate will change in the afterlife. Such adulteration of the gospel follows from the false interpretation that the Kingdom of God which Jesus proclaims to the poor is equivalent to the Kingdom of "the heavens," as a kind of promise for the next life. The gospel, however, is a historical message. If Jesus calls the poor blessed and tells them to rejoice, it is because they will cease to be poor when the Kingdom of Justice comes on earth. The Beatitudes are already an indication of God's intervention. Hope is proclaimed that a change in history in favor of the oppressed is now under way. The gospel is not a kind of resignation or consolation for the less privileged but a catalyst for commitment, a call to "hold high one's head with the coming of the day of liberation" (Luke 21:28).

Instead of saying: "Happy are you, the poor," Jesus says: "Happy are we, the poor." "We who weep, we who hunger..." Jesus was poor, as poor and oppressed as the people of Capernaum to whom he addressed the Beatitudes. This is too easily forgotten, making Jesus some kind of a religious guru who "makes himself poor," disguises himself, so that the poor will understand him better, making his apostolate a gesture of divine condescension with the suffering people. This is a distortion of not only a portion but the very essence of the gospel. It misrepresents the plan of God, who wished to reveal himself concretely in the person of a humble peasant of Nazareth. In fact, up to this day, God continues to manifest himself in the life and struggle of the poor.

There have been speculations on who these poor people were to whom Jesus addressed the Beatitudes. Much has been said about the "poor in spirit." In Luke it says: Happy are the poor; in Matthew, it is: The poor in spirit. (In other translations we have: Those who know how to be poor, those who opt to be poor.) Surely, Luke's rendition is the most original. Jesus addresses himself to those who actually have nothing, those who suffer hunger. The "spirit" which Matthew added later on is in line with the preachings of the prophets of the Old Testament, who often discoursed on the "humble in spirit," the "downcast in spirit," the *anawim* (the poor). *Anawim,* a key word in biblical texts, corresponds with the unfortunate, the oppressed, the helpless, the hopeless men and women who rely on God's mercy because they are rejected by the rich and powerful. Luke stresses the fact of the poor's external oppression. Matthew, on the other hand, focuses on their spiritual need (which is always present in people suffering from external oppression). Matthew and Luke wrote for different readers. The church addressed by Luke was generally composed of oppressed men and women within the powerful structure of the Roman Empire: slaves and urban people of various social orientation exploited by the harsh conditions of life. Matthew catered to the Jewish church, which was still easy prey to influential thinking of the Pharisees, who taught ideas like: Decent people are good and obey moral laws, and so on. His "poor in spirit" are those who lack morality, the sinners, people of ill-repute. Notwithstanding this difference in nuances, Luke and Matthew successfully get across the prophetic message of Jesus: the Kingdom of God is his gift to the poor of this world. Although Matthew presents us with eight Beatitudes and Luke only four (including his lamentations against the rich), the texts should not be misunderstood as an index handed to us by two different types of people. Both evangelists speak of one and the same reality: "Happy are the poor," and this sums up all the Beatitudes. Everything boils down to this prescription: Happy are the poor because God is on their side. They are not happy because of "their good comportment" but because they are poor. The situation they are in, oppression and exploitation, has earned for themselves God's sympathy. God prefers the poor not because they are "good" but because they are poor. This message of Jesus is absolutely revolutionary. Aside from saying that moral norms as criteria for God's benevolence do not count, the message further states that God puts himself in the context of historical conflicts: the side of people on the bottom of the ladder.

The meaning of the term "poverty" can be distorted. In the Bible, poverty as a state of oppression is a scandalous condition because it is against life. Therefore it is against the will of God. Poverty must be rejected, fought against, and eliminated. It is not fate but the consequence of human abuse of others. The Christian attitude toward poverty must be that of God: reject it and show a preference for the poor. It is an option which does not end in mere denunciation and words of condemnation. The old Mosaic laws were not mere words; they were social laws intended to avoid poverty and defend the poor. Every effort to fight and suppress poverty is therefore a step toward promoting the Kingdom of God even if those who are involved in it do not believe in God or in Jesus.

Therefore, poverty should not be introduced as a Christian ideal. To opt for poverty — in present-day situations of injustice being experienced in various countries — becomes a Christian preference only when it is in solidarity with the poor in their struggle against poverty. Taken in another light, poverty shall be understood as "infancy" before the Lord: such as the attitude of humility, with no power, with no aspirations. This "poverty-infancy" tandem is in line with this biblical interpretation. However, it is obvious that a person who accumulates wealth and privilege at the expense of others shall never be poor in this sense if he or she does not first rid her- or himself of wealth and power.

(Matt. 5:1–12; Luke 6:20–26)

29

The Poor Man's Wheat

It was Saturday when the hailstorm destroyed the wheat crops that were about to be harvested. In Israel, Saturday is a day of rest. Women do not light their stoves, nor do men go to the field. The seventh day of the week is consecrated to God. But that Saturday was not a day of rest for us. We were gathered on the Mount of the Seven Fountains facing the lake together with the farmers from Capernaum who had lost their harvest.

A Man: This year's gonna be very bad. It's gonna be a year of hunger.

An Old Woman: Everything's gone. The storm did it all!

Another Man: Not all, old woman. Eleazar's farm wasn't totally destroyed, and he has plenty of wheat.

A Man: Phanuel's farm was also spared. Those rascals own so much land and their barns are so numerous that not even heaven can destroy them.

Another Man: The rich always land on their feet like cats. They're never losers. Now they'll increase the price of flour to that of gold!

Woman: Are they trying to kill us?

Man: What else can we do but tighten our belts? We can't go against the will of heaven!

Old Woman: But we can do something about the hoarders.

Man: Really? And what can we do? Shall we confront them on their farms?

Old Woman: Why not? What did our ancient laws say? That the poor may gather the excess on the rich men's farms so no one goes hungry in Israel.

Man: Old Deborah is right. Moses commanded the rich to give away excess food that the less fortunate might have something to eat.

195

Woman: Did Moses really say that? Then let the law of Moses be fulfilled, dammit!

The wife of a farmer named Ishmael made the last statement. After she spoke, everyone looked at each other indecisively. The men scratched their heads while the women whispered among themselves.

Woman: What are we waiting for? Didn't the stranger from Nazareth and all of you say that God's on our side and that things are heading for change? Why don't we give him a little push so that things will change soon? Let's gather the grains in Eleazar's farm!

Man: Yes, let's all go!

Old Woman: Hold it, hold it! All right, we all go there, but without haste and without making trouble. This was how Moses led the Israelites through the desert. It's much better to claim justice the right way!

All: That's very well said, grandmother! Let's go, everybody.

With Ishmael's wife and old Deborah at the lead, we all started to go down the hill and headed toward the vast tract of land starting from north of the Seven Fountains. We passed through miles of fertile land owned by the powerful Eleazar.

Man: Are you all out of your mind? Where are we headed? This can't be!

Woman: And why not?

Man: How can we slip freely into his farm?

Woman: This miser Eleazar has all his barns filled with the previous harvest.

Man: Yes, but...

Woman: No more buts. This man has more than enough!

Man: While we have nothing! Come on, everybody, let's all go! In the name of God!

We were like an army in tatters. We went splashing through the fields, sliding down the muddy slope as we approached the posts that marked Eleazar's property. The storm had been so strong, it had destroyed some of the crops, but the farm was so huge, grain lay scattered here and there, undestroyed.

Man: Look, there is still so much wheat left!

Old Woman: Let's start! And don't you worry; Ruth started this way. See how well it turned out for her in the end.

We dispersed through the inundated wheat fields, like ants swarming in confusion after a storm. We were all covered with mud up to our knees. Then we started to cut the sturdy stalks that had withstood the violent storm. The men took out their knives and began to harvest. Behind them were the women who were gathering the wet wheat in their skirts.

Old Woman: Gather all you can! Everything! Fill your skirts with whatever you gather!

Man: Listen, old woman, aren't we doing something wrong?

Old Woman: Oh, my son, I don't know, but they say that a thief who steals from another thief is forgiven for one hundred years.

Man: And what do you say to this, young man from Nazareth?

Jesus: Well, I think we've got to ... oh!

Man: Be careful, Jesus!

Jesus slid and fell on his butt into the mud pool. When we saw him, his face was covered with mud, and we all laughed boisterously.

Man: Hey, man, don't eat the soil!

Woman: This stranger looks just like Adam when God created him in paradise!

Jesus laughed as well, as if someone had tickled him. His tunic was wet and he was supporting himself on a few rocks. Finally, he managed to get himself out of the mud pool.

Jesus: What a life, my friends. ... A while ago, we were all weeping, now we're laughing. And how things change. We can change things with the help of our hands, with God's hand supporting us. Yes, we can move on! Tomorrow, everything will be different. We shall rid ourselves of the present pains, and there'll be no more tears nor screams. We'll all be happy and God'll be happy, too, because he's on our side. God'll lend a hand and will help us build a new world out of this old clay.

We continued pulling the stalks. Jesus was gathering beside me, and I remember him still laughing over his fall. Peter, James, and Andrew were helping a group of farmers who had penetrated the inner part of the farm.

When we had finished cutting enough wheat, Eleazar's foremen arrived. They were rushing toward us, with poles and hunting dogs.

Foremen: Thieves, thieves!

There was great confusion. Most of us were able to jump over the posts with our arms and the women's skirts full of wheat. Others left the wheat and their sandals, fleeing like scared rabbits, leaping from one mud pool to another. Some of us went back, to face Eleazar and his men.

Eleazar: Who concocted this plot against my farm? Who gave you the right to steal from my property?

Woman: We came here in the name of God!

Eleazar: Oh really? Or could it be in the name of the devil? He who steals is the devil's brood!

Man: He who sucks the blood of his laborers like you do is father to the devil!

Eleazar: You shut up or be beaten up! This way you'll learn how to respect the law, you thieves!

Man: We weren't stealing. Why call us thieves?

Eleazar: So you're not stealing. What do you call it then? I caught you with your hands in my wheat, pulling up the few stalks that were left after the storm. And you say you're not thieves!

Woman: We ain't no thieves. We simply obeyed God's law.

Eleazar: Shut up, you big mouth! Don't you ever mention the name of God with your filthy lips!

Eleazar's men forced us to return to one of the yards of Eleazar's house. With him were his two friend scribes, Abiel and Josaphat.

Abiel: I tell you, Master Eleazar, you gotta find out who's behind this conspiracy, who the mastermind is.

Eleazar: Who're your leaders, huh? Who advised you to steal from my property?

Old Woman: It's hunger. Yes, we're dictated by hunger. We need wheat for our children!

Eleazar: So? If you weren't so lazy, you wouldn't experience hunger. Hunger comes from laziness!

Woman: It's the result of people's greed, people like you!

Eleazar: If you shout at me again, I'll have your tongue and hands cut off! But what's got into your head? You think I'll allow such a brazen act in broad daylight like this? I'll inform the Roman captain, and you won't leave jail without paying damages. You all hear me?

Jesus, who was quiet until then, replied to the landowner.

Jesus: Aren't you contented with the wheat that is kept rotting in your barns? And you still want to deprive us of the excess grain that you have?

Eleazar: And where did this young man get such temerity? Well, you listen, stranger: I'm gonna kick you and the rest right into jail!

Jesus: Then you'll have to put King David in prison too.

Josaphat: What did this damned fellow say?

Jesus: I said David did something worse than what we did, yet David became a great saint.

Abiel: What nonsense are you talking about? What has King David got to do with this?

Josaphat: With whom do you think you are talking, peasant? We're teachers of the law from the school of Ben-Sira.

Jesus: Well, if you're really teachers, then you'll remember David and his companions. They were hungry, and entered not into the farm but the temple of God, where they ate the consecrated bread on the altar. Do you realize that? God didn't punish them for having stolen bread because they were hungry. A starving human being is more sacred than the holy temple of the Almighty!

Josaphat: Oh dammit! What's this insolent talking about? Your own words betray you. You must be their leader. Go tell the tribunal your story about King David, so you'll get the beatings you deserve!

Woman: We only got what belonged to us, according to Moses!

Eleazar: Shut up, you bitch! All this is mine and nobody else's. Do you hear? All this land extending down to the Waters of Merom belongs to me and nobody can take even a single grain of wheat from it!

Jesus: We have taken only a few stalks while you have stolen the whole land, which is worse. The Scripture says that the land belongs to God and nobody can take possession of it. You're the thief, not us.

Eleazar: I'm getting impatient, you thieves! I was the one being robbed, yet you expect me to bear your impertinence?

Abiel: And the worst thing is they did it today.

Josaphat: Today is the Sabbath, a holy day. These people have violated the law on two counts: by stealing and working on the Sabbath. Do you realize the crime that you've committed against the sacred law of God?

Jesus: The law is made for people, not people for the law. If you really understood the law, you wouldn't accuse us of any crime. The first law that God commands of us is: We should have enough in order to live.

All: Dammit! That was very well said!

Eleazar: Enough of this silly talk! We shall all go to the synagogue right now and let the tribunal hear you!

The noisy crowd was getting bigger. Several farmers, men and women alike who were waiting outside the farm, joined us on our way to the city. The landowner and the scribes advised the Roman soldiers to maintain order and to take us to the synagogue, where the teachers of law would judge what we did.

•

This episode is in a way related to the previous account. Jesus proclaims that God is on the side of the poor — that he suffers and struggles with them. Jesus puts into practice the message of this proclamation, and the poor who believe in it rely on him for the consequences as they move on to realize their liberation. The gospel is not merely words of liberation but deals with the act of liberating being undertaken by Jesus' followers. At the same time, in our communities the gospel cannot end up with mere accusations, with mere words. It should be translated into concrete action — organization, commitment, struggle — inspired by the message of Jesus.

The culture of the Mediterranean, where Palestine is located, is a "wheat culture." In Central America, the culture of the Mayas and the Aztecs is a "corn culture." Similarly, we speak of the culture of various tropical countries as "banana cultures" or "rice cultures." Wheat was the principal crop of Palestine and constituted the bulk of agricultural provision to the cities. Famine corresponded to scarcity of wheat.

Galilee was known for the quality of its wheat. In the fields around the lake as well as in Capernaum, there were vast wheatfields, mostly owned by a few landowners. Feudal estates were common in the north. One of the goals of the zealot movement was agrarian reform, which earned the sympathy of the farmers and the small landowners. On the other hand, the big landowners collaborated with the Romans, who assured them of retaining ownership of vast tracts of land.

When the first tribes of shepherds came to Israel, land was distributed among families, according to the area they occupied. The ownership of land was a family inheritance, and, from the religious point of view, God was considered the owner of all land (Lev. 25:23). To go beyond the limits of family patrimony was a violation of the will of God. Nevertheless, in Jesus' time and before his time, there were big landowners who on various occasions acquired lands by putting fraudulent landmarkers on their farms (Job 24:2). The prophets repeatedly denounced these economic trends (Isa. 5:8; Hos. 5:10), which were further encouraged during the period of Roman domination. From the economic point of view, the most tangible consequence of the Roman occupation was the process of extending feudal property at the expense of communal ownership. This led to the rapid impoverishment of the small farmers, who then became hired laborers in the service of wealthy landlords.

To stop this greed, there were laws in Israel limiting property ownership and excessive accumulation of the same: the Year of Grace, the Sabbatical Year. There were other laws to protect the poor, the orphans, the widows, and the foreigners according to which the landowners had to yield part of their harvest and surplus products from their farms and trees (Lev. 19:10; Deut. 24:19–22). The residents of Capernaum pulled the wheat grains on a Sabbath day. The law of the Sabbath was the core of the legal system in Israel in Jesus' time. A willful violation of this law, and after a first warning, was sufficient reason for a death sentence. The law of the Sabbath prohibited any type of work or effort on this sacred day. Just as Jesus proclaimed, in his time, the supremacy of people over the law of the Sabbath, we Christians must proclaim with the same strength the social meaning of ownership (property) in the manner Pope John Paul II formulated it when he spoke of "the social obligation of ownership."

The most ancient tradition of the church has pointed out that when a poor person, out of necessity, takes what is an excess from a rich one, that person should not be rebuked nor be considered a thief. A thief is one who takes what the other needs. On the question of what is "mine" and what is "yours," St. Basil said to the rich and the powerful: "Tell me, which things are yours? You took them from somewhere and here you are claiming them as yours? You claimed as your own what used to be property of all. Now, who is the thief? What other name can you give to someone who does not clothe the naked when he can very well do it? You refuse to give bread to the hungry; you hide in your chest the cloak to clothe the naked, and you let the sandals rot in your house rather than give them to the barefoot" (Homily *Destruam*).

The peaceful, mass action undertaken by the residents of Capernaum to fight for their basic right to life is supported by the ancient Mosaic law. Jesus was similarly inspired in justifying the above by citing the episode of King David in the sanctuary of Nob (1 Sam. 21:1–7), where he took the consecrated bread so that he and his men would have something to eat. The great freedom with which King David acted was the same style that Jesus would always resort to, in order to show how a law became worthless if it was oppressive to people and to life. St. Paul would later on say that the law of the Christians is no other than the law of freedom (Gal. 5:1–18).

(Matt. 12:1–8; Mark 2:23–28; Luke 6:1–5)

30

The Withered Hands

Eleazar, the landlord, caught us picking the heads of wheat on his farm after the storm destroyed the crops in Capernaum. The scribes who were his friends dragged us into the synagogue to judge our act. It was still the day of the Sabbath.

Abiel: Go inside, you band of rascals!
Josaphat: Now let's see what you have to say to the rabbi. Thieves, bandits!
Abiel: Come on, and make the guilty ones pay!

Although the synagogue had a number of wide entrance doors, many people had to climb through the windows in order to get in. They didn't want to miss anything in that altercation. Half of Capernaum was there. The rabbi, who was getting impatient, walked from one side to another, without looking at us.

Abiel: Rabbi Eliab, these men here have instigated the people to steal wheat from Eleazar's farm.
Josaphat: They trespassed onto somebody else's property!
Abiel: If they had only been ordinary thieves, we wouldn't have brought them to you! They stole on the day of the Sabbath! They've desecrated the law of Moses.
Rabbi: Oh? And that's why they're here? May I know why you did it?
A Man: Because we're hungry!
All: That's right!
Rabbi: Silence! Only one will speak!
A Man: We've lost our crops, rabbi. We need food.
A Woman: Our children will starve to death!
Rabbi: Quiet, all of you! I said only one must speak! Let's see, you, come over here! Yes, you!

The rabbi grabbed Nito by his tunic sleeve. He was the son of Anna, a good but not very bright boy.

Rabbi: Answer me: Did you break into the farm of landlord Eleazar to get some wheat?

Nito: Yes, rabbi!

Rabbi: That farm belongs to Eleazar, did you know that?

Nito: Yes, rabbi.

Rabbi: If a farm belongs to somebody, its harvest belongs naturally to him. Did you know that?

Nito: Everybody knows that, rabbi.

Rabbi: Then why did you steal wheat which isn't yours?

Nito: Because I was hungry, rabbi.

Rabbi: But the wheat belongs to Eleazar.

Nito: It is I who was hungry, rabbi.

Rabbi: Come here, rascal. What right have you to go into somebody else's property and steal what is not yours? Come on, answer me.

Nito: Well, because, . . . pardon me, rabbi, what did you say?

Rabbi: Excuses, excuses. That is all you can do, come up with excuses. You do something wrong, after which you deny having done it.

Nito: But I did go, rabbi. All of us here slipped into his farm to pick some heads of wheat. I picked several of them.

Rabbi: Oh, really? So you brazenly took what wasn't yours?

Nito: Well, of course. In fact, after this, I'll go back to gather some more.

A Woman: Eleazar has a lot of wheat on his land, while we don't have any!

John: God can't allow people to starve to death while others live with a full stomach!

Rabbi: This is out of control. We're in the synagogue, in a sacred place! Besides, today is the Sabbath, a holy day! What's happening here?

Abiel: Rabbi Eliab, this group of fishermen were the ones who instigated the people. Apparently, this stranger from Nazareth has put some crazy ideas into their heads.

One of the scribes with a bony body pointed an accusing finger at us. Then he stared at Jesus, who looked so relaxed, as if nothing was happening at all.

Rabbi: What have you got to say, Nazarene? Did you start all this trouble?

Jesus: People will do anything when they have an empty stomach.

Rabbi: Listen to me, you insolent farmer. This country has laws that must be obeyed, you hear? And what does the law say, huh? Do not steal! Do you hear?

Jesus: What about the man who hoards wheat on his farm, isn't he a thief too, rabbi?

Rabbi: The law says: Do not steal. Do you understand? *Do no steal!*

Jesus: And the one who pays very low wages, isn't he a thief, too?

Rabbi: That's enough! You're all guilty for having violated the law. Furthermore, you did it on the day of the Sabbath. What does the law say about this? You shall observe the Sabbath as a sacred day. You will work for six days, but the seventh day shall be a rest day, which is dedicated to the Lord. That is what the law says. Is that clear?

Jesus: But God made the law for people, and not people for the law.

John: That was very well said!

Rabbi: Shut up, damn you! Speak only when asked!

A Man: You better keep quiet, John — this is getting complicated and dangerous.

Rabbi: What do you want, huh? Do you want to put an end to everything and destroy the laws that Moses gave us?

Jesus: On the contrary, rabbi. We don't want to destroy them but to give them real meaning.

The rabbi was already very furious, but he tried to control himself.

Rabbi: Brothers, sisters, please ignore this stranger who's here to cause trouble and confuse you. You have done something terrible, which I hope will not be repeated. You have violated the law of the Sabbath, which is the work of God. You are fully aware that when the shadows cover the walls of the city on the eve of the Sabbath, you are commanded by the law to shut all doors in the whole of Israel until the end of the sacred day. The Sabbath is a day of rest. No one's allowed to make any purchases, any sale, not even to walk more than a mile. No one's to transport wheat, wine, grapes, or any merchandise. No one's to lift weights, to cook.

The law of the Sabbath was so rigid, its prohibitions so numerous, that when the rabbi started to cite the interminable list of "don'ts" of the law, we felt as if the yoke of the oxen rested on our shoulders. We breathed a sigh of relief when Eliab had finished. Then Jesus broke the silence.

Jesus: I wish to ask you teachers of the law a question: What if the only sheep you had fell into a pit on the day of the Sabbath. Would you not pull it out, even if it was forbidden by law? What is allowed to be done on the Sabbath: The good or the bad? To save life or to lose it? What do you think, gentlemen?

There were whispers of approval from everyone present, and this gradually heightened like a rising tide.

A Man: Jesus is right! He explains things better than the rabbi!
Abiel: This is getting us nowhere, Rabbi Eliab. This man's dangerous, and you have to teach these people a lesson.

Then the scribe with the bony body extended his arms like a bird about to fly and fixed his eyes on us.

Josaphat: Thieves! Charlatans! God will punish you for what you've done on a Sabbath day! Thieves! God'll paralyze your hands, because they've offended him by stealing! The Lord's curse'll be on you, who're violators of the law! Your hands'll all be paralyzed!

The screaming voice of the scribe shook the synagogue and made us all tremble. Then there was a commotion in one corner, at one end of the temple. Everyone turned to see what was happening.

A Man: Hey, rabbi, here's one whose hand's already withered, but he's not a thief!
Asaph: I am an honest man! I wasn't involved in that stuff!
A Woman: He's always had this disease. It's an old one. The scribe's making a new curse.

Asaph, the fruit vendor, had had his right hand paralyzed for many years. When he saw that everyone was looking at him, he wanted to hide himself and leave the synagogue, but the bony scribe wouldn't let him go.

Josaphat: Hey, you, with the withered hand! Don't hide yourself. Come here, to the center!

Everyone around him pushed Asaph to the center of the synagogue. His face was all red.

Josaphat: Do you see this man? Do you see him well? Same way, God will paralyze the hands of those who have stolen wheat. The Lord's curse is on you!

His voice echoed like thunder. Then there was silence afterward. Everyone expected lightning to strike the roof of the synagogue and burn our hands. We heard Jesus' voice instead.

Jesus: It's the Sabbath, Josaphat. It's also prohibited to curse on this day. Don't ask for God's malediction. God never does anything evil on Sabbath nor on any other day of the week. You claim to be an authority on the Scriptures, yet you're wrong. God didn't make the law to be a burden to people and to crush them. God wants everyone to be free, so they won't become slaves of the law. God won't paralyze our hands. On the contrary, he'll make them free so that they can continue with their struggle and with their work, just as he will cure the hand of this man. Asaph, extend your hand!

Asaph, the fruit vendor, stretched his arm and began to move it. There was great uproar. We all rushed toward him to touch his hand and to see if what we had witnessed was true.

A Woman: Praise the Lord! Never before have we seen anything like this!

A Man: If this ain't the end of the world, then it's gotta be the eve!

The rabbi, who was very indignant, shouted from the lectern.

Rabbi: All of you, get out of the synagogue! You've desecrated the temple of God! Out, out you go!

Neither the scribes nor the rabbi succeeded in driving us out of the synagogue. There were so many of us, and pandemonium was such that it was impossible to drag us out. The good news about the healing of Asaph spread through the whole valley of Galilee like wind blowing through the trees. From that day on, the teachers of the law began to plot against Jesus.

•

The Israelites gathered every Saturday in the synagogue in order to pray and worship the Lord. It was there that Jesus and his companions were judged for having violated the law of the Sabbath, which was a day of rest. Jesus' words and actions before the rabbi and the people stress that in order to worship God truly, one must take into account the liberation of the poor.

The Israelites trace the law of the Sabbath back before the time of Moses, to the very designs of God's creation. Tradition has it that God created people on the sixth day, after which he set the seventh day as a day of rest. This order of creation indicates — as Jesus himself has said — that "God made the law for people," that is, for good. Jesus considers this precept about the Sabbath as God's gift to human beings, a gift of free time, that people might not be enslaved by work. Jesus has rejected as a burden for the people the tradition and customs perpetuated by the rabbis and Pharisees for generations.

The traditional concept of the Sabbath became tedious on account of the "do's" and "don'ts" that people had to observe on that day. In Jesus' time, there were thirty-nine types of work listed as prohibited — the one exception when the law could be relaxed was when one had to save a life. Jesus was not satisfied with this as the only exception and rebelled against this uptightness as contrary to the will of God.

Christianity in other contexts has sometimes been reduced to a mere catalogue of laws which are not necessarily intended to liberate but to suppress. The ideal of Christian life has at times been equated with the scrupulous fulfillment of negative norms: "You cannot..." "It is prohibited..." "God will punish you if you do this..." This is a terrible caricature of religion and an attitude that is wholly anti-Christian. Jesus always puts people above any law.

A Christian, by definition, is a free person before the law.

Jesus was a constant violator of the principal laws of his time. That is why he was a rebel in the eyes of the teachers and lawmakers of his town. Judging him on this basis, we would say they were right. When Jesus insisted through his words and actions that the Sabbath was made to protect people's needs and not to suppress them, he was making an interpretation contrary to common practice. Any law that suppresses a person and does not allow him or her to live has no value whatsoever.

The rabbi was the religious authority in the community. In this episode, there were two teachers: the doctors or theologians and Jesus. The mission of the former was to interpret the laws and to monitor their implementation. They acted as faithful allies of the landlord and defenders of his interests, as justified by the religious law of the Sabbath. What Jesus did for Asaph, the fruit vendor, by healing his paralyzed hand, brought home a point that a curse with which a false religion threatens a person cannot win over the grace of God who wants people to live and be free.

This episode is related to the two previous narratives. The sign that God makes through Jesus strengthens the proclamation of liberation through the Beatitudes. He blesses the liberating action carried out by the poor people of Capernaum. The three chapters constitute a triptych-summary of a catechetical scheme often repeated in the gospel: proclamation-practice-sign.

(Matt. 12:9–14; Mark 3:1–6; Luke 6:6–11)

31

The Story of the Sower

In those days, Jesus was already popular in Capernaum. The people sought after him to listen as he spoke about the Kingdom of God. I think they also came to listen to his stories since he had a knack for storytelling. We who belonged to the group became more excited each day.

Peter: This is it! The people are beginning to open their eyes.

James: I told you, Peter, this brown one from Nazareth's very smart. I always thought that with him, we'll go far.

Peter: Hey, guys, why don't we go to the wharf? We'll all roast to death here inside! Let's go, Jesus!

We left Peter's house when the sun was about to drown itself to the lake. The heat was terrible that day. There was not even a breath of air in our midst. We sat at the lakeshore beside the wharf, awaiting the cool afternoon breeze. Suddenly, old Gaspar, his wife, the twins from the big house, and my father, Zebedee, appeared with Samuel, the limping one, and a number of fishermen.

A Woman: Hey, you from Nazareth. You spoke with firmness in the synagogue the other day. Come on, tell us in all honesty, you can trust us. What are you really up to?

Jesus: Not I, neighbor, but the One from up there.

Woman: What do you mean the One from up there?

Jesus: That's right, God is weary of waiting and said: "Be prepared, because my turn has come."

A Man: God said that?

Jesus: Yes he did, and cast the seed in the air.

Man: What seed are you talking about? You?

Jesus: What else but the seed of the Kingdom, my friend.

Woman: We ain't getting nowhere. Not even Solomon can understand you!

Jesus: That the Kingdom of God has come, my companions! There's no need to wait anymore. It's already in our midst!

Woman: If it's true, then where is it? At least I should see it around.

Jesus: Nor do you see the wind, but it blows. The sun eagerly reflects its rays even if it hasn't risen from behind the mountains. The Kingdom of God is like that. You don't have to look above or below you. Nor do you have to go far looking for it, for it's just around you. It's in our midst! In everybody's midst. Where there are two or three of us who want a change, then the hand of God is there!

Men: If that's so, then count my fingers and my hands, and everybody else's! You'll find out how many we are!

Jesus: Yes, we're a considerable number now. I just hope we won't have the same fate as my uncle in Nazareth.

Another Man: What happened to him?

Jesus: To my uncle, Jonathan, and...

Peter: Hey, we can't hear anything from here! Speak louder, dammit!

More and more people gathered at the lakeshore. They came from their houses, sweating after a long day's work. Even the men who were drinking in the tavern came closer.

Jesus: As I was saying, this uncle of mine, Jonathan...

Peter: Not even Joshua's trumpet can silence the people. It's a big crowd we have here.

James: And damn this heat!

Peter: Listen, red hair. I've got an idea. Why don't we move in to Gaspar's boat. We give it a little push and from the water we'll be able to see the people better and everybody can hear. What do you say, Jesus?

Jesus: Are you out of your mind, Peter? Why do we all have to go into the lake?

Peter: Don't tell me you're scared of the water, brown on.

Jesus: No, well... but... this water is already a little murky.

James: To hell with these farmers! They're even more scared of the water than the cats are!

Peter: Come on, forget all this fuss and let's go to the boat. Unfasten the rope and stretch it a few cubits!

James, Peter, and I went with Jesus on Gaspar's boat, staying a little way from the shore.

One Woman: Where the hell are you all going?

Peter: We aren't going anywhere, lady. We're just looking for a better place. With this noise, we won't understand each other. Go ahead, Jesus, with your story about your uncle Jonathan.

Jesus: You see, my uncle Jonathan went out every summer to sow his little piece of land, just like all the farmers did. I was a little boy then when this happened, but I remember when one day I saw him cross the village carrying a sack of seeds on his shoulders, and I ran after him.

> *Little Jesus:* Uncle Jonathan! Uncle Jonathan! Wait for me, uncle!
>
> *Jonathan:* And where's this little brat going in such a big hurry?
>
> *Little Jesus:* I'm going with you, Uncle, so you can teach me how to sow.
>
> *Jonathan:* Oh? So you want to learn how to till the soil instead of being a carpenter like your father? Very well then; I'll teach you to be a good farmer. Come, little boy, let's begin on that end. I'll teach you how to scatter the seeds and sing the planting songs. Listen . . . La, la, larara . . .

Jesus: So we reached the small farm. Uncle Jonathan and I passed through the posts marking the land. Then he slipped his big brawny hand inside the sack, took a handful of seeds, and threw them at random.

> *Jonathan:* This is good seed, my boy! May God bring the rains soon that the bushes may take root well!

Jesus: He took another handful again and threw the seeds into the air.

> *Little Jesus:* Hey, Uncle, the seeds are coming out from the sack.
>
> *Jonathan:* What're you saying, snot-nose?
>
> *Little Jesus:* I said some of the seeds are falling from the sack. Look, Uncle, there!
>
> *Jonathan:* Of course my son; that always happens. Some seeds fall on the other side of the posts while some fall along the path.
>
> *Little Jesus:* Do you pick them up again, Uncle?
>
> *Jonathan:* No, my boy. Don't waste your time on that. Leave them for the birds so they can have something to eat, the poor creatures. Come, keep on walking. In a short time, the sun'll be up and we'll be sweating like pigs. La, la, larara . . .

Jesus: Then, when I was already grown-up, I began to liken some people to those seeds that fall along the borders of the farm. It reminds me that one has to work hard so that this world will be just. These seeds also remind me of people who are indifferent, who don't care about others, but think only of themselves. Their hearts are calloused and dry, as dry as the soil along the roads. The Kingdom of God cannot thrive there.

Jonathan: Now, my boy, slip your hand into the sack and take all the seeds that you can and cast them into the air, like I do. Do it firmly, dammit! Haven't you eaten yet?

Little Jesus: I have, Uncle. I drank a jug of milk before coming here.

Jonathan: You gotta prove that to me. Come on, throw the seeds far and away! That's it! No, not over there. What are you doing?

Little Jesus: Why not, Uncle?

Jonathan: You rascal! Can't you see those thistles? If you sow along this part where the bushes grow, and since the thistles grow taller than the bushes, then the plants choke and die. Remember that, little boy. Come on, don't doze off. We got lots of work to do. La, la, larara . . .

Jesus: When I grew up, I thought that money and the easy life were the thorns growing by our side. There are people who talk a lot about justice and they firmly agree with my thought. They want so many changes for the world, and beautiful words fall from their lips. But when they're asked to share what they have with their neighbors, they have a change of heart, and they shy away. Yes, my friends, money's the bad seed that's in conflict with the Kingdom of God.

Little Jesus: Here, Uncle, look! There ain't no thorns here. Gimme a handful to sow along this part!

Jonathan: Yes, my boy, this is good soil. But don't be deceived. You gotta be very careful, as you can never be sure. Come, put a piece of stick here.

Little Jesus: Where?

Jonathan: Here, remove the soil. Dig a little.

Little Jesus: Hold it, Uncle. Hey, these are rocks! And there are plenty of them!

Jonathan: That's why, my boy, you shouldn't be too trusting. Those seeds you have sown will grow, but when the summer heat comes and the soil is not very deep the seeds will not grow roots, and the young plants will get scorched and wither. Come, my son; we have to move fast or else the sun will fry our heads too. La, la, larara...

Jesus: In time, I thought that the seeds that fell on rocky ground were like people who really want to do something for others, and so start out with enthusiasm and hard work, but later, when problems come their way, when the powerful try to stop them and begin throwing people in jail, putting their lives in danger, then they lose heart and back out. These people don't have good roots.

Little Jesus: What about this part, Uncle?

Jonathan: Yes, here, my boy. Look at this soil; it's black and fertile, like that dark girl in the Song of Songs. Yes, this will give good harvest!

Little Jesus: Shall I sow the seeds, Uncle?

Jonathan: Why, of course, son! And use both hands! Come on, move fast! And do it with enthusiasm, dammit, because this land will yield plenty, I assure you! La, la, larara...

Jesus: This is the good soil that produces good people: those who have a big heart, those who get involved with people in spite of their fears, those who risk their lives and their money, working tirelessly to give their children and their children's children a world different from ours. These are the kind that God needs for his Kingdom!

Jonathan: Pff... There ain't no more seeds left, my boy. The earth is full of seeds. You gotta take care of 'em so that they won't perish. In a few days, God willing, and with the rains, everything'll be covered with young plants. And in a few months, they're gonna be as tall as the bushes, with sunlight and rain cultivating the grains. You'll see, snot-nose, how beautiful this farm will become... Some bushes will produce heads that yield thirty grains, others sixty, and still others yield a hundred grains. Yes sir!

Little Jesus: I'll go with you on that day, Uncle.

Jonathan: But of course. We gotta leave early, after a good shot of wine to give us strength. After which comes the time for harvesting, as the Lord has set it!

Little Jesus: Are you gonna teach me how to cut the crops, Uncle?

Jonathan: Sure, I'm gonna teach you how to cut and sing. I see how willing you are to work, although apparently, music isn't your cup of tea! Come on, listen to me closely, and sing with me. La, la, larara...

Jesus: Yes, my friends, let's all open our ears and listen to the story of the sower! Everyone must look inside to see which soil one is like!

It was night already when Jesus finished talking. The tide was beginning to rise and the boat we were in was moving gently. The people returned to their houses, whispering among themselves on the road. We returned to the wharf and stayed a little while talking with Jesus. At night, after a long and hot day, the wind began to blow over the vast round Sea of Galilee.

•

The parables are perhaps the texts in the gospel where we can "hear" Jesus most faithfully and "see" the environment where he grew up and developed himself. In the parables where he makes use of farm images, we see Jesus the peasant, who was used to working on the farm since childhood. To sow the seeds randomly, despite a chance of wasting, would apparently reflect the lack of skill of the sower. But that isn't so. The parable of the sower describes in detail the usual manner of planting crops in Palestine. This parable corresponds — like that of the mustard seed — to the beginning of the gospel preaching. In telling this story, Jesus manifests his unlimited trust in the Lord who, in the end, despite the usual losses and difficulties that accompany this agricultural activity, will provide the sower with abundant harvest at least on a piece of land. Jesus is so confident that this will happen, and so great is his joy over God's plan, that he exaggerates the final yield to a large extent. He speaks of a yield of thirty, sixty, and even a hundredfold of the harvest. In Palestine, a 7.5 yield from a harvest was regular. A tenfold yield was a good harvest. In speaking of God's generosity, Jesus often exaggerates his comparisons. It is a way of saying that such generosity has no bounds and that God surprises us with more than we expect when we perform our work. Aside from this being the "parable of the indefatigable sower," it is likewise known as the parable of the "lands." A very ancient catechetical tradition adopted by the gospels tried to decipher the meaning of each element of this particular story of Jesus. This led to the formulation of a catalog with four types of people, according to their reaction to the message of the gospel (the word). In this line, "to listen to the message," we must not translate it or understand it as simple intellectual knowledge of God. "Orthodox" people declare that they "believe in everything that the Holy Mother Church" dictates, but this does not hold water if they don't live the message. The evangelical message repeats that no one understands God and knows nor accepts his word if one does not accept others, particularly the poor (James 2:14–23). The Christian God is accepted or rejected only through an attitude of justice that is acted upon. The Latin American bishops meeting at Medellín formulated it thus: "Where there is unjust social, political, economic, and cultural inequality, there is a rejection of the gift of peace of God, and much more, a rejection of the Lord himself" (Document of Peace).

In this episode, Jesus concretizes the way of "listening to the message": "working for justice in this world," "sharing what one has with others," "working for others," "risking one's life and money," and so on. These are the various translations of the essence of the biblical formula, which is "working for justice." The prophets likewise converted into concrete examples what ought to be done to remain faithful to the word of God (Isa. 1:10–20; 58:6–10).

(Matt. 13:1–23; Mark 4:1–9; Luke 8:4–8)

32

They Say He's Crazy

The story of stealing wheat in Eleazar's farm spread like wildfire through the whole of Galilee. Our group was already known in Capernaum, and the people whispered about us in the market and square. Rumors spread all over the cities, around the lake, and eventually reached Nazareth.

Susanna: Mary, Mary, where are you?

Mary: What's up, Susanna? Tell me what's happened? Has any one of your children fallen ill, cousin Simon?

Simon: Not mine, but yours. Haven't you heard yet?

Mary: About what? Has anything happened to Jesus? What've they done to my son?

Susanna: They're gonna do something to him if you don't tie him up!

Mary: For God's sake, tell me what's happened.

Simon: He and his group of bums slipped into the farm of Eleazar, the most powerful landlord in the whole north. Have you seen old Ananias, the landowner here? Well, he's a tame cat next to a lion like Eleazar.

Mary: Why did they have to slip into his farm?

Simon: As you might expect, cousin Mary — to steal some wheat. Your son's a thief.

Mary: What? That's absurd.

Simon: But he is. And the worst thing is that they did it on the Sabbath.

Susanna: Besides, Jesus said before the tribunal that he doesn't observe the Sabbath because he doesn't want to; that the laws were made for people and not the other way around; that he can do anything he wants!

Mary: I can't believe that. It can't be.

Simon: He's crazy, Mary; your son's out of his mind. Ever since he was hit on the head by Rachel's son, something's gone wrong with him.

Susanna: No, man, no. This started after he went to the Jordan to see that hairy man baptizing in the river. That's where he had a slip. I told you, Mary, your son's changed since then.

Simon: He also said that those who are up would go down and those who are down would go up. He's inciting the poor against the rich.

A Neighbor: That means he ain't crazy. Damn! That's what we need here — someone to turn the tables.

Simon: But it's crazy, and dangerous. Eleazar's already denounced him. He's blacklisted.

Susanna: Mary, you gotta do something fast!

Mary: But I can't believe a single word you're saying: I never taught these things to my son.

Neighbor: Well, he learned all that when he went away!

Susanna: He was also seen in Jasmine Street, the red light district, you know... Ahem!

Simon: And they saw him drinking in the tavern by the lakeside, with Matthew, the tax collector, damn him and his pals!

Woman Neighbor: There must be something between him and Matthew's wife, because I was told he's often seen in their house up 'till late in the evening, and...

Mary: That's enough, that's enough. It can't be, it can't be my Jesus. He must be sick.

Woman Neighbor: Sick? Ha! He's just brazen! That's what it is!

Simon: He talks a lot, that's why, and he bums around. That's what he's been doing since he left Nazareth. Tell us, Mary, has he ever sent you some dinars to buy beans? He doesn't even think of his mother!

Susanna: Not quite, Simon. The truth is...

Simon: Where there's smoke, there's fire. Cousin Mary, something's wrong with your son. Either he's out of his mind, or he's become brazen. If he's joined a bunch of scoundrels, then he's likely to become one. If you'll take my advice, go and fetch him right away.

Susanna: That's right, Mary! Bring him back to Nazareth and let him stay here. He was brought up here, so here he should stay. Very soon he'll forget about this idea of the Messiah and liberation. He'll go back to his tools and bricks: his real life. You are his mother and he will obey you. Go, look for him at Capernaum.

Mary: But Susanna, I can't go there all by myself.

Susanna: Your cousins'll go with you, won't you, Simon?

Simon: Sure, Mary. We'll accompany you. I'll go tell my brother, Jacob.

Susanna: I'm going too. And when I see that son of yours, I'll really settle with him, by damn! I'll give him a piece of my mind, and he'll remember me for that. He's no right to behave like this.

The next morning, before sunrise over the plain of Esdraelon, the group of Nazarenes started their journey to Capernaum to look for Jesus. His cousins went, and so did Susanna and a neighbor who didn't want to miss any detail of the event. Mary, in tears, was with them.

Mary: But why? Why does he let me suffer all this shame? My God, why?

Simon: Don't worry, Mary. Whatever happens, we'll bring him to Nazareth! Take it easy; leave everything to us. We'll teach Jesus how to obey his family. Dammit! Hurry up, Mary!

The journey was shortened by the outrage they all felt, making them walk rapidly. When they reached Capernaum and crossed the Gate of Consolation, they inquired at the first house in the village.

Simon: Pardon, Madam, would you know where this tall, brown, and bearded guy lives? He's half-bricklayer and half-carpenter, . . . came from Nazareth a few months ago.

A Woman: You mean . . . Jesus of Nazareth?

Mary: Exactly. Do you know him, Madam?

Woman: But of course! Every one knows him here. He lives in Zebedee's house, by the wharf. Salome takes care of him more than a mother does.

Mary: I'm his mother.

Woman: Oh, really? Well, are you here to visit him?

Simon: We came to fetch him. Our cousin is out of his mind.

Woman: No, what happens is that this brown-skinned guy is so frank, he tells the truth to the rabbi's face and to the landlord's, and he reasons things out before the Roman governor. I'd say he's a prophet.

A Man: What? You mean this peasant is a prophet?

Another Woman: They say there's a thin line between a prophet and a nut. If you're his family, you'd better take him with you. Many strange things have happened since he came to this city.

Woman: What are you saying, you meddlesome woman? Jesus is a good man. Didn't he cure Bartholomew, huh? Don't you remember anymore?

Another Woman: Oh really? Or better, he cured him with magic! The Nazarene must have made a pact with the devil.

Woman: Oh yeah? What about Caleb, the fisherman? Didn't he cleanse him of leprosy? Didn't he cure Asaph's hand, the fruit vendor, huh? I swear by God, this Jesus must be a good quack doctor!

Man: A quack doctor? I swear the only medicine he can think of is to steal wheat from a neighbor's farm. If you don't believe me, then go ask the old man, Eleazar!

Woman: To hell with you! The Nazarene is a decent man.

Simon: Say whatever you want to say, we're his family, and we're gonna get him outta here right now. Could you tell us where he is now?

Another Woman: Come with me. I'll take you to Zebedee's house.

Man: Hey, guys, don't get lost! Hurry, hurry up! This is getting interesting!

The word spread around, from house to house. The women left the stoves they were tending and their brooms, to join the group of Nazarenes. The men who were idling their time away in the square stood up and went toward them. As usual, they were preceded by the kids as they shouted through the narrow street that reeked of onions and rotten fish.

John: What's the commotion about? Have they murdered King Herod?

A Woman: Hey, John, they're looking for the stranger!

John: What's happened? Maybe they're soldiers coming with fat-neck Eleazar.

Man: These ain't no soldiers. It's his mother who walked all the way from Nazareth, with his cousins. His entire family's here!

Jesus: What's the matter, John? Who is it?

John: Can't you hear their screams, Jesus? Your mother and relatives are out there looking for you.

Jesus: My mother? Something must have happened!

John: Go and meet them, Nazarene!

Jesus: What's all this screaming about? Has someone passed away in Nazareth?

Susanna: You're the one who's gonna kill us of shame, Jesus. I can't believe you could do this to your mother!

Jesus: What are you talking about, Susanna? What's all the trouble? Have you all gone crazy?

Susanna: You're the crazy one. Who ever taught you to steal wheat, huh? And to be inciting the people, huh? To make them rebel against the rich? Since when did you learn to get drunk with tax collectors and associate with prostitutes, huh? Who ever taught you to live like a rogue and a vicious person? Speak up!

Simon: Let's do the interrogation later, Susanna. You don't wash your dirty linen in public. Come on, Mary, tell your son to pack his things; we're going back to Nazareth right now.

Mary: Jesus, son, let's go. You're gonna go back to Nazareth with us. Your cousin's right. Since you left home, you've done nothing but foolish things. Come, we're leaving.

But Jesus did not move; he didn't even bat an eye.

Susanna: Are you deaf? Didn't you hear what your mother said?

Jesus: My mother? I'm sorry, Susanna. This woman who claims what we're doing is silly can't be my mother. Her face may resemble my mother's, but she can't be my mother. My mom never listened to gossip. She was always courageous, speaking of a God who wants to see his children proud and confident. She taught me to become responsible, to ignore what others would say. This woman isn't my mother. Neither are these people my family. I don't even know them.

Simon: I told you so, cousin Mary. He's delirious! Now he claims not to know us!

Jesus: I really don't know you. My mother, brothers, and family are someone else: they fight for justice and are not like you who hinder their struggle.

Simon: Stop all this nonsense! Now, will somebody please lend me some rope. Our relative is out of his mind. There's nothing we can do but tie him up!

Jesus: You're wasting your time, cousin. The truth cannot be suppressed by tying it up with ropes. God's word is like the wind; it can't be stopped by chains or ropes. The messengers of this word have to be as free as the wind. What we have to say, we say from the roof. And what must be done, we do openly.

But the Nazarenes were not convinced. Fuming mad, they stayed in front of our house and continued the fight. The truth was, during those months and even the following months, Jesus was called many names. They called him crazy, a drunk, a glutton, and a troublemaker. A lot of people never understood him. It's not good to sew a piece of new cloth on an old suit. One cannot put new wine into old wineskins.

•

Jesus scandalized his neighbors in the synagogue of Nazareth when he spoke to them with great conviction about liberation and the Kingdom of God. They were not the only ones scandalized. His own family — his mother, his cousins — could not comprehend his actions or his words. They really thought he was crazy. The freedom with which Jesus violated laws and faced authorities to argue about the ancient customs of his people scandalized his family, brought up in a highly traditional peasant society. For them, such freedom was perilous madness.

In their gospels, Mark and Matthew speak of Jesus' "brothers and sisters." Four of these brothers are even named: Simon, Joseph, Judas, and James (Jacob) (Matt. 13:55). Surely, the Greek word used by the evangelists is "brother," but it's a literal translation in Aramaic. One must realize that in Jesus' language, this word "brother" likewise encompasses distant relatives: nephews, second cousins, and so on, such that when the gospel of John says that Peter was Andrew's brother — son of the same parents — John specifies it by adding to "brother" another word that may allow the translation as "brother in the flesh," which undoubtedly defines the relationship (John 1:41). A large amount of data about the gospels and tradition unanimously show us that Jesus was the only son of Mary.

In the episode, Simon appears as one of the cousins of Jesus. If Mary's objection to her son's actions is above all emotional, a result of her fear of an impending danger, his cousin's attitude is a lot more ideological. Simon is a concerned poor man who is moved by financial concerns; materialistic and skeptical, he rejects any change, any novelty, especially if the prime mover of this novelty is a friend or a relative. The very serious conflict between Jesus and his family must be defined within the level of rumor-mongering. This gossiping is typical of small towns, where everything that shatters existing norms is judged with severity, and the absence of more significant happenings magnifies the trivialities.

The evangelical text about Mary's confrontation with her son has hardly been taken seriously. This is a less known text and is rarely preached. Nevertheless, it is a Marian text of great significance. It brings us close to Mary, as we see a mother who fears for her son who does not understand her, and who even opposes her by taking a step different from what she has desired. Like any other mother, Mary suffers anguish in seeing her son getting embroiled with the authorities for fear of losing him. This is the real Mary. Mary undertook a long and difficult road to faith, during which she experienced uncertainties and vacillations. The beginning of Jesus' activities in Capernaum was, for her, an especially difficult moment which she could not accept. It was so difficult that three of the evangelists took this conflict into account, even if they were aware that their lectors might find it rather disconcerting or scandalous.

The family was a very significant institution in Israel. Family ties were so strong that they lasted for life. The veneration and respect of children for their parents belonged to a deeply rooted tradition in the country. This notwithstanding, fidelity for justice's sake is for Jesus the first and foremost of all obligations. He firmly situates it over and above family considerations. If this episode highlights Mary's human frailty, it likewise focuses on the freedom which always characterized Jesus.

(Matt. 12:46–50; Mark 3:20–21, 31–35; Luke 8:19–21)

33

We Have Enough to Worry about Each Day

Simon: Tie him up, tie him up! You've heard him! He's lost his sanity! He's crazy!

The fishing village seemed like an agitated beehive when Jesus' relatives came to look for him, saying he was crazy. The Nazarenes amassed at the front door, preparing ropes that would tie Jesus up while the neighbors of Capernaum shouted and laughed as they witnessed the family squabble.

Mary: Hold it, cousin Simon. Don't do that. Let me talk to him. Let me pass. I'm his mother.

Mary forced her way through our house where Jesus was.

Mary: Please, don't mind him! My son is sick and he doesn't know what he's saying. He's sick.

Jesus: No, mother. I know what I'm saying. You just wasted your time and your trip. I'm not going back with you.

Mary: Jesus, don't be discourteous in front of these people. Aren't you ashamed of yourself, talking to me like that?

Jesus: That's okay, mother. I'm sorry, . . . but listen to me: they've poisoned your mind with silly talk. I must say this, even if they are neighbors of mine: rumors spread like wildfire in Nazareth. I'm not aware of what they've told you about me, but whatever it is, if you just believe one-eighth, then you've got only a little truth.

Simon: Oh? So, in spite of all the nonsense you uttered before, you still have the nerve to call us liars, is that right?

Jesus: Cousin Simon, the truth is . . . Oh well, the truth is, you're a blabbermouth.

Mary: For God's sake, son, what's gotten into you? How could you speak that way to your relatives? You've changed a lot, Jesus. You weren't like that before.

Jesus: Maybe it's you who've changed, Mamma. You used to tell me before: "One's gotta do what one oughtta do, regardless of what people say." What's happened to you now?

Mary: I'm scared, son, so scared. There are a lot of soldiers and spies all over. The situation's getting worse every day.

Jesus: That's why we must do something soon. Or would you rather have the same situation as we have now, where people starve to death right before our eyes until the same happens to us?

Mary: It's not that, Jesus, but... things get so complicated. Tomorrow they might just tell me that you've been imprisoned and...

Jesus: Don't think of what will happen tomorrow. We have enough to worry about each day.

Mary: These days I'm reminded so much of your father, Joseph.

Jesus: Well, as far as I can remember, there are no cowards in father's family. He hid those poor fellows when the soldiers were after them. He saved their lives.

Susanna: Yeah, and lost his instead. Do you want your mother to lose you too?

Mary: Don't make me suffer this way, Jesus, I beg of you. Why don't you just stay put in Nazareth? You can earn a living by making horseshoes, and patching roofs. Then get yourself a wife, raise your own children, that I may one day see my grandchildren. Why can't you be just like the rest, Jesus? Why?

Mary dried her tears with a striped scarf she wore in her hair. She didn't want to be seen in tears, as she felt humbled and embarrassed in the midst of the people around her. The Nazarenes were ridiculing Jesus, and the people from Capernaum were making fun of the Nazarenes. Both caused her much pain.

Simon: Don't waste your tears on this rascal son of yours, cousin Mary. Your son doesn't want to work, that's it. He'd rather involve himself in politics than work. So much silly talk, but little work. Tell me, how will your mother live if you don't even earn anything to buy firewood? Have you got any savings at all? Have you got any business at hand? Why, you don't even have a lot to bury yourself when you die! This one thing I should tell you, Jesus: Don't look for help at my door later, for I'll not lend you a single cent, do you hear?

Jesus: I never borrowed anything from you, cousin Simon. I work with my hands like you do. I owe you nothing. My mother does not feed on your bread, nor does she take clothes from your family. This one thing I must tell you too: You seem to worry too much about the food that you eat, your own food, that is. Well, that's right. You must earn your daily bread by your own sweat. But look at the birds of the sky, the sparrows, the seagulls ... They neither sow nor reap, nor have they saved anything, yet they don't lack anything to eat. Every time I see them, I ask myself: Aren't we worth more than these birds?

Simon: Yes, you go ahead with your stories and those sweet words. But the words can't be eaten, do you hear?

Jesus: Look at the flowers, cousin, those white lilies that grow in the field, with no one tending them. They don't spin or weave, ... but whenever I see them, I wonder: Dammit, not even King Solomon, in his elegant, woolen suit, was clothed better than any of these. If God takes care of the grass that grows today but is burned tomorrow, how can he not care for us who are his children?

After Jesus had said this, Simon, his cousin, grabbed the small bag of money that was tied to his waist and proudly shook it. The people crammed together all the more to see his face better.

Simon: Listen, dreamer, ... this is what counts. I don't care about the rest. The lilies of the field? The birds? All that's nothing! When you look up at the sky, to see the sparrows pass by, don't look with an open mouth — no bread will come down from heaven, but something else! No, my cousin, no. Only fools will listen to you. One must take life seriously.

Jesus: Not quite, Simon.

Simon: Do you expect us to beg the Lord for food with our arms crossed?

Jesus: No, Simon. One has to work. But you must also trust in God. He knows our needs — shelter, clothing, and food. If we do our part, then he'll not fail us. But you must also think of the needs of others who have less than you. I believe that if we concern ourselves about the needs of others more than ours, then our own needs will be taken care of.

Mary: Oh, son, that's easily said, ... but when life becomes so difficult ...

Jesus: But Mamma, you yourself taught me this. You said: "Happier is he who gives than he who receives." Don't you remember anymore? "Help your brothers and sisters and God will help you." You would tell me that day in and day out. Well, I want to help my people to be free, even if I have to pay the price that all the prophets have paid.

Mary: Your words scare me, son. I beg of you, Jesus, don't get yourself into trouble.

Jesus: Mamma, please, don't try to twist the road that you yourself have paved for me. Nothing is resolved with fear. Nor can you solve problems that have not come. There is enough to worry about each day.

My brother James and I remained inside the house so as not to provoke the Nazarenes the more.

James: What a cousin Jesus has! It's as if a mad dog had bitten him!

John: And this Susanna is too much!

James: The mother can't even say a word!

Salome: What else can the poor woman do? It's her son and she must take care of him.

John: For God's sake, Jesus is already thirty years old!

Salome: For a mother, her son's age doesn't matter.

James: Of course, and that's the problem. For you mothers, we never grow up, and you want to control our whole life.

Salome: That isn't so; what we want is that parents and children support one another. We mothers suffer in anguish for whatever happens. At least I can say I'm still fortunate because I have you near and you two have been behaving well. But who knows, one of these days...?

John: Mamma, here you go again.

Salome: Well, you started it. Ever since this Jesus came here, you've been overacting. Listen to me, you crazy pair, he who plays with fire, gets burned. So stop fooling with politics. Do you hear me? Get out of it.

James: Well, well, Mamma, a fight in here and one outside is one too many. Come, let's see what's happening in the street.

Outside, the squabble among the Nazarenes continued. Simon, Jesus' cousin, was getting impatient.

Simon: Hurry up, Mary. Jesus is out of his mind. You heard him talk, didn't you?

Mary: Please, Jesus, let's go back to Nazareth.

Jesus: No, Mamma, I'm staying here. We're trying to do something so that you and I and all the poor of Israel will inherit God's promise.

Mary: You don't have to do it for me. And you're slurring the memory of Joseph, may he rest in peace. Haven't you any respect for your late father?

Jesus: My father would be happy to see me doing this. He was never a coward in the face of danger. On the contrary.

Mary: Are you disobeying me, your mother? Jesus! For the last time, I beg of you: come with me to Nazareth.

Jesus: I'm not going.

Mary bit her lip in a desperate gesture. Then she broke into tears, disconsolately.

Susanna: Let's go, Mary. Take it easy.

Mary: What do you want me to do, Susanna? Nothing is left for me. I had a husband, but I lost him. I had an only son, and I've lost him too. Nothing's left anymore.

Susanna: Try not to think about it for now.

Mary: I don't understand, Susanna. . . . Why does Jesus have to do this to me, why?

Simon: Because he's brazen. He's rebellious and insolent. Let's get this over with, once and for all. Jacob, give me the ropes! If he doesn't want to come of his own will, then we'll have to drag him like a beast!

Mary: Please Simon, don't do that. Leave him alone, if he doesn't want to come.

Simon: What? And let him do as he pleases, involving himself in politics and putting us on the spot, which could imperil our lives as his relatives? I'm not going to pay for what he does. He's gonna come with us, whether he likes it or not!

Simon and James (Jacob) approached Jesus with two sets of rope. Jesus stood by the door of our house.

Jesus: I may be involving myself in politics, cousin Simon, while you waste your time in matters you don't really care about. And will you please refrain from telling lies to my mother? You do nothing but spread lies and mess up people's lives. Why don't you live and let live?

Simon: I dare you to say that again. Come on!

Jesus: You mess people's lives . . .

Simon punched Jesus in the face. The people milled around all the more. Jesus, wobbling, wiped the blood that was starting to flow from his nose.

Simon: Come on, fight like a man! Unless you're not one! Come on, give it back to me. Defend yourself, coward, or I'll hit you again, and make a man out of you, sissy!

Jesus crossed his arms and went near Simon.

Jesus: I have nothing against you, cousin. Why don't you leave me alone?
Simon: I want you to fight me!
Jesus: No, I won't give you the pleasure. You may beat me, if you want, but I'm not fighting back.

Simon waited with clenched teeth and fists. Jesus remained calm, without removing his gaze from his cousin, who, once again, lost his patience.

Simon: Idiot... You're an asshole! I always thought you were nothing. Now I'm convinced you're even worse than I thought! Puah! Let's go, Jacob! Let this puppet stay where he pleases! Hurry — we've got a long way to go!

The Nazarenes undertook the journey back to their village. Simon and Jacob went ahead of the group, letting out their outrage by hitting the stones along the road with their canes. Mary, Jesus' mother, held Susanna's arm for support, feeling very depressed because of the incident in Capernaum that afternoon.

•

In this episode, Jesus' conflict with his mother is overshadowed by his conflict with his cousin Simon. The materialistic personality and indifferent attitude of the cousin give occasion to focus on the well-known words of Jesus about the birds of the sky and the lilies of the field, which are not at all easy to explain without resorting to an alienating interpretation. This is because these words of unconditional trust in God's providence — if not explained well — may prove to be offensive to those who, in their misery, are forced to struggle merely to survive.

Certainly, one must "eat in order to live" and not "live in order to eat." However, poor people are constrained to be "materialistic," exerting most of their effort to get food for the day. This is the general situation in many countries today. Jesus does not denounce the urgency with which the poor look for means to survive. That would be in contradiction to the rest of his message. What he criticizes is the selfish ideology of the hoarder, the materialism of the greedy and that of the egoist who only think of themselves and their own well-being, in utter disregard for the needs of others. For those who seek to break the vicious circle of having to earn more, and offer their lives in the service of others, these words of putting one's trust in the Lord sound different. The one who fights for justice amid economic difficulties is aware that God is watching and will provide, in addition, the means to continue the fight.

A person must not be a production machine. Nor should she or he be a consumer machine. To have more in life may conceal the true Christian ideal, which is being more: being happier by giving and receiving. Mary's being a widow accentuates her fears. In Israel, a single woman with no man in the house was extremely helpless. In this episode, Salome, in her conversation with James and John, manifests her great understanding of Mary's situation. Mothers find it difficult to let go of children, to stop influencing them, and to accept their children's decision to engage in risky undertakings. For a newborn child to have his or her own life, the umbilical cord connecting them to the mother must be cut. Throughout the whole of life, this act must be repeated in order for the mother and son or daughter to grow and develop into mature personalities.

(Matt. 6:25–34; Luke 12:22–34)

34

The Sons of Ephraim

A pair of small lamps illuminated Peter's house, producing shadows on the walls. That night, like almost every night, we stayed after dinner talking, and Jesus told us the story of old Ephraim.

Jesus: Yes, that man had a heart as huge as the Sea of Galilee. His name was Ephraim and he had six children. The first four were girls and the other two were boys. His wife died when the last child was born. Ephraim became a widower and had to work very hard to raise his six children. He had a small piece of land at the right side of the hill of Nazareth. There he sweated it out from morning till night, plowing and sowing. He worked like an old mule to provide them with their daily bread. The years passed and his daughters got married. Ephraim was left with his two sons: Reuben, the elder one, and Nico, the youngest. One morning one of Ephraim's neighbors saw him, and they talked:

Neighbor: Good morning, Ephraim! How's life treating you, neighbor?

Ephraim: Well, as you can see my friend, working very hard!

Neighbor: But your sons are already helping you, aren't they?

Ephraim: Of course. Right now, the elder one is plowing one side of the field. It's almost sowing time for us, my neighbor.

Neighbor: Ah, that son of yours, Reuben, is a grand boy, yes sir. He's very dependable, but your other son — he's something else!

Ephraim: Poor Nico.

Neighbor: Don't defend him, Ephraim. Everyone here knows your son's misadventures. All he does is run after the girls. He's a bum, that's what he is. You gotta talk to him, Ephraim. Correct him while there's still time. He isn't growing up properly.

Ephraim: This boy grew up without a mother, neighbor. I had to

231

be mother and father to him. Do you understand? I know him well. He isn't a shameless boy, definitely not. He's just a little confused.

Jesus: That night, Nico, the youngest son, came home very late.

Ephraim: Where could he have gone? This is strange, Reuben, because your brother always comes home to eat.
Reuben: Oh yes; he knows how to come home on time to eat. How brazen can he get? He doesn't bend his back to work, but he'll bend forward to eat. Oh, Papa, I'm done. I'm going to bed now.
Ephraim: I can't sleep until he comes home, son. I'll wait for him.

Jesus: Nico came home past midnight. The old man, Ephraim, was waiting for him.

Nico: Cheers to life, cheers to love! Hic! Hey, Papa, you're still up? Hic!
Ephraim: Son, why did you come home so late? I was worried about you.
Nico: Old man, life must be lived! Hic! I was with some friends. We have some plans, you know. We're leaving this little town. It's so boring here. Papa, I'm bored to death here, and I can't stand it anymore.
Ephraim: But son, what're you talking about?
Nico: I'm leaving. Tomorrow I'll be off. I don't want to stay here stagnating. I want to see the world.
Ephraim: Nico, my son, you're drunk. You don't know what you're saying.
Nico: Listen, Papa. I know you're keeping some money from the previous harvest. Gimme what's due me. I'm gonna enjoy life. Cheers to life, cheers to love!

Jesus: The next morning, old Ephraim took from a hole in the yard the money he had been saving from the last harvest and gave his son what was due him. He was old enough to claim his inheritance. He wrapped the money in a piece of handkerchief and gave it to him hoping, up to the last minute, that his son wouldn't go away.

Ephraim: Well, son, if that's your decision . . .
Nico: Hey, old man, stop being sentimental. Money's supposed to be enjoyed and not kept.

Ephraim: And . . . where are you going?

Nico: Anywhere I can have some fun!

Ephraim: Son, send me news about yourself through the traders coming here.

Nico: Nobody ever comes here, Papa, because this is a dead town. I'm sick and tired of everything and everyone here. I'm going now, Papa, goodbye!

Jesus: Ephraim saw his son off as he disappeared down the road without even looking back. The father followed him with tear-laden eyes until he was lost on the horizon, among the olive trees along the road.

Reuben: Damn him, Papa! Why did he get the money he didn't earn?

Ephraim: Your brother is free, son. If he wanted to leave, I'll not tie him up like a donkey. He isn't my slave either. He's my son.

Jesus: At the port of Japhia, Nico started to squander the money he got from his father. Months passed by. He was in the company of women, got himself drunk, or would simply gamble. All the money that Ephraim had saved by working like an old mule was squandered in a short time. Meanwhile, in Nazareth, his father never stopped thinking of him.

Neighbor: How's life with you, Ephraim, just like any other day?

Ephraim: Yes, my neighbor, here I am still waiting. The caravans from the south pass at this time. My son could be in any one of them.

Neighbor: He's not coming back, Ephraim, after having been given such a large amount.

Ephraim: I don't know anything about him. It's as if he died.

Neighbor: Exactly. Consider him dead and suffer no more. Forget about him. You have five others left and they're good. Forget about this black sheep.

Jesus: But how can a mother or father ever forget the child they've brought up? How can they cease worrying about the child who's part of their guts? Though his son forgot him, Ephraim never forgot his son.

Nico: Hey, potbelly, bring me another jug over here; my throat's so dry! Hik! Besides, my girlfriend here also wants to have a shot! Isn't that right, precious one?

Jesus: Another month passed and another. Nico continued to squander his money. One day he bet all he had left and lost.

Nico: Damn the luck! What the hell can I do now?

Jesus: He then looked for a job but found none. Things did not go well in Japhia. The harvest had been poor because of the drought that year. Money was scarce and there was hunger everywhere. Finally, after several days, a man contracted him to work on a pig farm in exchange for a measly wage.

Nico: What a miserable life! I'd gladly eat those carob beans instead of tending the pigs, but if the owner saw me, he'd kill me with a beating. By the horns of Beelzebub, I've never felt so starved before!

Jesus: So weeks passed. Nico was dying of hunger while the pigs all got fat. He was filthy, stinking even more than the pigs, and he did nothing but complain.

Nico: Here I am, a shabby and miserable man, while at home they're probably enjoying a nice and hearty meal. They may be poor there, but they always have something to eat. I've got to return. I can't bear this anymore. I'll tell the old man: Look, Papa, I'm sorry, I was wrong, things have been bad for me. Say whatever you want; yell at me; do anything you please; but please, help me. I'm sure the old man will soften up and give me some money. Yes, I must return.

Jesus: And so he decided to return.

Ephraim: It's been more than three years since your brother went away.
Reuben: He's your son, and not my brother. For me, it's like a hundred years ago.
Ephraim: If I only knew where he was, I'd look for him.
Reuben: You could use up ten sandals and still not find him. That son of yours is dead. Forget about him once and for all, Papa.

Jesus: That morning, like all mornings for more than three years, Ephraim went out to the road during the passage of caravans from the south, hoping to get some news from his son. When the sun peeped over the horizon and illuminated the road, the poor father saw something coming from afar. Someone coming near. His heart told him it was his son, and old Ephraim, like a child, ran to receive him.

Ephraim: My son, my son!

Jesus: He embraced and kissed his son.

Ephraim: My son, you've returned!
Nico: Papa, look, I'll explain.
Ephraim: There's no need to explain. You've returned and that's enough! Come, let's go. Neighbor, help me get the best tunic in the chest and get me the wedding ring of his mother for him to put on, and a pair of new sandals too. My son's in tatters. You, servant, bring the fat calf and roast it fast. My son's hungry and he's so thin, he has to eat well. He isn't dead! He's alive! He was lost, but I've found him!

Jesus: Soon, the whole of Nazareth was in Ephraim's house. The old man told the whole town that Nico, his son, had returned. He was home again.

Woman Neighbor: Where have you been, you rascal? Here we thought you had left the country.
Another Woman: How many girlfriends did you have? See how happy your father is today. Look, he's dancing with Susanna!
Nico: The truth is I've never seen him so happy.
Woman Neighbor: Ever since you left, he's been waiting for you everyday. He always said you'd come back.
Another Neighbor: You did come back, young man! Come, let us dance to that!

Jesus: At noontime, Reuben, the older brother, came back from work on the farm. As he approached the house, he heard the music playing and he wondered.

Reuben: Hey, you, what's all the noise in the house?
Neighbor: Why, didn't you know? Your brother, Nico, is back! There is a big feast going on in your house. Your father even or-

dered the slaughter of the fattened calf for the celebration. Run and catch up!

Jesus: The elder brother was enraged when he heard this and didn't want to enter the house. Old Ephraim was informed what happened and he ran to look for his older son.

Ephraim: Reuben, my son, Reuben, your brother's back! He's back safe and sound! Come inside, we've been waiting for you.

Reuben: But Papa, you know very well how that bastard squandered your money in wine and with whores. Now you offer him the fattened calf for his food and a party. You're out of your mind, Papa!

Ephraim: Yes, my son: I'm crazy. I'm mad with joy. I was told that your brother was dead, but as you can see, he's back with us. We'd lost him, yet we've found him. How can I not be happy? If I only had three calves, I would have killed all of them so we could have even a better celebration!

Reuben: Of course. I have spent my whole life with you, working and obeying you every time, yet you've never offered me even a young goat to celebrate with my friends.

Ephraim: Why didn't you tell me, son? You know fully well that what's mine is yours. You know how I love the two of you.

Jesus: Ephraim embraced his older son with the same joy with which he embraced Nico. Then they went inside the house. Reuben embraced Nico and smiled. He hadn't smiled for a long time. After a few days, when his daughters and their families came to Nazareth for a visit, Ephraim had his two sons seated around the table, and everyone in the family was there.

That is the story of old Ephraim, that old father whose heart is as big as the lake. If you understand, then you understand our Lord.
It was Jesus who taught us how to love God as our Father.

•

The parable of the prodigal son should be called the parable of the good father because it is he who is the real protagonist in Jesus' story. This is one of those parables used by Jesus to teach those who listened how God is. Ephraim's character — that of generosity, patience, and infinite capacity to forgive — best describes the greatness of God's heart.

In his talks, Jesus did not resort to abstract language in expressing concepts and ideas. He used concrete images. In this parable — without discussing it directly — he tells how God can forgive. He describes this with various symbolism. When Ephraim found his lost son, he clothed him with a new tunic. In the Middle East, such a presentation of new clothing is a gesture of great appreciation, and in biblical language it symbolizes the coming of salvation. The father also gave him a ring and a pair of sandals to wear. The ring typifies the full trust one gives to another, while the sandals represent a free person (the slaves never wore them). Lastly, the banquet; meat was eaten only on special occasions. To partake of a meal together at the same table was indicative of the forgotten past and a sign of complete communion. In presenting these images, Jesus tells us how God can be forgiving to one who repents and goes back to him.

The parable consists of two parts; it tells about the two types of attitude shown to God by the two sons. For them, the father is the same: understanding and easy to forgive with open arms. But the older son does not share in the joy. He has done no wrong all his life but neither has he understood who the father is. Here, Jesus invites those who are "good and just" to share in the joy of seeing those who were lost — the less fortunate — also seated at the table and participating in the banquet. For people like the older brother, the gospel always turns out to be scandalous. Because of their merits accumulated in the course of time — prayers, observance of the commandments, and sacrifices — they not only want the Lord to reward them with heaven, but also wish to deprive the rest, particularly the sinners, of the same blessings. Sadly enough, this attitude is common among a great number of people who call themselves Christians.

In this story, Jesus compared God to the father with the big heart. He taught his disciples to call on God "the Father" as he always did. In all the books of the Old Testament, it is said that God treats his children as "a Father," but on no occasion does anyone address him as "my Father." (The invocation "Our Father" is used in collective prayers, in the name of the whole community.) The immense trust with which Jesus addressed the Lord as "Father," as *Abba* (Papa), the Aramaic word affectionately used to mean "father," is an outstanding characteristic of his personality. In the whole literature of prayers in ancient Judaism, not a single prayer is found invoking God as *Abba,* not even in the liturgical or private prayers. At this point, Jesus was not heir to the tradition of his ancestors. Instead, he opened a new road unknown to anyone and replete with theological consequences which have enabled us to get to know God more profoundly. Thus, through him, we definitely come to know God as our "Father."

(Luke 15:11–32)

35

Sliding through the Roof

In those days, Peter's house was the most frequented in Capernaum. As the sun hid itself behind Carmel, our group, together with a number of village folks, gathered there to discuss our own problems.

Rufa: Yes, that's fine. We need justice, equality, and reforms, but... what about our souls?

Peter: What souls are you talking about, mother-in-law?

Rufa: Yours, Peter, and mine and everybody else's. If after all this mess we all die and are condemned, then what?

John: But old woman, why are we going to be condemned?

Rufa: Because we're all sinners, dammit! We gotta worry about cleansing our souls!

A Man: The soul can wait — we've got to feed our stomachs first. The Messiah's coming with enough food for everyone!

Rufa: Well, I'm telling you, first and foremost we got to clear our conscience with the Lord; there'll be enough time to worry about what to eat. Am I right or wrong, Jesus?

Jesus: A bird needs two wings to fly. It can't fly with a broken wing.

Rufa: What do you mean by that?

Jesus: God doesn't separate things from each other. Everything goes together, like the body and soul, heaven and earth, the past and present.

That night, the cold wind blew over Mt. Hermon. Rufina, Peter's wife, started to prepare soup with roots as an ingredient. The whole neighborhood smelled its aroma, and everyone came to partake of it. In a short while, the house was filled with people.

A Man: Hey, I can't hear a word they're saying.

A Woman: I heard something about a bird having two wings in order to fly and... Stop pushing, will you? Look who's here, the sons of Floro, and the old man too!

Another Man: How come the old fox is here?

Son: We want to get in. We brought our father here all the way from the other end of the town.

Another Woman: Well, you better go back to where you came from! Don't you see there ain't no more space because of the crowd here?

Four young men carried an improvised small bed made of a fishing net and two paddles. Lying on it was Floro, a weak and paralyzed old man. His eyes were red and bulging like those of a frog.

Son: Give way, please!

Man: But how can you get this cripple inside? There isn't even room for a needle in there! Go away, go away!

Floro's sons tried to slip through the door, through the kitchen and through the yard, but in vain. There was a big crowd. But Floro wasn't about to give up without seeing Jesus. And then an idea occurred to him.

Son: It's terrible here, Papa. We better get outta here.

Floro: No way. I'm not budging here without seeing Jesus.

Son: But Papa, there's nothing we can do. We can't get in there.

Floro: Bring me up to the roof then.

Son: How's that?

Floro: Bring me up to the roof, then lower me through it. For me it would be easy to do.

The four sons removed the paddles and rolled the net around the old man. They raised him up to the roof of the house while Jesus continued to talk about the Kingdom of God.

Jesus: Yes, to move forward, a bird needs to move its two wings in harmony, just as rowers of a boat need to work in harmony. In the Kingdom of God, everything goes in unison; everything...

Rufina: What's happening here? Peter, for God's sake, come over and look at this! They're boring a hole in our roof! Come, Peter!

Peter: What's the matter, crazy woman?

Rufina: Look, Peter; some people are scaling the roof!

Peter: Dammit, what's happening here? Hey, you come down immediately or else! Are you outta your minds? Bring me the broom, Rufina, and I'll break their necks if they won't come down.

In a matter of seconds, Floro's sons slid downward, breaking the middle beam as the roof collapsed over our heads. Amid falling dust and broken posts appeared Floro, the paralytic, like an octopus trapped inside a net.

Peter: Look what you've done! You beasts, idiots, you sons of a bitch! You've ruined my roof! Who's gonna repair this now, huh?

Son: We lost our grip and slid.

Peter: Damn! You'll have to pay for this!

Son: The roof posts are a little rotten, so...

Peter: That's none of your business! Who ever told you to scale my roof?

Son: Papa told us to.

Peter: Papa, Papa! You call this cretin "Papa"?

Jesus: That's enough Peter. It's really nothing.

Peter: Oh yeah? Have you ever seen a man falling from the sky like a mashed bird, huh? He could've harmed my mother-in-law and might've killed me!

Jesus: That's all right. Nobody got hurt.

Peter: But look, everything's ruined: my roof, my windows, everything!

Jesus: Don't worry, I'll fix it tomorrow. Remember, I'm an expert in roof repairs.

Rufina: You're an expert in repairing roofs while this old man is an expert in destroying them! Is that right, Floro? You don't know this man, Jesus. He's Floro, the cripple. Don't take pity on this sly fox. Do you know how he broke his legs? He was scaling walls and slipping through rooftops in order to steal. Scoundrel, I'll give you a good beating!

Peter: Why the hell did you have to pass through the roof and not through the door, huh? Come on, speak up. Your legs may be paralyzed, but not your tongue!

Floro: Because I'm crippled.

Peter: You're a bandit! That's what you are, and these four sons of yours are even worse. Come on, get this rascal outta here!

Jesus: Hold it, Peter, that's not the way to handle this. Let him speak first. Why have you come, Floro? And why did you do this?

Floro: Because I wanted to get in. An old woman at the door was driving us away because there was no more room inside. I really wanted to see you.

Peter: Why didn't you stay by the window to listen, like the rest?

Floro: Because I wanted to see this man called Jesus who came to the city and cures the sick. My legs are paralyzed.

Rufina: Your sickness is in your hands, you thief! God will not heal you!

Peter: Look, Jesus, this man, as you can see, is a thief. Now he's useless, but before . . . If I told you now, you wouldn't believe me!

John: This old man stole the candleholders from the synagogue without even blowing the candles out!

Peter: If you lost a dinar, you would find it inside his pocket. He even stole bread and olives so that he and his children would have something to eat!

A Woman: He's a thief and a drunkard!

A Man: And a gambler!

Rufa: He's a troublemaker too!

John: Let him go to hell; he's as sinful as his sons!

Jesus: Is this true, Floro?

Floro: Yes, sir. That's all true. I'm a scoundrel. But my sons are not. My children are good.

Another Man: Good? Every time Floro and his sons went to the marketplace, it was like a plague had taken over, because they ravaged everything!

Floro: That's a lie. My sons are honest and decent.

Jesus: Are these four your sons, Floro?

Floro: Yes sir. They're the older ones. The two pairs are twins.

Jesus: Do you have more children?

Floro: I have ten more at home. I have fourteen children.

Jesus: Fourteen? Dammit! You have more than the tribes of Israel!

Floro: My wife gives birth to two at a time.

Jesus: Why did you steal? Didn't you have a job?

Floro: Yes, but it wasn't enough with fourteen mouths to feed. My wife would say they'd die of hunger. I worked during the day and stole at night. Yet it was still not enough! I became desperate and cursed the Lord. Yes sir, I committed every sin in violation of the law. I can't be forgiven. I'm a sinner yet my children are not. I brought them up to be good and hard-working.

A Man: Your children are as insolent as you, old liar!

Floro: No, no, please don't say that. They are not like me.

Another Man: A chip off the old block!

Floro: No, spare them please! They're good. Believe me, stranger, my children aren't like me.

Jesus: It's all right, Floro. Take it easy. Look, you trust your children so much. And God trusts you. In the Kingdom of God, everyone has a place, even if he has to slip through the roof. Be happy, Floro: God forgives your sins. Believe me, he's forgiven your sins.

The paralytic looked at Jesus surprisingly with bulging eyes. He was smiling, though. Everyone was stunned by Jesus' words.

Man: What did you say, stranger?
Jesus: That God has forgiven Floro.
Man: And who're you to say that? This old man's a scoundrel. He can't be forgiven.
Jesus: Are you sure?
Man: Of course!
Jesus: Which is easier to say: "Your sins are forgiven" or "Your legs are cured"?
Man: Neither of the two. The first is a blasphemy. The second is impossible.
Jesus: You're wrong, my friend. There is nothing impossible with God. Haven't we said before that in the Kingdom of God everything goes to-gether, like the body and soul? Come, Floro, you can get up now and go home with your sons.

Then the incredible happened. Old Floro stood up, stretched his legs with great ease, then hefted the net and oars that had served as his bed over his shoulders. His face was radiant with great joy. He looked at us and started to walk. Stunned and afraid, our gaze followed his steps until he was out of sight. Never had we seen an event like this.

•

In Jesus' time, and even today, a great number of Middle Eastern dwellings have had flat rooftops. These used to rest on a base of beams covered with branches, above which there was a layer of flattened clay. In ordinary houses this beam structure was made of sycamore wood. In big buildings, wood of stronger material, like cedar, had to be used. This type of light and provisional construction — wherein the roof could be raised during hot weather — explains how Floro, the paralytic, could be lowered from the roof to the interior part of Peter's house. The neighbors who were gathered on that day not only occupied the entire space of the house, which was extremely small, but also clustered in the yard, which was shared by several families in the neighborhood.

Dualism is deeply rooted in religious thought. On the one hand, one speaks of sacred things, persons, and places; and on the other, of profane things, persons, and places. People are said to have a soul (that is, spiritual, lofty, worth emulating) and a body (material, with baser instincts that ought to be controlled). Likewise, one speaks of the material and the spiritual, or the natural and the supernatural. For centuries, many Christians have tried to differentiate salvation from the promotion of the human (or liberation in Christ from temporal liberation). The future awaiting people is likewise seen as distinct and opposed to the present: heaven as opposed to earth; the beyond as opposed to the here and now. In reality, none of these dualisms has a basis in the message of the gospel. The words of Jesus and his attitude totally discard these false divisions by proclaiming that all people are equal (all are holy), that God fills in the universe he himself created, and that eternal life begins the moment people opt to defend the life of others.

The miracle that Jesus performs on the crippled man, Floro, is a sign that God does not consider any differences of this type. God simultaneously frees the paralytic of his sickness and frees him from the burden of his weakness, his sins. For God — according to Jesus' signs — the body and soul go hand in hand. God is interested in the complete person. None of these dualisms matters anymore in the gospel. Nor do the dualisms in action matter. In our struggle to transform our history from misery and injustice to that which is authentically humane, we construct the history of our salvation, the Reign of God. In other words, we are beginning our heaven here on earth now. And that is why we find God in people.

God knows the individual history of each man and woman. Therefore, he knows the ulterior motives of our actions, and, like a just judge, he is aware of the extenuating circumstances whenever we "sin." Extreme need — and such is the case of Floro, who had so many mouths to feed — is a great extenuating circumstance of our human debility. When confronted by Jesus, the paralytic "sees" his complete life and accepts it as is, and, considering his limitations, he confesses this life in all sincerity. God, through Jesus, likewise sees and accepts it. He forgives him, and cleanses him of all his faults and even elevates him. Such accounting is made clear: Jesus is the messenger of God's unconditional forgiveness and brings joy to people's tormented hearts.

We must not "read" Jesus' miracles as proofs of his might or majesty. What is majestic isolates, and what is powerful makes us tremble; it scares us. If the miracles by Jesus had had this effect, they would have been contradictory to the plan of God, who wanted to be near us through Jesus. Each of these signs brought the poor and the humble of Jesus' town closer to him. They saw themselves in him who was a friend they could love and a leader they could follow. Those who stayed away from him, who definitely did not admire him, were those who believed that God was with them through their prayers and laws. Therefore, there was no need to support a poor peasant who was capable of discoursing on religious matters and enkindling the hope of a people terribly overcome by too much suffering.

(Matt. 9:1–8; Mark 2:1–12; Luke 5:17–26)

36

As Small as Mingo

Canilla: Jesus! Jesus! Wait!

Jesus: What's the matter, Canilla?

Canilla: Teach me the three fingers trick.

Jesus: Again? I already taught you that yesterday.

Canilla: But I forgot.

Jesus: I'm gonna do it tomorrow.

Canilla: No, I want it now.

Jesus: Okay, watch it closely so you will learn. You hide your thumb this way. Then twist your little finger this way and...

Canilla: I know it! I know it already. Look! Am I doing it right?

Jesus: Better than I do. Now, go and teach it to Nino, who still hasn't learned to do it.

Canilla: Yes, I'll show this to Nino.

Jesus: And then in the afternoon you go to Peter's house with him. I want to know if you're learning how to write the alphabet in the synagogue.

Canilla: Goodbye, Jesus!

Jesus: Goodbye, Canilla!

The children of Capernaum had become Jesus' friends in a short time. They always followed him, so he would teach them a trick or tell a story. The boys were running to and from the street the whole day. The rabbi met them only once a week to teach them how to read, while they did nothing but play and do mischief the rest of the time. The same thing happened in Peter's house.

Mingo: You're a pig, pig, a filthy pig!

Peter and Rufina's four sons were moving about from morning till night, and not a day or night passed without someone crying, laughing, or picking a fight. Rufina spent the day running from the kitchen to the garden and back, also picking a fight with them. Old grandma Rufa had her own chores to attend to. When Peter returned from his fishing, he was always in for a surprise.

Peter: What's it this time, woman? How did the children behave today?

Rufina: Like rogues, as always. Little Simon wounded Mingo on the head with a piece of iron.

Peter: He has a cut on his head? And what did you do?

Rufina: And what could I do? I washed his head with water from the lake and put a patch on it. Oh Peter, I'm afraid these boys will kill each other.

Peter: They're gonna kill us first. What little brats. Sito! Sito! Come over here!

Rufina: Don't hurt them, Peter. He already received a good strapping from his grandma. Leave him alone.

Peter: They gotta learn their lesson, Rufina. We have to correct them while we can.

Rufina: But they're still kids. It doesn't really matter yet.

Peter: Sito, I told you to come over here!

Rufina: Listen, instead of beating him, why don't you just pick his lice. Mamma was too busy to do it. I'm sure his head is full of them.

One day, like any other day, the three daughters of my brother James went to play with Peter and Rufina's sons. When the seven children got together, the garden of old Jonas's house looked like the Sea of Galilee on a stormy day.

Little Simon: Now, I laugh and everybody cries! Ha, ho, ha, ha!

A Girl: Now, do it the other way around! I cry and you all laugh! Boo hoo.

Another Girl: I'm bored. Let's play something else, Sito!

Mingo: Let's play soldiers!

Little Simon: Okay!

Girl: What about us?

Little Simon: Mila and you will be the lions. Come on! Let's go look for some swords!

Girl: What about me: what am I gonna be?

Little Simon: You're gonna be another lion! The swords! Where are the swords?

After a while, at midafternoon, Jesus arrived at Peter's house.

Jesus: How's everything, Rufina?

Rufina: I'm here, Jesus, in front of the stove, as always.

Jesus: Hmmm . . . ! The soup smells good.

Rufina: You can stay for dinner if you want. Dinner'll soon be ready. Everything gets delayed because of these boys. Right now, Reuben is suffering from diarrhea, and he takes most of my time.

Jesus: Maybe he's got worms.

Rufina: Of course, what else could it be? It's either the worms or some other sickness. This never ends! Well, Jesus, are you gonna stay for dinner?

Jesus: No, Rufina, thanks. I came to look for some poles I asked Peter to keep for me here. I need them in my work. Would you know where he put them?

Rufina: Oh Jesus, with so many things in my head, I don't remember where they are now, but I saw them yesterday. Why don't you ask Peter?

Peter: Oh yes, your poles ... They were just here in this corner! Where are they now?

Jesus: I wanted to do the repair that I promised our neighbor on the other side, while it's still early.

Peter: Yes, of course! But where the hell are they now? Rufina!

Rufina: Don't ask me, Peter, I don't know.

Nina: Ay, ay, ay!

Little Simon: I killed you, I killed you!

Nina: Oh, Uncle Peter, look at Sito! Uncle Peter!

Peter: Damn these children! Little Simon!

Jesus: Peter, look, she's bleeding.

Peter: Rufina, Rufina! Run! Little Simon, come here quick! Here are your poles, Jesus. They're all broken! Okay, who gave you permission to play with these poles?

Little Simon: They were our swords, Papa!

Peter: Swords, huh? And what were these swords for?

Little Simon: So that we could kill the lions. She was the lion.

Peter: These poles aren't yours, damn! They belong to Jesus and he needs them for his work. All right, pull down your pants, quick! You too, Mingo, show me your buttocks!

Rufina: Don't beat him, Peter. He's too small.

Peter: Yeah, he's too small to be beaten, but look at the mischief he's doing. Rufina, take the girls to their house. Now, to hell with these boys! Here, take this ... so you'll learn to respect what's not yours, dammit!

Jesus: Peter.

Peter: Insolent! Disobedient! You wretch!

Jesus: That's enough, Peter.

Peter: Bad seed! You good for nothing!

Jesus: Peter, for God's sake, I can replace those poles.

Peter: You shut up too, Jesus! These boys gotta learn their lesson!

Mingo: Oh, oh, oh...ohhh...!

Peter: Now, you two will stay here kneeling on these stones until I tell you. Do you hear? Do you hear me well?

Little Simon: Papa, we're sorry. I'm scared. It's dark here. Please forgive us.

Peter: So you're scared, huh? Well, you're gonna stay here till I tell you. And you better be ready, because the moment you move, the witch will come and take you with her long fork to the bottom of the lake!

Rufina: Don't scare them, Peter! How dare you, Peter!

Little Simon and Mingo were left in the yard, with a punishment of kneeling on stones. Peter went inside the house. Jesus was beside Rufina by the stove.

Peter: Pff!...I'm sorry, Jesus. Your work was ruined. I'll get other poles for you.

Jesus: Don't worry, Peter. I'm sorry for the children. You have beaten them very hard. And they're still kids.

Peter: They're kids, all right, but look at the mischief they do. No Jesus, don't defend them.

Jesus: Forgive them, man. They didn't know it was wrong.

Peter: Right, but they did it, and that's it.

Rufina: Yes, Peter. Listen to Jesus, and let the children in. They'll catch cold outside. Come on, forgive them. Tell them that the soup is ready.

Jesus: Come on, Peter, soften up. Don't be too hard with the boys.

Little Simon: And then, Papa, Mila said "grr," and Mingo took her by the tail and...

Jesus: See, Peter? They've forgotten their punishment. Children forget and forgive so easily. That's the good thing about them.

In my country, children hardly mattered, and that's the truth. They were taught the basic things; they received a good beating; and we grown-ups never conversed with them or asked their opinion. They mattered only because when they grew up, they could work. But not with Jesus. He could see something great in children.

Every time Jesus went to Peter's house he loved to chat with the children. He would sit in the yard under the lemon tree and soon Peter's boys and their neighbors, as well as James's daughters, would come running to him. Jesus gladly obliged them with his stories. That day, Jesus was teaching them some tongue-twisters.

I don't know how Jesus managed to attract the children to himself. I think he acted a bit like them and played with those brats like he was one of them. That day, when Peter and Andrew came home from fishing, they looked through the window and saw the children swarming like bees as they flocked around Jesus.

Rufina: I wonder why Jesus doesn't get married and have his own children. He surely knows how to pamper them. Look how fascinated they are with him, what with the stories he tells them each day!

Peter: Well, they better get back their senses right now. We gotta discuss something in Zebedee's house right now and Jesus has to come with us. Hey, kids, beat it, and don't bother us! Out! Out! Out of here!

Jesus: But the children are behaving well here. Let them stay with me.

Little Simon: Papa, Papa! I just learned a new tongue-twister today! That night...

Jesus: Oh Peter, you just don't know....

Peter: Oh hell, you're more patient than Job with these children!

Jesus: The truth is, I'm very fond of children, Peter.

Peter: Of course, because they're not your children. If you had your own to support today and tomorrow and the day after tomorrow, then it would be different.

Jesus: Peter, Peter...

Peter: Yes, I know, they're still hiding under the skirts of their mother and...

Jesus: And that's the best thing about them. They're kids, and, unlike us grown-ups, they're happy being what they are. We think we're important; we become serious; we crack our heads solving the most difficult problems in the world, while this kid, well, look at him: he sleeps, not a care in the world.

Rufina: He's tired, Jesus, he fell asleep sucking milk.

Jesus: See how good he looks with his mother, Peter. He fears nothing in his mother's arms, even on your lap. Sometimes I think that the entrance to the Kingdom of Heaven should be small, so small that only the children could go through it. Yes, that's it: we adults would have to bend our heads, leaving behind our pride, grudges, fears, everything. We'd have to make ourselves small, like Mingo or Little Simon or Mila, so we could get through that door.

Before he went to sleep, Jesus caressed Mingo, held him in his arms for a while, and kissed him. Oblivious of everything, Mingo slept soundly on his mother's lap.

•

In Jesus' milieu, children mattered very little. Certainly, they were considered as God's blessing, but a human's worth became a reality only when reaching majority age. In terms of the law, obligations, and religious rights, children were of little concern, as is shown in the writings of the period: the young were often grouped with the deaf-mutes and idiots. Other groups looked down upon were the sick, the slaves, women, the crippled, homosexuals, the blind, and so on. In the same manner that Jesus had an authentically revolutionary attitude toward women, his actions toward children — very much related to how he related with women — were surprising during his time. He made children privileged heirs of the Kingdom of God. This means that children are closer to God than adults, and as such they already have their own worth, and not just for what they will be when they grow up. Jesus' position had no precedent in the traditions of his ancestors. It was absolutely original.

Jesus' attitude toward children was not an empty theory nor an idea floating in the air. It was put into practice. Jesus shared much of his time playing with children, laughing and joking with them, talking to them about their small problems. These moments of sharing — devoid of sermons and many words — show how adults should act toward children. Their attitude should be founded on respect for their smallness, without expecting from them what they cannot give at their early age. In other words, to follow the classic formula of Paul: in order to win the children, be like a child (1 Cor. 9:23).

The children who were close to Jesus were not like those found in pictures: well kept, in spotless tunics, piously asking for a blessing with angelic faces. The children in the poor districts of Capernaum were street children, inured to wanting and to working at an early age, untidy, creatures full of lice, wearing rundown sandals, like present-day street children in our cities, like our peasant boys who are consumed by work and hunger even before they outgrow their infancy.

When Jesus talked to adults about "being like children" in order to enter the Kingdom of Heaven, he was not asking them to be as pure as children (as in being chaste). The idea that the child is more chaste than the adult, in this sense, is alien to Jewish thought. Rather, Jesus is referring more to the attitude that we must have before God — a Father who welcomes us in his arms. Being a child basically means learning to utter *Abba* ("Papa," "Daddy"). Jesus always addressed God with this word, full of trust, affection, and familiarity. *Abba* is the Aramaic word by which children call their father, and it is the first word that the baby babbles. Addressing the Lord in this manner means that Jesus has set aside all fears of a God who takes account of our failures. It conveys seeing in God a home, a refuge, and a big heart.

(Matt. 19:13–15; Mark 10:13–16; Luke 18:15–17;
Matt. 18:1–5; Mark 9:33–37; Luke 9:46–48)

37

The Cry of Lazarus

That year was a bad one in all of Galilee. The summer storms had ruined all the harvests. The wheat crop, the rye, and the olive groves were destroyed. Hunger came like a plague and knocked at every door, and the epidemics and desperation followed. The farmers sold at any price the fruits of the next harvests which had not even been sown. The usurers had a heyday and loaned money with an interest rate of 80 to 90 percent. More and more beggars migrated into the cities each day. Capernaum was not spared from them.

Jesus: Look, John, there they go again.

John: Yeah, they'll sit in front of Eleazar's house and stay there the whole day waiting for the garbage to be disposed so they can scavenge melon skins or some scrap meat.

Jesus: No, no, it can't go on like this.

John: Today it's the peasants, but tomorrow, it's gonna be us, Jesus, the fishermen of the lake. Then the artisans. This will never end.

Jesus: Let's join them, John. Let's stay in front of Eleazar's house.

Beggar: What are you talking about, Nazarene? About God? Bah! God doesn't listen to us. He's deaf.

Jesus: No, he's not deaf. You haven't shouted loud enough for him to hear. Is that right, John?

John: Exactly. Come, let us shout all together until the rocks tremble and split!

Jesus: Until the God of Heaven hears the screams of the hungry and gives us a hand.

Beggar: Well, what are we waiting for? Let's all scream!

All: Aaah! Aaah! Aaah!

Jesus then began telling another of his stories.

Jesus: One night, God was taking a rest up in heaven, and Abraham passed in front of God's door.

253

God: Ah, my friend Abraham, come...

Abraham: At your service, my Lord.

God: Abraham, what's going on down there? I hear a lot of noise? Don't you hear it? Listen well.

Beggars: Aaah! Aaah! Aaah!

Abraham: It's like the rumbling of thunder promising a storm. Or it could be the roaring of an impending earthquake.

God: You're wrong, Abraham. Nothing of the sort. Listen well.

Beggars: Aaah! Aaah! Aaah!

God: These are men and women weeping and screaming. And the children too. Don't you hear? They're my children, Abraham! Something terrible must be happening to them. Come, go down immediately to earth and find out what's the matter. I'll be waiting for you.

Abraham: At your service, my Lord. I'm going right away.

Jesus: And old Abraham put on his sandals, took his cane, and headed as rapidly and obediently as before, when he left Ur of Chaldea, for an unknown land. Soon enough, a perspiring Abraham returned and faced the Lord.

God: So you're back, Abraham.

Abraham: Yes, my Lord. I was there for only a few seconds and my ears almost burst because of the noise. The yelling of the people was like boiling water, or a volcano about to explode. Their cries can be heard from all four corners of the earth.

God: Tell me what's wrong. Why are my children screaming?

Abraham: Because they're hungry.

God: They're hungry? Why, that can't be. When I created the earth at the beginning, I planned everything well. Do you think I'm irresponsible? No, I planted many fruit trees, sowed many seeds that would give them abundant food, and created the birds that fly in the sky and the fish in the rivers and the animals that provide delicious meat on earth. I created everything so that people would have food to eat. This doesn't include the wealth that's hidden in the bowels of the earth and in the seas. They can't be hungry. Everything was well planned. There's sufficient food for everyone on earth. Why is this happening now?

Abraham: You have forgotten one important detail, Lord.

God: What is it?

Abraham: Human beings. They've taken it upon themselves to divide the land. Do you see what I mean?

God: "The one who divides gets the lion's share." Is that it?

Abraham: Exactly. This is what a group of people have done, so they can own everything. They have all the food hoarded in their barns.

God: What about the rest?

Abraham: They're the ones shouting at the doors of the rich, waiting for the garbage to be thrown out of the window so they can get the spoils and eat them. They're starving.

God: I can't believe what you're saying, my friend Abraham. Is this what my children on earth are doing?

Abraham: Just as I have said, my Lord.

God: Hearing all this, Abraham, I'm about to lose my patience. I'm so enraged that I feel I want to summon all the clouds in heaven, as I had done before, during the time of Noah, to bring the floods and submerge the earth in water. I'm too ashamed to have them as my children, whose hearts are made not of flesh but of stone.

Abraham: What can we do now, my Lord?

God: Have you forgotten that I am the judge of heaven and earth? Michael, Raphael, Gabriel, and Uriel, come right away!

Jesus: And, without batting an eyelash, the archangels presented themselves before the Lord.

God: I will mete out judgment on earth. I want you to descend to earth immediately and bring me one of those crying out in hunger, that he may give his declaration. Then bring me one of those who are feasting, one whose stomach is full. I am going to question the two. Come on, move fast!

Jesus: So the four archangels turned and immediately descended to earth, where the screams were heard. Michael and Raphael grabbed one of those dying of hunger by the shoulders, while Gabriel and Uriel did the same to a rich man who was also dying, not of hunger but of extreme self-indulgence. The two were brought before God's tribunal.

God: The meeting may now come to order. You, what's your name?

Lazarus: Lazarus, my Lord.

God: You're one of those creating a lot of noise down there, aren't you?

Lazarus: Yes, Lord.

God: Will you tell us why you and your friends are screaming so much?

Lazarus: Because our children are dying of hunger, because our wives don't even have a drop of milk in the breast with which to feed them. Our men are so weak that their knees tremble for not having eaten for seven days. That's why we're crying out loud. Day and night we do this, that justice may fall upon us. Look at me, my Lord. You can count my ribs one by one. I'm all skin and bones. My wounds are all over my body and dogs come to lick them and I allow this because their saliva eases the pain.

God: Stop, my son. That's enough. Do you want to ask him anything, Abraham?

Abraham: You said you're hungry. Some say this happens because you hate to work, that you're a bum.

Lazarus: No, father Abraham, it's not true. All our lives we do nothing but work and sweat. We toil like animals. The rich drink our sweat and suck our blood. They wring us like grapes in the pressing field, and like olives under a millstone. These are the people who hoard everything but won't even give the crumbs from their table.

Jesus: God was teary-eyed while he listened to poor Lazarus's account. Then God stood up, walked a few steps, and faced the rich man.

God: Who are you?

Epulon: My name is Epulon.

God: What can you say about the declaration of Lazarus?

Epulon: Well, to tell you frankly, I don't know anything about it.

God: Of course you do! Unless you're deaf! I know you can hear perfectly well. Why didn't you listen to these people seated in front of your house and crying out in hunger, begging you to share with them what you had in excess? I heard them from heaven. Why didn't you hear them when you were just beside them?

Epulon: Lord, I ... There was a lot of noise at the party, so I couldn't hear.

God: Liar! Now you'll hear. Open your ears because I am going to pass judgment: you're being accused of murder, rich man, Epulon, for having killed your brothers and sisters of hunger or having allowed them to die, which is the same thing.

Epulon: But Lord, the farm, as well as the wheat and barns, are mine. They're all my property. Why should I give to someone whose name I don't even know?

God: Mine, mine, all you can say is mine! Who gave you the right to claim what's not yours? I created this world and everything in it. I created it from the beginning and it's mine. I lease to anyone I like. Who are you? You were naked when you came out of your mother's womb and will return naked to the womb of the earth. The only thing that's yours are the ashes; they're your only property.

Epulon: Have mercy, Lord, have mercy on me.

God: You never had pity on your brothers and sisters. You wished to be alone, and you'll remain alone forever.

God: Lazarus, come and take a rest. You've suffered enough.

Lazarus: I can't, my Lord. How can I when my companions continue to scream down on earth? Don't you hear them?

God: You're right, son. Look, I've thought of something better. I'm going down with you to earth. Abraham!

Abraham: At your service, Lord.

God: Lend me your sandals.

Abraham: Yes, my Lord.

God: You stay here, Abraham. Here you'll find peace and glory, but on earth, there's hell from the egoism of some. I'm needed down there by my children who are crying out for justice.

Abraham: Lord, are you out of your mind? How can you leave your house in heaven?

God: It's all right. My home is down there with the homeless, with thousands of people like Lazarus, who know not where to go. Goodbye, Abraham, and take care of everything until I come back. Let's go, Lazarus, and hurry. We'll start a Kingdom of Justice for the poor people of the world. From now on and forever, I'll be with you each day, until things have finally changed.

Beggar: But things have remained the same, countryman. We're tired of screaming, and the landlord's house remains closed. Eleazar is selfish and cruel, like the rich man in your story.

Jesus: We can't expect much from him and from people like him, but look, other doors will be opened for you. Hi, Anna, will you come over for a minute!

Neighbor: What's the matter? What's this noise? My ears are almost bursting because of it!

Beggar: We're hungry.

Neighbor: Well, the truth is I don't have much to spare, but . . . Let's see if can add more water to the soup!

Old Samuel opened his door too, and Joanne, the wife of Lolo. Deborah did the same, as well as Simeon the hunchback.

The poor people's doors were opened to welcome poorer ones. Yes, the Kingdom of God was close to us.

•

In Palestine, as in the rest of the ancient world, natural catastrophes — which people did not know how to prevent or control — were a cause of great starvation periodically besieging the country. Intense droughts, hurricanes, and torrential rains destroyed the harvests, the main source of income for most people. The poor crop yields caused an increase in the price of basic foods. The number of beggars grew in the cities and on the roadsides. Speculators and hoarders took advantage of the situation, which is exactly what happens nowadays.

There exists in all cultures stories describing the twist of fate befalling people in history. These are ways of expressing people's rebellion against acts of injustice committed in history. On the basis of this, Jesus narrated the parable of the rich man, Epulon ("opulent"), and the poor man, Lazarus. In this parable, Jesus tries to show his listeners, dramatically, the demands of justice in the gospel. The name Lazarus — meaning "God helps" — is important in the parable: God helps the poor; he helps one who has been seen as worthless.

In the parable, God judges the rich and the poor in the persons of Epulon and Lazarus. He shares in the pain experienced by the poor, and he condemns the rich, who are deaf to the poor's cry of anguish. Wealth hardens people's hearts and plugs their ears. That is why the rich cannot enter the Kingdom of God — which is a kingdom of equality — unless they renounce wealth.

In our present world there is enough food for everyone everywhere. There are sufficient raw materials to provide every family a decent way of life. It is not true that the world is overpopulated. The majority of the third world countries are underpopulated. It is also a fallacy that population is the cause of poverty for millions of people. Many people have little or nothing because a few people have an excess. God does not condone this situation. He created the world in abundance: its riches, fruits, mines, all for everyone's benefit. But the ambition of a few widens the gap between the rich and the poor day by day. God hears the cries of anguish, of protest and rebellion, of the poor, and he responds by taking their cause as his own. God grieves by their side and fights with them too. The cause of liberation of the poor in this world is God's cause. The message of Jesus in the gospel has to do with the realization of equality among people in this world.

Although the parable talks of something beyond, of justice that God will give in the next life, the constant message in the gospel is applicable to the present. That is why, in this episode, God wears Abraham's sandals and goes down to earth to immediately start the liberation of the hungry: this is Jesus, God's messenger, who tells us that God is in a hurry to carry out his plan to distribute the earth's riches among his children on earth.

To be a Christian is to say "This is ours," and not "This is mine." The rich persist in defending property and, in doing so, contradict God's plan. St. Ambrose said: "Don't give to the poor what is yours, but give him back what is his. This is so because you claim as your own what is common property and what has been given for the benefit of all. The land belongs to all, and not only to the rich." It is Christian to share, to create a community, and to share one's wealth. The poor are often freer and more capable than the rich of sharing the little that they have, and of learning the value of saying "ours."

This parable has always been used to discourse on hell and a cruel God who denies the rich man, Epulon, even a drop of water. But Jesus does not want to frighten anyone with the flames of hell nor present a vindictive God. What he wants to show us is the severity, the radicalness, of God's judgment, which cannot be swayed by the rich people's alibis. It is very clear that in the Kingdom of God, there is no place for those who refuse to alleviate the misery of others: only those who share their food with the hungry shall find a place beside God.

(Luke 16:19–31)

38

It Happened in Nain

In those days, great was the misery all over Israel. Hunger spread to all the cities by the lakeshore and throughout the farms. There was starvation in poor people's houses, and it became their constant companion day and night.

Naomi: Here, son, take it. Just make do with this piece of bread and . . .

Abel: I can't stand this! Damn! I work like a beast under the heat of the sun, and this is what I get: a piece of hard bread?

Naomi: What can I do? There's nothing more than this. We're indebted to everyone, and nobody wants to lend us a single cent anymore.

Abel: It's not you, Mamma. How long will we put up with this? Tomorrow it's gonna be the same thing — filling up the barns of this fortunate Eleazar and then back here to chew a crust of hard bread for supper. This isn't life, dammit!

Naomi: Abel, my son, don't curse, for God might punish us.

Abel: That's it! Here we are living in misery, and worse, God comes to punish us! Well, let him do what he pleases, for all I care. To hell with God and with Eleazar, and with everyone! Oh, oh, this pain!

Naomi: Son, what's the matter?

Abel: Nothing, it's nothing, Mamma. I'm going to lie down. Leave me alone.

Naomi: Are you feeling bad, my son?

Abel: I'm tired, I feel like they beat me several times, and I feel cold all over my body.

Naomi: Oh, Lord God! When will you ever remember us, when?

Woman Neighbor: Let me look at him, neighbor. Oh, yes, this boy is burning with fever. He looks sick.

Naomi: Holy God! What am I gonna do? What am I gonna do?

Woman Neighbor: Don't worry. Let me prepare some bitter lemon for him, and you'll see how soon he'll get well.

Naomi: Do you think so, neighbor?

Woman Neighbor: He'll get well, you'll see. If he doesn't, then what can we do? Don't be sad, Naomi; if this is really meant for him, then let's just accept it.

The doctor came that night.

Doctor: Your son is serious, lady. The high fever has consumed his whole body.

Naomi: He hasn't uttered a word for two days, Doctor. He doesn't even know who I am.

Doctor: I can't do anything.

Naomi: Is he going to die?

Doctor: This question of death is God's concern and not ours.

Naomi: If he dies, what will I do? He's the only one I have, the only one.

That young man was the only one Naomi had. Her husband had passed away several years before. Since then, Naomi worked on the farm in order to raise her son. Her hands became callused and her youthful face developed wrinkles. That year, hunger struck Naomi's house, as it did the rest of the houses of Israel. This was followed by sickness. That day at dawn, death came to that house.

Naomi: Abel, my son! Abel! Abel!

Woman Neighbor: Don't call him anymore, Naomi. He's gone.

Naomi: It can't be! It can't be!

Woman Neighbor: Learn to accept it, woman. God gave him to you, and God took him away from you.

Naomi: But I needed him! He was the only one I had! I live because of him! Now, what's the use of life?

Woman Neighbor: Better resign yourself, Naomi, and have patience.

Naomi shut the eyes of her son, Abel, and, assisted by her neighbors, washed his body and wrapped it in a clean white sheet. Soon the mourners came, those women who wept for our dead and informed everyone of death through their songs. Their plaintive cries were heard through all the houses of the small town of Nain. Naomi's friends came to console her and to prepare her son's burial.

Woman Neighbor: Oh Naomi, your son was seen working with you in the field up until last week. The mourners have gathered beside the dead body. Some men have played vigil music with their flutes, while the others have prepared the little bed on which to place the dead boy during interment.

Another Woman: It's destiny, Naomi, which is written in the book of heaven. No amount of tears can erase it. Accept your fate.

Naomi: I'm all alone. I'm all by myself. I have no husband to give me other children, nor children who can give me grandchildren. What use are my breasts, my womb, and my hands?

Woman Neighbor: Be resigned to your fate, woman.

Naomi: Why? Why me? He's the only one I have!

Woman Neighbor: It was a case of bad fever.

Naomi: But he was very young. He didn't have to die! He didn't have to die!

Woman Neighbor: Accept your fate, woman, accept your fate.

During those days of hunger, Peter and I went with Jesus to Nazareth. Jesus wanted to send Mary, his mother, some money and to see how she was. Before returning to Capernaum, we passed by Nain, where a cousin of his lived. Nain was a small town on the outskirts of Mount Gabial and was very closely guarded by the heights of Mount Tabor. As we were approaching Nain, we heard from afar the mournful music of the flutes and the plaintive cries of the women.

Peter: What a curse! This is the third death that we've seen on the road. Since we left Capernaum, we've done nothing but come across funerals.

John: It must be another case of black fever. There must be an epidemic here.

Jesus: What epidemic? It's hunger, John. We poor are dying of hunger. There was no harvest, prices have gone up, taxes have gone up, and as a result people die of hunger.

Along the road leading outside the town, we saw the funeral heading toward us. The mourners, dressed in sackcloth, beat their bare chests, and pulled their hair while crying in anguish. Behind them was the dead man being carried by four men on an improvised bed. He was wrapped in a white sheet. Then we saw him. He was a young man. There was no trace of beard on his face. Beside him must have been his mother, anguish written all over her face. She was crying and tearing her dress off while lifting her arms to heaven. Many men and women from the town accompanied her. We followed the cortege when it passed in front of us.

Woman Neighbor: Oh my God! Oh my God! Poor Naomi! Poor woman!

John: Who died, madam?

Another Neighbor: Abel, Naomi's son. His mother was widowed six years ago. He was her only child. What a misfortune! He died so young.

Jesus: He didn't have to die.

Woman Neighbor: But he died. He had the black fever, which is deadly.

The funeral cortege passed through the narrow and dusty road bordering the hill of Nain. At the far end was the small cemetery.

Woman Neighbor: He died this morning at sunrise!

Jesus: He didn't die, woman. Don't say that. Better say: They killed him. Yes, yes, ... he was killed by those who overpriced the little wheat that the rains have left us! He was killed by those who continue to enrich themselves while the children of Israel are dying of hunger.

The people behind the cortege turned to Jesus, who raised his voice while uttering those words, amid lamentations and flute sounds. The commotion that ensued spread fast enough, and the men carrying the dead stopped walking. Everyone was looking at us.

Neighbor: Hey, what are those strangers shouting about at the back? Respect the dead, dammit!

Woman Neighbor: This man is saying that Abel was killed not by black fever nor any other fever, but that he died of starvation.

Another Neighbor: It doesn't matter anymore. He's dead.

Naomi: My son! My son! Oh my son!

Neighbor: Keep on moving! Stop this silly talk! Come on! Continue playing the flutes!

Naomi: My God, why did you take him away from me? Why?

Without uttering a word, Jesus moved through the flute players and the farmers from Nain. Peter and I followed him. Jesus stopped by the boy's mother and in a low voice began to say the prayer for the dead of Israel. Beside him, the mourners continued weeping, in keeping with their job.

Naomi: My son! My son's dead. He was the only one I've got.

Neighbor: Hey you, what's your business disturbing the funeral?

Jesus went near the boy's mother.

Jesus: Now, now, stop weeping, woman.

Naomi, her eyes full of tears, turned to Jesus.

Naomi: I've lost everything I had! Everything's gone! Everything!

Neighbor: Come on, Naomi. You must accept your fate.

Naomi: No! I don't want him to die! No, no!

Jesus: Neither does God want your son to die. Neither does he accept it.

John: Hey, Jesus, let's get away from here. There's nothing we can do.

Jesus: Stay, John. I want to see him.

Then Jesus went near the small bed carrying the dead boy and looked at him; he also had tears in his eyes. The mourners were gathered around the corpse, their hair disheveled. They were crying in deep sorrow. They never stopped.

Jesus: What was your son's name?

Naomi: Abel, his name was Abel.

Jesus: Of course, Abel. . . . History keeps on repeating itself. Abel, where are the Cains who killed you? How long, oh God of Israel? How long will you turn a deaf ear to your many children dying of hunger? How long shall our mothers mourn the early death of their sons? The blood of this Abel is clamoring to God from this earth. This boy didn't have to die, he can't die. Abel, stand up, Abel!

Jesus bent over the dead boy, took him by the arm, and helped him to sit. Abel opened his eyes. His eyes were big and scared, as if he woke up from a long nightmare.

Naomi: My son, my son!

Seeing this, the men dropped the small bed on the ground and ran like hell. They were followed by the mourners and the flute players, as well as by the other neighbors from Nain. They were running and screaming, horrified. Peter was as white as chalk, while my legs were trembling. Only the mother was left with us, who was looking at her son with tears still in her eyes, but she did not dare touch him.

Naomi: Abel, Abel, my son!

Jesus looked tired, like one who had just fought a hard battle. Soon, what happened in Nain spread through the whole of Galilee. And the people were saying: "We have a prophet in our midst. God has come to help his people."

•

Hunger is the door to many diseases. In earlier times of drought or loss of harvests, epidemics came about (plague, fevers), and no one knew their origin, much less how to fight them.

Nain is a small city, around fifteen kilometers from Nazareth. Its name means "beautiful." It is situated by the mountainside and is closely sheltered by the height of Mount Tabor. At present, a small Franciscan church serves as a reminder of Jesus' passage through this village.

The Israelites had many ways of showing their sorrow for the dead: they ripped off their clothes, loosened their hair, beat their breasts, and poured ashes on their heads. They mourned their dead with ritualistic weeping from the time the news of a death became known up to interment. At times, this was a scandalous ritual. Not only the relatives and neighbors but the professional mourners as well came to weep for the dead. Generally, a group of flute players were present during the wake and would even play during the funeral. They wept, screamed, or sang "lamentations," which almost always commenced with an "ay." These lamentations continued even after the burial for a period of seven days, which was the duration of mourning in Israel.

When Jesus replied to John the Baptist's question about what he was doing in Galilee, he enumerated five signs for the coming of the Kingdom of God: that the blind would see, the crippled would walk, the lepers would be cleansed, the deaf would hear, and the dead would be brought back to life (Matt. 11:1–6). All these are signs of the messianic time. Luke included this episode in his gospel. The good news that Jesus brings us is this: God rebels against the death of his children. He does not want death to be considered as a final destiny. He is the God of the living and, therefore, fights against death.

In the episode, the widow's son is called Abel. It is a way of telling us of a "type" of death. Abel, the second son of Adam and Eve, slain by his brother Cain, will forever be the type of the just person killed unjustly. To die of hunger is to die unjustly; it is murder. God does not want any of his children to perish in this manner. The act of Jesus, bringing Abel back to life, is therefore not a gesture of pure compassion, but God's firm manifestation of his rebellion against this unjust death. As in Genesis, in the face of hunger, we are always confronted with this question: "What have you done to your brother?" (Gen. 4:9).

In the face of millions of people dying of hunger, no one can say: I am not responsible; this problem does not concern me; I cannot do anything.

Hunger is actually the number one problem in the world. Two out of three persons living on this planet suffer from hunger or malnutrition of some kind. Hunger is the prelude to a long string of diseases (some hereditary), countless family problems, and death. Many entire countries suffer from hunger. In a society where hunger is a chain that binds the majority of people, the Kingdom of God will begin when this situation disappears and a new life begins by way of good nutrition. There is nothing more unjust than dying due to hunger in a world where a few countries squander food each day, as people become blind to the misery of their brothers and sisters.

Death is always more painful when it comes prematurely and unexpectedly: when one is young, when one has hardly had a chance to live. There are countries near us — Haiti, for example — where life expectancy does not exceed forty years. (In developed countries, it reaches seventy-five years.) In many Third World countries, it is a fact that millions of men and women die "before their time." Those who die of hunger, even if they die in their beds, die because they are killed. Their blood, like that of Abel's, cries out to God from earth.

(Luke 7:11–17)

39

A Storm by the Lake

Jesus: ... and then this Samaritan came with his camel!

Zebedee: Well, guys, this is enough for now, don't you think? Let's end all these stories; tomorrow we gotta start work early. Come on, let's all go to sleep.

John: Hey, old man, don't be a kill-joy. Go to sleep if you want, and leave us alone. What happened again to the Samaritan, Jesus?

Jesus: Well, this man goes and ...

Zebedee: Don't you have ears? I told you to go to sleep! You sleep so late and then doze off in the boat. You, Jesus from Nazareth, will you shut up now and reserve your stories for the next time?

John: Just let him finish with this one, old man. He's halfway through it. Come on, what happened to the Samaritan?

Zebedee: No. Get up early tomorrow morning so you can go fishing with us, and you can tell us all the stories you want in the boat. But now, this small talk is finished, do you hear?

We would often get together with Jesus to play dice and to hear his stories and laugh at jokes he'd already told several times. Sometimes we would meet at Peter's house, and other times at the house of Zebedee, my old man, to take time out from the day's work. The wee hours of the night simply slipped away without our knowing it.

Peter: Yes, why not, Jesus? Come and join us in our fishing tomorrow. Ever since you came to Capernaum, you never dipped your finger into the water.

Jesus: Who, me? Go fishing? No way. That's not for me. I know nothing about fishing.

Zebedee: It's high time you learned, dammit! "There's always time for learning," as my late father used to say.

Salome: Yeah, he always said that, but he never learned himself. He was more stupid than a laborer!

Jesus: No, Peter, leave me alone with my bricks and tools. We from the inland are not real lovers of water.

John: Cheer up, brown one! There's always a first time.

Peter: Tomorrow will be a good day for fishing, yes sir.

James: I'm not sure about that, Peter. They say that the Great Coffer is shaking.

Salome: You don't have to go very far then. Today the sun was as red as tomato, which is a bad sign.

Peter: What nonsense are you talking about? The lake is as still as a poor man's jawbone!

James: This lake is treacherous, Peter. Everything's so quiet and the wind from Mount Carmel will suddenly come pounding down the lake.

Peter: Don't be a soothsayer, James. I tell you, the weather's very fine.

James: Philemon, the crippled, was called a soothsayer, and where is he now? Buried at the bottom of the lake!

Peter: Go to hell, red head! The weather has been fine today, and it'll even be better tomorrow!

James: I bet there's gonna be a storm tomorrow! The Great Coffer's shaking!

Zebedee: Hell, that's enough! If you're not telling stories, you're fighting. Go to sleep everybody! We gotta get up early to work!

The Great Coffer was the name given to a number of rocks found between Bethsaida and Capernaum. The old seamen used to say that from there, they could hear the agitated waves of the Great Sea whenever a storm was approaching.

Zebedee: Come on, lazy bones, get up! Didn't I tell you? Now you can continue with your storytelling! On your toes, everyone!

It was only about four o'clock in the morning when my father, Zebedee, was already starting to wake us all up.

Zebedee: Hey, you, Nazarene, didn't you say you were coming? Well, hurry up! Rub that sleep out of your eyes and move fast.

After taking some hot root soup that Salome had prepared, we headed toward the wharf, as we always did, everyday.

Zebedee: To the boats, guys, for the weather's good and we gotta take advantage! Today's gonna be a lucky day!

We sailed out in two boats with our big nets. Zebedee, Peter, James, Jesus, and I were on the first boat. On the second were Andrew, the twins, and old Jonas. The last of the evening stars were still shining in the sky. Gradually, we were moving away from the shore as we paddled through the lake. The wind barely blew and the sail was hanging by the mast.

Zebedee: Hey, John, what's the matter with that fellow? Look at his face.
John: He's as white as flour.
Peter: Farm people aren't used to this. They get dizzy with the splash of water.
James: Or they're scared of the water!
John: Hey, Jesus, why don't you lie down over there? Maybe your fear'll go away!
James: It'll pass. Leave him alone.
Zebedee: The net, guys, get the net ready! My nose is telling me there's a school of fish over here. Strengthen the buoys, Peter. You, James, loosen up a little. Hey, you guys on the other boat, let's all cast the net!

While we were getting the big net ready, Jesus went near the rail and held on with both hands. He was very dizzy. Later, he threw himself down on the headrest of the stern and curled himself up on it. Soon he fell asleep.

James: Hmmm . . . I don't like this. The wind is blowing strong. . . .
John: Yeah, all of a sudden it's blowing very hard.
Zebedee: Take in the sail a little, if you don't want the wind to sweep us like it did to Habakkuk! Peter, don't let go of the net — it's loaded with needlefish! Pull hard!
James: For the love of Satan, this wind is blowing still harder! A storm is brewing!
Zebedee: Damn, gather all the oars and let's go back to the shore! These waves are going to swallow all of us!
Peter: You guys on the other boat! Jonas! Pull in the net and let's go! A storm is coming!
Jonas: All right. We're going ahead. Good luck!
Zebedee: Dammit! This guy's still sleeping. Look at him — he's all curled up like a frog!

John: Hey, Jesus, wake up. There's a storm coming, one of the worst. You better get up. Hey, he's not moving. I think he's dead.

Peter: He's scared to death, that's what he is. Poor guy, this is the first time he went fishing!

Jesus: How did I ever get into this?

Zebedee: Our man has finally resurrected. What's he saying?

John: What were you saying, brown one?

Jesus: I was asking how I ever got into this mess.

Peter: What's the matter, Jesus? Are you scared?

Jesus: Of course, what do you think?

Zebedee: What about the story you were telling us last night? Come on, tell us now.

James: Damn, these waves will ruin our sail!

The stern suddenly creaked terribly. A huge wave lifted us into the air, hurling the boat back into the lake, amid the storm's fury. We were drenched to the bone. Peter and I hurriedly tried to fasten the sail, but unfortunately missed, and it was torn to pieces. The wind blew before us, shaking our boat violently each time.

James: I told you, Peter, I told you not to set out into the lake today, as the Great Coffer was trembling!

Peter: Go to hell, James! How was I supposed to know that?

James: It's because you're so stubborn. I warned you not to go away from the shore. But you're so stupid, you even brought more men than ever on the boat. This boat's gonna sink because of our weight!

John: Well, why don't you throw yourself into the water to lighten our load?

James: Take it easy — before long we'll be joining the crippled Philemon down there, and it's all your fault.

Peter: Listen, beast: no one expected this to happen!

James: Oh really? Didn't you see the sun turn red, redder than my hair, yesterday?

Peter: Then why did you come, imbecile? You could've stayed behind.

James: So I'm the stupid one, am I? You deserve a punch in the nose!

Peter: Just try, you pig, and you'll know who I am!

James: I warned you about the Great Coffer.

Jesus: That's enough, James, and shut up, Peter! To hell with both of you. Why don't you do something instead of bickering with one another? We're all going to drown here and you waste time arguing on who's right.

Zebedee: Well said, Jesus. These two are wasting their energy. I wonder which is worse: to face the storm or to put up with these two nuts. Come on guys, let's take a turn toward the starboard. If we row with all our might, then we can save our skin. Each one take his own oar and we'll row at the same time. Harder, fellas, let's go, yahhh!

All: Yahhhh!

Zebedee: God helps those who help themselves! Let's go, yahhh! Push harder, come on, yahhh!

All: Yahhhh!

Zebedee: As though it were Beelzebub's neck, go, yahhha!

All: Yahhhh!

Zebedee: Don't stop, dammit, let's go, yahhh!

All: Yahhhh!

Zebedee: Don't be scared, just go, yahhh!

All: Yahhhh!

Zebedee: Men of little faith, go, yahhh!

All: Yahhhh!

Zebedee: Up with our faith and down with the oars, go, yahh!

All: Yahhhh!

Old Zebedee led us in synchronizing the rowing of our boats. Gradually, in full force and with our veins about to explode, we were advancing in the midst of that dark and stormy sea. Since he did not know how to row, Jesus was given a jar to bail out the water that entered the boat.

After our long bout with the waves, when the storm had calmed down, we saw the darkened rocks along the coast. Slowly, we touched bottom with our oars as we drew near the rocky ground which formed an opening between the cliffs. Not too far away, we could see a small city.

Peter: Look, imagine where we've landed. We're on the other side of the lake. This is Gerasa.

James: Gerasa? What the hell are we doing here? This is the land of pigs!

Zebedee: Rejoice that you've finally touched land, even if it belongs to the Gerasenes! We very nearly ended up on the bottom of the lake.

John: That's true, old man. That would've been scary!

Zebedee: It was the Nazarene who must've been really scared.

Peter: When that strong wind nearly smashed us on the side, you were almost scared to death, weren't you Jesus?

Jesus: The truth is, I was never so scared in my life.

James: Don't laugh now, Peter, but you also smell like piss.

Peter: Well, listen, Jesus was like the captain of the boat when he yelled at us and said: "That's enough and shut up!" I think even the sea was scared by that scream and so it calmed down.

Zebedee: Come on, guys, let's take something to warm our stomachs. Let's see if these pagans are hospitable enough to attend to castaways like us.

Many years later, every time we remembered that storm in the lake, Peter would say that the huge waves calmed down when Jesus yelled. I don't know, but my fear then was so great that I couldn't remember what happened exactly. There was only one thing I was sure of: that each day, Jesus seemed to us an extraordinary human being. From him we learned how to be united in order to overcome any difficulty.

•

The geographical structure of the Sea of Galilee beside the river Jordan, flanked on the north by tall mountains, hastens the formation of heavy storms accompanied sometimes by strong winds and huge waves. Peter and his companions, like expert seamen, knew, by means of different signs — the color of the sky, the wind's direction — the possibility of an impending storm. Nevertheless, since these storms come unexpectedly, they could not ever really be absolutely sure.

We cannot read all the texts of the Bible, whether of the Old or New Testament, in the same manner and use the same criteria. The Bible, besides being the word of God (and this does not always mean "historical word"), is a collection of stories which the people of Israel have transmitted from parents to children through the centuries until such time that they were put into writing. In these accounts, the people tell us what they have lived, felt, thought, and sung. Consequently, some books are historical narratives; others are religious outlines or sketches, catechetical summaries, theological outlines, or refrains; and others are poetry. These are what we call the "literary genres" of the Bible. Not taking this into account, one may, out of confusion, look only for "what happened" in the Scriptures, what is strictly historical, while the deeper meaning of faith found in the symbolic teaching of a number of accounts may lose out.

The gospels tell us of six miracles Jesus performed in relation to nature. These have to do not with the cure of human beings but with natural elements. In one of these accounts Jesus calms a storm simply by raising his voice. In each of these texts, there is an attempt to come up with an outline for catechesis in order to transmit an idea.

It must be remembered that for the Israelite mentality, the sea — for example, the Sea of Galilee — was considered a haven of bad spirits and demons, the powerful and occult forces which represented danger for people. That Jesus was able to calm the waves is a symbol of power which God had given him. It was a way of proclaiming that he was the Messiah, the Lord, and therefore a way of saying that a poor peasant's weakness, like that of Jesus, is stronger than all the powers working against the community.

It is likewise true — and this is the central message of this episode — that the weakness of the poor is strengthened and efficient when the poor are united, when they become organized, when they row together in the same direction. These "miracles" in relation to nature — for example, controlling lightning and thunder — are thus always acts of unity and criticisms of power.

(Matt. 8:23–27; Mark 4:35–41; Luke 8:22–25)

40

In the Land of the Gerasenes

After the storm we disembarked in Gerasa, on the other side of the lake. Our boat with its tattered sail was moored near one of the black and pointed rocks by the cliff. Old Zebedee, Peter, Jesus, my brother James, and I started to walk through the rocky ground along the shore toward the small town at the end, about a thousand meters away.

Zebedee: These pagans must be very fond of pork. Look how many swine there are! It's an enormous herd.

John: Who could this man be, running toward us? He's making some signs.

Andronicus: I see you're strangers! Where do you come from?

Peter: From Capernaum, my friend, from the other side of the lake.

Andronicus: That far? And you traveled in such bad weather?

Zebedee: We were caught by the storm. We went out fishing and almost died.

Andronicus: It's not surprising. Trypho announced it.

Peter: How's that? Who said what?

Andronicus: Yesterday, Trypho went around Gerasa announcing to the people that a storm was coming, and that the sun was as red as a ball of fire.

John: And who the hell's this guy?

Andronicus: He's the adviser of the entire land of Gerasa, a friend of the gods and the demons: he's Trypho, the sorcerer. Strangers, listen to me, if you want a piece of good advice.

Zebedee: Well, as they say in my homeland, he who listens to advice doesn't perish young. Come now, what's your advice?

Andronicus: If you want to cross the lake again, you'd better consult the powerful Trypho first. He'll tell you whether to go or not. He'll unfold for you the mysteries of the sea and the land, as well as the sky.

Peter: If indeed he knows so much, let him tell us where to eat a good piece of lamb's head, as we're already starving to death.

Andronicus: You may have a good laugh now, but when you're in front of Trypho, you may not feel like doing so. Come with me, strangers.

Jesus: Hey, you haven't told us your name yet.

Andronicus: My name is Andronicus. I work as a swineherd for Aesculapius. All the herds you see belong to him. Come, follow me.

Andronicus, the swineherd, led us around the town. Behind it, by a grove of oak trees, was the town cemetery. At the far end was an open cave.

Zebedee: Where are you taking us, pal? We have no need to reserve a space in this place yet!

Trypho: Ahh, ahh, ahh!

John: Pff! At the rate we're going... If I don't take something to warm my stomach, chances are you'll have to bury me in this place!

Trypho: Ahh, ahh, ahh!

John: Hey, Andronicus, who's the one shouting?

Andronicus: That's precisely where we're going, strangers. In that cave, Trypho communicates with the living and the dead. Follow me!

We followed the Gerasene, passing over stones and tombs until we reached the entrance of the stinking cave. We covered our noses as we went inside. Then we saw the famous sorcerer: his body was huge and hairy, barely covered by a dirty rag around his waist. His arms and feet were in chains. He was a madman.

Andronicus: Trypho. *Kumi kerti!*

Trypho: Ahh, ahh, ahh!

John: What's he telling him, Peter?

Peter: What do I know? Even the devil doesn't understand this jargon of the Gerasenes. Hey, Andronicus, what are we supposed to do?

Andronicus: Shut up. The sorcerer is invoking the spirits of the dead.

Trypho: Ahh, ahh, ahh!

Andronicus: Trypho wants to know what you want.

Jesus: Nothing. Tell him that we're here to greet him.

Zebedee: Tell him we're leaving before he hits us with his chain.

Andronicus took a piece of stick and made a sign to Trypho. Then the sorcerer approached us, with his two fists raised, like they were two hammers.

Trypho: Ahh, ahh, ahh!

Andronicus: The spirits want you to ask questions and you'll receive a reply.

John: Come on, Peter, ask him anything.

Peter: What am I gonna ask him?

John: I dunno. Ask him who's gonna win at dice tomorrow, or if you'll have good fortune this year. Ask him to read your palm.

Peter: Hmm ... I don't think he can do that.

Andronicus: You'd better make up your mind. The dead can't wait for the living.

John: How about you Jesus, anything in mind?

Jesus: Well, yes, I'll ask him something.

Andronicus: Ask him anything, stranger. Trypho is endowed with so many powers. He knows everything and discovers everything.

Jesus: Well, if that's the case, then ask him what should I do with Cleotilde. My knees tremble before her and I get dizzy when I'm with her.

Andronicus: Marratina!

When the mad man Trypho heard the swineherd's command, he bent to pick up a stone on the ground and began to hit himself with it. Then he gave out a loud cry. He pulled off his tatters and, half-naked and bleeding, rolled over the ground, entangled in his own chains. After a short while, Trypho remained still, like a wounded animal.

Trypho: Ahh, ahh, ahh!

Andronicus: Shh! The dead spirits are now answering your question, stranger: she's not the right woman for you. She can't give you a child. Leave her and look for someone else.

John: Ha, ha, ha!

Andronicus: Hey, imbecile, what are you laughing at?

John: Ha, ha, ha! Cleotilde is the name of Zebedee's boat. You know, this brown one is scared of the water and gets dizzy whenever he's on the boat! Ha, ha, ha! Your dead spirits are fake!

Andronicus: If you don't have faith, then get outta here and stop bothering me. Have you come to provoke me? Trypho doesn't want to be bothered.

Peter: Jesus, let's go. This man can't predict anything. He's crazy.

Jesus: Yeah, we'd better go.

Andronicus: Hold it, strangers. Trypho doesn't do this for free. It's one dinar for every consultation.

Zebedee: A what? Friend, the storm picked our pockets clean. We don't even have a copper. You have barked up the wrong tree.

Andronicus: You gotta pay, otherwise you're gonna be cursed by the spirits before nightfall.

Jesus: Hey, Andronicus, who did you say you were working for?

Andronicus: For Aesculapius, the wealthiest proprietor in Gerasa. He trades purple in Damascus. He owns enormous herds of swine, as well as cattle, donkeys, and camels.

Jesus: I see, and this poor fellow also works for him, doesn't he? I guess you're his business administrator, aren't you?

Andronicus: Hey, what do you mean?

Jesus: I say this Aesculapius and you make big money out of the screaming of this poor man.

Andronicus: What nonsense are you talking about? Pay me the dinar, and get out of here.

Jesus: No, my friend, we're not going yet. Come, I want to consult the "great Trypho" again.

Andronicus: He's resting now. He can't answer you.

Jesus: Yes he can. Trypho, my brother, listen to me. They're exploiting you!

Trypho: Ahh, ahh, ahh!

Andronicus: Marratina!

Peter: He, with his ahh, ahh, ahh, and the other with his *marratina*, make an odd combination.

When the swineherd gave the order again, the mad man attacked Jesus who bent over, so Trypho landed on the ground. Thick and white saliva came bubbling from his mouth. This fit lasted for a few minutes. Then Jesus leaned over the poor creature and whispered something in his ear.

Jesus: Trypho, my brother, they've abused you plenty, by using your sickness to suck money from gullible people. They use their ignorance in order to enslave you more. The Lord doesn't wish to see you this way. Come on, Trypho, get up. James, John, help me remove his chains. Maybe we can take the lock off with a sharp-edged stone or a knife. And you, Andronicus, get outta here, fast!

Peter: Jesus, you're crazier than him. He's dangerous. He can hurt you.

Jesus: No, you'll see. Come, Trypho, and keep still. We won't hurt you.

Trypho: Ahh, ahh, ahh.

Trypho went near Jesus like a tame dog and let him cut open the chains. He was free.

Meanwhile, Andronicus, the swineherd, rushed to his patron, Aesculapius, and told him what happened and what the strangers from Capernaum had done. The news spread like wildfire. The Gerasenes left their houses and headed for the cemetery, to find out what was happening.

Woman: Tell me, what did you ask the sorcerer?

Jesus: I asked where the money of the foolish victims went.

Woman: What was his reply?

Jesus: Trypho stood up and said: "To the pockets of Aesculapius!" Believe me, countrymen, that was the only true prediction he made. The swine of Aesculapius got fat from your money.

While Jesus was talking to the Gerasenes, Trypho remained seated on a rock, his head buried in his hands. The women washed his wounds and his welts. They had also placed an old tunic over his shoulders. As we were about to go back to our boat, Trypho stood up and looked at Jesus, grinning at him like a child.

Trypho: Let me go with you.

Jesus: No, Trypho. You belong here. When people see you working and living like the rest, the people will say: There are no sorcerers or witchcraft. Only God is powerful. Go and tell your neighbors how good the Lord has been to you.

Trypho: Yes, yes, I'm gonna tell everyone! I'll tell everybody!

So he left and started to tell everyone in all the towns of the Decapolis what Jesus had done for him. Aesculapius, with the loss of his business, told people that the strangers from Capernaum scared his swine and that a herd of pigs hurled themselves over the cliff and drowned. Since then, this story spread through the land of the Gerasenes.

•

Gerasa (or Gadara) was a city by the eastern shore of the Sea of Galilee. It was part of the so-called Decapolis (a league of ten cities), a territory with Greek customs, and was inhabited almost entirely by foreigners. For the Israelites, it was a pagan area, the land of the Gentiles. The ruins that are presently preserved range from two hundred to three hundred years after Christ. The swine (or pig) was an impure animal for the Israelites. To eat its flesh was strictly prohibited, and it was a symbol of rejecting the Jewish religion. The

Israelites considered swine herding as degrading. In Gerasa, which was a foreign territory, inhabited by non-Jews, such religious scruples did not exist.

Throughout history, people have put great faith in magic, prophecies, witchcraft, and various forms of superstition. When Christian faith takes on aspects of these religious expressions, it is harmed, for these expressions are associated with fear, with a blind faith in destiny and in what is "written," and have very little to do with a life of freedom and responsibility. What is even worse, however, is the business that derives from these beliefs. Someone is always ready to make a profit from gullible people. These "religious deals" happen within the Catholic faith. The devotion to a number of saints and to miraculous relics that are sold to the people, almsgiving to please a particular saint, and the pilgrimages which translate into an income for agencies of tourism are all forms of this religiosity "used" to the advantage of some people. We should be wary whenever economic benefits are associated with religious belief. The criterion for the validity of any of these was given by Jesus himself when he said: "Give for free what you have received for free," and "You cannot serve the Lord and money." In order to be close to the real God, a God who wants people to be free and happy, one must gradually shed these primitive religious ideas which are an authentic "opium of the people" because they numb people's senses, paralyze and prevent them from seeing clearly the true face of the God of Jesus, a God who wants his children accountable to history and committed to transform the world. The miracle that Jesus performed on Trypho is a sign that God frees us from the chains of false religion. And it is a sign which not only frees him — a man mentally deranged and used as a business tool — but also frees the people, who, upon discovering the secrets of "fortune-telling," shed their many fears.

The story of the possessed man from Gerasa is an example of a text that has been "adorned" in order to make it and the gospels more spectacular and more dramatic. Over the years, events that impress people are exaggerated and magnified when retold, thus making them appear more marvelous. Certainly, behind those hundreds of pigs that hurled themselves into the devil-infested sea — as the gospel describes it — there were several legends transmitted from one person to another, legends which the evangelists, without any possibility of confirming them, put into writing in order to derive a message of faith from them.

(Matt. 8:28–34; Mark 5:1–20; Luke 8:26–39)

41

This Is a Decent House

Salome: So what now? Aren't you comin'?

John: Where to, old woman?

Salome: To the house of Simon, the Pharisee, where else? His son was introduced in the synagogue today, and he's giving a party to celebrate.

John: I'm not a party-goer, much less if the party's in the house of that fellow.

James: Come on, John, cheer up. Simon always serves good pastries. What about you, Peter? Aren't you comin' either?

Peter: That stingy old man won't throw a good party.

Salome: You say he's a miser, but look, Peter, he's invited the whole family. You know how it is here in Capernaum, everyone's a relative of everybody. Imagine, half the city is going there to eat.

James: Yeah, let's all go. Don't be a kill-joy. Go tell Rufina, Peter. Hey, Andrew, don't just stand there like a scarecrow. What's the matter, Jesus? Aren't you coming?

Jesus: I'm coming, James, although I'm not a relative of this fellow Simon.

James: It doesn't matter. You're our friend, and friends of the family are relatives too. I tell you their house is gonna be teeming with so many people, like a barrel of olives.

The redhead insisted that we all go. Soon, we found ourselves in the streets of the money-lenders, in front of the house of Simon, the Pharisee. While we were waiting outside the door, we saw two women beside the wall. We knew them, and in fact, the younger one was making some gestures to Jesus.

Mary: Psst! Hey, Nazarene! Pssst! How're you? This is a friend of mine, Selena.

Selena: Who's he?

Mary: He's a nut.

Jesus: Hi, Mary! I was thinking about you. How's life?

Mary: It's a job, friends. You have to take advantage of the times. Isn't that right, Selena?

Jesus: And how — I could smell your perfume from the other street!

Selena: Yeah, friend, and since we're night owls, you don't see us, you just smell us!

Mary: You may laugh now, silly girl; later, you might spend three hours waiting here for nothing.

Selena: Well, you shouldn't complain, because with this brown one around, your problem is solved for the night.

Mary: That's none of your business, Selena. I already told you this is something else.

Jesus: Mary and I are friends.

Selena: So I see. The trouble is she's so well made-up and I can't compete. It's all right, friend, you won. I give up.

Mary and Selena each had a bottle of jasmine oil hanging around her neck. This was the perfume prostitutes always used.

John: Come Jesus, they're gonna open the door now!

Jesus: I'm coming, John. Wait!

Mary: Go, join your friends, or you'll be left out. You don't have to say with us.

Jesus: I don't mind. Aren't you coming inside?

Mary: Who, us? Ha! Didn't I tell you, Selena? This guy's crazy!

Jesus: No, Mary, I'm serious. Why don't you come inside with the rest?

Mary: We'd like that — to at least be able to eat some pastries...But this is where we belong. "This is a decent house, the house of Simon, the Pharisee." That's what they'd say when they kicked us out. May the devil swallow him up, the damned old miser!

Jesus: Why do you speak ill of him? What's he done to you?

Mary: To me, nothing. But to all the unfortunate who owe him money ...That's how he became rich: by lending ten and collecting twenty, and squeezing necks if they fail to pay on time.

John: Hey, Jesus, what's the matter? Aren't you comin'?

Jesus: What about these ladies, John, can't they go inside?

John: Who, these two whores here?

Mary: Oh yes, let's go in. After all, business is bad. At least, we can gobble up something warm inside!

Jesus: What do you think, John? Can we let them in?

John: Well, I don't think anyone will notice. Come on, and mix with the group.

Mary: Wow, this is gonna be fun! Well, as they say, better be on time than be invited! Let's go, Selena, move on!

Selena: No, no Mary. I'd better stay here and wait for a customer. You go ahead. If you get bored, then come out and let's exchange places.

Mary: Well, you're gonna miss something. See you soon!

Selena: Don't forget to bring me some of the goodies!

We joined Peter and the rest of the group. When we were already passing through the entrance, one of the servants with a serious face cut through to Mary the Magdalene.

Servant: And where do you think you're going? This is a decent house, do you hear? Out, out, outta here!

Jesus: Hey, friend, has this woman done you any harm? If not, leave her alone.

Servant: Look, Nazarene...Of course, you aren't from here, so you don't know. But this woman beside you is a whore. So...

Jesus: So, we who are with her are also indecent. Do you have anything else to say?

Servant: To hell with you, stranger! Well then, you can go inside with her, but I warn you, insolent woman, don't make trouble. And you, make sure you give yourselves a nice bath later, so you won't smell like jasmine oil!

Mary: Son of a bitch. Puah! "This is a decent house." Yeah, he won't make his eyes impure by looking at me. But when he goes to my house tomorrow, he's gonna be the first John at my door! What a filthy creep!

Jesus: Leave him alone, Mary. If you don't want them to mess around with you, then don't mess around with them, either. Come, let's go inside!

The garden was very spacious and there were many people. We from the poor district were seated toward the end, on straw mats, and were served dates to fill our bellies. The tables in front, well decorated and full of the best food, were reserved for the businessmen and the rich relatives of Simon, the Pharisee. One of them came near us.

A Man: Well, well, Mary, what a good catch you got. How did you get the Nazarene?

Mary: Damn you son of a bitch! Get outta my sight! I ain't working now!

Man: That's all right. Don't get mad. I was just kidding!

Mary: Didn't I tell you, Jesus? I don't belong here.

Jesus: You asked for it, Mary. Who ever told you to put on so much perfume? Not even a carpenter's brush could remove the smell! Come on, forget it and eat something.

Then came Benneth the cripple, who was wobbling and carrying a half-finished jug of wine.

Benneth: Look who's here, a siren on our shore! Mary, my dear one, I've been looking all over the place for you. At last, I've found you! Hik!

Mary: Go away, dirty old man, and sleep it off!

Benneth: Don't treat me that way, precious one. I may have drunk too much wine, but you're overdressed too! Hic! Ain't I right, my friend? This woman's better without so many clothes on!

The crippled Benneth rushed toward Mary, and suddenly tore off her dress. Then Jesus pushed the drunk man, who slipped and fell on his back. Soon a commotion ensued in that corner of the garden. To make matters worse, the bottle of jasmine that Mary was carrying around her neck rolled on the floor, broke into pieces, and the whole place began to smell like a carnival.

Servant: What the hell's going on here? I warned you, bitch; I don't want no trouble!

Jesus: You started it.

Servant: Will you shut up, stranger! Now, you're gonna know who I am, you whore!

The servant raised the tray he was carrying in a threatening gesture. Mary leaned over and threw herself at the feet of Jesus, as if asking for protection.

Servant: Stay away from her — I'm gonna teach her how to respect a decent house!

Jesus: James, John, help me!

My brother and I rushed over to the servant, but the other neighbors fell over us.

A Man: Here, take this for being such a troublemaker!

The matter would have gotten worse, if at that moment, Simon the Pharisee had not come, having been warned of the trouble. Simon was the owner of the house.

Simon: What's going on here? Can't we have our celebration in peace?
Jesus: There's nothing here. We were just conversing.
Simon: Conversing? What's this woman doing on the floor? Is she conversing too?
Servant: She's one of the women from Jasmine Street.
Simon: Oh? And what is this whore doing in my house? Who let her in?
Jesus: I did, Simon. She came with me.
Simon: And who are you to dirty my house?
Servant: He's the man from Nazareth. I'm sure you've heard of him. He's known as a prophet.
Simon: So you're a prophet! I didn't know that the prophets of today allowed themselves to be cuddled by whores. Now get this woman out of my house! I'd rather smell a cat's urine than the perfume of a sinner!

Mary remained on the floor. With her hair disheveled, she cried shamefully at Jesus' feet.

Simon: I said get this woman out of here! My house is a decent one!
Jesus: Simon, if you'll allow me, may I ask you something?
Simon: What do you want? Come on, make it fast. This perfume is making me dizzy.
Jesus: Listen to this story, Simon: There were two men who were indebted to a moneylender. One owed him fifty dinars and the other, five hundred dinars. But both of them lost their harvest and did not have a single cent to pay him.
Simon: And the moneylender sent them to prison accordingly.
Jesus: On the contrary, he felt pity for them and so he wrote off their debts. Now, tell me, Simon: Which of the two men should feel more grateful to the moneylender?
Simon: What a question! The man who owed him five hundred dinars, of course. He was pardoned for a greater amount, so he should be more grateful. What's this got to do with this prostitute?
Jesus: A lot. But I doubt if you'll understand, since you've never forgiven anyone; neither have you ever felt the need to be pardoned. But this woman needs to be forgiven, and therefore, knows how to feel grateful.

Simon: What does she have to be thankful for?

Jesus: Of course, she has nothing to thank you for. When we, the poor, entered your house, we were put here at the back; you didn't even come to welcome us; nor did you give us water with which to wash our hands. She doesn't have to thank you for anything. But the Lord, yes, has forgiven her for all the debts she owed him.

Then Simon the Pharisee firmly gripped the handle of his cane and looked at Jesus with hatred.

Simon: Get this woman out of here! And the Nazarene too, and everything that smells of jasmine. I prefer to smell a cat's urine to a sinner's perfume!

Jesus lifted Mary from the ground and left with her. We, too, went away from there, and so did the rest of the people from the poor district. I think it was after that party in Simon's house that Mary of Magdala started to change.

•

An old proverb of the rabbis in Jesus' time went like this: "Don't speak too long with a woman in the street." This meant with any woman and not only with a prostitute — though speaking with a prostitute was worse. On many occasions Jesus violated the customs of his people with respect to relationship with women. Within this freedom toward tradition, he showed special treatment to the "bad women" who profoundly scandalized the "good" people of his time.

Jesus continuously reiterated God's preferential interest in sinners, that they were closer to God than the pious ones and the observers of the law. This provoked angry protests, especially among the Pharisees. One must bear in mind that these Pharisees were not always from the upper class. They also came from a more common class. What characterized them as a group was the pride which they flaunted, being members of a community of the chosen people of the Lord. And this was because they fulfilled the laws and the religious practices with many scruples. That is why they despised the "immoral" and "damned" creatures of God. All throughout the gospels, Jesus accuses them of hypocrisy to their face and tries to make them see how they, more than anyone else, alienate themselves from God because of their pride.

Even today, we are not wanting in Pharisees. There are many people who gloat over their "decency," their good education, their good family —

and in most cases, the money they have — which separate them from the lowly. They not only think of themselves as superior and more important, but have also come to identify Christianity with social class, and their morality with appearances. All this pretension has nothing to do with the gospel. Christian virtues are primarily attitudes of solidarity and equality among people, in contrast to feelings of pride or discrimination. On no occasion did Jesus claim special treatment or preference for himself, as great men and women surrounded by servants, luxury, and distinctions do, just to highlight the importance they want extended to themselves. What Jesus demanded was that the poor and marginalized be treated with respect and deference. He did not want any privilege for himself but equality for all.

Jesus told Simon the Pharisee a short story: that of the two debtors. It was a parable about forgiveness. Through this story, Jesus pointed to the sinner as the one who really "knew" how to forgive, and therefore the only one to be grateful. The Pharisee, proud and despising, would never understand this, since he did not believe he should be pardoned for anything. Neither did he know what it meant to be grateful. Gratefulness for having been forgiven — a basic dimension in a person's relationship with God — is not within the reach of a self-righteous person.

(Luke 7:36–50)

42

The Roman Captain

Cornelius was the captain of the Roman troops in Capernaum. His huge house was always guarded by soldiers. Matthew, the tax collector, often went to see him because he was a friend.

Cornelius: Will you have some more wine, Matthew?

Matthew: Yes, a little more. It's very good. Is it from Cana?

Cornelius: Yes.

Matthew: Hey, you haven't drunk anything. Is anything the matter?

Cornelius: I'm just worried, Matthew.

Matthew: What's wrong? Are the zealots conspiring again?

Cornelius: No, it has nothing to do with politics.

Matthew: What's your problem then? Do you need money? If you want, . . . I can lend you.

Cornelius: Nothing of that sort. It's about Mark.

Matthew: Who's Mark?

Cornelius: One of my servants, who has been with me for ten years.

Matthew: What's wrong with him? Is he leaving you for another master?

Cornelius: No, but he's sick. He's been very weak lately and hasn't taken anything to eat. He has terrible pains. I've sent for all the doctors in Capernaum and they say his condition is serious, that he's going to die. I keep thinking about this.

Matthew: For the love of the Almighty, how could you be so concerned about a servant? Come on, pour me some more wine, my cup is empty.

Cornelius: I love him like a son, you know. I trust him more than anybody. I don't want Mark to die.

Matthew: Well, I don't know. If he's very sick . . . I don't know . . . Hey, maybe . . .

Cornelius: Maybe what?

Matthew: Nothing, this wine is putting ideas into my head. I don't know, but I've heard about Jesus, the Nazarene, well, you know him too, I guess. They say he's a healer. They say he cleansed the skin of a leper, and cured an insane man. They even say that there in Nain, he brought a dead man back to life. I think these are just stories invented by people. But it seems this Nazarene really has a knack for healing. There are farmers who know a lot about herbs.

Cornelius: And and so?

Matthew: Tell him to see your servant. You can't lose anything by trying. What do you think, huh? Don't tell me this is a silly idea, dammit!

Cornelius: I also thought about that last night, Matthew, but...

Matthew: But what?

Cornelius: This Jesus has spoken hard against the Romans. We have spies all over the place. Besides, the men he goes with, well, we know their leanings.

Matthew: They're agitators, and Jesus isn't far behind. But that's another matter. Didn't you say you were so worried about this servant of yours? Well, ask Jesus to see him.

Cornelius: Do you think he'd come, Matthew? I'm a Roman soldier, and you Jews are so fanatical.

Matthew: Well, if you don't have the courage to ask him, then I'm gonna do it, dammit! He's a friend of mine. I invited him to have dinner at home and he came. I think he can help you, Cornelius.

Cornelius: I think so too, Matthew.

At noon, when Matthew had finished collecting taxes from the caravans from the north, he went to the fishermen's barrio by the wharf to look for Jesus in my father's house.

Neighbors: The devil's publican! Go join your own kind, you filthy bastard! Traitor!

Matthew was wobbling, as always, because of the alcohol in him. The people spat at him, as expected, as they insulted him. But the spirit of the wine numbed his hearing. We were having lunch when Matthew arrived.

John: Hey, filthy man, what's your business around here?

Matthew: I'm looking for the Nazarene.

John: And may I know why?

Matthew: It's personal. Is he here?

Jesus: I'm here, Matthew, what do you want?

Behind Jesus were my parents, James, and his wife. People also began to mill around the narrow street. They were curious to know what Matthew was looking for in the barrio. Zebedee, my father, was the first man to raise his voice. Then the yelling spread like wildfire.

Zebedee: What are you doing here, you son of a bitch? Don't you dare set foot in my house!

James: You haven't lost anything here, drunkard! Go to the other corner of town and do your thing there!

Neighbors: Out, out!

Matthew: Go to hell, all of you! I said I came to see you, Nazarene!

Zebedee: Jesus, what have you to do with his kind?

Jesus: I don't know what he wants, Zebedee. You haven't allowed him to speak yet. Did you say you were looking for me, Matthew?

Matthew: Yes, and the rest can all go to hell!

Jesus: Okay, what's the matter, Matthew?

Matthew: Cornelius, the Roman captain, wants you to go to his house.

Jesus: What for?

John: This is a trap, Jesus. Don't trust him.

Matthew: His servant is ill. He wants you to see him.

James: Tell the Roman captain and his servant to go to hell! You can join them too!

Matthew: Now you talk too much, redhead, and so do all of you here, but when you had to build the synagogue, you had to ask the captain to grant you permission.

John: Ah, but that was a long time ago!

Matthew: Yeah, what about last year, when you were in trouble? You had to look for the captain to help you get out of trouble, huh?

Zebedee: Will you shut up now, swine? You're a good for nothing leech! Get outta my sight before I squeeze your neck! I don't even want to see your shadow around! Get outta here!

But Matthew did not leave. He wiped his mouth with the sleeve of his tunic and looked at Jesus.

Matthew: So, are you coming or not?

James: Of course he isn't coming!

Jesus: Hey, James, let me answer that, will you? Yes, I'm going with you, Matthew.

Zebedee: Listen Jesus: once you set foot in this Roman captain's house, you will never come back to my house, ever! Do you hear? Do you hear me right?

Jesus: I'm not deaf. No need to scream, Zebedee. Let's go, Matthew.

Jesus and Matthew forced their way through the people and headed down the street. My father, red with rage, pounded the wall with clenched fist, then went inside the house. All of us followed him. Outside, tongues wagged furiously as they talked about what had happened.

Captain Cornelius's house was at the outskirts of Capernaum, beside the headquarters. Jesus and Matthew, closely followed by a bunch of curious people, left the city and headed for the captain's house.

Matthew: I hate your friends, Nazarene.

Jesus: They return the favor, Matthew. Hate begets hate. It's always the case.

Matthew: As you can see, this doesn't matter to Cornelius. Your friends may detest him, but he's always tried to help them, whenever possible.

As they were nearing the captain's house, Cornelius came out to the street. The people pressed hard against Jesus while Matthew tried not to miss a word they were saying.

Cornelius: Greetings to you, Jesus! I'm glad Matthew has persuaded you to come.

Matthew: I had a hard time doing it. That old man Zebedee even cursed him for having agreed to come to your house. He also says Jesus can't set foot in his house anymore.

Cornelius: Zebedee said that?

Matthew: Yes, and more, he spat on me when I knocked at his door.

Cornelius: And who are all these people with you?

Matthew: The nosy ones as always. For lack of entertainment here in Capernaum, they gotta look for something to amuse themselves.

Cornelius: I'm really sorry, Jesus. I never thought this would cause you so much trouble.

Jesus: That's all right, Cornelius. And don't worry about Zebedee. Barking dogs don't bite.

Cornelius: Look Jesus, I'm not really worth all the hassles you've gotten into by coming to my house. As you've seen, I didn't even dare look for you myself.

Jesus: Matthew told me your servant was sick.

Cornelius: Oh yes, Mark. I've heard about your having cured several sick people. I'm helpless, you see. He's burning with fever. I thought you ...

Matthew: Cornelius wants you to cure him, if you can.

Jesus: I would like to see him. Let's go.

Cornelius: No, Jesus. I don't mean to give you problems. But look, the God you believe in as you Jews always say is the master of life and death. If he can command sickness to go away, then Mark will be healed.

Jesus: Do you believe so, Cornelius?

Cornelius: Well, when they give me orders, I obey. When I command one of my soldiers to come, he does come. And when I dismiss him, he leaves. Isn't your God the master of all of us? Then there's no need for you to go inside. All you have to do is to command this sickness to go away in the name of this God you believe in, and the sickness will leave.

Jesus was amazed at what the captain said, and he turned to the people who were following him.

Jesus: Dammit, this man who's a foreigner has more faith in our God than all of us put together!

A Woman: What did you say, Nazarene?

Jesus: That the day will come when outsiders, like Cornelius, will sit at the same table with our father Abraham.

A Man: Now look who's talking! How much were you paid by the captain to give those compliments?

Jesus: Really, I'm telling you: they'll enter the Kingdom of God, and many of those who think they will be inside and are so sure of themselves, will be left outside.

Woman: What's he talking about?

Man: Are you with us or not, Jesus?

Matthew: To hell with all of you! If you're not creating trouble, you're out to promote dissent. Get outta here, you gossipers and scandalous lot, outta here, all of you!

Woman: You get outta here, you drunken traitor!

Jesus: Leave 'em alone, Matthew. Let's go now. Stop worrying about your servant, Cornelius. God'll grant what you expect from him.

Cornelius returned to his house amid whistles and yells of the people. Jesus was peeved and raised his voice.

Jesus: You've got eyes and yet don't see, ears and you don't hear.

Man: What the hell is there to see? That captain is a Roman beast. The Romans are our enemies. He who praises the Romans is as much beast as they are!

Jesus: You've got eyes but don't see, ears but don't hear.

Woman: There you go again! You're the blind one, Nazarene!

Man: He's not blind, but has sold himself. Come on, show us how much this captain paid you!

Woman: Down with Rome and with all traitors!

The disturbance lasted for some time. When the people got tired of yelling, they returned to Capernaum and spread the story of what happened. Having taken another route, Jesus returned to the fishermen's barrio, where we were waiting for him. Meanwhile, in Captain Cornelius's house, Mark's fever had subsided.

•

Although Matthew was an official not of the Roman Empire but of Herod, he still needed to maintain very good relations with the Roman soldiers. Rome retained Herod on his throne. Due to the strategic position of Capernaum, the city had a Roman garrison headed by a centurion (a captain). He was the military authority over the troops (the smallest unit of the Roman infantry was one hundred soldiers). The Roman soldiers were hated by the Israelites, who considered them as the country's invaders. They symbolized the imperialist power of Rome, which, in those times, ruled the greater part of the known world. National pride and the desire for freedom of the Israelites were a constant source of confrontation with these foreign soldiers. As far as Jesus' friends were concerned (who were greatly influenced by the zealot spirit — obviously nationalistic and anti-Roman), this hatred and rejection were difficult to overcome. If Jesus' act of accepting Matthew, the publican, marked the first serious conflict within the group of the apostles, his open attitude toward the Roman captain would certainly be a cause for another crucial discussion among them.

As regards the Roman occupation, the Israelites were — and still are — an extremely nationalistic people. Their awareness of being the chosen people of God was at the root of this sentiment.

In Jesus' time it was generally believed that the coming of the Messiah would be the day of God's judgment over all nations and therefore a time of vengeance against them. Jesus tried to put an end to these ideas. In the gospel, nationalism is replaced by universality. Although Jesus associated with foreigners only on isolated occasions — one of which was this one — his acceptance of them was a sign that God does not favor any particular race or nation.

In this episode, the focus is not so much on the servant's healing, as on its significance for our faith: the need to transcend nationalistic barriers or obstacles.

(Matt. 8:5–13; Luke 7:1–10; John 4:43–54)

43

The Wheat and the Weeds

That afternoon, after fishing, we all gathered in the house. Jesus' visit to Cornelius, the Roman captain of Capernaum, enraged everyone. For several hours we did nothing but nag him about it. My father, Zebedee, was the most vocal of all.

Zebedee: Wait till he comes. I'm gonna give him a piece of my mind. Dammit, I'm gonna say things to his face which no one has ever told him. I can't stand the shame that he's caused us, and I'm not about to tolerate bootlickers of the Romans. The bootlickers are as filthy as the Romans, because they support their dirty tricks.

John: Take it easy, old man. Come on, relax.

It was already dark when Jesus peeped in the door.

Jesus: Zebedee, Zebedee, may I come in?

No one answered.

Jesus: I asked if I could come in.
Zebedee: Go to hell, Nazarene!
Jesus: I didn't set foot in the captain's house. I didn't enter his house. I didn't stain my sandals by stepping on the Roman's yard.
Zebedee: Who do you think you are anyway? Do you think you can just come and go with nobody ever questioning you? Or don't you know who this Matthew is, that blood-sucking tax collector? And don't you know who this Cornelius is, that damned captain who's possessed by the devil like all the rest of his kind? You've been staying with us in Capernaum for six months and still you don't know who these slobs are? Now, answer me.
Jesus: I think I know them better than you do, Zebedee.
Zebedee: Oh, yeah? Better than I do? So, why don't you join them in their hang-out and gnaw bones with the country's traitors! I can't provide shelter to chameleons who conveniently change their colors.

Jesus: Does this mean that I can't come in?

Zebedee: Come in, dammit, come in. You can't just stand there like a beggar. After all, I already lost my cool before noontime, even before this swine, Matthew, came to see you.

Jesus went inside the house and looked at everyone. Then he sat on the floor, with crossed legs. We were expecting an explanation from him, but he didn't say anything.

Zebedee: Damn you, Jesus? Have you swallowed your tongue?

James: Let's make this clear, Jesus: we are here everyday trying to figure out how we can get rid of these Romans, and here you go to the house of their chief, Cornelius, no less. May the lightning strike him dead!

John: Once you said that the Romans are squeezing our necks and that things have to change; but now, the whole barrio has seen you with this traitor, Matthew, on your way to the captain's house. What's the matter with you?

Zebedee: May the gates of hell open up and swallow you, Jesus. We can't understand you. Well, aren't you gonna speak up?

Jesus: Zebedee, Captain Cornelius isn't a bad man. Believe me.

James: He's not a bad man, dammit, but he's a Roman! That's enough.

Jesus: Yes, he's a Roman. So what?

John: The Romans are our enemies.

Jesus: Cornelius is a Roman. We're Jews, and the others are Greeks. So what? You don't eat the skin of the fruit but the flesh inside, right? This captain has the skin of a Roman, but inside him is good fruit.

James: Then beware that you don't choke on this fruit!

Zebedee: Nonsense, Jesus, this is nonsense. I think you're getting to be scatterbrained. If we say we gotta get rid of the Romans, so be it! And that's final!

Jesus: Well, look, old man, I think what happened to Titus and Abdon will also happen to you.

Zebedee: What do you mean? And who the devil are they?

Jesus: They were Renato's companions.

Zebedee: What're you talking about, dammit?

Jesus: Renato was a farmer who owned a small parcel of land, out there behind the hills of Nazareth. When the rainy season came, Renato planted all his land with wheat. His wife came out to see him:

Wife: What now, old man? Are you tired?

Renato: Yes, I'm tired but happy, woman. I expect a good harvest this year, you'll see.

Wife: And we'll be able to buy sheep, won't we?

Renato: Not one but four, woman. We're gonna buy a goat too. It's gonna be a good harvest, you'll see, you'll see.

Jesus: But Renato had a troublesome neighbor who was envious whenever things went well with his neighbors. One midnight, this neighbor got up and slipped onto the land where Renato had sown wheat.

Neighbor: Ha! I'll sow bad seed on the farm and will destroy his harvest. Then I'll die laughing seeing the expression on the stupid man's face, ha, ha, ha!

Jesus: So while everyone was sleeping, the evil man sowed bad seeds on the land of this poor man, Renato. After a few days, the seeds began to sprout and the land began to clothe itself with a green mantle of young blades. The wheat and the weeds began to grow together. When Titus and Abdon, friends of Renato, passed by and saw the disaster, they ran to their friend and told him.

Renato: Hey, what's the matter, huh?

Titus: Open the door, Renato! It's us!

Renato: What seems to be the trouble?

Abdon: Don't you know?

Renato: What?

Abdon: There are weeds on your land! We looked closely and saw a lot of weeds growing.

Renato: That can't be. I chose the seeds very carefully. I sowed wheat seeds of good quality.

Titus: But the whole farm is loaded with weeds.

Renato: Hell! Who would've wanted to cause me harm?

Abdon: You can figure it out for yourself. Everyone knows him.

Renato: Do you think he's capable of doing such a thing?

Abdon: Why, of course, man. He's capable of doing it and more. This neighbor of yours is evil.

Renato: How I wish I could squeeze his neck and . . .

Titus: Take it easy, Renato. There's no need to worry. Tomorrow,

Abdon and I will give you a hand. The three of us will rid your farm of the weeds that are growing and your problem will be solved.

Renato: Thank you, my friends, thank you. I'm counting on you.

Jesus: The following morning...

Renato: Hey, wait a minute. What are you pulling? Let me see.
Titus: These are weeds, look.
Renato: No, man, no. That's wheat.
Titus: Look closely, Renato, these are weeds.
Renato: Don't be silly, Titus, I tell you, these are wheat stalks!
Titus: What do you say, Abdon?
Abdon: Let me see. I don't know, they look the same to me.
Titus: I swear by Abraham, these are weeds, Renato!
Renato: And I insist that it's good wheat, Titus, and you're up-rooting it! Pff! One problem after another. That neighbor of mine destroyed my land and now you're killing my harvest.
Abdon: Okay, Renato, what do you want us to do then?
Renato: Look, friends, please pardon me. I'm grateful that you've come, but, let's leave this for another day. Will that be okay? Since we can't see the fruit yet, it's too difficult to distinguish wheat from weed. Let's wait for them to grow together, until we can separate one from the other. After all, the harvest won't be damaged.
Titus: You're right. It'll be worse to pull out the wheat thinking it's weeds. It's too soon to know.
Renato: I'll let you know when it's harvest time. Then we'll burn the weeds while we put the wheat in the barn. Is that okay?
Abdon: Sure, it's okay, Renato.

Jesus: So the days passed by, and the wheat grew together with the weeds. When harvest time came, Renato and his friends separated the wheat heads from the weeds easily. This time, they were not mistaken. They learned patience and committed no mistakes.
Zebedee: So I'm likened to Titus and Abdon, Renato's friends, huh?
Jesus: I think so, Zebedee. You said: "Cornelius is a weed, so out with him! He's got to be pulled out."
Zebedee: Yes, I said it, and I'm saying it again.
Jesus: Well you see, God isn't that way. He's more patient, because he knows that people are like trees: we are known by the fruit. If a tree yields

good fruit, then it's a good one even if it has an ugly skin. But if the fruit is bad, the tree is bad, notwithstanding its good appearance. What matters is the fruit, Zebedee. Come on, tell me, have you ever seen a vine with thorns bearing grapes?

Zebedee: No!

Jesus: And have you ever seen a bush of thistles with figs on their branches?

Zebedee: Nope!

Jesus: So...

Zebedee: I still maintain that Cornelius is a Roman wolf. Tell me who your friends are and I'll tell you who you are!

Jesus: Of course, that way of looking at things is easier. We point an accusing finger; we put a label on other people's foreheads saying: You're the bad ones, we're the good ones. "My God, send forth your fire from heaven and destroy all these scoundrels!" But the Lord simply smiles and says: Hey, how can you tell wheat from weeds? "Because this one is Roman, and that one is a Jew, and this Pharisee is a pious man, and that one is a rebel zealot, and this Sadducee is a traitor, while this man is a priest of the temple!" God takes away all labels and burns them in the garbage. Show me the fruit and then we talk. Don't you think, Zebedee, we should focus more on what one does than on the label one has?

Zebedee: There is only one thing that matters to me, Jesus.

Jesus: What is it, Zebedee?

Zebedee: That the captain is a Roman. And just the sight of him makes me throw up. That's why your having gone to his house was traitorous! It'll always be so for me until the end of the world!

John: Take it easy, Papa. You might faint. Be calm.

Jesus: When that day comes, perhaps you'll understand everything, Zebedee. It's only at the end when we see things clearly. The matter of separating wheat from weeds belongs to God, not to us.

My father, Zebedee, kept on grumbling. And so did my brother, James, and Peter and I. We spent several hours arguing with Jesus. Not one of us understood the story of the wheat and the weeds then.

•

The nationalism of Zebedee, his children, and certainly the majority of Jesus' disciples was one of intransigence and generated much prejudice.

In Zebedee's case, it was especially political prejudice against the Roman authorities and collaborators like Matthew. The biases of Jesus' friends were not of the moral or religious kind, on account of their social condition, but they were intransigent in political matters. Understood in a strict sense of superiority or power, nationalism can be a very dangerous feeling, and it may run counter to Christian universality. Jesus' gospel is a message that tends to do away with barriers among nations in favor of a profound solidarity among all people.

In the face of this intransigence, Jesus narrates a parable to his friends. The parable of the wheat and the weeds is a call to understanding and tolerance. Jesus makes them see the hazards of prejudgment and the value of patience until harvest time. In Palestine there is a type of plant known as "poisonous weed," which is a bad grass very similar to wheat. When it grows, it is difficult to distinguish one from the other. If — as told in the parable — there is much of this kind of grass growing in a field, it is dangerous to pull the weed out prematurely. The roots get entangled under the ground with those of the wheat. It is better to wait till harvest time to pull the weeds out from among the bundles of wheat. This way, one will not be mistaken. It is a common practice among farmers to make use of the weeds by drying them and using them for fuel. Palestine is a land that lacks forests, and, therefore, combustible material is scarce.

In this parable Jesus wants to tell us that no one is empowered to dictate who is who, to put on labels, and therefore to discriminate against others. People cannot read hearts, and the wish to classify others as "good" and "bad" may cause them to commit big blunders. Only in the movies can it be clear right from the start who is good or bad.

The parable refers likewise to judgment day when God will proclaim the harvest at the end of history, during which the chaff will unmistakably be separated from the grain. When Jesus talks about judgment, he also talks of God's patience. God is patient because he is good and gives every opportunity to people. He is patient as he is wise, and does not fall into the trap of appearances: he judges people according to their actions, not by position, nor the garments worn, nor the function people discharge.

For a long time we Christians have avoided concrete commitment in history, hoping to have a clearer understanding of who are the good people and who the bad ones. This manner of behavior is indicative not only of a lack of realism but of pride as well. We want to be "gods." Only God is capable of differentiating wheat from weeds; and only at the end shall he separate one from the other. Meanwhile, everything is together in the course of history. Those who do not commit to anything and consider themselves pure sin the most. Certainly, they have not done anything sinful, but they have not accomplished anything either — big or little — and, therefore, shall be accountable.

(Matt. 13:24–30)

44

The Fig Vendor

That day at dusk, James, Peter, and I were with Jesus at Joachim's tavern near the wharf. We were all seated on the floor, playing dice.

James: Five and three! This round is mine too!
Peter: Hold it, redhead, it's still my turn! Bring me that cube.
Jesus: Come on, Peter, save the honor of the sons of Jonas!
Peter: Hold your breath, fellas, here I go. . . . Five and four! I win!
John: Damn this stone-thrower! He got it from his sleeve.
Innkeeper: What's going on here? Who's winning?
John: At the moment, this redhead and the big-nose. But they say they haven't gone far enough.
Innkeeper: Because those who are behind drink a lot! Hey, you losers, don't give up! Right now I'm bringing you a pitcher full of the best wine from Galilee, and you can all have a good toast. This will give you good luck in the game, in your fishing, and while you're in bed with your wives!
John: Dammit! There you go again with your gimmicks, Joachim!
Melanie: Figs, figs! Very good, and as sweet as honey!
James: And there goes that woman again!

It was Melanie, the fig vendor, who came at that moment.

Melanie: Figs, figs, buy my delicious figs!
James: There goes that woman again!
Jesus: Who, James?
James: The fig vendor.
Jesus: I see her often in the market.
Peter: She's everywhere. If you're not quick enough, she'll even follow you to the toilet just to sell her damned figs!

Melanie started to linger by the inn, carrying her old and dirty basket of fruit on her head. She was a very thin woman always dressed in black. She shouted of her wares in a shrill voice, like a raucous bird, and smiled at every prospective buyer of her ripe figs.

James: What a cheap woman! And she's in terrible condition.

Jesus: Why, what's the matter with her, James?

John: The whole town knows about it. It's something unbelievable, Jesus. She's different from other women who have their period every month. For many years she hasn't stopped bleeding.

Peter: That's it, she's in bad shape. No doctor has been able to cure her. Apparently, this woman had money before, but spent it all on doctors. Now, she has nothing.

John: All the healers of Galilee know her, but no one has ever found the cure for her.

Peter: But she continues selling figs to earn more money to pay more doctors.

Melanie: Figs, figs, buy my delicious figs! They're as sweet as honey, figs, figs!

James: No, we don't want your figs.

Melanie: They're very good. Look, they're full of honey. Look.

James: Go sell them somewhere else! We don't want your figs.

Melanie: Why don't you try them, stranger?

Jesus: I don't have a single cent with me, woman.

Melanie: Hey, aren't you the one who...?

James: Stay away from here, we said! Beat it!

The fig vendor continued to hang around the inn, as we kept on making fun of her and her sickness.

Jesus: Isn't she married?

James: But Jesus, what man would be willing to put up with such a disaster? She's not a woman or anything. She can't even have a child.

Jesus: But she works very hard. I see her around the whole day with her basket of figs.

Peter: Sure, because she pokes her nose into everyone's business. The only work that women engages in is chatting. I guess the Lord took the woman not out of Adam's ribs but from his tongue. Oh, these women! The trouble with them is that they're so weak, and wear themselves out so easily.

Jesus: Rufina's not weak, Peter. Without her, what would happen to your home, huh?

Peter: Rufina works hard, all right, but she's always complaining. You gotta always treat her with affection, you know; otherwise she's out of her mind. I tell you, women are like straw blown by the wind.

Jesus: You can't say that of Salome. She's a very strong and a very smart woman.

John: Well, she happens to be my mother, Jesus, so that's something else.

James: Women are weak, dammit. Look what happened to Jairus's daughter.

Jesus: Why?

James: Well, poor creature, a few days ago, the girl caught a bad cold, and look at her now: she's dying! And all because of a cold. That's because women are weak and sickly.

Jesus: Why is she dying? Is she that serious?

James: This morning, I was told she was about gone.

Peter: Women die more often than we change shoestrings! We ought to thank the Lord for making us men, dammit! What do you think?

John: Hey, fellows, the pitcher's empty! Let's go to the inn next door. They serve better wine there.

James: That's right. Let's drink to our good fortune in being men and not women! Let's go!

Peter: That's a superb idea. Indeed this raisin wine is already burning my throat.

John: Are you coming with us, Jesus?

Jesus: No, but go if you want...I'd like to see this girl.

John: Which girl?

Jesus: The daughter of Jairus. I know her father. He's a good man. He and his wife must be very worried about the girl if she's that bad.

James: Bah, do it next time, Jesus. We're tired.

Jesus: Tired? Ah, I thought you never got tired. You don't have to go if you don't want to. But I'm going.

Peter: Okay, okay, let's go there.

We grudgingly decided to go with Jesus. As we were leaving the inn, Melanie, the fig vendor, was there again.

Melanie: Figs, figs, buy my delicious figs. They're as sweet as honey!

James: There you go again with your figs! We're sick and tired of them, don't you understand? Out of our way!

Melanie's deep and brilliant eyes turned to Jesus.

Melanie: How about you, stranger?
Jesus: I already told you I didn't have money. I'll buy from you next time.
Melanie: Wait, stranger, I was told you've healed many people, that you have the hands of a doctor. I... I'm sick. If you could...
John: Let's go, Jesus, don't mind her! Go away with your basket of figs and leave us in peace!
Peter: Hey, what's that noise?

The mourners of Capernaum, those women hired to weep for our dead, hurriedly crossed the street grieving, with their hair loose. People came out of their homes when they heard their cries and gathered in the street.

A Woman: Jairus's daughter has passed away! His daughter died!

Jairus was one of the caretakers of the synagogue in Capernaum. We all liked him, and when we learned what happened, the whole neighborhood rushed to his house. We went too. Melanie, the fig vendor, went, and she was following us closely. In front of Jairus's house, people were all squeezing to get in.

James: This woman has been following us from the pub, Jesus, haven't you noticed?
Jesus: Yeah, I know.
James: She's a bore, I tell you.
Jesus: She's a brave woman, James. She's not intimidated, even if people laugh at her to her face. She knows what she wants.
James: And what's it that she wants?
Jesus: She wants to get cured. That's it. She has no husband nor children. At least, she wants to have good health.

While we were waiting in front of Jairus's house, Melanie pushed her way toward Jesus, and from behind, called him.

Jesus: Hey, who's pulling my cloak?
James: Who else? Look at her, the disgusting woman!

Melanie finally succeeded in getting near Jesus. She looked at him full of hope.

Melanie: You can cure me! I know you can cure me!

Jesus: What's your name?

James: They call her "the bleeding woman"! Ha, ha ... That's how she's known here.

Jesus: From now on, nobody will ever call you by that name, Melanie.

For many years, the woman hadn't heard her name uttered with so much respect and affection. And for many years, she hadn't felt as much life in her body, worn out by sickness and suffering. As she stood up, she felt like a tree that wakes up from winter ready to share its flowers in bloom.

Jesus: You may now go in peace, woman.

We saw her pass through the crowded street, with her head high and in such great hurry, as if she had wings.

John: What's happened to her Jesus? Has she gone crazy or what?

Jesus: No, John. We're the crazy ones. A woman's life has as much worth as a man's in God's weighing scale, but we men have tipped that balance. Come on, let's go see the girl.

We went inside Jairus's house. The mourners' cry and the smoke from the newly burned incense filled the little air that we could breathe.

A Man: In a way Jairus is lucky; he still has the boys. If someone had to die, better to be the girl. What do you think?

James: Between two evils, the lesser one.

Peter: Let's get outta here, Jesus. We'll all choke to death here. Besides, once a person is dead, he's dead. Nothing can be done about it, except to weep. There are already enough women weeping here.

Jesus: I wonder why they're crying, Peter. This girl isn't dead. She's just asleep.

The people who were near us heard Jesus and they began to laugh.

A Man: Hey, listen to this man. He says the girl is just sleeping!

Slowly, Jesus inched his way to the room where Jairus's daughter lay. Peter, James, and I followed him. The mother was weeping beside her daughter, scratching her face and tearing her garments. Jairus was leaning against the wall and raised his face when he saw Jesus enter the room.

Jairus: Jesus, here she is. We thought she was going to live, but now, she's gone.

Jesus: Don't cry, Jairus.

Jairus: It's okay. Men weep too. People console me by saying that I have three boys left, and that women should weep for women. After all, she's only a girl, but I ... I loved her very much.

Jesus: God loved her too, and understands you, Jairus. He weeps as much when he loses a daughter as when he loses a son.

Jesus moved closer and gently looked at the girl. She seemed to be sleeping. No one would think she was dead. Jesus leaned over the girl and took her hand.

Jesus: Come on, young lady, wake up. Get up.

And, as if waking up from a long sleep, Jairus's daughter stood up and smiled.

•

According to the civil and religious laws, as well as the customs of Israel, woman was inferior to man. The civil laws relegated her to the place of a slave and a minor, who needed a man as master. A woman's testimony was not valid in court for she was considered a liar. From the religious point of view, she was also an outcast. She could not read the Scriptures in the synagogue, nor could she bless the food on the table. An important detail in the language: the Hebrew words that mean "pious," "just," and "holy" do not have a feminine form. It is therefore believed that a woman could never be what these words denote. There was a prayer recommended for men to recite everyday, which went like this: "Praise the Lord for not having made me a woman."

Women's exclusion from social life was more common among upper-class society and in the big cities than on the farms and in small towns. Nevertheless, in the whole country the little importance granted to the woman was attributed to her ability to perform domestic chores. She was appreciated basically for her fecundity. A barren woman was practically worthless, and a fertile woman was appreciated more if she gave birth to a boy than to a girl. The birth of a girl was sometimes cause for indifference or sadness, as the popular saying "Woe to him whose children are girls" attests. Nurtured by this environment from the time of infancy, Jesus' disciples were therefore male chauvinists who despised women, more so if the woman was someone like the fig vendor in this episode.

Selling was a common occupation among poor women. In the case of Melanie, it was her only way to survive, and her nondependence on a man made her even more destitute than most women. Her sickness — the gospel says it is a "hemorrhage" — is menorrhagia. It is an irregular form of menstruation characterized by continuous bleeding. Aside from the inconveniences and bodily weakness caused by the disorder, Melanie was perennially considered "unclean" as all women were considered during their menstrual period (Lev. 15:19–30). The fig vendor's case was, for several reasons, an extreme example of social discrimination: first, she was a woman; second, she was sick; finally, she was sterile and all alone. This also explains why she was shy to ask for Jesus' help. Melanie's healing and the miracle done for Jairus's daughter are indications that God does not discriminate between sexes, that man and woman are equal in the eyes of God. The gospel is feminist, since it vindicates the fundamental equality and dignity of both genders before God (Gal. 3:28). This is one of the revolutionary aspects of the message of Jesus.

Only if we take into account the basic chauvinist character of the society in which Jesus was part can we fully appreciate the novelty of the gospel's message, the profound amazement caused by Jesus' attitude toward women. In many countries, male chauvinism is a very important social component. The Kingdom of God shall come to the fullest only when women are appreciated as equals of men and given the same opportunities and rights. Only then can a woman develop herself to the fullest as a human being, without any social, economic, or religious impediment.

(Matt. 9:18–26; Mark 5:21–43; Luke 8:40–56)

45

A Question from the Prison Cell

John, the prophet of the desert, continued to be a prisoner in Machaerus. King Herod dared not kill him for fear of a people's revolution. Neither did he set him free for fear of Herodias, his wife. Thus, John remained imprisoned for months without seeing the light of the sun, rotting in a dark and humid dungeon near the mountains of Moab.

Matthew: Pssst! Jailer!

Jailer: It's you again?

Matthew: We want to see the prophet.

Jailer: Who do you think you are, huh? You can go to hell and leave me in peace!

Thomas: W...w...we want to bring some food to the pro-prophet, John.

Jailer: It's not allowed. The law is the law.

Matthew: What about five?

Jailer: Five! Puah! Risking my life for five filthy dinars!

Thomas: Ufff...We'll,...make it seven. Is that okay?

Jailer: Damn you! Okay, gimme the money. Hey, you, watch out! Make a scene and they'll cut off your tongue. And you better hurry, huh? I don't want any hassle!

Matthew: John, John, what a joy to see you!

The Baptist: Thomas, Matthew, what a surprise! How did you get in?

Matthew: Don't worry. Somehow, we always find a kind soul.

Thomas: H...h...how do you feel, John?

Baptist: Not so good, Thomas. This sickness is consuming me inside. I spit a lot of blood.

Matthew: We brought you something to eat. Look...it's not much, but...And this syrup from fig leaves, according to a friend of mine, is very good to loosen up the lungs.

308

Baptist: Thanks. What would happen to me without you? I think even the Lord forgets us prisoners.

Thomas: Don't talk that way, John. T...t...tell us what you need and w...w...we're gonna do whatever's possible to get it.

Baptist: Yeah, I want to ask you a favor, something very important to me. I need, I need to know if I'll die peacefully.

Matthew: What're you talking about, John? Have faith. Herod will set you free soon. He's gotta do it. The people are protesting a lot and...

Baptist: People forget what they don't see. They haven't seen me for a long time.

Matthew: You'll be outta here soon, I'm sure. You'll go back to the river and the people will come to listen to you and you'll continue to baptize in Israel.

Baptist: No, Matthew, no... This sickness is killing me. I feel terrible. My days are coming to an end.

Thomas: Don't say that, John.

Baptist: I'm not afraid to die, Thomas. When I began to preach justice, I already knew it would end this way. No prophet perishes in bed. But it doesn't matter. I did what I had to do.

Matthew: Speak up, John. What do you want to ask from us?

Baptist: Down there at the Jordan, I met a Galilean who came to be baptized. I want to know what's happened to him. His name is Jesus, and he's from Nazareth. Have you heard anything about him?

Matthew: Yes, news about him has spread as far as Judea and even Jerusalem.

Thomas: S...s...some say he's a healer.

Matthew: Others claim he's a sorcerer. Or even an agitator.

Thomas: Still others s...s...say he's another prophet.

Baptist: It doesn't matter what people say, but what he says. I need to know what he's doing, what he thinks.

Matthew: Do you want us to see him and bring you news about him?

Baptist: Yes, that's what I want. Please go to Galilee, but let no one know. It would be dangerous for him and for you.

Thomas: I think h...h...he lives in Capernaum.

Baptist: So go to Capernaum. And tell this on my behalf: John, the son of Zechariah, is asking you: My days are numbered. Will I die peacefully? I have sown the seed: Will somebody water it? I had an ax in my hands. Will someone give the necessary blow? I have set the light. Will someone blow the flame and kindle the fire? Please tell him I'm sick, that I hardly have the strength to speak. I shouted and bellowed, announcing the coming of the Liberator. Has my voice been lost in the wilderness?

Matthew: Anything else, John?

Baptist: Yes. Ask him if we gotta keep on waiting or if the one who was to come has already come. I hope my dreams haven't been in vain.

Thomas: W ... w ... we'll journey to Galilee right now.

John: Be off soon. I promise not to die before you return.

Thomas and Matthew were part of John's group of disciples when the prophet was preaching by the riverbank. Now they were staying in Jericho, and they went to Machaerus whenever they could to visit him. That same morning they started their journey to the north, to Galilee of the Gentiles, to comply with the wish of the imprisoned prophet.

Thomas: W ... w ... we have to be very cautious, Matthew. Things are getting worse.

Matthew: You bet. The truth is, I wouldn't want to end up like John and rot in a prison like that.

Thomas: N ... n ... neither would I. We mustn't be seen talking often with this Jesus. Let's keep a distance from him.

They passed the night in Perea and then in the Decapolis. On the third day, they reached Tiberias. They crossed the lake and went up to Capernaum.

Matthew: Pssst! Friend, would you know where this man Jesus, the one from Nazareth, lives?

A Man: What, what do they say?

Matthew: Don't be afraid. We can be trusted.

Thomas: We want to know wh ... wh ... where the Nazarene lives!

Man: You, you ... yo, yo ... you ...

Matthew: Let's go Thomas. This fellow is worse than you.

By asking here and there, they finally found our house. My mother, Salome, told them that Jesus was on the wharf, and would be every afternoon, waiting for our return from fishing. Thomas and Matthew approached Jesus from behind.

Matthew: Pssst ... hey, you.

Jesus: Who me?

Thomas: Yes, y ... y ... you.

Jesus: What?

Thomas: Who're you?

Jesus: That's what I want to know: Who're you?

Matthew: We're looking for a certain Jesus of Nazareth.

Jesus: Well, you've found him. I'm Jesus.

Thomas: Aa ... aa ... are you sure?

Jesus: As of this moment I'm sure. I dunno if tomorrow I'll change my mind.

Matthew: At last we've found you. We came from the south.

Thomas: Yes, f ... f ... from Jericho.

Matthew: To be exact, from Machaerus.

Jesus: From Machaerus?

Matthew: Ssh! Don't shout. They might hear us. Things are very bad, and since the Passover is near, there's more vigilance than ever.

Jesus: But are you sure you came from Machaerus?

Matthew: Yes we're sure!

Jesus: Are you John's friends?

Thomas: Yes, we saw John in his prison cell.

Jesus: How is he?

Matthew: He's fine, no, he's sick. He's very pale, like a worm who hasn't seen light for several months. He used to be tall and sturdy like a cedar, but now, he's as limp as a rag. They've finished with him.

Jesus: Is he very ill?

Matthew: Yeah, he is. He spits blood. He won't last long.

Jesus: I've got to see him before he dies. Is there a way?

Matthew: You won't be able to get through. They'll easily recognize you as Galilean. The Galileans are blacklisted.

Thomas: We bribed the jailer so we could go near him and talk to him briefly.

Jesus: I have to go there. I need to talk to John and ask him a few things.

Matthew: John also wishes to ask you something.

Jesus: Did you bring any message from him?

Thomas: Yes. John w ... w ... wants us to tell you: "My days are numbered. W ... w ... will I die in peace?"

Matthew: He also told us to tell you: "I shouted out the coming of the Liberator. Has my voice been lost in the wilderness? Shall we keep on waiting or has he come, the one who was to come?"

Jesus became pensive and stared blankly at the black stones of the wharf.

Thomas: W . . . w . . . what do you want us to tell John?

Jesus: Tell him that things are going fine, slowly, but fine. We have started here in Capernaum. We're still a small number, but we proclaim the Kingdom of God, we fight against injustice, and we try to do something so that things will change.

Thomas: And h . . . h . . . how do the people take it?

Jesus: They're beginning to open their eyes. Those who were deaf are beginning to hear. Those who were oppressed are becoming hopeful, and they're beginning to rise and move on. Even the poorest, those who are starving to death, share whatever little they have, and they help one another. The people are getting on their feet, yes, they're waking up.

Matthew: Who have joined you?

Jesus: A lot of people, especially those who were left behind, of course. Tell John that in the Kingdom of God, the last shall be the first to enter; those who have no place anywhere: the sick, the prostitutes, the publicans, the lepers, the most trampled upon — these are the people who'll have a place with us.

Thomas: Don't you have p . . . p . . . problems with the bigwigs?

Jesus: Yes, of course. That's obvious.

Matthew: So what now?

Jesus: Nothing. We'll move on and continue to announce the good news of liberation to the poor, that God is on our side; that it breaks his heart to see this world twisted and he wants to straighten it.

Matthew: John will be very happy to hear this. I assure you he will.

Jesus: Yes, and tell him, for my part, that the ax has not lost its sharp edge, that the fire has not been extinguished, that the seed he has sown shall bear fruit in time. John will understand. He is one of those who understand the way of the Lord. He's got a keen sense of smell for this. I'm sure he won't be disappointed with what we've been doing up until now, and what we shall still do.

Peter: Hey, brown one, we're back.

Matthew: Who're they?

Jesus: They belong to my group.

Peter: Dammit! Who're these guys, Jesus?

Jesus: The truth is, I haven't asked them who they are.

Matthew: My name's Matthew.

Thomas: My name's T...t...Thomas.

Jesus: You know what, Peter? They're able to talk with the prophet, John, in his prison cell.

Peter: Oh, really! Hey guys, hurry up! We have news from the prophet John!

Matthew: For God's sake, don't shout! The guards might...

Peter: To hell with them! Let's have some hot soup first, then tell us what you know about the prophet. Long live the movement!

Andrew came and then James. The rest of us on the other boat followed with the old man, Zebedee. All of us went with Thomas and Matthew who told us of the happenings in the south and in the prison cell of Machaerus.

•

Very little is spoken of Thomas in the gospels. It is John who occasionally mentions his name, and he calls him "the twin." He is known as the "doubter." Matthew is mentioned throughout the book of Acts, and he was chosen to take the place of Judas to fill up the group of the twelve apostles after Jesus' resurrection. In this episode, Thomas and Matthew appear as John the Baptist's disciples, who later on join Jesus' group. Thomas stammers. He is ingenuous, a little stubborn, and a coward. The character of his friend, Matthew, is less defined.

John the Baptist, the prophet who influenced Jesus and inspired him decisively in his initial activities in Galilee, wants to know from his confinement in the dungeons of Herod's palace what the Galilean whom he had met at the Jordan is doing. Jesus' reply to his messengers shows his awareness of being the heir of the prophetic tradition of his people and, with the help of his friends, of setting up the messianic Kingdom which John himself and the rest of the prophets had announced.

It was in the synagogue of Nazareth that Jesus proclaimed the message of liberation to his countrymen for the first time. On that occasion, Jesus described the signs that accompanied such liberation. Now, after a period of activity in Galilee, he sends the message to John that what has been proclaimed is beginning to be fulfilled. Up to that moment, Jesus' activity would have been what we would refer to nowadays as a task of "conscientization." Through words and signs, Jesus inspired among the poor of Capernaum and the neighboring villages hope for freedom and an awareness of their dignity. The Kingdom of God starts precisely when a person is assured in his or her heart that all people are equal and that inequality among people is contrary to the will of God. With this as a starting point, people find strength to fight for a just and free world. Before engaging in any act of liberation, the Christian must carry this message at heart since this is essential to the gospel. There cannot be a liberating act without a prior liberating conscience.

The prophetic text of Isaiah on which Jesus based his mission (Isa. 61:1– 2) spoke of the blind, the deaf, and the dead. An interpretation reducing the signs of the messianic Kingdom to simple and isolated healings with which Jesus manifested his power would distort the gospel. The blind are not only those who could not see and whose sight Jesus — in his capacity to make people overcome limitations — recovered for them but also those who, wallowing in injustice and becoming its victim, could not rise from that situation and became blind to any opportunity to get out of it. The deaf are not only those who refuse to hear in spite of having ears but, worse, those who hear not the voice that speaks of liberation, as pain has numbed sensitivity to hope for things to change. He or she is deaf who is passive and fatalistic. The dead are those who have never lived like human beings, those who have wept and sweated and been oppressed by others who have treated them like animals. When the blind begin to see, the deaf begin to hear, and the dead rise from their tombs of misery, then the Kingdom of God is near. The gospel is the good news of liberation, a complete liberation which will come from beyond this world to free us from death. It has already begun on this earth.

(Matt. 11:2–6; Luke 7:18–23)

46

The Kind of Fasting
That God Wants

Thomas and Matthew, the messengers sent by the prophet John from the prison cell of Machaerus, stayed in my house. Many people came that afternoon. We were all anxious to hear their news. Later, at night, the group stayed for dinner. With crossed legs, we sat on the mat spread on the floor while we waited for Salome to bring in the soup.

Peter: Hmm! The soup smells good!

Salome: Dip the spoon down to the bottom to get the good pieces of fish.

Salome put a big boiling pot in the middle. The smell of the soup pervaded the entire house.

Salome: Zebedee, old man, mind your manners! Let the guests serve themselves first!

Zebedee: You're right, lady. But I'm hungry!

Salome: Come on guys, Thomas and Matthew, don't be shy.

Matthew: No, after you. You start and we follow.

Thomas: Ain't you gonna b...b...bless the food?

Zebedee: Hell, that's right. Come on James, give the blessing.

James: God of Israel, give us food and appetite, and bless this food, amen.

All: Amen!

Zebedee: Come on fellas, let's all enjoy a good piece of fishtail — there's no better fish than what we have here in Capernaum!

Matthew: You better start, Mr. Zebedee.

Zebedee: No, Matthew, no. You start. Not that there's enough, but at least the soup is hot.

Thomas: No, no, you f...f...f...first.

James: Maybe our guests don't like fish.

Thomas: Yes we do, b...b...but we can't eat it.

Salome: You can't eat it? Are you sick in the stomach?

Matthew: Oh no, it's not that. It's just that we can't eat it.

Peter: But why? Who told you not to eat it?

Matthew: We ourselves did.

James: You did?

Matthew: Well, Thomas and I made a vow not to eat fish nor anything that comes from the sea if we got back safe and sound to Judea after this trip.

Thomas: We had to make some p...p...p...penitence.

Peter: Oh, of course, of course...Now I understand, dammit!

Zebedee: Well, man, that's no problem. You're my guests. Salome, old lady, go and kill a chicken and hurry. Get some olives so we can have something to munch.

Salome: Right away, old man, right away.

Zebedee: Just be patient. It will be done in a minute!

Matthew: No, please don't do that, Mam Salome! Don't bother. Hold it please.

Thomas: N...n...n...neither.

Zebedee: How's that again?

Thomas: N...n...n...neither can we eat meat.

Peter: And why can't you eat meat?

Matthew: Because we're fasting. We promised not to take a bite of meat until the feast of the Passover.

Thomas: W...w...we must make some penitence.

Everyone remained silent, with our eyes fixed on the boiling pot that made our mouths water. But no one dared extend a hand to help himself.

James: Well, fellas, let's shift from food to something to drink. What do you think? That's it, old lady, bring us some jugs of wine to celebrate this meeting and...Don't you drink wine either?

Thomas: We swore not to taste a drop of w...w...wine until the prophet John is free from jail. We must make some...

Zebedee: Penitence, of course. One must make some penitence. Now I understand why this fellow's tongue has dried up — for not having drunk or eaten anything.

Salome: Shut up, Zebedee, don't be rude. They're our guests.

Zebedee: Of course, of course, and in my house, the guests call the shots.

The atmosphere became tense. With bowed heads, we all started to fiddle with our fingers, or to scratch our beards, or even to nibble our fingernails. It was Jesus who broke the deafening silence.

Jesus: Hey, Salome, the soup's getting cold, isn't it? Hmm...It smells so good! Let me see how it tastes.... "The best fish can only come from Capernaum." Oh yeah, it's delicious, dammit! It's super delicious!

Jesus dipped the spoon inside the pot, took some fishtails, and filled a plate of soup to the brim. Then he took a slice of bread and began to eat just like that. We were all stunned. My father, Zebedee, who was at the other end of the mat, gaped at Jesus' plate, his eyes green with envy.

Jesus: Can I have a little wine?

Jesus reached out to where Salome was. She was waiting, like a statue, with a jug of wine in each hand.

Jesus: My throat is so dried up...ahhh! "The best wine, the wine from Capernaum," one ought to say this, too. Serve me a little more wine, please, Salome. Thanks.

That ended my father's patience.

Zebedee: To hell with all of you! What're we supposed to be doing here, huh? Are we gonna eat or not?

Jesus: Are you hungry, Zebedee?

Zebedee: Of course I am! I'm already feeling pains and stomach cramps, and you're eating so calmly, devouring all the fishbones that you can get hold of!

Jesus: Well, then you eat, too, man. What's keeping you from doing so?

Zebedee: Well this guy here has said "one must make some p...p... penitence so that the prophet John can be released from prison"...

Jesus: Thomas, do you really believe that this fox, Herod, will set him free simply because you have refrained from eating fishtail?

Thomas: Herod, no, b...b...but God.

Jesus: God? God's already happy seeing you go to and from the prison cell visiting the prophet and bringing him necessities.

Thomas: That's not enough. God also punishes the body in order to p...p...pu...purify the spirit.

Jesus: Are you sure he commands that? I don't know, I think you're imagining a very, very serious God.

Salome: And how do you imagine God, Jesus?

Jesus: I don't know, a happier one...How shall I tell you?...Yeah, that's it, a joyful one. A very happy God. Tell me, Salome: What's the happiest thing on earth?

Salome: For me, it's a wedding.

Jesus: Well then, God is like a bridegroom in a wedding. He invites us to his party. Then you come and say: "I don't dance, I don't eat, I don't drink, I don't laugh." Hey, what did you come to my wedding for? What boring guests have come to my house!

Zebedee: Well said, Jesus! You took the burden off me!

Peter: Therefore, fellas, come and get it!

Thomas: Wait a moment, wait a moment! It's not as s...s...simple as that.

Zebedee: What's it this time? For heaven's sake, what's happening now?

Matthew: Do whatever you please. But John, the baptizer, said it very clearly, as clearly as the water from the sea: "Be converted, repent, and sacrifice!"

Everyone froze: Peter, with raised spoon; Andrew and James, with their hands in the air, extended toward the pot of soup; old Zebedee, who had already chewed a fishtail, and was about to swallow it, felt a lump in his throat.

Thomas: If we don't make sacrifices, we c...c...can't be lifted up to God.

Jesus: Do you think so, Thomas? How about the trees that grow and reach out to heaven?

Thomas: I d...d...don't understand you, Jesus.

Jesus: Look, I'm gonna tell you a story that happened to me when I was a little boy. I had sown some orange seeds in front of our house. The seeds took root and the bush began to grow. But I was impatient. I wanted to see the orange blossoms soon and gather the ripe oranges.

Rabbi: But Jesus, my boy, what're you doing?

Boy: Pruning the leaves.

Rabbi: Can't you see it's a very young plant?

Boy: Of course, rabbi. I'm helping it grow.

Rabbi: You're doing it more harm. You'll only kill it by pulling its leaves. Just leave it alone. Oranges don't need to be taken care of. Come on, go to bed, it's already late, and God created night for us to rest.

Jesus: And so, while I slept and worked, the bush grew up to be a tree that bore flowers and fruits in due time.

Peter: So...

Jesus: So, I think the Kingdom of God is like a seed that grows and grows without pressure from us: fasting, promises, penitence... Don't you think all these will end up choking the plant?

Salome: To my mind, Jesus, this life's already full of too many sacrifices. We can't have more.

Zebedee: Yes sir. Let Mr. Eleazar and all the rich men do the fasting. We've been fasting throughout the year for their sake. Yeah, guys, dip the spoon into the pot before the soup gets cold!

Thomas: One moment! I'm not yet c...c...convinced.

Zebedee: Look, stutterer, let's finish this once and for all, because you're getting on my nerves. Will you or won't you let us eat? What the hell's the matter with you?

Thomas: I say th...th...th...that...

At that time, Dimo, the blind man, peeped through the door.

Dimo: God bless the food and all those gathered here. Mam Salome, could you spare an extra piece of bread for this poor creature?

Salome: There's enough of everything, old Dimo. What do you want? Bread, wine, fish? Take your pick.

Dimo: Whatever it is that you wish to give.

Salome: Come on in Dimo and join us. I'll serve you some good soup.

Dimo: Thank you, thank you. The truth is, my children, I'm starved.

Zebedee: Not as much as I am, old man. But at any rate, enjoy your meal.

Dimo: Thank you, my son, thank you.

Zebedee: Funny, the outsiders sit at the table and eat, while we are all dependent on what this stutterer has to say. That does it, fellas. I'm going to the pub.

Jesus: No, Zebedee, you wait. There's no need for you to go. Can't you see? Just look at old Dimo: you've already fulfilled what God wants you to do: "By sharing your food with the hungry and receiving the homeless into your house." God doesn't want us to starve; he wants us to struggle so that others won't be hungry. This is what the prophet John and the rest of the prophets preached. Am I not right, Thomas?

Thomas: Well, it's b...b...be...because...

Peter: So, why don't we all help ourselves to the food now?

This time, everybody dipped spoons into the big pot. Jesus had another serving of the soup for that day; he had worked hard and therefore felt hungry. Matthew and Thomas ate fish and drank wine and shared a good laugh with old Dimo, who started to tell stories about when he was a fisherman on the lake.

•

In the Bible, fasting was considered a kind of human humiliation before God. It was practiced to make prayers more effective, in moments of danger and trial. The religious law specified days of fasting, during which people were to refrain from eating in remembrance of the great national calamities and to ask for divine intercession. Fasting was also done as personal devotion. In Jesus' time, the practice was given even greater significance. The Pharisees and the rest of the religious fasted twice a week, on Mondays and Thursdays. John the Baptist, a truly austere prophet, probably inculcated the need for fasting among his disciples. That is why Matthew and Thomas appear as faithful observers of this custom in this episode. Fasting, like many other religious practices, was severely criticized by the prophets of Israel. They had become a kind of spiritual blackmail through which unjust people thought they could win God, neglecting what is essential in the religious attitude: justice. In their worship, in the use of incense and prayers and severe forms of penitence, they sought merit before God in order to save themselves. The prophets protested against this caricature of God and religion and clearly pointed out the kind of "fasting that God wants": Freeing the oppressed, sharing one's bread, opening prison doors (Isa. 58:1–12). Jesus certainly acknowledged this prophetic message.

A mistaken notion about religion might make us believe that God loves us more or grants us more favors if we make sacrifices. Sometimes there is nothing wrong with this. When a person feels sick or is confronted with a serious problem that cannot be solved, when a person is scared, then he or she turns to heaven. Since people believe that their fate depends on God, they seek to satisfy God. Out of these beliefs come promises (pilgrimages, use of special clothes, prayers...) and sacrifices (fasting, other corporal mortifications, hair shirts, flagellations...). Generally, these practices reflect the idea of a horrible God: God must be a sadist who is appeased by our pains, who softens only with our sufferings. This God is not the God of the Bible, not Jesus' God. Let us remember those idols of stone before which primitive people sacrificed animals so that the smell of blood would pacify their ire. The God Jesus speaks about, the God he calls "Papa," does not want to see us suffering and afraid; he wants to set us free; he understands and waits for us. He is a God who cannot be bought, who wants us to love him. He only asks justice and humility from us: he does not want us to feel superior or inferior to anyone (Mic. 6:8).

In order to rid Thomas and Matthew and the others of this commercial concept of merit needed in order to win God, Jesus tells the parable of the seed that grows alone. It is a way of telling us to be humble, that salvation does not depend on us. We go to sleep peacefully, with the assurance that God watches over our lives. This is not in contradiction to the work that God entrusts to us to change the course of history. Our work is an indispensable complement. We need to work, but not to the point of exhausting ourselves, trusting that God is most concerned that we succeed in our work. To avoid egoism, we must not worry about our fate as much as we do about the fate of our brothers and sisters.

In the first Christian community, the practice of fasting was accepted as a preparation for the selection of church leaders (Acts 13:2–3). Fasting is not mentioned in any of the letters of the apostles. Later, through the centuries in Christian civilization, the custom was imposed. One must take into account that fasting was a common practice in many Oriental religions, as a form of hygienic measure or health practice. It was believed that fasting once a week could be beneficial for the body. A lot of doctors recommend this practice even today. The practice of refraining from eating meat and substituting fish instead, which has persisted to the present time, has economic rather than religious origins. In the twelfth century, great quantities of salted fish were marketed; the fish were stored in the monasteries, which had the monopoly on this product. From here came the religious law of abstinence. These are only two examples, indicating that we must always analyze and try to find out how these practices of penitence came about. Not one of them can be traced to Jesus. The message of the gospel is demanding, but not in this respect. It demands justice, equality, and freedom. Jesus brings out God's mercy for the sinners and his special affection for the oppressed, never his fastidiousness with respect to merits that we can do. Jesus was a joyful man who was accused of being a wine drinker and a glutton by those who engaged in fasting. Jesus told us that the Kingdom of God was like a banquet, a wedding, and a feast. Yes, and this is what is authentically Christian.

(Matt. 9:14–17; Mark 2:18–22 and 4:26–29; Luke 5:33–39)

47

Our Daily Bread

Thomas and Matthew stayed the whole night talking to us about the prophet John, the maltreatment he was receiving in the prison cell of Machaerus, and the lung disease he was afflicted with. We were all fuming mad at Herod, the tyrant who had had the prophet locked up for several months and who had been the people's oppressor for many years. When it was past midnight...

Peter: Well, fellas, it's very late. Don't you think it's time for us to go to sleep now?

John: Hey, Peter! Save a place for me in your house, so Thomas and Matthew can sleep here.

Peter: Of course, John, come. There's always a place for everyone. Shall we go, Jesus?

Jesus and I went with Peter and Andrew to spend the night in their home. Jesus did not utter a word along the way. He looked extremely worried.

Peter: Goodnight everyone! Sleep well and don't snore a lot!

Since the house was small and there were many people inside, Jesus and I slept on a mat by the door.

Jesus: Ufff...

John: What's wrong, brown one?

Peter: Nothing, John. I just can't sleep.

John: It must be the heat.

Peter: Yeah, maybe. Know what? I'm gonna take in some fresh air.

Jesus went outside the house. The entire city was dark and quiet. Above him the stars were sparkling bright, like little lamps hanging from the sky. Jesus breathed deeply to take in some air, and went down the street leading to the wharf. Only the rhythmic rushing of the waves could be heard, as well as the soft and routine breathing of the sea, as if the Sea of Galilee was also asleep at that moment. Jesus looked for a rock to sit on. He stayed there for some time, his gaze lost in the darkness around him.

Jesus: Father, you are in heaven as well as on earth, with us. Blessed are you. In your name we rest our hope. May the day of our liberation come soon. May your justice from heaven be fulfilled on earth too. Provide for our food tomorrow. Give us today the hunger to struggle for tomorrow's food. Forgive us our sins and teach us to forgive. Let not fear overcome us. Free us from our oppressors. Free the prophet John from prison. Free our people. Make us all free, our Father!

After a while, Jesus returned to Peter's house. He lay down on the mat, by the door, and slept at once. Then it was dawn.

Rufina: Get up guys, the cocks are already crowing! Wake up, grandmother Rufa. Come on. Hey, Peter, it's time to get up! Jonas, father-in-law, Jonas! I know you're awake, huh! Little Simon, my son, put on your sandals now. Shh! you might wake Mingo up! Andrew, for heaven's sake! Hey, you two, move fast!

John: Hell, I could have slept the whole morning!

Rufa: My dear, have you seen my sandals?

Mingo: Mamma, I want some milk. I'm hungry!

Rufina: Peter, for God's sake, get up and milk the goat!

Peter: Right away, woman, right away.

Rufina: John, on your toes, and wake Jesus up. We can't open the door with him lying there.

John: Leave him alone, Rufina. He spent the night outside, that's why he's sleeping like a log now.

Peter: Hey, you, Jesus, move over — no one can pass through that door. Jesus!

Jesus: Hmmm . . . Leave me alone, Peter. I'm sleepy.

Rufina: You spent the night bumming around the whole town of Capernaum, and now you don't want to get up.

Peter: And what the hell was this fellow doing during the night, huh? Searching for bats? Hey, Rufina, get me the broom so I can hit the sleepyhead. You'll see how fast he'll get on his toes!

Jesus: Okay, okay, Peter, I'm getting up. But you'd better be ready tomorrow, for I'm gonna wake you up with a bucket of cold water in your face!

Peter: Now, may I know what you lost that you had to go out on the street at midnight?

Jesus: Nothing, Peter. I felt warm, so I went out for some fresh air. Then I prayed.

Peter: You prayed? At that time of the night?

Rufina: How's that? Is there anything wrong, Jesus?

Jesus: No, woman. I was just praying.

Rufina: But one prays when one has many problems, doesn't he?

Jesus: Well, I guess it's the prophet John who has a bigger problem in his prison cell, don't you think so? I was praying for him, that the Lord may help him and give him strength. Haven't you prayed for John?

Peter: Yes, yes. Well, no. The truth is, it never occurred to me. What about you, Rufi?

Rufina: Oh, Peter, you know I have a lot of things in my head.

Peter: The truth is . . .

Rufa: The truth is, we've forgotten all the good customs in this house, and nobody prays anymore. I dunno why everything gets lost in this house. Where are my sandals?

Rufina: Here they are, Grandma, and stop complaining. I'm sure Mingo hid them under the stove.

Rufa: Imps!

As always, that was a day of hard work. When it was dark we would get together at Peter and Rufina's house.

Peter: Say, Jesus, tell me something: Are you gonna pray for the prophet John again tonight?

Jesus: Why not?

Peter: I just thought, we could pray for him together. What do you say?

Rufa: That's a good idea my son. They say that when you pray at home, God's blessings enter.

Rufina: Hey men, all of you move over here and let's pray!

Everyone was amenable to the idea, and so, one by one, we seated ourselves, forming a small circle on the earthen floor of Peter's small house. A small lamp was burning in a hole in the wall.

Jesus: Grandma, we shall pray together for the prophet John, that God may release him from prison. Will you start the prayer?

Rufa: What did you say, my son?

Jesus: That you start with a prayer that you already know.

Rufa: Oh yes, my son, I know a lot of prayers that my mother taught me. Let me see...Let me think...a prayer to release somebody from prison...I think the best will be Psalm 87. Here goes: "Oh Lord my God, day and night I ask you to hear my prayer, incline your ear that you may hear my plea. My God, I lift up my hands to you. Why do you reject me? Why do you hide your face from me?"

Peter: One moment, mother-in-law, one moment. Go slow, dammit. Is there a fire somewhere that you have to do it that fast?

Rufa: If I don't do it that way, I won't remember the last part of the prayer.

John: Well, I got stuck in the first part. I don't even remember the number of the psalm.

Rufa: It's Psalm 87, about the prisoners. Well, if you want I can also pray Psalm 88, but that is an intense prayer. You gotta be careful.

Jesus: What do you mean, it's an intense prayer? What's it about, Grandma?

Rufa: Well, it's really a strong prayer. It doesn't fail; it asks God for seven curses against the enemy. Do you see? Of the seven, if one doesn't apply then the other one does. My mother taught me that every prayer has its own intention. If you want to earn money, you pray Psalm 64. For a safe trip, it's Psalm 22. For chest pains, the prayer of the four angels. When there is a storm, it's Psalm 28. Businessmen pray Solomon's prayer, and so forth and so on.

John: Midwives pray Psalm 126 in reverse, otherwise, the baby is a breach!

Rufa: Hey, what are you laughing at?

Jesus: Nothing, Grandma. You speak of prayers like they were kitchen recipes.

Mingo: Papa, let me have some bread!

Peter: Again? Haven't you eaten yet?

Mingo: But I'm still hungry.

Peter: You better shut up, we're praying.

Rufina: Come on, Grandma, continue praying.

Rufa: You continue this time. I've lost my concentration.

John: Go ahead, Rufina, it's your turn.

Rufina: You see, I don't know any prayer by memory. I just invent my prayers.

Peter: Well, that's better, Rufina. Come on, begin.

Rufina: Okay, let me think..."Oh God, Oh King, Almighty and most Holy Lord, most admirable and most powerful Judge of the high heavens..."

Peter: If you keep on going up, Rufi, you might fall!

Rufina: Hey, Peter, be a little more respectful, will you? We're talking to God.

Jesus: That's right, Rufina, but you don't have to exaggerate. God prefers simple things. Talk to him like a friend, like you were face to face with him.

Rufa: Take care not to get burned, son. Look, God is like the sun: you can't look at his face. One can't see God's face because he makes your eyes small, and you die!

Jesus: You believe that, Grandma?

Rufa: That's what the sacred books say.

Jesus: I dunno, but for me, whoever wrote that didn't know God very well, because with God, you can be trustful.

Rufina: Yeah, but neither should you abuse that trust. After all, God is God.

Jesus: After all, God is our Father. You can always trust your father.

Mingo: Mamma, I'm hungry, gimme more bread.

Rufina: Quiet, Mingo! Can't you see we're praying?

John: Come on, Peter. It's your turn now. At the rate we're going, the cocks will be crowing before we're done.

Peter: Okay. It's my turn now. Ahem...

Mingo: Papa, I'm hungry!

Peter: Quiet, I said!

John: Come on, Peter.

Peter: Hold it, John. I don't know where to begin. I can't think of anything.

Mingo: Papa, gimme some more bread, I'm still hungry!

Peter: My goodness, how can you pray with these little brats around? Go get another piece of bread, and shut up. These kids are really getting on my nerves!

Jesus: Look, Peter, I'm beginning to think that Mingo knows how to pray a lot better than all of us.

Peter: What did you say, Jesus?

Jesus: Mingo never stops asking you and Rufina for a piece of bread,

and he succeeds in getting it. You have granted his wish just to get it over
with. The same is true with God. If we, whose hearts are smaller than this
fist, give the best to our children, how can God not grant us the best too,
he whose heart is greater than the sea?

Peter: So...

Jesus: So we can pray with all confidence and say to him: Our Father,
in heaven, holy be your name, your kingdom come.

That night, by the Sea of Galilee, Jesus taught us how to pray.

•

Sleeping on a bed was a luxury in Israel. Only the rich had beds, but these
were not exactly like the ones we have at present. On some occasions,
these beds served as dining tables during the day. The country folk slept
on mats or straw mattresses which were laid on the ground, and people
covered themselves with blankets.

On several occasions, the gospel refers to Jesus' custom of praying in
silence at night (Luke 5:16). In all probability, Jesus complied with the
traditional prayers of his town: at dawn, at dusk, before meals, in the synagogue on Saturdays, and so forth. But he did not confine himself to what
was mandated. He talked to God in a personal manner, outside the bounds
of liturgical laws, when he felt the need, when he was confronted with a
problem, when he had to make a decision. He did not pray out of obligation, but simply because his relationship with God was such that he had
to talk to him as if he were a father.

In teaching the Lord's Prayer to his disciples, Jesus veers away from
the customary. The prayers of the Israelites were in Hebrew. The Lord's
Prayer, on the other hand, was in Aramaic, the common language spoken
by the people. Jesus calls God *Abba,* an informal word in Aramaic. This
shows that Jesus prayed to God in his mother tongue. And when he taught
his friends how to pray, he taught them a community prayer in Aramaic.
With this, Jesus took the prayer from the sacred and liturgical milieu, and
situated it within the familiar and daily life of the people.

In Jesus' mother tongue, the Lord's Prayer sounds like this: "Abba,
yitqaddas semaj, tete maljutaj..." Jesus teaches his friends to invoke God
as *Abba,* as "Papa," "Daddy." He uses the same word that children used
to refer to their father. *Abba* is a typical first utterance of an infant. In Aramaic, the baby begins to speak by saying *Abba, Imma* (Papa, Mamma). In

Jesus' time, *Abba* was used not only by little children but by grown-ups as a sign of their close affinity to their parents. For Jesus' contemporaries, it was inconceivable to address God in such a familiar manner. For them it was impolite. But we must not think that for Jesus *Abba* was a vulgar word. On the contrary, it was a very significant word. When he tells his disciples to call "no man your father on earth" (Matt. 23:9), he is emphasizing the importance of seeing God as our "Father" (*Abba*).

The Lord's Prayer outlines an entire attitude toward life. Of the two versions in the gospels (Matt. 6:9–13 and Luke 11:2–4), that of Luke is older and retains the more original words of Jesus. The Lord's Prayer underscores the attitude of complete trust in the Lord: we can call God *Abba* because we are certain we are his children and that he loves us (Rom. 8:15; Gal. 4:6).

The idea of forgiveness is foremost in the Lord's Prayer, because the entire prayer leads the heart toward the future: toward the Kingdom that is to come, toward God's justice on the last day of judgment, toward that final bread of life that will satisfy all forms of hunger. At that time, only God and his forgiveness will save people. By forgiving one another, we move forward toward that day. By sharing our food as well. All prayers seek the coming of the Kingdom of equality, justice, and freedom, the Kingdom of God. A mere repetition of the Lord's Prayer without undergoing a profound change in attitude distorts the very message of Jesus, which is opposed to the routine prayers uttered by the lips but not by the heart.

In this episode Jesus prays for the release of John the Baptist. Praying for others was very important in the prayers of Jesus. This appears on several occasions in the gospels (Luke 22:31–32; John 14:15–16). Although it may not seem so at first, this is very significant. In Israel, praying for others was not a common practice. Interceding for others was typical of the prophet, of the man who, in a special way, felt he had the responsibility for the problems of his people. Jesus' manner of praying shows the awareness that was gradually developing within, that he was getting closer to the legacy of the Jewish prophets. In this episode, the way Rufa and Rufina prayed and Peter's vacillation reflect the praying customs of the simple folks of Israel. In general, God was viewed in their prayer as a remote king. Praying was considered a manner of rendering homage. It was assumed everything must be done like a ceremony, like what customarily was done in the presence of kings. Thus, the tendency to employ fixed and solemn formulas, set forth by ancient traditions. Naturally, prayer was also associated with the idea of merit. It was believed that prayers helped in obtaining favors from God. If community prayers were at all recommended, it was because they reached heaven with greater impact. When Jesus looks to the child's spontaneity, his simplicity, and his trusting insistence to serve as our model for prayer, he is in fact revolutionizing prayer for Israel and for the religions of other nations.

(Matt. 6:5–15; Luke 11:1–4)

48

The Thirteen

The feast of the Passover was already near. As happened every year, every full moon of the month of Nisan, all of us children of Israel would look toward the direction of Jerusalem, desiring to celebrate within its confines the great feast of liberation of our people. Caravans were organized in all provinces throughout the country, and in every town pilgrimages were formed to visit the Holy City.

Jesus: Why don't we go together this year, guys?

Peter: I like the idea. When do we leave?

Jesus: In two or three days would be fine. Don't you think so, Peter? John, Andrew, what do you say?

John: There's nothing more to say. We all go.

Peter: How about you, James?

James: There will be many of us Galileans going to the feast. That might mean trouble, don't you think? Things get heated up during the Passover.

Jesus: That means five of us already.

The following day was market day. Peter went to see Philip the junk dealer.

Philip: So you're going to Jerusalem. What for? To look for trouble and incite a revolution, or to pray? Come on what is it?

Peter: Philip, we're going to Jerusalem, that's it. Are you coming or not?

Philip: Okay, okay, big nose. I'm going. You can't just leave me out.

Peter: That makes six of us.

And Philip informed his friend:

Philip: Nathanael, you've got to go!

Nathanael: But Philip, how can I leave my shop? Besides I'm still suffering from this corn that I got from our trip to the Jordan.

Philip: That was a great trip, Nat. And this will be even better. Make up your mind, man. You'll regret it for the rest of your life if you don't come.

Nathanael: Okay, Philip, I'll go. But bear in mind that I'm doing this for Jerusalem and not for you!

Philip: So that makes seven of us.

In those days our friends from the zealot movement were passing by. They were Judas Iscariot and his friend, Simon. They were also persuaded to go to Jerusalem for the feast. With those two, we became nine.

John: Hey, Andrew, I heard that Jacob of Alpheus and Thaddeus were planning to go to the capital too. Why don't we ask them to join us?

With Thaddeus and Jacob, the two farmers from Capernaum, that made eleven of us.

Jesus: Hey, Matthew, are you going to Jerusalem for the feast?

Matthew: Yes, why do you ask?

Jesus: Who are you going with?

Matthew: With myself.

Jesus: So you're going alone.

Matthew: With myself is enough.

Jesus: Why don't you come with us? We're planning to go as a group.

Matthew: Puah . . . And who will form this "group"?

Jesus: Andrew and Peter, Zebedee's sons, Judas and Simon, Philip, some others . . . Come with us too. . . .

Matthew: I don't like those friends of yours. The feeling is mutual, I guess.

Jesus: We're leaving tomorrow, Matthew. If you make up your mind, be at Peter's house tomorrow at dawn. We'll be waiting for you.

Matthew: You better wait for me sitting down, so you don't tire yourselves. Know what? You're nuts, the nuttiest person I've ever met in my damned life!

Thomas, prophet John's disciple, was the last to learn about the trip. His friend Matthew had already gone back to Jericho while he spent a few more days in Capernaum.

Thomas: I am a . . . a . . . a . . . also going with you. I . . . I . . . I . . . like the idea.

That first trip to Jerusalem together proved to be very important for all of us. But how different our ideas were then from what Jesus said about the Kingdom of God!

The sun had not yet peeped through the mountains of Bashan, but we were already causing a stir in the neighborhood. We were going to Jerusalem to celebrate the Passover. A number of pilgrim groups had already left from our barrio. A lot more would be traveling in the next few days. One after the other, with our sandals well secured for a long journey, we gathered at Peter and Rufina's house.

Peter: Look who's coming, guys . . . Philip! Hey, big head, don't tell me you're going to Jerusalem with us?

Philip: Of course, Peter. Here I am. I'm a little late, because of my cart. Its wheels are not oiled.

James: Why did you bring it? Are you going to Jerusalem with this damned cart?

Philip: Well, yes, red head. I'm like a snail that carries his house wherever he travels.

Peter: Are you out of your mind, Philip?

Philip: I'm as sane as you are. During these journeys is when business is brisk, fellows. People take along their savings to Jerusalem. Very good. I carry my wares. I sell while you pray. A piece of comb here and a necklace over there. As far as I know, I won't be molesting anyone.

James: No, way, Philip. We're not going with you and this trash. The cart stays here.

Philip: It goes.

James: The cart stays here.

Philip: Then I stay too!

John: Jesus, why don't you convince this guy? He listens to you.

Then Jesus winked at everyone, a sign that we might just play along with him.

Jesus: Philip, why don't you leave your cart and your junk here? The pearl is worth a lot more.

Philip: The pearl? What pearl are you talking about?

Jesus: Shh! A fine pearl, this big. You have a flair for business. You would be interested to be part of a business group, wouldn't you?

Philip scratched his enormous head and looked at everyone with a look of connivance.

Philip: Speak up clear, brown one. If we need money, I'm willing to sell my cart, even my sandals, if need be. Then let's negotiate for that pearl and get a clean share of it. How much are they asking for that pearl?

Jesus: A lot.

Philip: And where is it, in Jerusalem?

Jesus: No, Philip, it's right here with us.

Philip: Here? Of course, I understand... a smuggled piece. Do you have it, John? You do, Simon? Okay, okay, I promise to keep quiet. My lips are sealed. Okay? You can trust me. But tell me, how did you get it?

Jesus: Listen: Thaddeus and Jacob were working on a farm. While they were plowing it, they came across a treasure hidden in the ground.

Philip: A treasure? And what did they do with it?

Jesus: They hid it again. They went to see the owner of the farm and they bought it from him. They had to sell everything to be able to buy the farm. So the treasure remained with them.

Philip: But what was the treasure they found?

Jesus: The same pearl that I told you about before! They discovered it.

Philip: The pearl? But pearls are found in the sea, not in the earth. What's all this mess I'm getting into, Nazarene?

Jesus: Listen, Philip. The truth is, it all started in the sea, as you say. Peter and Andrew set sail on the sea and cast their nets, pulling them back full of fish. And when the fish were all sorted, they got the big surprise of their lives because...

Philip: Because it was there that they found the pearl.

Jesus: Yeah, and they left everything, the nets, the boats, the fish. And they kept the pearl, which was worth a lot more!

Philip: And so, the treasure from the farm... Ah, of course, I understand. And then... Wait. I don't get this. Such a big head, Jesus, but little brains. Explain this business to me.

Jesus: Philip, we have abandoned all our things, our fields, our nets, and our homes for the pearl. Leave your cart behind, too.

Philip: Okay, okay. But at least, show me the pearl, so that...

Jesus: The pearl is the Kingdom of God, Philip. Come on, leave all your junk and come to Jerusalem with nothing in your hands. Forget about your combs and necklaces for a few days, and celebrate the Passover with an open mind.

Philip: You band of rascals, if you keep on pulling my leg, I'll end up with a limp. All right, all right, I'll put Salome in charge of my junk until my return.

Matthew arrived when we were just about to leave. Although it was still very early, he was already half-drunk.

James: Have you left something behind, you stinking bastard?
Jesus: Welcome back, Matthew. I knew you'd come.
John: What?
Jesus: Matthew is coming with us. Didn't I tell you?
James: Did you say he was coming with us? Did I hear right?
Jesus: You heard it right, James. Matthew is coming with us.
James: To hell with you, Jesus! What do you mean by this?
Jesus: That the feast of the Passover is for everybody. And the gates of Jerusalem, like the gates of the Kingdom of God, are open to all.

Jesus' words and Matthew's presence infuriated all of us. James and I were about to hit them both when Simon and Judas pulled us apart.

Judas: You shut up, red head. Stop that yelling. Do you understand?
James: What? There's nothing to understand here. Jesus is an imbecile.
Judas: You're the foolish ones. Jesus has planned this thing very well.
John: What do you mean?
Judas: The frontier of Galilee is very well guarded, John. They fear a popular uprising. We're all blacklisted, especially Jesus. With Matthew around, it's different. We get more protection. Do you understand? Matthew knows all the swine guarding the frontier.
John: Do you think it was for this reason that Jesus invited Matthew?
Judas: And why not? Jesus is smart. He thinks of everything.
John: And why is Matthew playing along?
Judas: Matthew is a drunkard. Give him more wine and he'll follow you like a meek lamb.
James: You're right, Judas. This Nazarene is clever. He's the man we need! Come on guys, let's go!
Thomas: W . . . w . . . wait a w . . . w . . . while.
John: What's it this time, Thomas? Have you forgotten something?
Thomas: No, no, it's not that. Have you n . . . n . . . n . . . noticed how many we are?
James: Yeah, we're thirteen. With this swi . . . , I mean, with Matthew, we're thirteen.

Thomas: T . . . t . . . they say that n . . . n . . . number b . . . b . . . brings bad luck.

Peter: Bah, don't worry about that, Thomas. If one of us gets his head cut off, then we shall be twelve, a round number, like the tribes of Israel. Come on, guys, let's go. Jerusalem is waiting for us!

We were thirteen. Peter, the stone-thrower, led the group. His sun-burnt face always carried a smile. On his side was Andrew, the skinny one and the tallest of all. He was the quietest also. My brother James and I were imagining Jerusalem like a battlefield where all the Romans would be destroyed by the strength of our own hands. Philip, the vendor, tied around his waist the horn with which he used to advertise his wares. From time to time he blew his horn. He did not want to part with it. Beside him, as always, was Nathanael. The morning sun shone on his bald head. He walked very slowly. Thomas the stutterer was looking on both sides with eyes full of curiosity. He did nothing but talk with his half-tongue about the prophet John, his master. Matthew, the tax collector, his eyes red with alcohol, walked with wobbly steps. Jacob and Thaddeus, the farmers from Capernaum, walked together. Simon, the tough, freckled guy, was with Judas, who was wearing a yellow scarf around his neck, a present from a grandson of the Maccabees. We were twelve; thirteen, with Jesus of Nazareth, the man who dragged us into this adventure along the roads of our town to announce the coming of God's justice.

•

The number twelve had a special meaning in the ancient Middle East, probably because the year was divided into twelve months. In Israel, this was an important number, signifying totality. It synthesized the entire people of God, using only one number. Thus, Jacob's sons were twelve, who became patriarchs that gave names to the twelve tribes that inhabited the Promised Land. A very ancient tradition in the gospels recalls how Jesus on various occasions chose the twelve disciples, as the nucleus among the many who followed him. These twelve disciples spread his message after the Passover and carried forth his cause. In the texts of the New Testament, "the number twelve" refers to the twelve individuals — whose names we have — yet at the same time, "twelve" designates the new community, heir of the people of twelve tribes. The nucleus twelve is particularly preferred in the book of the Revelation; it appears in the measurements of the new

Jerusalem, in the number of the chosen (144,000 = 12 x 12 x 1,000), and so on.

This numerical stereotype of "twelve" is transformed in the episode about the thirteen men. It is a way of indicating Jesus' integration into the group. Jesus was not an "outsider" from the heavens; rather, he was linked to history and to a specific people. He came from a town, from a social class, and worked with his brothers and sisters side by side, in order to create a community where God was to be the only Lord and everyone else would be equal.

Three times a year, on the feasts of Passover, Pentecost, and the Tents, it was the practice of the Israelites to travel to Jerusalem. A huge number of foreigners from the neighboring countries also traveled to the capital. The feast of the Passover attracted the greatest number of pilgrims every year. Since it occurred in the spring, the trip was made easier, as there were no longer any rains in February or March, and thus, the roads were more passable. Looking for a companion for the road was an essential part of the preparations for the trip. There were more bandits during this period, and no one dared travel alone. This explains the existence of great caravans for the feasts.

In this episode, the announcement to go to Jerusalem to celebrate the Passover passes from one mouth to another; thus, the twelve get together to go with Jesus. One and another become convinced for various reasons. Jesus calls them, and they, too, call one another. God has called us through Jesus, the new human, so that we shall also become renewed men and women, capable of giving life for the sake of others as artisans of peace and justice. But God's call, this vocation, never comes to us from above as if words of invitation were blown down into us. God invites us through the community. The Christian community, of which Jesus is a part, is the one calling us, teaching us, and receiving us; it is the one forgiving us, helping us to overcome our fears, our limitations, and strengthening our hope. One goes to the new land of Jerusalem in community. Jesus' group was not homogeneous, of one stripe. All came from the popular class, but the story and motive of each one were different and maybe even contradictory, or at least in conflict. Jesus united all of them, as happens when a leader coming from the community is capable of achieving unity amid diversity, thus making the group move together. In the Christian community, the members are not herded into groups, nor are they called to render the same service. Variety is a value that must be nurtured. The same happens in society. When the day of justice comes and everyone is given the same opportunity to develop self as a truly free person, then we shall see the beauty there is in variety.

Jesus convinces Philip to join the trip by telling him two parables: that of the pearl and that of the treasure in the field (Matt. 13:44–46). Hidden treasures are a favorite theme in Middle Eastern stories. In those times, the stories also had a historical basis. The innumerable wars that shook Palestine through the centuries forced the people, during their moments of escape, to bury all their valuable property until their possible return, which often never came. Pearls were much-coveted during ancient times. They had a highly symbolic value, especially related to fertility. They were the precious fruit of the water, which grew hidden in shells and developed like a human embryo. The skin divers would collect them in the Red Sea, in the Persian Gulf, and in the Indian Ocean, and they were often used in necklaces. Through these parables, Jesus seeks to emphasize the importance of an attitude of surprise in life.

One is surprised if suddenly and unexpectedly one finds a treasure or a pearl of enormous value. One is surprised and becomes extremely happy. Jesus wants to tell us that when one finds the meaning of the Kingdom of God, the great joy of this discovery can bring one to the deepest experience, just as the "treasure" made one lose interest in everything else in life. No price seems too high to preserve what was found. The love for the Kingdom of God is a passionate and enthusiastic love. Philip leaves his cart behind and forgets about his merchandise. Others will leave their apathy and get to work for the sake of others. Still others will rid themselves of their egoism and will learn how to form a community. Still others will forget even their life and will risk it over and over for the sake of justice. This trade-in of values without regret and with utter joy is a sign of the Kingdom of God.

(Matt. 10:1–4; Mark 6:12–16)

49

In the City of King David

It was very early in the morning when we set out on our journey. Behind us the sun began to caress the circular blue Sea of Galilee, showing signs of its first light of dawn. Alongside was Capernaum, lazily shaking off her drowsiness. We did not even turn our backs to bid our city goodbye, but only set our eyes for Jerusalem. The joy of the Paschal feast filled our hearts and there was really no time to look back.

Peter: Hey guys, be sure you've got your sandals well tied and your canes in order because we've got three days ahead of us on the road!

On our first night we camped out in Ginae. Then we took the road toward the mountains up to Gilgal. We then passed through the arid and yellow lands of Judea. Our eyes were fixed on any sign of the holy city as we climbed from hill to hill. Suddenly, everyone gave out a loud cry.

John: Run everybody — we can see the city!

From one of the roads, on top of Anathoth, the city seemed resplendent to us. The walls of Jerusalem shone above Mount Zion. Its white palaces, strong gates, and massive towers sparkled. At the center was the holy temple of the God of Israel, its most precious gem.

Peter: Long live Jerusalem and all her pilgrims!

Jerusalem, the city of peace, was the treasure of all Israelites: the capital of our country, conquered by Joab a thousand years ago, where King David entered dancing, as he carried the ark of the covenant and where King Solomon constructed the temple made of cedar, gold, and marble, admired all over the world. For the last leg of our journey, we joined the caravans of pilgrims from the north, from Perea and Decapolis, to partake of the Paschal lamb in Jerusalem. We entered through the Fish Gate. Beside this was the Antonia Tower, the building most hated by all of us: it was the headquarters of the Roman garrison and the palace of Pontius Pilate whenever he stayed in the city.

339

Peter: Spit on it and let's get away from here. The mere sight of the eagle of Rome upsets my stomach!

John: Swine! If only I could kill you by squeezing your necks!

Jesus: Don't kill anyone now, John. Right now we gotta look for a place for ourselves. With so many people, I'm afraid we'll all end up sleeping in the open air.

Peter: Follow me guys! I've got a friend who lives near the Gate of the Valley. He's like a brother. His name is Mark.

We walked on until we reached Mark's house. Mark was outside his home, and Peter greeted him.

Peter: Dammit, Mark, we meet at long last! Friend, my dear friend, gimme five, man!

Mark: Peter? Peter the stone-thrower, the biggest rascal in the whole of Galilee! But what are you doing here? Herod's men must be after your head, ha, ha, ha!

Peter: We've come to celebrate the Passover in Jerusalem, like faithful followers of the law of Moses, ha, ha, ha!

Mark: Tell that to the soldiers, Peter. You must have smuggled something from Capernaum!

Peter: Well, yes, I have smuggled in a dozen friends. Hey guys, this is Mark. I love him more than Cleotilde, my boat! Mark, you can trust all of them! We've formed a group. We're planning to do something. This dark one here is Jesus, the noisiest of the group, and this freckled fellow is Simon...

Mark: Well, well, let's have the introductions later. Now let's go inside. I've got a half-barrel of wine, earmarked especially for a dozen Galileans to drink!

Peter: Now? Are you out of your mind? We just came!

Matthew: So what? We're all tired from the journey. We can, ... we can have a little toast, since those thieves from Samaria made it difficult for us.

John: To hell with you, Matthew. You only think of drinking.

Peter: Mark, you'd better tell us where we can spend the night.

Mark: Well, let's go to Shiloh's inn. You can stay there for a couple of days. The place is big enough, and the smell will suit you Galileans. Come on, let's go there. But always stick with your group. With so many people around, it's so easy to get lost in the crowd.

On the days of the Passover, Jerusalem seemed like a huge cauldron teeming with 20,000 inhabitants from the city, 125,000 pilgrims from all over the country, plus herds and herds of lambs filling up the atrium of the temple, waiting to be sacrificed on the altar stone.

Thomas: One moment, one moment! Before we go and look for an i...i...inn, why don't we all go the temple of God. First things f...f... first. He who doesn't visit the temple when he comes to Jerusalem, gets his r...r...right hand paralyzed and becomes m...m...mute.

John: Thomas is talking from experience.

Peter: That's right, fellas, let's all go to the temple and say hello to the angels!

John: Let's give thanks for having gotten here safe and sound!

Jesus: That's it. That the Lord of Israel may bless all of us who have come to celebrate the Passover!

Thousands of pilgrims shoved each other just to pass through the arches of the famous temple of Solomon. There was shouting in the air, prayers and promises, merging with the pervading smell of burned fat from the sacrificed animals. A number of money-changers stood by the walls as several junk-dealers shouted out their merchandise. It was like the Tower of Babel all over again.

Mark: Damn these vendors! Their screamings could bust your eardrums! Let's all go to the atrium of the Jews. They must be going up the steps now.

John: Who are they, Mark?

Mark: The penitents. They're here to fulfill their vows during the year. Look, there they are now!

A group of men in sackcloth, pouring handfuls of ashes on their heads, were climbing the steps of the atrium. Thick rosaries of amulets were hanging around their arms and necks. Their knees had become rough from having knelt on stones.

Peter: Why are they doing this, Mark?

Mark: They fast for seven days before the feast, and now they present themselves before the priests.

Jesus: And these priests haven't told them that God prefers love to sacrifices?

Mark: That's exactly my point. So they want to fast? Well, why don't they hide it so that nobody gets to know what they're doing? Isn't that right, Jesus? Come on, let's go up.

We climbed the steps. There, in one corner, in front of the priests' atrium, was a group of men whose faces were covered with the blank veil of prayers. They were praying ceaselessly, the psalms of the congregation of the pious. They were the best Pharisees of Jerusalem.

Peter: Well, look at them. They're like parrots, repeating the same thing all over. I wonder if their tongues don't get twisted by this.

Mark: They claim to be praying to God, but through the corners of their eyes, they're spying on everyone.

Jesus: That's what they want: for people to look at them. If they wanted to seek the Lord, they would pray in private.

Mark: Hey, look who's coming!

When we were about to cross the Beautiful Gate, the sound of trumpets was heard and the crowd moved to one side. All of a sudden there was a long line of beggars by the gate's ark. Then four Levites carrying a sedan chair appeared. They stopped beside the beggars and put the chair down on the ground. They opened the curtains and Joseph Caiaphas, the high priest of that year, dressed in white tunic, descended slowly. With the eyes of an owl he looked nervously on all sides. He wanted to flaunt his almsgiving to the people, yet he did not want to take any chances. During the feast last year, a fanatic had thrown a dagger at him.

Matthew: What a first-class scoundrel we have run into!

Thomas: Don't say that, M ... M ... Matthew. He's God's h ... h ... high priest.

Matthew: What a priest! His kind is only interested in making people adore him! Look what he's doing....

Caiaphas went toward the beggars and gave them denarii like he was distributing candies to children. He gave the alms with one hand, while the other hand displayed a golden cord, a symbol of his authority, which the beggars were kissing as a gesture of gratitude.

Jesus: If I were God's high priest, I wouldn't allow my left hand to know what my right hand was doing. He's no more than a hypocrite.

Peter: Nathanael, Jesus, Andrew ... Let's go. It's getting late and we haven't a place to sleep yet.

Mark: Don't worry too much about the inn. If there's no place in Shiloh, you may go to Bethany. The Galileans have an encampment there.

Meantime, you gotta finish the half-barrel that I'm offering you; otherwise, I'm gonna report you to the police!

We returned to Mark's house, and his half-barrel of wine.

Mark: I toast to the thirteen countrymen who came all the way from Galilee to visit the house of this humble merchant of olives!

Peter: Wait a minute, Mark. We didn't come here to visit you, rascal. We came for Jerusalem. I toast the holy city of Jerusalem!

Mark: Don't believe that, Peter. This city's no longer as holy as you think it is. Do you know why? Because anyone who visits the temple loses his faith and leaves it there! If it were only the temple ... Look, do you see those lights? They're from the palaces of the rich neighborhood. Then go and look at the huts in Ophel and the shanties beside the Gate of Trash. Then the swarm of farmers coming to the city to look for a job ... And what do they find? Nothing but misery and black fever. This city stinks, I tell you. I know this city through and through.

Jesus: You're right, Mark. It's built on sand, so it'll collapse.

Thomas: Jerusalem's foundations are of p ... p ... pure rock.

Jesus: The only solid rock is justice, Thomas. And this city is built on ambition and inequalities.

Mark: Well, guys, we'd better head for Bethany now. Let's go!

The streets were jammed with people and animals. The smell of baked unleavened bread pervaded the air, competing with the perfumes of the most popular prostitutes of Jerusalem. Early during the day they could be seen displaying themselves and their well-painted faces. In every corner of the squatters area, there were bets on dice and other games. All pubs were full of drunk men as the children sneaked away with the leftovers from the tables. We went out through the walls and crossed the Kidron, which in spring was overflowing. We ascended the Mount of Olives, until we reached Bethany, where the Galileans always found shelter to spend the days of the Passover. Behind us was Jerusalem, full of din and lights. Hunger, injustice, and hypocrisy sleepily, yet happily, guarded the walled gates of King David's city.

•

The trip to Jerusalem, during great pilgrimages of the Passover, was done on foot. Capernaum is about two hundred kilometers from Jerusalem. Jesus and his fellow pilgrims in caravans probably took this route in four or five stages. When they were close to the holy city, the pilgrims would sing the so-called psalms of ascent (Psalms 120 to 134). Among the most popular was the one that is still sung today: "I rejoiced with those who told me: Let us go to the house of the Lord! And now we have set foot within your gates, O Jerusalem" (Psalm 121).

Jerusalem (which means "city of peace"; peace = "shalom") is one of the most ancient cities in the world. It is built on a rocky plateau, flanked by two deep valleys: the Kidron and the Gihon. A thousand years before Jesus' birth, Jerusalem was conquered by King David from the Jebusites and eventually became the capital of the kingdom. In the course of history, Jerusalem was either totally or partially devastated on more than twenty occasions. One of the most terrible destructions occurred 586 years before Christ, when the Babylonians razed even its foundations to the ground. Still another took place seventy years after the death of Jesus, this time at the hands of the Roman troops in their desire to suppress the insurrection of the zealots. Jerusalem was and still is a city surrounded by walls, which were opened by a dozen doors. The numerous wars and destructions experienced by the city explain why in the present Jerusalem there are recent establishments superimposed on old constructions. Nevertheless, we can count on innumerable authentic memories of happenings during Jesus' time. Since the time of the prophets up to the writings of the New Testament, Jerusalem was the symbol of the messianic city, of God's abode, the city where at the end of time, all people would congregate for the feast of the Messiah (Isa. 60:1–22; Mic. 4:1–5; Rev. 21:1–27). Jerusalem is also known as Zion, for having been built on top of a mount bearing this name.

Jerusalem was the country's capital and the center of political and religious life of Israel. It is estimated that in Jesus' time approximately 20,000 persons lived within the walls of the city, and a total of about 5,000 to 10,000 inhabitants dwelt outside the city. (The total population of Palestine was from 500,000 to 600,000 inhabitants.) A total of about 125,000 pilgrims flocked to Jerusalem during the feasts of the Passover, overflowing the city with people. The multitude of national and foreign visitors was a boon for trade and profit but encouraged disorder and trouble, making the city a real sea of humanity, where people from the small towns and countryside converged, stunned and confused.

Within the walls, among the great establishments of the city, the temple stood out. It was a magnificent and elegant building whose area was equivalent to one-fifth of the area of the entire walled city. This would give us an idea of the impressive construction which was the center of religious activity in the country and the seat of economic power. Along the northern part of the temple was the Antonia Tower, a walled fortress that served as a garrison during Roman domination. From this fortress, the soldiers watched over the temple's vast expanse, to which the tower was joined by two staircases. This vigilance was intensified during the Passover, when there were more people than usual. Mark is mentioned for the first time in the book of the Acts of the Apostles (12:25), accompanying Paul on his trip from Jerusalem to Antioch. He was a cousin of Barnabas, another companion of Paul on his trips. On different occasions, Mark — his complete name was John Mark — is seen together with Paul and also with Peter, who was very fond of him, to the degree that he called him "his son" in one of his letters (1 Pet. 2:13). Through some details of the New Testament, we learn that Mark was from Jerusalem, where his mother lived, that Peter became a family friend, and that the first Christians regularly met at his house (Acts 12:12). From the second century on, he has been considered the author of the second gospel. On the basis of this, Mark appears in the episode as a resident of Jerusalem and Peter's friend. He is frank, happy, and practical. Around the temple of Jerusalem, one could always see, particularly during the days of the Passover, men and women fulfilling their religious vows, beggars, and a multitude praying or doing penitential acts. What Jesus taught about almsgiving, fasting, and praying in this episode could be summarized in a simple manner: a rebuff of exhibitionism, of scandalous words, of the desire to flaunt one's religiosity. It was the practice, for example, to announce the time of afternoon praying by the sound of trumpets. Some Pharisees saw to it that they were in the middle of the street, by chance, when this happened, so that they could pray before the eyes of everybody. In this manner, people would see their religiosity. In his criticism of hypocrisy of this type, Jesus talks of praying in the secrecy of one's room, of subtle fasting, and of almsgiving without the knowledge of anyone.

Jerusalem was a big, beautiful city whose elegant buildings were known throughout the ancient world. But in the midst of all this luxury, and side by side with the houses of the powerful traders and rich families, were the poor people's huts, the houses of the low salaried whose jobs were looked down upon, and who therefore lived miserably. And beggars filled the streets and the periphery of the city. Jesus, in this episode, compares this Jerusalem of the very rich and of the very poor to a city that is built on sand (Matt. 7:24, 27). God cannot tolerate inequality. If there is no justice, there can never be a firm foundation; and a corrupt society will have its downfall from below. Jesus rejects the important people responsible for this situation: the rich, the priests, the religious who alienate people with their false idea of God just to maintain their situation and privilege.

(Matt. 6:1–18)

50

Bethany's Pub

A little distance from Jerusalem, at the other side of the Mount of Olives, is Bethany, a small, white town surrounded by date trees. The name means exactly that: the land of date trees. We Galileans always ended up looking for an inn in one of the pubs of Bethany, every time we went to Jerusalem.

Lazarus: Martha, why don't you take a look at the bread in the oven? I think it's burning! And you, Mary, you'd better stop talking and have six more sleeping mats ready! La, la, ra, la, ri! This is the best time of the year, yes sir! Jerusalem is bursting with pilgrims!

Mary: And my kidneys are going to explode, from too much bending and standing, preparing these sleeping mats. Listen, brother, the place is already full. You can't even drop a needle here. If anyone comes around looking for a place, tell him there's no more space.

Lazarus: You listen, young lady: Don't you know that refusing a Galilean brings bad luck? You become mute and worms start coming out of your ears. We can still take in twenty. I know this inn better than the palm of my hand. Hey, Martha, give me a hand with this soup, the customers are already waiting!

Martha: I'm coming, man! I only have two hands.

Lazarus's inn at Bethany was called "The Beautiful Palm Tree." It was full of people, camels, and mules during the great feasts of Jerusalem, celebrated thrice a year. The feast of the Passover was the most popular of all. At that time the inn was teeming with people and animals, and the air was thick with the smell of wine, sweat, and cow dung. Lazarus was happiest during this time of the year.

Lazarus: What can you say about my soup, huh? Go ahead, have another serving. We still have an extra pot of soup! I don't want anyone to feel hunger in my house. Here one eats well and sleeps well. You can tell all about it when you go back north!

Lazarus was a big, fat man whose long beard ended on his big belly. He was born in Sepphoris in Galilee and left for Judea at a very young age. Since then, he managed his own business. He never married and, when asked, would say that he was married to his inn, licking his black beard with gusto as he said it.

Lazarus: Martha, go and prepare four heads of lamb. These countrymen of ours want to taste the specialty of the house.

Martha: You know it takes time to do it. I can't be everywhere at the same time.

Lazarus: That's all right, woman, there's really no hurry.

Martha: Yeah, you're not in a hurry, but these people are hungry. I don't like people waiting for me.

Lazarus: Come on, do as I say, and be quiet. If they don't like it, then we ourselves will gobble it up!

Martha: You just had lunch, Lazarus! You seem to have bats in your belfry!

Martha, Lazarus's elder sister, was a strong woman, with robust arms and agile legs. She had been working in the tavern ever since she was widowed. She was very hardworking, and Lazarus was very fond of and trusted her. Since Martha started working at the inn, business became brisk. Mary, his other sister, was very different.

Mary: Oh, Lazarus, oh!

Lazarus: What's wrong, Mary?

Mary: Do you know what Salim, the camel driver, has been telling me? He said he saw a dozen thieves in Samaria. They were carrying knives in their mouths and were sliding like scorpions, crawling underneath the stones!

Lazarus: There you go again with your stories.

Mary: But Lazarus, what if one of those who came last night from the north is one of them, like that one-armed person? I don't like him at all.

Lazarus: If he lacks an arm, how can he be a thief, Mary?

Mary: He's got the other hand, Lazarus! I tell you, he's strange. I was searching in his bag and I saw a brilliant object. Couldn't he be one of the group? This camel driver I've been telling you about told me that the thieves were in search of jewels.

Lazarus: Well, if that's what they're after, then they'll leave empty-handed. Here they'll find nothing but pots of soup and mice!

Mary: Lazarus...

Lazarus: Mary, you're not going to scare me with your stories of thieves.

Mary: No, I don't mean that. Look, this camel driver I'm telling you about — I think he would make a good husband for Martha. Don't you think so? He seems an honest man, and he's got big strong hands. He would know how to protect her.

Lazarus: Protect her from whom? Martha can take care of herself! Cut the small talk. Have you prepared the sleeping mats?

Mary: Oh, I forgot! It skipped my mind while talking to that camel driver.

Lazarus: Hell, you always forget everything! Hurry and prepare them now! Come on!

Mary was Lazarus's other sister. She had big eyes but was a little cross-eyed and ugly, but very cheerful. One would suddenly notice the smile on her lips. She was abandoned by her husband a few months before, and since then, also worked at the inn with Lazarus.

Martha: Mary, go and prepare the sleeping mats as I told you! There are more Galileans coming!

We arrived at the Beautiful Palm Tree after noon. We were all tired, dirty, and hungry from the journey. As we neared the inn, Lazarus came to receive us at the door.

Lazarus: Say, how many are you?

John: Count everyone you see here.

Lazarus: Six, eight, twelve, thirteen: they say this number brings bad luck.

Thomas: I told you so.

Lazarus: But for me, a Galilean has never brought me bad luck! On the contrary! You're all from there, aren't you?

Peter: Almost all of us. Well, except this guy with a yellow scarf and the freckled one.

Thomas: I come from Judea t...t...too.

Jesus: Very well, my friend, is there a place for us or not?

Lazarus: But of course, Galileans! If there is room for seven sheep, then there is room for the entire herd, don't you think? Besides, you just came in time to feast yourselves on some lamb heads that are being prepared.

What? You don't smell the aroma? They were intended for our other customers, but they simply didn't have enough patience to wait. It was written
in the book of heavens that these lambs heads would end up in your bellies.
Come on in!

*When we entered Lazarus's inn, Martha was cleaning up the extra food
that had been served earlier to four dozen countrymen. Some were still left at
the corners of the spacious yard, drinking and playing dice. Goats were chewing
crumbs of bread on the ground, while a camel was slowly passing before our eyes.*

Lazarus: Hey, Martha, you might as well cook a pot of chick peas!
Then, have some wine ready! We have more customers coming in who
are hungry! And you, Mary, come over here, quick! Sit down, friends,
the food will be served any minute now. Well, now tell me, what's the
news about Galilee? When will you cut off Herod's head? Where have you
come from?

John: From Capernaum. We met together there so we could come and
celebrate the Passover.

Peter: And tell us what's happening here in Jerusalem. We've seen a
number of soldiers everywhere.

Lazarus: That has been so every year. But this year there are more
guards than mice. They put in more reinforcements every year, so you've
got to be extra careful!

Mary: How many have come, Lazarus?

Lazarus: There are thirteen of them, so you'd better prepare thirteen
sleeping mats.

Mary: But Lazarus, do you know what that means? They'll be stepping
on each other.

Lazarus: Go. When will God make you understand, Mary? You'd better
attend to our countrymen while I go get something over there. Don't
mind this sister of mine. If you do, you might get involved in a hassle you
can't escape.

Mary: Where do you come from? You're a Galilean, right?

John: Yeah. I live in Capernaum.

Mary: Oh, in Capernaum! I met a fellow there by the name of Pamphilus. He told me a lot of things! He said Capernaum's a very beautiful
city, with more gardens than Babylon. It's so huge one needs two pairs of
sandals to be able to go around the city. He also told me about the big fish
in the lake, which are of four colors — praise the Lord — as well as the

tall palm trees, whose leaves can be used for protection against the sun. Goodness, how I'd love to travel through the north and see that place! But being tied up to this tavern, how can I? Ah, when I get old, I'll really go around the country, even on a camel. Then I'll go to Capernaum, where Pamphilus is from. How about you? Are you also from that place?

Peter: No, I come from further north, from Bethsaida.

Mary: There was a man from that place who fell in love with me. But he was cross-eyed, like me. Well, he was worse. We couldn't understand each other. When I looked at one side, he looked at the other. It was such a mess! Two cross-eyed people can never get married! Hey, you, where are you from?

Jesus: From Nazareth.

Mary: From Nazareth? Oh, I've never heard of that place in all my life!

Jesus: Neither have I, Mary, until I was born there.

Mary: And where's that place, huh?

Jesus: Far, so far that when the devil shouted three times, nobody heard it.

Mary: Oh, that's funny!

Jesus: Nazareth is a very small town, unlike Capernaum. But small things are important too. Consider this riddle for example: It's as small as a mouse but it guards the house like a lion. One, two, three: Guess what it is!

Mary: Small as a mouse... It's a key! I guessed it! I guessed it!

Jesus: Listen to this one: It's as small as a nut, has no feet, but can climb a mountain.

Mary: Wait: a nut going up the mountain... A snail! Ha, ha, ha. Tell me another one!

Jesus: You won't guess this one right. Listen well: It has no bones, it is never quiet, with edges sharper than scissors.

Mary: It has no bones... I don't know.

Jesus: It's your tongue, Mary, which never rests!

Mary: Oh, that's funny! Hey, what's your name?

Jesus: Jesus.

Thomas: They call him b...b...brown one.

Mary: Do you have a bad throat? If you wait, I can give you a prescription: two measures of water and two herbs that have been soaked for three days. Gargle with this concoction and you'll see how your tongue will loosen up.

John: You must have taken too much of the same solution.

At one end of the tavern, Martha was getting impatient.

Martha: Lazarus, Lazarus! Don't you know that Mary does nothing but chat and leaves all the work in the kitchen to me? Why, tell her to give me a hand!

Lazarus: Damn these women! Why don't the two of you work it out together?

Then Martha went to where we were all seated. On top of her striped dress she was wearing an oil-stained large apron that smelled of garlic and onion.

Martha: If you'll excuse me, but there's much work to be done, and this sister of mine does nothing but chat. Stop talking to her please, so she can give me a hand. Otherwise, we'll never get done.

Mary: Martha, listen to this: "As small as a mouse but guards the house like a lion." Huh? It's a key!

Martha: Come on, Mary, for God's sake, we'll never finish anything.

Jesus: But Martha, why do you worry so much? We're all hungry, but we can eat anything. There's no hurry, really. Listen to this other riddle, Mary! It's as small as a cucumber but it keeps on shouting along the road...

Mary stayed a little while to chat with us. We had a good laugh together. Her cheerfulness was contagious and we needed it a lot more than bread and salt. At any rate, when Martha brought us the heads of lamb that Lazarus had advertised, we gobbled them all up in a jiffy. I remember we didn't leave anything on the table — not even the bones were spared.

●

In Jerusalem, lodging was a big problem during feast days, because of the multitude of pilgrims present. This was reflected in a saying of the period that one of the ten miracles performed by the Lord from his temple was squeezing all the people into the city. It was impossible, though, that everybody could be housed in inns situated within the walled city, and a number had to go to neighboring towns for their accommodation. It was improbable that people camped out in the open air, as the nights in Jerusalem during these feasts are extremely cold. In this episode, the group stays in Bethany, a small town situated about six kilometers east of Jerusalem, beyond the Mount of Olives.

In the relatively big Jewish city there were lodging places for transient pilgrims or trading caravans. These inns had a big yard surrounded by a fence, with small rooms where people as well as animals sought shelter for the night. It is in one of these inns, very disorganized and messy due to the continuous flow of people, that this episode about Lazarus and his sisters, Martha and Mary, is set. Although the gospels give us few details about the family, religious tradition introduces them as middle-class, on the way up, people who received Jesus into a comfortable and quiet house and who saw him as a spiritual advisers. This picture has no basis whatsoever in the evangelical texts. Historical data about inns located in Bethany put them in another light: they were run by townsfolk working for a living who had no refinements. Their friendship with Jesus was the result of frequent contact with him and his friends every time Jesus traveled to the city with his friends. In the episode, Lazarus appears as a strong and generous man who is happy with his work. He drinks and eats a lot. Martha is a widow, a practical woman, serious and hardworking. Mary, the younger sister, who was abandoned by her husband, is cheerful, talkative, spontaneous, and confused. The three work hard to maintain "The Beautiful Palm Tree," which is their business and their home.

Luke's text, which serves as basis for this episode, has been utilized on many occasions to compare (and contrast) prayer and action, contemplative and active life, to the point of restricting the message of these words only to religious: making the issue one of living an active life or living a cloistered life. Our episode, however, brings the two ways of faith under one roof: prayer and action exist together, in the same room brimming with life.

The challenge to the Christian who fights for the liberation of his brothers and sisters consists of putting prayer into action. One does not pray on one side and act on another. Rather, a person prays within the same process of liberation, of seeing God where he is: in the faces of the poor. The courage necessary in order "to give life" for the sake of the people and the patience needed to lead the poor toward the path of freedom find maturity in prayer.

(Luke 10:38–42)

51

Two Copper Coins

The next morning we went up the temple to recite the Passover prayers, according to the custom of our parents. Crossing through the Gentiles' atrium, we reached the Beautiful Gate. Alongside, as always, was a line of beggars and sick people, begging for alms with their raised hands.

A Beggar: For the love of God, please help this poor blind man! God will reward you for this, countrymen. God will reward you for this!

Woman Beggar: Strangers, take a look at my wounds, and have pity on me!

Judas Iscariot was the first to give a couple of coins to the woman showing us her wound-infested legs.

Woman Beggar: May God reward you with long life and good health!

Judas: Come on, Nathanael, don't be stingy. Give this poor man something too.

Nathanael: It's not that, Judas. My heart bleeds every time I see such misery, but . . .

Philip: But what? Come on, Nat, loosen your pocket. We're in a tight fix too, but these unfortunate ones are worse.

Nathanael: I know, Philip. But that's not the problem.

Philip: So what's the problem?

Nathanael: Tell me, what do we solve by giving a couple of coins?

Philip: Less, if we don't give anything.

Nathanael: Who should I give alms to, Philip? To this woman with rotten legs, or to that man who's bloated like a frog, or to that blind man over there, or . . . ?

Another Woman Beggar: For God's sake, take a look at my wounds and have pity on me!

Philip: Don't think too much anymore, Nat. Get a dinar and give it to this poor woman, so she can get something hot for her stomach.

354

Nathanael: Yeah, that's for today, Philip. What about tomorrow, huh?

Philip: Tomorrow, someone'll pass by who'll give her another dinar.

Nathanael: And what if he doesn't give?

Philip: Well, what can we do? One...

Nathanael: We'll all be sleeping peacefully, while this poor one is dying of hunger.

Philip: Okay, okay. I'm convinced. I'll give him two dinars.

Nathanael: What about the day after tomorrow, Philip?

Philip: You go to hell, Nathanael! You can't even part with your copper and here you are pestering me! I'm not heaven's treasure-keeper!

Judas: Hey, what's the matter with you? Hurry up!

Nathanael: We're coming, Judas, we're coming.

We passed through the Beautiful Gate and entered the women's atrium where the temple's treasury was located. There, beneath a small door, could be found the bronze chests where we Israelites put in our tithes. Voluntary offerings from people were also collected in these boxes. During the Passover, a number of pilgrims gave alms for the cult and for the maintenance of the temple. When we got there a rich businessman with a red turban and a pair of silken sandals was dropping a handful of silver coins one by one into the box.

Rich Man: That our temple may always shine, as these silver coins, amen!

A Woman: Psst, neighbor! Do you know that man? He's one of the nephews of the old man, Annas! He lives along the coast and raises cattle for business. Look at his ring! With the price of that ring, he could feed all the poor ones waiting by the gate.

Another Woman: Look at the man beside him, the one who's dressed like a Greek.

Woman: Isn't he the son of the merchant Antonino?

Woman: Exactly. That one is a good man, yes sir.

Woman: A what? Hah! You just don't know him! That guy treats his horses better than his servants! What a man!

A Man: So that the altar of God will never run out of incense, amen!

A Woman: Did you hear him? Here what's needed is bread to feed the hungry poor.

Another Woman: Shut up woman! How can you say that? I think you're beginning to lose your faith. I've got a feeling this boyfriend of yours is putting strange ideas into your head.

We also gave some donations to the temple's treasury.

Philip: What a line!

Judas: This is going to take forever.

Philip: What with this heat! Hey, Nathanael, why don't you cover your bald head with a piece of cloth? You might suffer from sunstroke! But...who's pulling my hand? What's happening here? Don't push, dammit, we can't even move here! This fellow's hair is almost in my mouth! But who the devil is tickling me?

Nathanael: Philip, it's this woman who wants to squeeze herself in.

Widow: Let's see, let me pass, m'son. Come on, yes, let me pass.

Philip: Hey, old woman, why don't you get in line like everybody else? And stop pushing.

A Man: But look at this hag! Who does she think she is?

Widow: Be a good boy, m'son, and let me pass. My grandchildren are waiting for me at home.

A very thin old woman was pushing her way among us. She was probably a widow, as she was dressed in black and her face was covered with a black veil. Unmindful of the protests among us, the woman made her way to the offering box.

A Man: Damn that old woman! She came last but wants to be the first!

A Woman: Well, at least she could hurry up!

The widow started to look for her handkerchief where she kept her money.

Widow: Wait a minute, m'son, where did I put my money?

She searched all her pockets, her belt, and her chest, but could not find her handkerchief. People were getting impatient.

A Man: Well, grandmother, did you come to give alms or to pray before this chest that it may take pity on you?

A Woman: Hey, you, get that hag out of here! We can't stay here waiting for her the whole morning.

Widow: But, where did I place my money, m'son? Could somebody have stolen it from me? There are so many bad people in the city now, and too many thieves!

A Man: And what can they steal from you, skin and bones? Not even the devil would be interested in you!

Another Man: If you don't know where the hell you kept your money, you'd better move now and come back when you find it!

A Woman: Get that witch out of there!

The voice of protest became more intense. Nevertheless, the widow kept calm. She continued to look for her handkerchief, which she finally found in one of the sleeves of her dress.

Widow: Here it is, here it is. That's why my father used to say that money that is well kept is sure money.

A Man: Hurry up, old woman, finish it up and go away!

The widow carefully removed the knot of the handkerchief and there appeared the two copper cents that she wanted to offer.

A Merchant: What a big fuss over two miserable copper coins! Beat it old woman, and don't stain the temple's treasury with your filthy coins!

Widow: What did you say, child? Speak louder — I'm a little hard of hearing.

Merchant: Better for you to swallow those filthy coins! We don't need them here!

Widow: What are you saying, m'son? One day a grandson of mine swallowed a coin, and his part here got swollen and . . .

Merchant: Go to hell, damned old woman! You're testing my patience! Go away, go away!

Widow: But, m'son, I . . .

Merchant: Out of my sight, I say!

The man grabbed the widow by the arm and pushed her outside the door. The two cents rolled onto the floor.

Merchant: Why don't you stay by the door with the other beggars? That's where you belong!

But the widow bent to the floor to look for the two cents that had fallen.

Jesus: Over here, there's one, grandmother! Take it.

Widow: Oh, thank you, m'son. With these eyes of mine, I'm as blind as a bat!

Judas: Here's the other one!

Widow: How can I ever thank you? What good-mannered boys you are!

Jesus: Save your thanks, grandmother, you're already out of line. Hey, you, hurry up a little.

The widow went near the offering box, accompanied by Judas and Jesus, who recovered the copper coins for her.

Widow: M'son, let me pass, give me some space.

Merchant: You again? I told you to stay away from here, you wicked old woman!

Jesus: And why, may I ask, does she have to leave?

Merchant: Because she made me lose my patience.

Jesus: She's here to give her offering to the temple, like you and everyone else.

Merchant: She's here to give the measly amount of two cents, which is worthless, do you hear?

Jesus: She's giving more than you are.

Merchant: Oh yeah? Don't tell me that. Do you know how much I'm going to give?

Jesus: No, but I'm sure you give from your plenty, while this poor widow gives what she has to live on. Her offering is more worthy in the eyes of the Lord.

Merchant: You're a funny man, Galilean! All you can say is in the eyes of God, in the eyes of God! But don't forget that the altar curtains and cups, as well as the priests vestments, are not paid for by the widow's cents but with lots of silver and gold.

Judas Iscariot went near the merchant.

Judas: The walls of the temple of God are covered with gold and marble, while God's children are dying of hunger outside. Don't you think something is wrong here?

Merchant: I say that's none of your business. The temple is a holy place, and there's little that's done to embellish it. God deserves a beautiful place and much, much more.

Jesus: People are the true temple of God. God doesn't live amid stones, but in the hearts of those who cry out of hunger by the gate.

Merchant: Now look who's talking! Can't you show any more respect for religion and sacred things?

A Man: What's going on here, dammit! First it was the old widow, now it's you! Will somebody call for a Levite to impose some order here?

At that moment, a priest was passing by the offering boxes.

Priest: What's this chatter all about? If you have nothing to give as offering, then go somewhere else and don't make trouble!

Jesus: Come on, grandma, drop your coins and go home!

Widow: How's that, m'son?

Jesus: I said, drop your coins and go back home!

Widow: Why, of course, ... the coins ... Heavens, where did I put them? You have given them to me, haven't you? Wait a minute, m'son, let me look for them.

Jesus: If you want, don't drop them here. You may just give them to those beggars by the gate.

Widow: Speak louder, m'son, for I'm deaf and I can't hear you well.

Jesus: No, you're not, grandma. The deaf ones are those who refuse to hear the cry of the many dying of hunger, while the coffers of God's temple are full.

Priest: Go, go, don't delay, there are many people waiting! Praise God for the generous souls who help maintain the temple and the splendor of its sanctuary!

The widow finally found her copper coins again and dropped them in the temple's treasure chest. Then, slowly, she moved away, as she passed through the street of the weavers and proceeded to her rambling house in the Ophel neighborhood.

•

In Jesus' time, Jerusalem was a center of mendicancy. Since almsgiving in Jerusalem was considered specially pleasing to God, beggars flocked to the city. They concentrated themselves near the temple, though many of them could not get inside if they were afflicted with diseases which were considered an impediment to being in God's presence. They were the lepers, the crippled, the insane, and so on.

For the Jewish religion, almsgiving was a very important deed. Jesus was not opposed to almsgiving. On the contrary, on various occasions he spoke of selling one's own riches so that one could give the money to the poor (Luke 12:12, 33).

What Jesus frowns upon is the attitude of those who give alms as a show or to cover up the injustice committed by employers against their laborers. In the entire ancient world, almsgiving and charity toward the poor were ways of encouraging equality among people. At present, in this economically complex world we live in, almsgiving, charitable works, and so-called development aid may be a beautiful smoke screen to cover the roots of injustice. When almsgiving becomes a substitute for justice, it must be rejected. When almsgiving stunts the growth of the receiver as a human being, it is not Christian. Acts of charity will always be needed in times of emergency, but if such acts fail to attack the structural injustice which causes poverty, then these charitable acts accomplish nothing but the perpetuation of poverty. This is not the kind of almsgiving that our Lord wants.

Beside the atrium for women was the so-called treasury of the temple, into which the Israelites placed their offerings. On the exterior facade of the atrium, there were thirteen wooden boxes in the form of trumpets, which were used to collect the compulsory as well as the voluntary contributions. The tithe was a compulsory contribution paid annually to the temple by all twenty-year-old male Israelites. In Jesus' time, the tithe was two drachmas (two dinars, equivalent to two days' work). There were other types of compulsory offerings for the cult: for incense, gold, silver, turtledoves, and so on. Voluntary almsgiving took several forms: for the atonement of sin, for purification, and so on. During holidays, a large crowd gathered around the treasury as people from all over the country came to fulfill their religious duty of giving their support to the cult. The temple's treasury was always known for its luxury and opulence. Here, the powerful people of the country left their wealth of incalculable value, in kind and in cash. Several families deposited their wealth, especially those of the aristocracy and the religious hierarchy. This made the temple the most important financial institution in the country. The building symbolized wealth and power. At every entrance were large doors coated with gold and silver. All this makes one appreciate what Jesus said about the widow's offering. She dropped a few coins into the treasury box, which was not even enough to pay for a day's meal. In magnifying the widow's generosity, Jesus, faithful to the tradition of the prophets, denounced the luxury of the so-called house of God, and more so, the assurance with which the rich thought of buying with their money the Lord's benevolence (Jer. 7:1–11).

The true God cannot be bought with money. God's temple is human beings (1 Cor. 3:16). The best tradition of the church was always critical of the wealth of the temples. "The Church," St. John Chrysostom said, "is not a showcase of gold and silver." St. John then offered that if we really want to honor the body of Christ, then we should not allow him — that is, his brothers and sisters, the poor — to be naked, hungry, or cold.

(Mark 12:41–44; Luke 21:1–4)

Suggestions for Using This Book

Just Jesus can be used in many ways. It is ideal for catechetical and liturgical dramatization. Here are listed liturgical and biblical references.

Volume 1, Chaps. 1–51
Volume 2, Chaps. 52–99
Volume 3, Chaps. 100–144

LITURGICAL REFERENCES

Cycle A

1 Sunday of Advent	Mt 24:37–44	Chap. 105
2 Sunday of Advent	Mt 3:1–12	Chap. 2, 6
3 Sunday of Advent	Mt 11:2–11	Chap. 45, 136
4 Sunday of Advent	Mt 1:18–24	Chap. 133
Christmas	Lk 2:1–14	Chap. 134, 135
Holy Family	Mt 2:13–15, 19–23	Chap. 137
2 Sunday After Christmas	Jn 1:1–18	Chap. 131
Epiphany	Mt 2:1–12	Chap. 135
Baptism of the Lord	Mt 3:13–17	Chap. 7, 8
Ash Wednesday	Mt 6:1–6, 16–18	Chap. 49
1 Sunday of Lent	Mt 4:1–11	Chap. 9
2 Sunday of Lent	Mt 17:1–9	Chap. 68
3 Sunday of Lent	Jn 4:5–42	Chap. 81, 82
4 Sunday of Lent	Jn 9:1–41	Chap. 79
5 Sunday of Lent	Jn 11:1–45	Chap. 102
Passion Sunday	Mt 26:14–27:66	Chap. 108–9, 111–16, 118–23
Good Friday	Jn 18:1–19:42	Chap. 113–14, 116, 118–23
Holy Saturday	Mt 28:1–10	Chap. 125
Easter Sunday	Jn 20:1–9	Chap. 125, 126
2 Sunday of Easter	Jn 20:19–31	Chap. 128
3 Sunday of Easter	Lk 24:13–35	Chap. 127
4 Sunday of Easter	Jn 10:1–10	Chap. 104
5 Sunday of Easter	Jn 14:1–12	
6 Sunday of Easter	Jn 14:15–21	
Ascension	Mt 28:16–20	Chap. 130
7 Sunday of Easter	Jn 17:1–11	
Pentecost	Jn 20:19–23	Chap. 128
Trinity Sunday	Jn 3:16–18	Chap. 56

Cycle B

Baptism of the Lord	Mk 1:7–11	Chap. 7, 8
Ash Wednesday	Mt 6:1–6, 16–18	Chap. 49
1 Sunday of Lent	Mk 1:12–15	Chap. 9
2 Sunday of Lent	Mk 9:2–10	Chap. 68
3 Sunday of Lent	Jn 2:13–25	Chap. 107
4 Sunday of Lent	Jn 3:14–21	Chap. 56
5 Sunday of Lent	Jn 12:20–30	
Passion Sunday	Mk 14:1–15, 47	Chap. 103, 108–9, 111–16
Good Friday	Jn 18:1–19:42	Chap. 113–14, 116, 118–23
Holy Saturday	Mk 16:1–7	Chap. 125
Easter Sunday	Jn 20:1–9	Chap. 125–26
2 Sunday of Easter	Jn 20:19–31	Chap. 128
3 Sunday of Easter	Lk 24:35–48	Chap. 128
4 Sunday of Easter	Jn 10:11–18	Chap. 104
5 Sunday of Easter	Jn 15:1–8	Chap. 111
6 Sunday of Easter	Jn 15:9–17	Chap. 111
Ascension	Mk 16:15–20	Chap. 128–30
7 Sunday of Easter	Jn 17:11–19	
Pentecost	Acts 2:1–11	Chap. 142
Trinity Sunday	Mt 28:16–20	Chap. 130
Body and Blood of Christ	Mk 14:12–16, 22–26	Chap. 109, 111
2 Sunday Ord. Time	Jn 1:35–42	Chap. 5
3 Sunday Ord. Time	Mk 1:14–20	Chap. 14
4 Sunday Ord. Time	Mk 1:21–28	Chap. 18
5 Sunday Ord. Time	Mk 1:29–39	Chap. 19
6 Sunday Ord. Time	Mk 1:40–45	Chap. 20
7 Sunday Ord. Time	Mk 2:1–12	Chap. 35
8 Sunday Ord. Time	Mk 2:18–22	Chap. 46
9 Sunday Ord. Time	Mk 2:23–3:6	Chap. 29, 30
10 Sunday Ord. Time	Mk 3:20–35	Chap. 32, 66
11 Sunday Ord. Time	Mk 4:26–34	Chap. 24, 46
12 Sunday Ord. Time	Mk 4:35–41	Chap. 39
13 Sunday Ord. Time	Mk 5:21–43	Chap. 44
14 Sunday Ord. Time	Mk 6:1–6	Chap. 22
15 Sunday Ord. Time	Mk 6:7–13	Chap. 60
16 Sunday Ord. Time	Mk 6:30–34	Chap. 57
17 Sunday Ord. Time	Jn 6:1–15	Chap. 57
18 Sunday Ord. Time	Jn 6:24–35	Chap. 58
19 Sunday Ord. Time	Jn 6:41–52	Chap. 58
20 Sunday Ord. Time	Jn 6:51–58	Chap. 58
21 Sunday Ord. Time	Jn 6:60–69	Chap. 58
22 Sunday Ord. Time	Mk 7:1–8, 14–15, 21–23	Chap. 98
23 Sunday Ord. Time	Mk 7:31–37	
24 Sunday Ord. Time	Mk 8:27–35	Chap. 67
25 Sunday Ord. Time	Mk 9:30–37	Chap. 36
26 Sunday Ord. Time	Mk 9:38–43, 45, 47–48	Chap. 63
27 Sunday Ord. Time	Mk 10:2–16	Chap. 36, 71
28 Sunday Ord. Time	Mk 10:17–30	Chap. 92

Cycle C

BIBLICAL REFERENCES

Matthew